ANDERSON'S
Law School Publications

Administrative Law Anthology
Thomas O. Sargentich

Administrative Law: Cases and Materials
Daniel J. Gifford

An Admiralty Law Anthology
Robert M. Jarvis

Alternative Dispute Resolution: Strategies for Law and Business
E. Wendy Trachte-Huber and Stephen K. Huber

The American Constitutional Order: History, Cases, and Philosophy
Douglas W. Kmiec and Stephen B. Presser

American Legal Systems: A Resource and Reference Guide
Toni M. Fine

Analytic Jurisprudence Anthology
Anthony D'Amato

An Antitrust Anthology
Andrew I. Gavil

Appellate Advocacy: Principles and Practice, *Third Edition*
Ursula Bentele and Eve Cary

Arbitration: Cases and Materials
Stephen K. Huber and E. Wendy Trachte-Huber

Basic Accounting Principles for Lawyers: With Present Value and Expected Value
C. Steven Bradford and Gary A. Ames

Basic Themes in Law and Jurisprudence
Charles W. Collier

The Best-Kept Secrets of Evidence Law: 101 Principles, Practices, and Pitfalls
Paul R. Rice

A Capital Punishment Anthology (and Electronic Caselaw Appendix)
Victor L. Streib

Cases and Materials in Juvenile Law
J. Eric Smithburn

Cases and Materials on Corporations
Thomas R. Hurst and William A. Gregory

Cases and Materials on the Law Governing Lawyers
James E. Moliterno

Cases and Problems in California Criminal Law
Myron Moskovitz

Cases and Problems in Criminal Law, *Fourth Edition*
Myron Moskovitz

The Citation Workbook: How to Beat the Citation Blues, *Second Edition*
Maria L. Ciampi, Rivka Widerman, and Vicki Lutz

Civil Procedure Anthology
David I. Levine, Donald L. Doernberg, and Melissa L. Nelken

Civil Procedure: Cases, Materials, and Questions, *Third Edition*
Richard D. Freer and Wendy Collins Perdue

Civil Procedure for Federal and State Courts
Jeffrey A. Parness

Federal and State Civil Procedure Handbook, *Second Edition*
Jeffrey A. Parness

Clinical Anthology: Readings for Live-Client Clinics
Alex J. Hurder, Frank S. Bloch, Susan L. Brooks, and Susan L. Kay

Commercial Transactions Series: Problems and Materials
Louis F. Del Duca, Egon Guttman, Alphonse M. Squillante, Fred H. Miller,
    Linda Rusch, and Peter Winship
    Vol. 1: Secured Transactions Under the UCC
    Vol. 2: Sales Under the UCC and the CISG
    Vol. 3: Negotiable Instruments Under the UCC and the CIBN

Communications Law: Media, Entertainment, and Regulation
Donald E. Lively, Allen S. Hammond, Blake D. Morant, and Russell L. Weaver

A Conflict-of-Laws Anthology
Gene R. Shreve

Constitutional Conflicts
Derrick A. Bell, Jr.

A Constitutional Law Anthology, *Second Edition*
Michael J. Glennon, Donald E. Lively, Phoebe A. Haddon, Dorothy E. Roberts,
    and Russell L. Weaver

Constitutional Law: Cases, History, and Dialogues, *Second Edition*
Donald E. Lively, Phoebe A. Haddon, Dorothy E. Roberts, Russell L. Weaver,
    and William D. Araiza

The Constitutional Law of the European Union
James D. Dinnage and John F. Murphy

The Constitutional Law of the European Union: Documentary Supplement
James D. Dinnage and John F. Murphy

Constitutional Torts
Sheldon H. Nahmod, Michael L. Wells, and Thomas A. Eaton

A Contracts Anthology, *Second Edition*
Peter Linzer

Environmental Protection and Justice
Readings and Commentary on Environmental Law and Practice, *Second Edition*
Kenneth A. Manaster

European Union Law Anthology
Karen V. Kole and Anthony D'Amato

An Evidence Anthology
Edward J. Imwinkelried and Glen Weissenberger

Family Law in Action: A Reader
Margaret F. Brinig, Carl E. Schneider, and Lee E. Teitelbaum

Federal Antitrust Law: Cases and Materials
Daniel J. Gifford and Leo J. Raskind

Federal Income Tax Anthology
Paul L. Caron, Karen C. Burke, and Grayson M.P. McCouch

Federal Rules of Civil Procedure
Publisher's Staff

Federal Rules of Evidence Handbook
Publisher's Staff

Federal Rules of Evidence: Rules, Legislative History, Commentary and Authority
Glen Weissenberger and James J. Duane

Federal Wealth Transfer Tax Anthology
Paul L. Caron, Grayson M.P. McCouch, Karen C. Burke

First Amendment Anthology
Donald E. Lively, Dorothy E. Roberts, and Russell L. Weaver

The History, Philosophy, and Structure of the American Constitution
Douglas W. Kmiec and Stephen B. Presser

Individual Rights and the American Constitution
Douglas W. Kmiec and Stephen B. Presser

International Environmental Law Anthology
Anthony D'Amato and Kirsten Engel

International Human Rights: Law, Policy, and Process, *Third Edition*
David Weissbrodt, Joan Fitzpatrick, and Frank Newman

Selected International Human Rights Instruments and
Bibliography for Research on International Human Rights Law, *Third Edition*
David Weissbrodt, Joan Fitzpatrick, Frank Newman, Marci Hoffman, and Mary Rumsey

International Intellectual Property Anthology
Anthony D'Amato and Doris Estelle Long

International Law Anthology
Anthony D'Amato

International Taxation: Cases, Materials, and Problems
Philip F. Postlewaite

Introduction to the Study of Law: Cases and Materials, *Second Edition*
John Makdisi

Judicial Externships: The Clinic Inside the Courthouse, *Second Edition*
Rebecca A. Cochran

A Land Use Anthology
Jon W. Bruce

Law and Economics Anthology
Kenneth G. Dau-Schmidt and Thomas S. Ulen

The Law of Disability Discrimination, *Third Edition*
Ruth Colker and Bonnie Poitras Tucker

The Law of Disability Discrimination Handbook: Statutes and Regulatory Guidance
 Third Edition
Ruth Colker and Bonnie Poitras Tucker

Lawyers and Fundamental Moral Responsibility
Daniel R. Coquillette

The Lawyer's Craft: An Introduction to Legal Analysis, Writing, Research,
 and Advocacy
Cathy Glaser, Jethro K. Lieberman, Robert A. Ruescher, and Lynn Boepple Su

Mediation and Negotiation: Reaching Agreement in Law and Business
E. Wendy Trachte-Huber and Stephen K. Huber

Microeconomic Predicates to Law and Economics
Mark Seidenfeld

Natural Resources: Cases and Materials
Barlow Burke

Patients, Psychiatrists and Lawyers: Law and the Mental Health System
 Second Edition
Raymond L. Spring, Roy B. Lacoursiere, and Glen Weissenberger

Preventive Law: Materials on a Non Adversarial Legal Process
Robert M. Hardaway

Principles of Evidence, *Fourth Edition*
Irving Younger, Michael Goldsmith, and David A. Sonenshein

Problems and Simulations in Evidence, *Second Edition*
Thomas F. Guernsey

A Products Liability Anthology
Anita Bernstein

Professional Responsibility Anthology
Thomas B. Metzloff

A Property Anthology, *Second Edition*
Richard H. Chused

FORTHCOMING PUBLICATIONS

The Lawyer's

AN INTRODUCTION TO LEGAL ANALYSIS, WRITING, RESEARCH, AND ADVOCACY

Craft

The Lawyer's

AN INTRODUCTION TO LEGAL ANALYSIS, WRITING, RESEARCH, AND ADVOCACY

Craft

Cathy Glaser
New York Law School

Jethro K. Lieberman
New York Law School

Robert A. Ruescher
St. John's University School of Law

Lynn Boepple Su
New York Law School

with the assistance of
Elaine P. Mills
Albany Law School

THE LAWYER'S CRAFT: AN INTRODUCTION TO LEGAL ANALYSIS, WRITING, RESEARCH, AND ADVOCACY
CATHY GLASER, JETHRO K. LIEBERMAN, ROBERT A. RUESCHER, AND LYNN BOEPPLE SU

© 2002 by Anderson Publishing Co.

Second Printing – July, 2002

Anderson Publishing Co.
2035 Reading Road / Cincinnati, Ohio 45202
800-582-7295 / e-mail lawschool@andersonpublishing.com / Fax 513-562-5430
www.andersonpublishing.com

ISBN: 1-58360-787-0

For Steve and Samantha
"To infinity and beyond . . . "

CG

For Elizabeth K. Lieberman (1914-2001) and J. Ben Lieberman (1914-1984),
word people.

JKL

To my Mom,
who taught me all I know about speaking plainly and getting to the point.

RAR

To Jim, Alex, and Alison Su,
whose unconditional love and support make everything possible,
and to Phyllis and Herb Boepple,
who inspired me to set high goals and to persevere.

LBS

Authors' Note

Key words defined for the first time appear in **boldface** and in the glossary.

Contents

Introduction

What Is the Lawyer's Craft?

The lawyer's craft can be described in five words: clear thinking and clear writing. Though easy to state, mastery of the craft comes only with much hard work.

You might suppose, as you begin your studies in law school, that only certain lawyers really need to write. In fact, however, most lawyers write often and a lot, regardless of the type of law they practice.

General practitioners spend a good deal of their time writing. They draft wills, contracts for house sales, partnership agreements, and many other documents. Corporate lawyers write a lot too. If a company plans to hire a senior executive, or rent office space, or buy another business, it is not likely to do so without a written employment contract, lease, or purchase agreement.

Trial lawyers do not win cases solely by their courtroom performance: the big day in court is preceded by months, probably years, of paperwork. Before the lawsuit starts, a trial lawyer might draft an advice letter to her client, evaluating the legal basis of the lawsuit, or a demand letter to the opposing side, asserting her client's legal position and rights. Certainly she cannot start the lawsuit without drafting a complaint outlining the legal and factual basis of her client's legal claim. She will also obtain documents and information from the opposing side by sending written discovery demands. These are only a few examples of the documents that trial lawyers draft before a trial begins.

Although law students may not fully appreciate the profound importance of writing skills to successful practicing lawyers, law school graduates quickly discover that to secure and retain legal jobs they must become professional writers. In the 1990s, the American Bar Foundation surveyed a large sample of recent law school graduates. The respondents ranked oral and written communication skills at the very top of a list of seventeen important skills and areas of knowledge— and by a wide margin. Those responsible for hiring them agreed. [Bryant G. Garth and Joanne Martin, *Law Schools and the Construction of Competence,* 43 J. of Legal Educ. 469, 473, 477, 489 (1993).]

Good Lawyers Must Be Good Writers

Legal writing is result-oriented: it is the lawyer's principal tool for achieving the client's desired results. People hire lawyers to accomplish specific tasks, like collecting money from a debtor, buying a house, or adopting a child. Good writing is not simply an aesthetic goal but rather an essential means to achieve these objectives. Poor writing reduces the likelihood of attaining them. The client who desperately needs to understand his legal options will not be well-served by a vague advice letter couched in legalisms. A busy judge may not even finish reading a brief that is rambling, wordy, or disorganized. A client's contractual rights may be compromised by an ill-conceived, incomplete, or ambiguous contract. A legal document is judged on how well it works, and how well it works almost always depends in large part on how well it reads.

If you are going to be a lawyer, then you are going to be a writer. To be a good lawyer, you must be a good writer.

What Is Good Writing?

Good writing effectively communicates ideas to another person. Just as a bad connection impedes a telephone conversation, imprecise, disorganized writing impedes written communication. In both cases, the goal of communication is frustrated: the listener cannot make out what the speaker is saying, and the reader cannot understand the writer. It is no consolation to anybody that the speaker heard himself or that the writer knew what he wanted to convey. The good writer helps the reader achieve the writer's level of understanding with minimal effort.

Good legal writing, like any other kind of good writing, is clear, precise, and well-organized. Much of this book is dedicated to the craft of writing legal memoranda and appellate briefs. Along the way, you will find help on composition, editing, research, citation, exam writing, oral reporting, and advocacy.

What Is Legal Analysis and How Does It Relate to What Lawyers Write?

If good writing is the effective communication of an idea from the writer's mind to the reader's, then good writing can only be as clear, precise, and well-organized as the ideas that the writer intends to communicate. Just as a perfect phone connection cannot overcome the shortcomings of rambling, incoherent speech, spare, grammatically correct prose cannot remedy sloppy thinking. To write well, you must first focus on clear, analytical thinking.

Writing based on sloppy thinking cannot be good writing. If you retained an architect to design your dream house, certainly you would consider his blueprint useless if the design omitted major structural beams. If the architect argued in his defense that the blueprint was precise and meticulously drawn, capable of communicating all the design specifications to the builder, you would undoubtedly point out that despite the blueprint's clarity, a house built to its specifications would not stand up. A lawyer who drafts a brief that eloquently misinterprets the law, or a sales contract that precisely expresses an unenforceable provision, is no different. She has not written anything useful.

For that reason, this book does not limit itself to teaching the craft of writing. It also teaches legal thinking, better known as legal analysis. After all, writing (a way of communicating ideas) and analysis (a way of forming ideas) are not really separate activities. Just as an architect designing a house often formulates the design plan at the drafting table, a lawyer often develops a solution to a legal problem with a pen in hand or fingers at the keyboard. The very act of expressing the idea in precise, clear terms in written form—whether in an architectural blueprint or a legal document—forces you to think about and refine the idea itself. As an architect drafts a floor plan, he develops and changes the design, moving doorways, rooms, and dimensions. Similarly, while a lawyer drafts a document, she develops a plan as she writes it, rethinking and reorganizing as she goes. Trying to express an idea clearly and precisely forces you to think about that idea more carefully. It is impossible to divorce good legal writing from good legal analysis: the two are integrally related. Therefore, to learn the lawyer's craft, you begin by studying the principles of legal analysis.

PART I

Legal Analysis

CHAPTER 1

Introduction to Legal Analysis

When you master this chapter, you will understand:

1. why lawyers analyze legal questions;

2. how legal analysis is based on a way of thinking that you use every day when you make decisions; and

3. what legal analysis is.

A. Why Lawyers Analyze Legal Questions

Lawyers are called upon to answer questions. Sometimes the question comes from the client ("Is this contract enforceable?") or from a judge ("Why has your client refused to pay the rent?"). Often the question is raised by the lawyer himself in trying to achieve the result his client wants. Suppose your client wants to open a restaurant. She may have a few questions, such as whether she needs a permit to operate the restaurant. After hearing her questions, you may think of others, such as whether she must provide parking facilities for her patrons.

Some legal questions have unequivocal answers, in the sense that the lawyer can answer the question definitively—the law's meaning is clear. Suppose the law provides that all restaurants must have permits from the board of health and that restaurants the size of your client's must provide parking for 25 cars. You can then advise your client with certainty that she cannot open the restaurant unless she has both a permit from the board of health and a parking lot for at least 25 cars.

But not all questions have definite answers. Lawyers know that even the most straightforward question might not have a conclusive answer. Finding the applicable law is just the first step. The next, and often harder, step is to understand how that law applies to your client's situation. Suppose that a few months after she opened the restaurant the owner asked you if she could fire a waiter who has refused to work on Friday nights for religious reasons. You look up the relevant law, and it provides that an employer can fire an employee only if accommodating his religious practice would place an *undue hardship* on the employer's business. Because the law is meant to apply generally to all employers, it does not, of course, definitively answer the question of whether this particular employer would suffer an undue hardship by accommodating this particular employee's practice under these particular circumstances.

Because no definite answer exists, you must form a reasoned opinion about how the law applies to your client's situation. Usually, that reasoned opinion is based on **cases**—written decisions by judges that resolve legal questions—dealing with the same law in similar, but not identical, situations. In essence, your opinion is a prediction of how a court might apply the law to your client's situation, based on how courts have applied it in cases involving similar situations.

Legal analysis is the process a lawyer uses to make these predictions. The term is not a loose, general one, a label for just any thoughtful statement about the law. Rather, it refers to a highly structured *approach* for making predictions about how courts will likely resolve legal questions. It is a method lawyers use to apply the generalities of the law to the specific question at hand.

B. Legal Analysis Is Not an Alien Mode of Thought

The way lawyers analyze legal questions is not inherently different from the way people analyze everyday questions. Consider the analysis needed to answer the following everyday questions:

- a husband wants to know whether his wife will like a scarf for her birthday.

- a teenager wants to know whether her parents will let her stay out late to attend her friend Rebecca's sweet-sixteen party. The party, held on a Saturday night, will be chaperoned by Rebecca's mother.

Both the husband and the teenager might try to answer their questions by using the same process: sifting through past experiences, identifying commonalities in those experiences, forming a rule from the commonalities, and applying the rule to their situations to predict an outcome.

The Husband's Question: Will his wife like the scarf?

Step 1: Sift through past experiences. The husband, when evaluating whether his wife would like a scarf, remembers previous gifts his wife has liked. In the past several years, she has liked jewelry, sweaters, blouses, shoes, and coats. But she did not like certain other gifts he gave her, including a CD-player, a book, and a set of coffee mugs.

Step 2: Form an understanding of why she liked some gifts and disliked others. To help him evaluate whether his wife will like the scarf, the husband identifies a common feature of the gifts she liked—all of them were wearable. The gifts she did not like could not be worn.

Step 3. Apply that understanding to evaluate whether she will like the scarf. Armed with his new-found understanding of what types of gifts his wife likes, the husband is prepared to assess whether his wife will like the scarf. He reasons that since the scarf is wearable, she will like it.

The Teenager's Question:
Will her parents let her stay late at Rebecca's party?

Step 1: Sift through past experiences. The teenager, when evaluating whether her parents will let her stay out late for this party, remembers her other requests and her parents' responses to them. She was not allowed to stay late at Mary's party because she had school the next day. Nor was she allowed to stay late at Paul's party on a Saturday night; her parents objected to the lack of adult supervision at the party. She was, however, allowed to stay late at Peter's party, which took place on a Friday night and was chaperoned by Peter's parents.

Step 2: Form an understanding of when she was allowed to stay out late for a party. To help her predict whether her parents will let her stay out late for Rebecca's party, the teenager tries to reconcile their past decisions, seeking to find a general rule that consistently explains their previous decisions so that she can predict whether they will decide this time to let her stay late. She derives this rule: she will be allowed to stay out late for parties only if they are chaperoned by parents and if she does not have school the next day.

Step 3. Apply that understanding to evaluate whether she will be allowed to go to Rebecca's party. Applying her new-found understanding to her present request, the teenager anticipates that her parents will let her stay late at Rebecca's party: the party is on a Saturday, so she does not have school the next day, and it will be chaperoned by Rebecca's mother.

The process described above—assessing the meaning of past events and applying that assessment to predict the outcome of a future one—is the essence of legal analysis. In legal analysis, you predict how a court will answer a legal question. In making that prediction, you consider not just any past events, but cases that have been decided. These cases help you understand the general rule that you must apply to the specific facts of your case to make a reasoned prediction.

Once you realize that legal analysis is a common form of reasoning, the process of legal analysis seems less foreign and intimidating. And although legal questions often demand more sophisticated rules than the everyday examples discussed here, the method of analysis (finding general rules and applying them to particular situations to predict the outcome) remains the same.

Do Exercise 1-A Now, p. 16

C. An Example of Legal Analysis

Suppose your client has been sued under a law that reads: "If a dog injures a person without provocation, then the dog's owner must pay the medical expenses of the injured person." Your client informs you that his dog, Spot, scratched Bobby Smith after Bobby inadvertently stepped on Spot's tail. Bobby's mother brought her son to the doctor and sent your client the bill. Your client wants to know whether he must pay the doctor's bill.

You might ask yourself some questions about the law as it applies to your client's situation, including: (1) is a scratch an "injury" and (2) is stepping on a dog's tail by mistake a "provocation"?

Suppose the law defines "injury" to include "any physical harm, however small, resulting from a bite, nibble, nip, chomp, snip, claw, scrape, or scratch at or upon a person." Then the question of whether a scratch is an injury is a legal question with a definite answer. The law explicitly says so; hence, Bobby's scratch *is* an injury under the law.

Suppose the law does not define the term "provocation." Then the second question—whether Spot was provoked—cannot be answered yet because the term "provocation" is too general to help. In trying to figure out if Spot was provoked, you might ask yourself: Did Bobby provoke Spot simply by stepping on his tail? Does it make a difference that Bobby was not trying to anger or taunt the dog, but did so only by mistake? When you ask yourself these questions, you have begun to analyze the question of whether Spot inflicted the injury "without provocation."

Legal analysis provides a method for predicting whether a court would conclude that Bobby provoked Spot when the law does not explicitly provide an answer. You have taken the first step by reviewing the law. You must then figure out how a general term in the law—provocation—applies to your client's situation.

Your next step, and the best way to predict how a general term applies to your client's situation, is to find out how the general term "provocation" has been applied in the past to somewhat similar cases (other people's situations). If you find a **controlling case**, a case that dictates the resolution of a legal question with facts just like yours (a case stating that an inadvertent step on a dog's tail is provocation), you can breathe a sigh of relief: your question has a definitive answer. The **holding** in that case—that is, the court's decision on how the law applies to the facts of the particular case—gives you a definite answer to your client's question, and no further analysis is needed.

But sometimes past cases will not definitively answer your question. Rather, they will only help you make an educated guess, a prediction, about how your client's situation will turn out.

If "provocation" is not defined in the law and you cannot find a controlling case resolving your question, you must further analyze the term. To do so, you would use the same logic used by the husband and the teenager in analyzing their everyday questions:

1. *Find similar cases.* You would find past cases involving similar incidents. That is, you would find cases in which dog owners asserted that they should not have to pay medical expenses because the injured persons provoked the dogs;

2. *Use these past cases to assess what constitutes provocation.* You would harmonize these past cases to come up with a definition of "provocation"; and

3. *Apply this definition to predict the outcome of Bobby's case.* Using your definition, you would predict whether a court would decide that Spot acted "without provocation."

These three steps are considered in detail below.

Step 1: Find Similar Cases

Because the law does not define provocation and you did not find a controlling case that answered the question, you must find **analogous cases**. Analogous cases have facts that are sufficiently similar to the facts in your client's situation. You can use these cases to predict how a judge would decide your client's case. Suppose you find the following three cases:

> *The Newspaper Case.* A delivery boy threw a newspaper over thick hedges and inadvertently hit a dog sleeping on the other side. The dog ran after the boy and bit him. The judge held that the dog was not provoked.

> *The Stick Case.* A girl hit a dog with a stick three times. The dog then bit the girl. The judge held that the dog was provoked.

> *The Stone Case.* A girl threw a stone at a dog but missed. The dog then bit the girl. The judge held that the dog was provoked.

These cases can help you predict whether Spot was provoked because judges generally follow the logic of previous decisions. Knowing how judges decided these cases and deducing the logic that led them to their decisions help you predict how a judge might decide your case.

Step 2: Use the Cases to Assess What Constitutes Provocation

Your next step is to make sense of the three cases by devising a definition from their holdings that explains what provocation is. In the law such a definition is called a **rule**. The goal is to find a rule that accurately and consistently explains the holdings in similar cases. To make sense of these three cases, then, you must explain why in the *Newspaper* case there was no provocation but in the *Stick* and *Stone* cases there was a provocation.

Sometimes a court states a rule explicitly. If the court in the *Stick* case had held that "When a person intentionally hits a dog, she is trying to anger or taunt the dog, so the dog is provoked," the court would have stated the rule explicitly. Since Bobby did not intentionally step on Spot's tail, you could apply the *Stick* case rule and predict that Bobby did not provoke Spot since he did not intentionally hit the dog and was not trying to anger or taunt it.

Do Exercise 1-B Now, p. 16

Sometimes, however, a court does not state a rule explicitly, and you must make sense of the case by devising a rule from its holding. If the *Newspaper*, *Stick*, and *Stone* courts did not explain their holdings, you would have to rationalize their holdings by devising a rule that explains in a more general way why the courts decided the way they did. Here are three rules that *attempt* to explain the three cases:

> Rule 1: If an object is thrown near or at a dog, the dog is provoked if the object hits him, but not provoked if it misses.

> Rule 2: An injury precipitated by a girl is provocation, but an injury precipitated by a boy is not provocation.

> Rule 3: A person provokes a dog if he was trying to anger or taunt the animal.

Rule 1 is wrong because it does not explain the results of *all* three cases. In the *Stone* case, the girl missed the dog, and still the judge held that the dog was provoked. Rule 1 is inconsistent with the holding of the *Stone* case. Because the rule fails to explain and reconcile *all* of the cases, it is incorrect.

Rules 2 and 3 reconcile all of the cases, but only one of them—Rule 3—does so in a way that makes sense.

Rule 2 is a ridiculous way of reconciling the cases. It turns on a fact—the sex of the person bitten—that surely is irrelevant. Common sense tells you that this rule cannot possibly be correct, and nothing in the cases suggests that they would have been decided differently if the sexes of the "provocateurs" were reversed.

Of these rules, Rule 3 is the best. It makes sense and is consistent with the holdings of the cases. Under Rule 3, the cases are explained and reconciled by the injured person's intent. The girls in the *Stick* and *Stone* cases intended to anger or taunt the dog, but the boy in the *Newspaper* case did not. Therefore, it is the intent of the person causing the injury that defines provocation.

Do Exercises 1-C(1) and 1-C(2) Now, p. 17

Step 3: Apply the Rule to Predict the Outcome

The last step in legal analysis is to use the rule to predict how a judge would decide your client's case—whether Bobby provoked Spot by stepping on his tail. If you apply Rule 3 (a dog is provoked if the person bitten was trying to anger or taunt the dog) to your client's situation (Bobby stepped on Spot's tail by mistake), then you could predict that a judge will probably decide that the dog was not provoked. Then you can advise your client that he is obligated to pay Bobby's doctor's bill.

The process described above—finding a rule in a case or devising a rule based on analogous cases and applying that rule to your case—is a cornerstone of legal analysis.

Do Exercise 1-D Now, p. 17

D. Legal Analysis Is an Art, Not a Science

Legal analysis is an art, not a scientific or mathematical method. The answer to a legal question is rarely definitive. Lawyers must use their creativity and analytical skills to identify legal questions, to find the law, and to predict an outcome in a client's case by applying the law to the facts. This is an integral part of the lawyer's craft.

Exercise 1-A

Read the following. Identify the commonalities in the Barnetts' vacation experiences so that Jane Kass can help them choose a vacation they will enjoy.

Jane Kass is a travel agent. Her friends Jim and Alice Barnett have asked her to recommend a vacation for them that they will enjoy. She asked them to describe their last three trips together and to tell her if they liked them. Three years ago, they spent two weeks at a small inn on the island of Nantucket and loved it. Two years ago, they visited London for a week and stayed in a large hotel in the downtown area. They found it full of city hustle and bustle and too busy to be restful. Last year, they went on a four-day cruise through the Carribean on an ocean liner. While they loved being on the water, they did not enjoy traveling with the large crowd on the ship, and they would have preferred to have stayed longer on some of the islands they visited.

Exercise 1-B

For each of the following, read the facts, state the rule, and answer the question.

1. The court has ruled that no divorce can be finalized until one year after the filing of a petition for divorce. Georgia and Jim Brown filed a petition with the court for a divorce decree on June 1, 2001. Jim Brown wishes to re-marry. What is the earliest possible date that his next wedding can be scheduled?

2. Courts in Arcadia have declared that no one under age 18 can enter into a contract. Skip Henley, age 16, has just signed a membership contract to join the local health club. His parents are upset that he must pay monthly membership fees for two years. Has Skip signed a contract that can be enforced?

Exercise 1-C(1)

Read the following. State a rule that would define undue hardship.

A law student has been called for jury duty in the state of Arcadia. Her jury summons says that potential jurors may be excused if service would cause an undue hardship. She asked the clerk of the court to explain reasons that might excuse her. The clerk told her that in one case, a self-employed baby-sitter who would have been unable to work while serving on a jury was excused. Serving on the jury would have caused undue hardship because she would have no income for the period of service. In another case, an accountant who had purchased non-refundable plane tickets to Los Angeles for his family's vacation, scheduled for the day his jury service was to begin, faced an undue hardship and was excused from service. In a third case, an investment banker who feared that he might lose an important client if he could not attend a previously-scheduled meeting was not excused, since this risk did not constitute an undue hardship.

Immediate financial loss that is certain to occur

Exercise 1-C(2)

Using the rule you identified in Exercise 1-C(1), predict whether the law student would qualify for an "undue hardship" excuse in the following situation.

A law student has an interview scheduled with an out-of-state law firm on the same day as her jury service. She knows that the firm is completing its interview process that same week. Jury service is scheduled to last two weeks.

Exercise 1-D

Arcadia has a shoplifting law that reads, "Shoplifting occurs when an individual in a store removes or hides goods with the intention of taking them without paying for them." Read the following facts and cases, and state a rule that explains when someone violates the shoplifting law. Then apply the rule to Johnson's case and predict how a court would rule.

Facts

Jack Johnson, age 16, lives in the State of Arcadia. He was detained for shoplifting in a music store. Jack was accused of taking two CDs. He claims he meant to pay for them and only stuffed them in his pocket while he looked at DVDs. He was apprehended by security guards before he left the store.

Cases

Three recent cases discuss the crime of shoplifting under Arcadia law. In one, a man who was carrying a large trash can walked out of a hardware store to determine if it would fit in his car. He claimed that he had no intention of taking the can without paying for it, but only wanted to see whether it would fit in his car. The court found that he was not guilty of shoplifting. In another case, a woman was arrested in the parking lot of a drug store with six bottles of nail polish in her pockets. Though she claimed she intended to pay for them but forgot, the court found her guilty of shoplifting. In the last case, a woman entered the fitting room of a clothing store. When she emerged, she was wearing four shirts, one under another. Each had the price tag attached. She was stopped in the adjacent parking lot by store security and charged with shoplifting. The court found her guilty of shoplifting.

taken items
tent to steal
ft the store

CHAPTER 2

Analyzing Legal Issues

When you master this chapter, you will understand:

1. how the American legal system is structured;

2. what a legal issue is; and

3. how to identify and analyze legal issues.

A. The Legal System

In Chapter 1, you were introduced to the principles of legal analysis and applied these principles to non-legal problems and simple legal problems. You learned how "legal" analysis is similar to everyday analysis: it is a logical way of identifying past similar situations, finding a rule that makes sense of them, and applying that rule to a new situation to predict an outcome.

In this chapter you will consider analysis in a more advanced legal context. But first you will need some basic information about the American legal system, including why the law so often is difficult to find and apply.

1. Why the law is rarely definitive

Before coming to law school, you probably thought that the trick to becoming a lawyer was in knowing where to look for the law and once you found it, using it. In fact, as you no doubt have already begun to sense, there often is no single place to look for "the law," that is, the specific rule that can dictate the resolution of a dispute or the outcome of a case. It may seem surprising that laws may be difficult to find or that rules may be so unclear or uncertain that the lawyer must spend a lot of time trying to figure out what they actually mean. Why the law is so often unclear, incomplete, uncertain, or ambiguous is itself a complex question. There are several reasons, each stemming from a different facet of the American legal system:

a. *The law is not always a part of a written code.* Much of "the law" consists of the judgments of courts about how particular disputes should be decided. Rules that emerge from judicial opinions lie at the heart of the common-law system, discussed at greater length below. Although much law is embodied in the opinions of the courts, it is rarely spelled out in **black-letter** form—that is, in a clearly-stated, precise, and well-settled rule. To discern the law, the lawyer often must synthesize the rules from the opinions of various courts that have considered an issue under different circumstances.

b. *Compromise fosters fuzziness.* **Statutes**—laws enacted by a legislature—are the result of political compromise. Legislators with different agendas and political outlooks must often compromise on the wording of a statute just to secure enactment. Similarly, the justices of the U.S. Supreme Court, and judges on other appellate courts, often compromise to obtain sufficient votes to decide the case their way. Such compromises frequently take the form of broad, ambiguous, and unclear language to appease the many sides of debates.

c. *Language is ambiguous.* Even when law is explicitly stated in rule form, language is inherently ambiguous, and what might seem to the legislator a straightforward declaration may turn out, when interpreted or applied by the courts in different cases, to be far from clear.

d. *Efficiency requires generality.* Even black-letter law is often necessarily stated in generalities to avoid the time-consuming and ultimately impossible task of listing every possible situation to be covered. For example, a statute might prohibit "deception" and "misrepresentation" in commercial dealings without spelling out what each such deceptive practice and misrepresentation might be.

e. *Fuzziness prompts still more analysis.* Because the law so often is unclear, disputes cannot easily be settled simply by referring to a rule. The rules must be interpreted, and that is why so many disputes wind up in court. But in deciding a particular case, a court might itself be less than clear, and so parties to future disputes may find it necessary to return to court to challenge interpretations of previous court rulings.

f. *Laws are imperfect.* Legislators are not infallible, and they have no greater ability to foresee everything that should fall within a rule than do most people attempting to predict the future. Likewise, the law-makers are often unable to foresee political, social, and economic developments that might require a rule, so when something new comes along, governmental agencies, courts, and lawyers might try to apply laws not designed for the purpose, leading to interpretations that the framers of the law might never have contemplated.

g. *Lawmakers are imperfect.* Sometimes laws are poorly drafted, owing to mistakes about the meaning of language and the purposes to be served by the law, failure to proofread, or a lazy or indifferent approach to writing.

For all these reasons, the lawyer faces a difficult task just in understanding what the law is. *That is why the mastery of language, the ability to read closely and to fathom meaning from dense prose, is such an important part of the lawyer's craft.*

2. The common-law system

Elementary civics textbooks often explain that the three branches of government—the legislature, the executive, and the judiciary—have different roles to play in making and enforcing law. In the elementary view, the legislature *makes* the law, the executive *enforces* it, and the courts *interpret* it. However, this view is much too simplistic to be useful to the law student in understanding the legal system. In reality, all three branches of government are actively involved in making law.

Historically, law as we know it originated in the courts. Roots of the **common law**—the law that was supposed to be common to all of England, not merely to the territory controlled by a particular duke or baron—emerged from courts established by the British monarchs in the eleventh and twelfth centuries. The courts did not announce rules the way Parliament would later enact laws. Rather, in resolving disputes brought before them, judges said they were being guided by ancient principles, customs, and traditions of the people. For centuries, common-law judges persisted in claiming that they were not declaring law, only "finding" pre-existing rules and principles. In fact, however, the common-law courts over several centuries fashioned, often out of whole cloth, large branches of law—what today we know as torts, contracts, and property law, among others. The common law is often called the "unwritten law," in contrast to the enactment of explicit laws by the legislature. But in fact the common law is written down, in the opinions of the judges stating the reasons they had for deciding each case as they did. Not surprisingly, this common-law system has led, and is continuing to lead, to a staggering number of written opinions.

Although the term "common law" is often used in a narrow sense to describe claims that are judge-made, as opposed to those created by statute, the common-law system has a broader sense, referring to the judicial tradition of deciding cases. The common-law tradition rests on two basic principles.

First, judges apply and construe the law on a *case-by-case* basis. That is, they discuss and interpret the law only so far as is needed to resolve the particular issue in the case before them. They avoid general, theoretical pronouncements, confining themselves to the job of determining how the law applies to the case at hand. In a slander case, therefore, the judge will decide only whether the particular words were slanderous under the circumstances. Of course, the judge may discuss the tort of slander generally, but only to explain and justify the reasoning behind the particular decision, not to create an all-encompassing definition of the tort. A general definition can be sought only by reading many decisions to see the contours and boundaries of the concept as the courts have developed it.

Second, judges use decisions in prior cases with similar facts to resolve present cases. This second principle is a corollary of the first: applying the law incrementally on a case-by-case basis would create chaos unless the cases were consistent with each other. This principle is called **stare decisis**, which is Latin for *to stand by things decided*. (*Stare decisis* is the shortened form of the Latin phrase *stare decisis et non quieta movere*, which means "to stand by precedents and not to disturb settled principles of law.") Specifically, *stare decisis* means that a judge in a particular court must follow decisions made by judges in courts to which that decision could be appealed. Under the principle of *stare decisis*, decisions by these judges are **binding authority**, and the judge must follow them.

Unfortunately for the student, the principle of *stare decisis* is not, and probably could not be, rigidly followed. If every decision were required to conform to previous ones, the first judge to rule would set the law for all time. The common-law system is much more flexible, allowing the law to change to adapt to changing circumstances. Flexibility is built into the general common-law system in two ways. First, judges can **distinguish** a later case from a previous one, by pointing to different facts that might require a different outcome. Often the differences are real, but sometimes judges purport to find distinctions that do not really exist; in creating the "fiction" of difference, they can change the law to suit their policy purposes. Over time, the continuing distinctions lead to new rules. Second, appellate courts, or so-called "higher" courts, are not legally bound to adhere to the principle of *stare decisis*. For any number of reasons, the United States Supreme Court, and state supreme courts, might decide that a previous rule was wrong and **overrule** the case or cases that established it.

Further complicating the picture of law-making is the role of the legislature. The common-law courts do not act in a vacuum. Legislatures, consisting of elected representatives of the people, are law-making bodies. The statutes they enact are superior to the rules announced by courts, in the sense that a statute can alter, modify, and even abolish a common-law rule, as well as other statutes previously enacted.

In the late nineteenth century in America, legislatures began to encroach on the common law by adopting statutes on matters formerly rooted in common-law principles. At first the courts resisted, sometimes refusing to enforce the statutes, almost always reading the statutes narrowly. But in time the courts conceded the legitimacy of legislative rule. Today it is well understood that statutes supersede common-law rules. For example, at common law in the nineteenth century, an employee could not sue his employer if the employee was injured by a fellow employee. This was the so-called "fellow-servant rule." But because this rule usually meant that injured employees had no remedies, legislatures in most states abolished the rule. When it then appeared that companies would be swamped with lawsuits, legislatures responded with workers' compensation statutes, which barred injured employees from pressing common-law claims against their employers, and in return gave injured employees the right to recover money in an administrative proceeding without having to prove that the employer was at fault.

Although the legislature can alter a common-law rule, or create law in areas in which the common law is silent, the common-law system continues to work. The legislatures are no more sealed off from the courts than the courts are from the legislatures. Courts must necessarily be involved in statutory law because people question the meaning of the statutes. The meaning of legislation is rarely free from doubt. Common-law principles therefore apply to statutory cases too. Frequently, definitions of statutory terms (such as "deadly weapon" or "intended use") develop on the same case-by-case basis that leads to common-law principles. When construing statutes, judges limit themselves to deciding only what is necessary to the particular case, not to explaining the statute's general meaning. And *stare decisis* applies as well: the court must construe the statute consistently with prior, binding authority. That is why no statute can be understood in the legal sense simply by reading it: the lawyer must be aware of the many cases that have considered and settled its meaning.

And so it should by now be clear why "the law" is no simple thing that can easily be looked up and then routinely applied to resolve a dispute or accomplish some other objective. The American legal system is complex and sprawling, and the law can only be "found" and ultimately understood by a diligent search for the appropriate statutes and cases and a careful reading and analysis of what they say.

3. Civil law: The difference between statutory and common-law claims

A person's right to sue another in a civil suit is based on *either* a statute or the common law. A **claim** is a set of requirements, which, if proven, establishes a person's right to a judgment against another. A statutory claim is based on a law enacted by a legislature. A common-law claim is based on law that is judge-made.

For example, many state legislatures have passed laws prohibiting employers from firing employees who report dangerous or illegal activities of the employer to the authorities. Typically, these whistleblower statutes give fired employees the right to sue their employers. An employee who believes his firing violated the state's whistleblower statute therefore has a statutory claim against his employer, and he may sue his employer, seeking a judgment against him.

Similarly, many state legislatures have passed "Dram Shop Acts." These laws give people who are injured by intoxicated drivers the right to sue business owners who sold or served liquor to the drivers. Before these laws were passed, courts in some states refused to hold business owners liable in such cases. Dram Shop Acts make business owners civilly liable when they sell or serve liquor to drivers who are later involved in car accidents.

In contrast, common-law claims are claims that courts have traditionally accepted, even though they have no statutory basis. Tort claims (such as negligence and trespass) are often rooted in the common law.

Whether judges interpret statutory law or common law, they do the same thing: apply general legal principles to the specific case. In both situations, judges look to prior cases to see how the statutory provision or general common-law principle has been applied in similar situations by other judges. The judge construing a statute, however, must often also consider the legislature's purpose in passing the statute and construe it consistently with that purpose.

4. The difference between civil and criminal law

In a civil lawsuit, one person (the **plaintiff**) sues another (the **defendant**) because the plaintiff believes that the defendant harmed him. The plaintiff's harm might be physical injury, mental distress, economic loss, or something else. Whatever the harm, the plaintiff wants a **judgment**, requiring the defendant to provide a **remedy**. Although the usual remedy is for the defendant to pay the plaintiff money (**damages**), sometimes the defendant must do something (**specific performance**) or not do something (**injunctive relief**). Civil law determines whether a plaintiff is entitled to a judgment against a defendant in a lawsuit and what that remedy will be.

In a criminal **prosecution**, a government (federal, state, or local) charges an individual (also called the defendant) with committing a crime, such as murder, burglary, or fraud. Crimes are created by statute and usually are compiled in a **penal code**. For constitutional reasons, there can be no common-law crimes. In a criminal case, the government seeks to punish the defendant for committing the crime. The punishment may be a jail sentence, fine, probation, or community service.

Sometimes one event becomes the basis for both civil and criminal lawsuits. For instance, the family of a victim killed by a reckless driver may bring a civil action against the driver for wrongful death; the state may independently prosecute the driver for the crime of vehicular homicide.

B. What Is a Legal Issue?

The first challenge the lawyer or judge faces when a legal problem arises is identifying the **legal issue**. A legal issue is a question about what the law means or how (or whether) it applies to the facts of a particular situation. The law, whether in the form of a common-law principle or a statutory provision, is often expressed in general terms. That generality is necessary because the law cannot anticipate and specifically address every conceivable situation. For instance, under tort law, a person has a claim against someone who slanders him. But what type of statements are slanderous? The law cannot list every comment a person might make and categorize it as slanderous or not slanderous. Certainly some comments are slanderous on their face and others are not. It is slanderous to call someone a criminal if you know he has broken no laws; it is not slanderous to call someone "honest" even if he is not. But other comments are not so clear-cut. For example, it may or may not be slanderous to call someone a "scoundrel."

Much of the actual practice of law (and *most* of the questions raised in law school) involve a middle ground between events that clearly fit and clearly do not fit within a legal rule. In this middle ground lies the legal issue: "Are these words slanderous?" "Did A trespass on B's property?" "Was that dog provoked?" Lawyers (and law students) must know how to recognize when the situation with which they are presented raises legal issues.

C. Identifying Legal Issues

Legal issues do not reveal themselves. Lawyers ferret them out by carefully considering their clients' rights and obligations in particular situations. Law students do exactly the same thing for fictitious characters in classroom discussions and on papers and exams.

In litigation, lawyers often uncover issues when trying to determine if a client has a good case (or a good defense). Typically a prospective client who wants to sue someone will tell his story and ask the lawyer, "Can I sue?" or "Do I have a case?" The client's questions—"Can I sue?" or "Do I have a case?"—are not legal questions. To answer these questions, you, as a lawyer, must ask yourself a different one: does your client have a legal claim against someone? It is by trying to answer *this* question that you come upon legal issues.

1. Identifying your client's claim

The law recognizes many distinct claims: negligence, slander, breach of contract, and so on. Some rights, and therefore some civil claims, are created by the legislature. These are statutory claims. Others have no statutory basis, but rather are created by courts. These are common-law claims. Claims, whether statutory or common law, have distinct requirements. The careful lawyer lays out the claim's requirements in a way that will promote a thorough analysis. Sometimes statutes or the courts express the requirements as a list. Each item on the list is called an **element**. By way of illustration, the elements of the common-law claim of civil trespass could be stated this way:

> D is liable to P for trespass if,
> 1. without P's permission,
> 2. D intentionally
>   (A) enters P's land; or
>   (B) causes someone or something to enter P's land; or
>   (C) remains on P's land; or
>   (D) fails to remove from P's land something that he had permission to place there but thereafter had a duty to remove. [Adapted from the Restatement of Torts 2d § 158.]

2. Matching the elements of the claim to the facts of your case

Listing the elements of a claim—breaking the claim into its components—helps lawyers focus on each requirement separately, allowing them to determine systematically which elements of their clients' claims are satisfied and which must be more carefully considered. For example, consider whether D trespassed on P's land in the following situation:

> D lives in a three-story house that borders P's land. D installed on this house an awning that juts out over P's property, knowing that the awning would overhang P's land. D did not obtain P's permission to install the awning.

To determine whether P has a claim of trespass against D, you must first lay out the elements of the claim and then match them up to the specific facts of P's case. In other words, you must determine whether the facts of P's case satisfy— that is, meet—all of the requirements of the claim.

Your first step is to understand the elements of trespass. D must act *intentionally* and *without P's permission*. The requirements listed in (A), (B), (C), and (D) are connected by an "or." When the law specifies one thing *or* another thing as a requirement, you need satisfy only *one*. Therefore, P has a claim for trespass against D if, without P's consent, D intentionally did *any one* of the things listed in these four requirements.

Your next step is to match the elements to the particular facts of P's case. You know that D acted intentionally—since he knew the awning would overhang P's land—and that he did not have P's permission. To establish his claim, P must *also* satisfy any one of the four items listed in (A) through (D). Matching just (B) will be sufficient to satisfy this element because (A) through (D) are alternative ways to establish the claim of trespass. P's case does not meet the criteria in (A), (C), and (D): D did not enter P's land; D did not remain on P's land; and D did not fail to remove from P's land something that he was under a duty to remove. Therefore, the only possible match is (B): "causes . . . something to enter P's land."

You must then determine whether D, by installing the awning over P's property, intentionally and without permission "cause[d] . . . something to enter P's land." There is no question about D's intent and his lack of permission. But did the awning "enter" P's land even though it did not touch the ground? *This question raises an issue.* Your matching of the elements of trespass to the facts raises a question that cannot be answered without further research and analysis.

- Once a lawyer determines the client's potential claim (or claims), he must see if the facts of the client's case satisfy all of the *elements* of the claim.

- A lawyer often discovers legal issues when trying to match the elements of a particular claim to the facts of the client's case.

Do Exercises 2-A, 2-B(1), and 2-B(2) Now, p. 35

3. About defenses

A plaintiff's right to a judgment against a defendant depends not only on whether the plaintiff has a claim, but also on whether the defendant has a **defense** to the claim. A defense is a set of requirements, which if proven, may defeat the plaintiff's right to a judgment on his claim. Even a plaintiff who satisfies all the elements of his claim may nonetheless be unable to obtain a judgment against the defendant if the defendant can establish a defense. For example, one defense to a claim of breach of contract is disaffirmance. Generally, the disaffirmance defense gives a person the right to void a contract that is not for necessaries (such as food, clothing, or shelter) if he is a minor.

Like claims, most defenses have elements too. The elements of the defense of disaffirmance to a breach of contract claim might be expressed this way:

D may disaffirm a contract he has made if
1.   he is under age 18 and
2.   the contract is not for necessaries, such as food, clothing, or shelter.

Approach questions about defenses as you would claims: identify the elements of the defense and match each of them against the facts. When matching, distinguish easy matches from problematic ones, recognizing that the problematic ones may raise issues. For instance, suppose Fred, a fifteen-year-old high school student, decided he needed a cell phone. He went to an electronics store and, in exchange for a free cell phone, signed an agreement for a very expensive annual calling plan. When the first bill came, Fred realized he had made a big mistake and did not pay it. The phone company sued him for breach of the agreement. To determine whether Fred may assert the defense of disaffirmance, you would match the elements outlined above to these facts. You could conclude that the first element is satisfied because Fred is under age 18. It is not as clear, however, whether the cell phone is a "necessary." Your matching the second element of the defense to the facts therefore raises a question that cannot be answered without further research and analysis.

Do Exercises 2-C(1) and 2-C(2) Now, p. 36

4.   How to identify an issue in a legal claim

Consider the following situation:

> Recently, Frank, an eleven-year-old, was hit by a reckless driver and died immediately. Frank's aunt, Susan Johnson, saw the crash in which Frank's body was hurled into the air. She was standing three feet away from the accident when it occurred. Johnson suffered severe emotional shock as a result of witnessing the accident. She has retained your firm and wants to know whether she has a claim against the driver for her anguish.
>
> Since Frank was three, his mother worked outside the home and Johnson took care of him during the day. She regularly prepared his meals, helped him with his homework, and drove him to after-school activities. Every summer, Johnson took Frank with her to Florida, where they would stay with Frank's grandparents (Johnson's parents).

Step 1. Identifying the claim. You should first ask: what claim might Johnson have against the driver? Sometimes the type of claim is obvious—a contractor who has not been paid for work satisfactorily completed has a claim for breach of contract. But sometimes a claim is not obvious, and the lawyer must do some preliminary research, looking for claims that might be supported by his client's situation. A lawyer often gathers the **necessary facts** and determines his client's claim concurrently: knowing which facts are necessary—the facts that will determine the outcome of the case—depends on knowing the elements of the claim, and vice versa.

From your research, you learn that Johnson may have a claim against the driver of the car for negligent infliction of emotional distress, which is a common-law tort claim in Arcadia, where the accident occurred.

Step 2. Identifying the elements of the claim. The controlling case in Arcadia on negligent infliction of emotional distress—the primary case in the jurisdiction that the courts follow—has listed the elements of this claim as follows:

> When the defendant injures a third person, the plaintiff has a claim against the defendant for negligent infliction of emotional distress if
> 1.   the plaintiff was closely related to the injured person;

2.   the plaintiff was present at the scene of the accident and aware that the third person was being injured; and

3.   as a result, the plaintiff suffered an emotional shock.

Step 3. Determining whether your client's facts satisfy the elements of the claim. After you have identified a possible claim and determined its elements, your next step is to match each of the elements to the particular facts of your case. In doing so, you determine whether the facts of your case satisfy the elements of the claim.

Easy matches: the second and third elements. A cursory review of the case law indicates that the second and third elements of negligent infliction of emotional distress are satisfied. The second element is satisfied because Johnson, from a distance of three feet, saw the car hit Frank. The third element is also satisfied: we know that Johnson suffered emotional shock from witnessing the accident.

A harder match: the first element. Whether Johnson is "closely related" to Frank is less clear. A quick review of the cases indicates that while spouses, parents, and siblings of a victim are *always* considered "closely related" to the victim, more distant family members, like aunts, uncles, and cousins, are only *sometimes* considered "closely related."

You have identified an issue: Does the relationship between Frank and his aunt satisfy the "closely-related" element of the claim of negligent infliction of emotional distress? Identifying the issue is only your first step. Now you must analyze it.

D. Analyzing Legal Issues

Analyzing a legal issue is a three-step process: (1) finding similar cases; (2) identifying a rule that explains the holdings in those cases; and (3) applying that rule to your situation to predict an outcome. Therefore, to analyze whether the relationship between the aunt and her nephew satisfies the "closely-related" element of negligent infliction of emotional distress you would

1.   find cases considering the "closely-related" element that are factually similar to your case;

2.   identify a rule that either is expressly stated in those cases or that explains their holdings; and

3.   apply that rule to your case to predict how a court would resolve the issue of whether Johnson and her nephew Frank were "closely related."

Step 1. Find Similar Cases. Your first step is to find cases involving similar facts. You might have a personal opinion about whether Johnson and her nephew were "closely related," but only the opinion of the courts, not your opinion, matters to the outcome of your client's case. So you do additional research, looking this time not for cases that generally list the elements of the claim of negligent infliction of emotional distress, but for cases that will help you predict how a court would decide the particular question of whether Johnson was "closely related" to her nephew Frank. In other words, you are focusing your research on the "closely-related" element of the claim, looking for cases with facts that are like yours.

You find nine cases in your jurisdiction, all binding authority, dealing with the "closely-related" element. Three of these cases consider whether a victim's spouse or parents are closely related to the victim. In these cases, the courts held that spouses and parents were closely related because they were members of the victim's immediate family. In three other cases, the court held that close friends of the victim could not recover because no "blood or conjugal relationship" existed between the friends and the victims. The three remaining cases involved aunts and uncles of the victim. Here are summaries of the facts and holdings of these three cases.

Case 1: Smith v. Jones

The uncle witnessed the death of his five-year-old nephew, who was killed by a reckless driver.

Relationship between uncle and victim. The uncle and nephew lived in the same neighborhood. The uncle visited the nephew's home almost every day and during those visits often read to his nephew or played with him. The boy slept at his uncle's house two nights a week (when the boy's mother, a single parent, worked at a nearby restaurant). The uncle took the boy to numerous baseball and football games during the year.

Holding on the issue. The uncle had a claim for negligent infliction of emotional distress because he was "closely related" to the boy. Characterizing the relationship between the boy and his uncle as "extremely close" and acknowledging that the uncle was a "father figure" for the boy, the court found them "closely related" even though the uncle was not a member of the boy's immediate family (*i.e.*, not a parent, sibling, or grandparent).

Case 2: Patrick v. Michaels

The aunt witnessed an accident in which her two-year-old nephew was severely burned.

Relationship between aunt and victim. The aunt and nephew lived in the same house in the suburbs for about a year. The aunt was a young professional, commuting to her job in the city and working long hours and weekends. She was living with her sister and brother-in-law until she saved enough money to buy an apartment in the city. She occasionally cleaned the apartment but never bathed the child, babysat for him, or changed his diapers.

Holding on the issue. The aunt was not "closely related" to the boy because she did not have a close, loving relationship with the child.

Case 3: Mills v. Donaldson

The uncle witnessed the hit-and-run death of his seven-year-old niece by a taxi.

Relationship between uncle and victim. The uncle moved into his sister's house five years before the accident, shortly after his sister's husband abandoned her and her four children (including the niece). Since then, the uncle, a construction worker who works long hours, has supported his sister and the children. Although not the primary caregiver for the children, he has developed strong emotional ties to them and, in addition to supporting the family, has assumed other responsibilities normally associated with parenting: disciplining and teaching the children, doing school work with them, and attending parent-teacher meetings at their school.

Holding on the issue. The uncle was "closely related" to the niece because he acted as a "surrogate father" to her.

Step 2. Identify a Rule. Cases and statutes often provide express rules that explain the meaning of an element of a claim. Sometimes, however, no express definition of the element is provided or the provided definition is too vague to give any practical assistance in predicting the outcome. There is no express definition here. You therefore must make sense of the three cases *as a whole* by identifying a correct and useful rule that explains and reconciles their holdings. Your rule must explain why the court held that the plaintiff in Case 2 was not "closely-related" to the victim but that the plaintiffs in Cases 1 and 3 were. Reviewing the three cases, you might determine that when considering whether aunts or uncles are "closely related" to nephews and nieces, the court looks at whether they had a relationship similar to that between a parent and child.

Often, making a chart that summarizes the holdings and necessary facts on an issue helps you identify a rule. A chart of these cases on the "closely-related" issue might look like this:

	Parental Relationship?	Closely Related?
Case 1: *Smith v. Jones*	Yes	Yes
Case 2: *Patrick v. Michaels*	No	No
Case 3: *Mills v. Donaldson*	Yes	Yes
Your case	?	?

After studying the chart, you might write the following rule:

> *Aunts and uncles are "closely related" to their nephews and nieces if they have frequent contact with them and assume significant parental responsibility for their welfare.*

Is this the correct rule? It is correct in the sense that it explains and reconciles the three cases. However, you could formulate a different rule based on the same cases. Arguably, the responsibility need not be "parental"; perhaps a close relationship that was not like that of a parent and child would suffice. The cases fall on the extreme ends of the spectrum of possible relationships. In two of the cases, the relationships were parental or nearly so (Cases 1 and 3); in the other, the relationship was nearly non-existent. You cannot be certain that the relationship must be parental because no case tests the "middle ground." Nonetheless, characterizing the required relationship as "parental" seems a defensible choice because in both Cases 1 and 3 the courts stressed that the uncles were surrogate fathers to the victims.

Remember, identifying rules is an *art,* not a science. You identify rules to predict how an issue in an *undecided* case will be resolved. The facts of your case will determine how broadly or narrowly you frame the rule.

Step 3. Apply Your Rule. The third step is to use your rule to predict whether a judge would hold that your client was "closely related" to her nephew. To make that prediction, complete the chart for your case. Was Johnson like a parent to Frank? Under your rule, she was "closely related" to him only if you can answer yes.

Johnson's relationship with Frank is analogous to the plaintiffs' relationships in Cases 1 and 3. (In both those cases, the court held that a parental relationship existed.) Like the plaintiffs in these cases, Johnson spent much time with the child and assumed many parental responsibilities. You could therefore predict that a court would be likely to hold that Johnson had a parental relationship with Frank. If they did have a parental relationship, you could then predict that a court would be likely to hold that Johnson was "closely related" to Frank.

Therefore, Johnson can satisfy the first element of the claim for negligent infliction of emotional distress.

You must conclude your analysis by answering the question that prompted your research in the first place: does Johnson have a claim for negligent infliction of emotional distress? Since you now know that Johnson can satisfy *all* three elements of the claim, you could conclude that a court would most likely find that she does.

Do Exercises 2-D(1), 2-D(2), and 2-D(3) Now, p. 37

EXERCISES

Exercise 2-A

Consider whether, in the following cases, D trespassed on P's land. Apply the elements of trespass set forth on p. 26 to the facts. Identify possible issues.

Case 1: D, running near P's property, slips and falls into T, who falls onto P's property.

Case 2: D cuts down a tree on a hill on his property. The tree rolls down the hill onto P's property.

Case 3: D owns a waste-processing plant. D's containment system fails; the stench of garbage invades P's property.

Case 4: D, with P's permission, parks his car in P's driveway for a three-month period during which D's house is renovated. After the renovation project is completed, D refuses to remove his car from P's property.

Exercise 2-B(1)

Read the following case excerpt. Identify the elements of a common-law fraud claim in Olympus.

> *Deluca v. Fletcher*: In Olympus, a person may be liable for common-law fraud if he knowingly makes a false statement of material fact to another person who justifiably relies on the statement and suffers damages by relying on the statement.

Exercise 2-B(2)

Read the facts in each example. Apply the elements of fraud that you identified in Exercise 2-B(1) to the facts. For each example, list issues that may arise from applying the elements to the facts.

Example A

Arthur Endicott, a builder, constructed a single-family house on a site adjacent to an abandoned industrial landfill. Margaret Wang, the purchaser of the house, claims that Endicott told her the surrounding property had never been used for industrial purposes. She learned of the former use of the adjacent property when a local newspaper ran a story about possible toxic contamination at the site. Wang asserts that she would not have bought the house had she known of its proximity to the abandoned landfill. She has not been able to sell her house; prospective buyers fear health hazards in the neighborhood.

Example B

Harvey Simpson was, until recently, the director of marketing for CFQ, a mid-sized corporation. Elizabeth Wagner, the president and chief executive officer of ZWE, a large multi-national corporation, offered Simpson a job as ZWE's vice president for marketing. Wagner assured Simpson that ZWE was financially sound. Simpson accepted the offer and resigned from his job at CFQ; he would make substantially more money and have more responsibility in the new position. On Simpson's first day at ZWE, Wagner told him that the company was experiencing financial difficulties and therefore had to eliminate the vice president for marketing position. Wagner offered Simpson a job as a salesperson in the marketing department; the salary for this position was slightly lower than the salary Simpson had earned at CFQ.

Exercise 2-C(1)

In Olympus, consent is a defense to a claim of common-law battery. Read the following case excerpt. Identify the elements of consent.

> *James v. Rogers*: In Olympus, consent is a defense to a claim of common-law battery if the plaintiff expressly or impliedly consents to the contact engaged in by the defendant.

Exercise 2-C(2)

Read the facts in each example. Apply the elements of consent that you identified in Exercise 2-C(1) to the facts. For each example, list issues that may arise from applying the elements of consent to the facts. Predict whether the defense of consent can be established in each example.

Example A

Paula Henson is a personal trainer at a gym. Ken Bernard is one of Henson's clients. During a strength-training workout, Henson grabbed Bernard's ankle and flexed his leg to his chest. Bernard doubled over in pain. He suffered a muscle injury which required arthoscopic surgery to repair.

Example B

Tommy Washington joined his high school's baseball team. At a recent game, Zachary Prescott, the pitcher for the opposing team, hit Washington on the chest with a ball when Washington was batting. Washington stopped breathing and was rushed to the hospital.

Exercise 2-D(1)

Read the following case excerpt. Identify the elements of a common-law battery claim in Olympus.

> *Walters v. Stern:* In Olympus, a person may be held liable for common-law battery if he intentionally touches another person in a harmful or offensive manner.

Exercise 2-D(2)

Read the following case excerpts. Use them to write rules for the "intentional touching" and "harmful or offensive contact" elements of battery identified in Exercise 2-D(1).

> *Alexander v. Riley:* Riley asserts that she did not commit common-law battery because she did not touch Alexander's body. This argument is without merit. In Olympus, the "intentional touching" element of battery includes any contact the defendant intentionally makes with the plaintiff's body, clothing, or objects in the plaintiff's physical possession. Riley deliberately

pulled on the plaintiff's shirt, causing it to rip. The "intentional touching" element is therefore satisfied.

Sakamura v. Turner: Turner maintains that he did not commit common-law battery because Sakamura suffered no physical injury. This argument is without merit. In Olympus, a plaintiff is not required to prove that he suffered physical injury to prevail on a claim of battery. "Harmful or offensive contact" is defined as touching that causes actual physical injury, pain, or discomfort or touching that causes pain or discomfort or that is offensive to the plaintiff's personal dignity. Turner slapped Sakamura in the face during a business meeting, causing Sakamura to suffer mild pain and great humiliation. The contact in this case was both harmful and offensive.

Exercise 2-D(3)

Read the facts in each example. Apply the elements of battery that you identified in Exercise 2-D(1) to the facts. For each example, list issues that may arise from applying the elements to the facts. Predict whether a claim of common-law battery can be established in each example.

Example A

Peter Conrad is a manager at FGH Corp. Jason Young is one of Conrad's subordinates. After suffering a skiing injury, Young walked to work with a cane. Conrad, believing that Young was faking the injury, teased him and then grabbed his cane. Young stumbled and bumped his head on the copy machine. He did not suffer any physical injuries.

Example B

Edward Finch and Sally Booker were standing next to each other on a crowded subway train during the evening rush hour commute. The train lurched. To maintain her balance, Booker grabbed Finch's arm. She cut Finch with a key she was holding in her hand.

No intent !

CHAPTER 3

Reading Cases and Writing Case Briefs

When you master this chapter, you will understand:

1. what a case is;

2. how reading cases helps you understand the law and analyze legal problems;

3. what a case brief is; and

4. how to write a useful case brief.

A. What Is a Case?

The word case has several meanings. Lawyers sometimes use the word case to refer to a lawsuit or other legal matter, such as a real estate transaction or corporate merger. They also use the word to refer to the arguments, law, and evidence that support a lawsuit: they speak of having "strong cases" and "weak cases." This chapter concentrates on a third meaning of the word case—a court's written decision, also referred to as an **opinion**.

Every case tells the story of a dispute that could not be resolved without resort to the courts. A court decides the legal question because the parties were unable or unwilling to settle the dispute themselves. Usually, once the court answers the legal question, its resolution becomes a matter of public record and the court's decision becomes legal authority to which other courts can turn.

Some decisions determine the *outcome* of the legal action—who wins and who loses. Many decisions do not address the ultimate merits of the action but rather resolve an *aspect* of it, such as the admissibility of evidence.

A case can answer a **substantive legal question**, a **procedural legal question**, or some combination of the two. An example of a substantive legal question is whether a defendant was negligent. An example of a procedural legal question is whether a court has **jurisdiction** over the parties, that is, the legal authority to hear a case involving the parties. Sometimes a case may decide both types of questions, such as the propriety of joining co-defendants (a procedural legal question) and the availability of an assumption of risk defense (a substantive legal question).

A court can write a decision at any stage of a legal proceeding when a legal question requires an answer. A trial court judge, for example, may issue a written opinion dismissing a complaint, deciding a legal question at trial, or granting a post-trial motion. A party who disagrees with a trial court's decision may appeal to an appellate court. If the appellate court finds that the trial court's decision was correct, it **affirms** the decision. If the appellate court finds that the trial court's decision was incorrect, it **reverses** the decision. Most opinions you read in law school come from appellate courts.

B. Why Lawyers and Law Students Read Cases

Lawyers and law students read cases for the same reasons. Lawyers read cases to understand the law, to determine how the law applies to a client's situation, and to predict how a court will view a client's problem. Similarly, as a law student, you will read cases to learn the law, to understand how the law applies to facts, and to resolve legal questions posed in the classroom, on exams, and in writing assignments.

1. Reading cases to learn the law

You must read cases to learn the common law. Cases establish and explain the elements of common-law claims and defenses. A court's decision, for instance, may tell you the elements required to state a common-law claim of false imprisonment or a common-law defense of contributory negligence. In addition, cases may determine general common-law principles, such as the distinction between an employee and independent contractor.

You also read cases to understand how the courts have interpreted statutes. As you learned in Chapter 2, cases often determine the applicability and scope of statutes. For example, while a statute may prohibit "consumer fraud," you likely will have to read cases to learn whether a car dealer's misrepresentation about the safety of a car constitutes consumer fraud under the statute. Cases also elucidate the meaning of constitutional provisions and administrative regulations.

2. Using cases to analyze legal problems

Once you understand the law established in a case or a group of cases, the next step is to analyze how the law applies to particular facts. The facts may come from a client's question or from a hypothetical scenario posed in the classroom, on an exam, or in a writing assignment. To determine if a case applies to your problem, ask yourself if it addresses the same legal question raised by your facts. If so, use it (together with other similar cases) to predict how a court would resolve your problem.

C. Understanding Cases

Read cases carefully and purposefully, constantly questioning what the text means. You must master the essence of a case so that you can explain it clearly. If you cannot explain a case directly and simply to a non-lawyer, you probably do not understand it. Moreover, you must learn to scrutinize the relationship *between* cases: do they deal with the same kind of facts, answer the same legal question, apply the same rule of law? Section D, p. 47, identifies and explains each part of a published decision. Learn the purpose of each part to help you read cases critically and master them.

A court's written opinion generally states:

1. the facts that gave rise to the dispute (including how the case got to court);
2. the issue—a question about what the law means or how (or whether) the law applies to the facts of the dispute;
3. the law applicable to the dispute;
4. the holding—the court's decision on the issue; and
5. the reasoning, including any relevant policy interest, that explains and supports the holding.

Many cases are very comprehensive; they lay out all of these components in great detail. Other cases are more abbreviated; a decision may explain these components summarily or may omit some of them altogether.

An appellate court opinion, usually decided by a panel of judges, may be unanimous; that is, all the judges agree on the result in the case and the reasons for it. If the appellate judges cannot reach a unanimous decision, the majority's opinion becomes the law; it is usually called the **majority opinion**. An appellate judge who disagrees with the result reached by the majority may write a **dissenting opinion** explaining how she would have ruled in the case and why. An appellate judge who agrees with the *result* reached by the majority but does not fully agree with the majority's *reasoning* may write a **concurring opinion**. A concurring opinion often presents alternative reasons for the result in the case. It is important to remember that a majority opinion sets out the law of the case. Dissenting and concurring opinions, although instructive, do not have any precedential value; they are not the law, although they often help to clarify what the majority has said.

In contrast to an appellate court case, a trial court case is usually decided by one judge or, in the case of a jury trial, by a jury that renders a verdict. Consequently, there are rarely dissenting or concurring opinions at the trial court level.

1. The facts of the case

Every case is based on a story: an employee is fired because of his race; a marriage fails and a spouse seeks a divorce; a drunk driver kills a pedestrian; a corporation defrauds its investors. The facts identify the parties and explain the basis for the legal action. Since each story is different, the facts of every case are unique. A court may recount the facts concisely and simply or in a lengthy and complicated manner.

All the facts in a case are not equally important. The **supporting facts** are not necessary to the outcome of the case, but assist the reader in understanding what happened. The **procedural facts** describe how the parties got to court and explain the court's rulings. The **necessary facts** are those the court relied on to reach its decision. Only after reading a case completely through, carefully analyzing the issues, rules, holdings, and reasoning, will you be able to discern which facts the court found necessary to decide the case as it did.

Judges may relate the facts in a variety of ways: they may provide a narrative summary, recite the facts as court findings, reprint the allegations of the parties, summarize the trial record (the testimony and exhibits submitted at trial), or use actual material from the trial record. You must identify all the necessary, supporting, and procedural facts in a case regardless of the manner in which they are presented.

2. **The issue: The question about what the law means or how (or whether) the law applies to a particular situation**

A legal issue is a question about what the law means or how (or whether) the law applies to a particular situation. A case often has more than one issue. The court might not discuss all the issues in one place. The court might intersperse them throughout the opinion. You must identify all the issues, wherever they appear in the opinion.

Some opinions identify the issues in a straightforward way: the court will use words like "The issue before us is . . . ." Occasionally the court will flag the issues for the reader by reciting what the parties have identified as the issues in their court papers. The court may then refine the issues in its own language, or it may continue with its analysis and decision. Whether the court delineates the issues or not, you must identify them and be able to state them clearly in your own words.

Issues are fact-sensitive when the answer to the legal question depends on the facts. A court may frame a fact-sensitive issue in broad terms, focusing on the claim or defense rather than on its elements. Note, however, that even when the issue is framed broadly in a case, the court usually analyzes the elements of the claim or defense separately. The following example illustrates a broadly framed issue; it focuses on the claim of slander, not on any of its elements:

- *Broadly framed issue*: The issue before us is whether a business owner has a claim for slander against a competitor who called him a cheapskate.

Alternatively, a court may frame a fact-sensitive issue narrowly, isolating elements of the claim. In the next example, the issue is narrow; it focuses on the "dwelling" element of a burglary statute:

- *Narrowly framed issue*: The issue before us is whether an abandoned car in which people live constitutes a "dwelling" under a statute that makes it a crime to burglarize a dwelling.

In contrast to fact-sensitive issues, some issues are purely legal questions, such as whether a statute is constitutional. The answers to such questions usually do not depend on particular facts. This chapter concentrates on the analysis of cases with fact-sensitive issues.

3.   The law applicable to the dispute

In every case, the court must decide what law applies to the parties' dispute. The court usually explains the law it is applying. The law may come from a statute, an ordinance, a court decision or a group of decisions, the federal constitution, a state constitution, or an administrative regulation. The following are examples of statements of law:

- *Law from a statute*: "Physical injury" means impairment of physical condition or substantial pain. N.Y. Penal Law § 10.00(9) (McKinney 1998).

- *Law from a court decision*: To state a malicious prosecution claim arising out of a criminal action, the plaintiff must establish that (1) the defendant caused a criminal action to be commenced against him; (2) the defendant was actuated by malice; (3) there was no probable cause for the action; and (4) the action was terminated in his favor. *Lind v. Schmid*, 337 A.2d 365 (N.J. 1975).

- *Law from the federal constitution*: People are protected from unreasonable searches and seizures. Fourth Amendment to the U.S. Constitution.

There may be more than one source of law that applies in a case. Here again, as with the issues, the court may recite all the applicable law in one place in its decision or may intersperse it throughout the text. You must identify all the laws applied by the court to understand how the court resolved the issues.

4. The holding: The court's decision on the issue

A holding in a case is the court's decision on how the law applies to the facts. *It resolves the issues in the case.* The holding is important because it tells you under what factual circumstances the court will make the same decision again.

If the court is called upon to decide more than one issue, a case will have more than one holding. Sometimes you will find the words "we hold" in the decision, clearly identifying the court's determination, but just as often you will not. You must identify all the holdings to understand how the court resolved the issues. The examples that follow illustrate how holdings might apply the law to the specific facts of a dispute:

Example A

Law on the competency of the testator (a person who makes a will): To make a valid will, the testator must be competent. Competence means knowing how much property one has, to whom one is bequeathing it, and who is being excluded.

Holding applying the law to the facts: The testator was competent when she made her will because she knew what she owned and understood that she left all her property to a friend instead of to her sons.

Example B

Law on undue influence: The beneficiary of a will exerts undue influence over the testator when he acts to procure the will in his favor.

Holding applying the law to the facts: The defendant exerted undue influence when he took the testator to his own attorney, was present during the entire consultation, participated in decisions about the disposition of the testator's estate, and convinced her to leave him all of her property.

A general pronouncement of law applicable to facts *unnecessary* to resolving the parties' dispute is not a holding; it is called a **dictum** (the plural is **dicta**). Because it is not the holding, a dictum is not the law and therefore is not binding authority in future cases. A court may write dicta to explain or support its decision.

Here is an example of a dictum in a malpractice case: "Even though the plaintiff's action is barred by the statute of limitations, the court notes that the elements for stating a malpractice claim appear to have been met." Since the court has dismissed the action because it is time-barred, the court's pronouncement on malpractice is not part of its holding. Because it is not a holding, the court's statement would not bind a judge who had to rule on a malpractice claim under similar facts. The judge in such a case could, however, use the statement to explain or support his decision.

5.   The reasoning: The court's rationale and support for its holding

The **reasoning** is the court's rationale and support for its holding in a case. The court may explain why the law requires a particular result when applied to the necessary facts of the dispute. It may point to a social or economic policy interest as support for its holding. In a dispute concerning a statute, the court may justify its holding by referring to the legislature's intent in enacting the statute. If there is a split of authority on an issue, the court may explain why it applied one rule of law instead of another. Here are examples of ways that courts might explain their holdings:

- *Reasoning turning on public policy:* Recognizing a claim for negligent supervision by a parent in this matter would open the floodgates to frivolous litigation. Minor childhood squabbles should be settled on the playground, not in the courtroom.

- *Reasoning turning on legislative intent:* The plaintiff is entitled to have his day in court on the question of whether he was denied a salary increase because of his sexual orientation. Indeed, the legislature, in enacting the statute prohibiting employment discrimination, recognized that the legislation's remedial goal of eradicating unlawful discrimination in the workplace will be realized only if the courts entertain all colorable claims.

Occasionally, a court does not explain its reasoning, but merely announces its holding. Avoid the temptation to speculate in such a case. Your inferences and speculations are not persuasive. If you need a case that explains the reasoning for the holding so that you can analogize it to your situation, continue your research.

D. The Parts of a Case: An Annotated Case

The components of a published decision are identified and analyzed below.* Remember, however, that every decision is unique. Decisions vary greatly in both format and substance. The sample annotation that follows identifies the common components of a case:

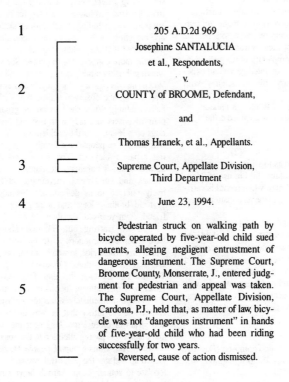

1

205 A.D.2d 969

Josephine SANTALUCIA
et al., Respondents,

v.

2   COUNTY of BROOME, Defendant,

and

Thomas Hranek, et al., Appellants.

3   Supreme Court, Appellate Division,
Third Department

4   June 23, 1994.

5
Pedestrian struck on walking path by bicycle operated by five-year-old child sued parents, alleging negligent entrustment of dangerous instrument. The Supreme Court, Broome County, Monserrate, J., entered judgment for pedestrian and appeal was taken. The Supreme Court, Appellate Division, Cardona, P.J., held that, as matter of law, bicycle was not "dangerous instrument" in hands of five-year-old child who had been riding successfully for two years.
Reversed, cause of action dismissed.

---

*   Reprinted from *Atlantic Reporter 2d* with permission of West Group.

SANTALUCIA v. COUNTY OF BROOME   775
Cite as 613 N.Y.S.3d 774 (A.D. 3 Dept. 1994)

1. Parent and Child 🔑 13(1)
    Exception to general rule, that parents are not liable for negligent supervision of their children, provides that parent owes duty to third party to shield them from infant child's improvident use of dangerous instrument, at least, if not especially, when parent is aware of and capable of controlling its use.

2. Parent and Child 🔑 13(1)
    Determination of whether particular instrument is "dangerous instrument" for purposes of imposing duty on parent to supervise infant child's use of such instrument, depends upon nature and complexity of allegedly dangerous instrument, age, intelligence and experience of child, and his proficiency with instrument.

> See publication Words and Phrases for other judicial construction and definitions.

3. Parents and Child 🔑 13(2)
    Determination as to whether parents had duty to supervise infant child in use of "dangerous instrument" may, when record is sufficiently developed, be made as a matter of law.

4. Parent and Child   13(1)
    Bicycle ridden by five-year-old child was not a "dangerous instrument," for purposes of imposing duty on parents to supervise a child who struck pedestrian; undisputed evidence established that child had been riding bicycle two years prior to accident, and that he possessed basic skills to ride it and had never had a prior accident.

———

Levene, Gouldin & Thompson (David F. McCarthy, of counsel), Binghamton, for appellants.

James N. Cahill, Endicott, for respondents.

Before CARDONA, P.J., and MIKOLL, WHITE, WEISS and PETERS, JJ.

CARDONA, Presiding Justice.

Appeal from an order of the Supreme Court (Monserrate, J.), entered November 24, 1998 in Broome County, which denied a motion by defendants Thomas Hranek and Jan Hranek for summary judgment dismissing the complaint against them.

On May 25, 1992 plaintiff Josephine Santalucia (hereinafter plaintiff), while walking on a path at Otsiningo Park, owned and operated by defendant County of Broome, was struck and injured by a 16-inch bicycle ridden by five-year-old Aaron Hranek. At the time of the accident, plaintiff was just finishing her second trip around the path which she knew, from her first revolution, was used for different purposes, including skateboarding, skating and bicycling. On her second revolution plaintiff noticed that the condition of the path had become more congested with people. She was walking briskly and passing other walkers. When she was struck by the bicycle and as she was falling, she observed a little boy with a helmet falling. While she was on the ground, plaintiff observed a lady with two, big heavy dogs on a leash, near the accident site. Aaron was one of five people on a family outing riding separate bicycles. The group included both of Aaron's parents, defendants Thomas Hranek and Jan Hranek (hereinafter collectively referred to as defendants), his eight-year-old brother, Joey, and a neighborhood friend, eight-year-old Mat-thew.

Before starting out, Thomas Hranek gave specific instructions as to the order in which they would ride, to watch out for people and stay clear of dogs. Once on the path, Thomas Hranek took the lead, followed by either Joey or Matthew, then Aaron and then his mother. Immediately after the collision, Aaron told his father that he was distracted and afraid of three large dogs near the path and that he was paying attention to the dogs as he went around this group of people. He then looked up and saw the plaintiff, however it was too late to actually stop. Aaron's bicycle had been given to him when he was three years old. Initially, it had training wheels; however, they were removed at the end of the previous summer. Other than crashes and falls as he learned to ride, Aaron never had any prior accidents with his bike. In his father's opinion, on the day of the accident Aaron possessed basic skills like any youngster and was good at riding his bike.

776   613 NEW YORK SUPPLEMENT, 2d SERIES

12 Following the accident, plaintiff commenced a personal injury action[1] against the County[2] and defendants, individually and as the parents and natural guardians of their son.

14 The complaint alleged, *inter alia,* that Aaron negligently rode his bike and defendants negligently supervised their son by entrusting to him a dangerous instrument,

15 his bicycle. Following discovery, which included examinations before trial of defendants and plaintiff, defendants moved pursuant to CPLR 3212 for summary judgment dismissing the complaint against them individually. The Supreme Court, reasoning that it

16 was up to a jury to determine whether, under the attendant circumstances, the bicycle was a "dangerous instrument", denied the motion. Defendants appeal.

17 [1-3] Parents are not liable for the negligent supervision of their children (*see, Holodook v. Spencer,* 36 N.Y.2d 35, 364 N.Y.S.2d 859, 824 N.E.2d 338); however, there is an exception to this rule. "[I]t is well-established law that a parent owes a duty to third parties to shield them from an infant child's improvident use of a dangerous instrument, at least, if not especially, when the parent is aware of and capable of controlling its use" (*Nolechek v. Gesuale,* 46 N.Y.2d 332, 338, 413 N.Y.S.2d 340, 385 N.E.2d 126). "Children might, at various points in their development, be permitted, and properly so, to use bicycles, lawn mowers, power tools, motorcycles, or automobiles, all of which are, in some contingencies, 'dangerous instruments'" (*id.,* at 338, 418 N.Y.S.2d 340, 385 N.E.2d 126). Thus, the determination of whether a particular instrument is dangerous "depends upon the nature and complexity of the allegedly dangerous instrument, the age, intelligence and experience of the child, and his proficiency with the instrument." (*Bottillo v. Poette,* 152 A.D.2d 840, 841, 544 N.Y.S.2d 47). Such

18 a determination may, where the record is sufficiently developed, be made as a matter of law, (*see, id.,* at 841, 544 N.Y.S.2d 47).

19 [4] Riding a bicycle has become, practically speaking, a natural stage of every child's development. It is very common to see very

young children, like Aaron, riding unassisted. Although a child's bicycle is a machine, it is not complex. Here, the undisputed evidence establishes that Aaron had been riding his bicycle some two years prior to the accident, and that he possessed the basic skills to ride it and never had a prior accident with it. The record is devoid of any evidence that his parents were aware that Aaron might not be able to control his bike on the path without placing third parties at unreasonable risk. Therefore, **19**

20 we hold, as a matter of law, under the circumstances herein, that Aaron's bicycle was not a "dangerous instrument" within the meaning of *Nolechek v. Gesuale* (*supra*) and grant summary judgment in favor of defendants.

21 ORDERED that the order is reversed, on the law, with costs, motion granted, summary judgment awarded to defendants Thomas Hranek and Jan Hranek and cause of action alleging negligent entrustment of a dangerous instrument dismissed.

22 MIKOLL, WHITE, WEISS and PETERS, JJ., concur.

---

13 1. Plaintiff's husband also brought a derivative action.

2. The County is not a party to this appeal.

1. Parallel citation

Although the case reproduced here is from the *New York Supplement, Second Series*, in volume 613 on page 774 (613 N.Y.S.2d 774), this **parallel citation—** 205 A.D. 2d 969—indicates a different reporter in which the same case can also be found: *New York Appellate Division Reports, Second Series*, in volume 205 on page 969. (For more information on reporters and citations, see Chapters 13 and 14.)

2. Name of the case

The name of the case, or caption, identifies the parties. The caption in this case is Josephine Santalucia *et al.* Respondents, v. County of Broome, Defendant, and Thomas Hranek *et al.*, Appellants. It also identifies the party who appealed. Here, the parties who are appealing, called the Appellants, are Thomas and Jan Hranek. (Jan Hranek is not named in the caption. You have to read the decision to learn that the "*et al.*" following Thomas Hranek's name refers to Jan Hranek.) The Respondents, who are opposing the appeal, are Josephine Santalucia and her husband. (Footnote 1 in the decision states that Santalucia's husband brought a derivative action. The "*et al.*" (an abbreviation for a Latin phrase meaning "and others") following Santalucia's name therefore refers to him. Footnote 2 states that the County of Broome, a defendant in the original action, is not party to this appeal.)

3. The court

The name of the court tells you which court decided the case. One of New York's intermediate appellate courts, the New York Supreme Court, Appellate Division, Third Department, decided this case.

4. The date

The date—June 23, 1994—is when the case was decided.

5. Editorial summary of the case

The editorial summary of the case is written by the book publisher. It is not part of the court's decision and therefore is not legal authority. You cannot rely on or cite to this summary. The summary is, however, a useful way to learn about the case and is helpful during research in determining whether a case might be relevant.

6. Headnotes

Headnotes are summaries of the law about specific issues. They are written by the book publisher. The headnotes begin with a boldfaced topic name and key number and are followed by a short summary of the issue and necessary facts. Like the editorial summary, headnotes are helpful in locating legal issues and cases, but they are not part of the court's decision and *cannot* be relied on or cited to as legal authority. For more on headnotes, see Chapter 13.

7. Names of lawyers who represented the parties

The names of the lawyers who represented the parties can be useful to a lawyer who wants to learn more about the arguments or evidence presented to the court, or who needs to refer a client to a lawyer specializing in similar cases.

8. Names of judges who decided the case

The names of the particular judges on a case can be helpful to a lawyer trying to predict how a court made up of one or more of these judges will decide a similar case because research into other opinions by those judges may help the lawyer shape the client's case.

9. Name of the judge who wrote the decision

Presiding Justice Cardona wrote this decision. Knowing the name of the judge who wrote the decision can be helpful to a lawyer trying to predict how this judge will decide a similar case.

10. Procedural posture of the case

The opinion begins here. This procedural posture statement tells you what happened in the lower court proceedings and the basis for the appeal. The trial court, the New York Supreme Court for Broome County, denied the Hraneks' motion for summary judgment to dismiss the complaint against them. The Hraneks appealed the lower court's decision to this intermediate appellate court.

11. Facts of the case

The court relates supporting facts that explain the context of the case and necessary facts that determine the outcome of the case.

Judges may provide the reader with facts in a variety of ways: they may provide a narrative summary, recite the facts as court findings, reprint the allegations of the parties, summarize the trial record, or use actual material from the record. The judge in this case related the facts in a narrative summary.

12. Commencement of the action

The court recites how the case began: the Plaintiff brought a personal injury action against the County of Broome and Thomas and Jan Hranek.

13. Footnotes

The footnotes explain that the Plaintiff's husband also brought a derivative action and that the County of Broome is not a party to this appeal.

14. Legal claims

The court identifies the legal claims alleged in the Plaintiff's complaint: (a) that the Hraneks' son negligently rode his bicycle and (b) that the Hraneks negligently supervised their son by entrusting him with a dangerous instrument, his bicycle.

15. Procedural history of the case

The court summarizes the key procedural events in the case: the parties engaged in discovery, including examinations before trial. Following discovery, the Hraneks moved for summary judgment. The trial court denied their motion. The Hraneks appealed this decision.

16. Issue

The court alludes to the issue by discussing the lower court's reasoning in denying the Defendants' motion for summary judgment. The issue is whether the parents negligently entrusted a dangerous instrument—a 16-inch bicycle—to their five-year-old son who had basic bike-riding skills and experience and no history of accidents.

17. Law

The bracketed numbers are not part of the decision. They indicate that the first three headnotes come from this paragraph. The court enunciates the law:

parents are not generally liable for the negligent supervision of their children. The exception to this rule is that a person injured by a child may have a claim for negligent entrustment of a dangerous instrument against the child's parents if the injury occurs because the parents allowed their child to improvidently use a dangerous instrument. A claim for negligent entrustment of a dangerous instrument must establish that (1) the injury resulted from the child's improvident use of the instrument, (2) the instrument was dangerous when used by the child, (3) the parents were aware that their child might not be able to control the instrument without unreasonable risk to third parties, and (4) the parents could control their child's use of the instrument. In deciding whether an instrument is dangerous, the courts consider the nature and complexity of the instrument and the age, intelligence, experience, and proficiency of the child.

18. Standard of proof

The court states the standard of proof: when the record is sufficiently developed, the court can determine whether an instrument is dangerous as a matter of law, without submitting the question to a jury. (For more on the standard of proof, see Chapter 15.)

19. Reasoning

The reasoning is the court's explanation for its holding in the case. The court explains why it found that the bicycle was not a dangerous instrument: young children ride bicycles without assistance. The child had adequate skills and experience to ride a 16-inch bike, an instrument that is not complex. Also, the parents were not aware that their son might ride his bike carelessly because he had no history of irresponsible riding.

20. Holding

The holding is the court's decision on the legal question in the case. The court held that the bicycle was not a dangerous instrument.

21. Procedural disposition of the case

The procedural disposition is the action the court takes in the case. The court *reversed* the lower court's order denying the motion for summary judgment. It granted summary judgment to the parents and dismissed the cause of action against them.

22. Concurrence

Justices Mickoll, White, Weiss, and Peters concurred with the result reached by Presiding Justice Cardona.

> **Do Exercises 3-A and 3-B Now, p. 58**

E. Case Briefs

A **case brief** is a concise written summary of a court's decision. Lawyers and law students write case briefs for a variety of reasons, but they almost always write them as notes for their own personal use. Both lawyers and law students write case briefs to understand particular cases, the relationship between cases, and how the law created in a case or a group of cases applies to particular facts. In addition, as a law student, you will brief cases to prepare for classes, develop course outlines, study for exams, and master cases to resolve legal problems for writing assignments.

Reasons for Briefing a Case:

- to understand the court's opinion;
- to predict the outcome of a case;
- to come up with arguments for a client;
- to master new case law in a particular area of expertise;
- to show a judge how "late-breaking" law relates to the proceedings; and/or
- to respond to a specific question about a case.

Case briefs are your personal notes on a case. There are exceptions, of course: a partner in a law firm might ask an associate for a formal written case brief on a particularly important or complex case. Usually, though, you are the sole reader of your case briefs. Case briefs therefore are highly individual in content and style, and their format depends on your reason for writing them.

Case briefs should not be confused with **court briefs**. A court brief is a formal legal document submitted to a court. It persuasively presents the facts giving rise to the lawsuit and the legal arguments that support your client's position. Appellate briefs are considered at length in Part III.

F. Writing a Useful Case Brief: Finding Your Own Briefing Style

You must devise a method of briefing cases that works for you. Because each of us learns in a different way, case briefs should be unique to their authors. Your goal in briefing cases is to understand what the law is and how it applies in different factual situations.

As a beginning law student, you should write case briefs that succinctly summarize the following parts of a court's decision:

1. the facts, including important procedural facts;
2. the issues;
3. the law;
4. the holdings; and
5. the reasoning.

This format will provide you with useful notes to prepare for classes and exams. A case brief of this type generally should not exceed one page and can be much shorter.

After you have gained some experience reading cases, you may decide to use a more abbreviated format for briefing cases. Rather than writing a narrative summary using complete sentences, instead you may chose to prepare a short outline of the parts of the case.

Some lawyers and law students brief cases by jotting notes in the margins of the text. This method of case briefing is not useful for a beginning law student. Mastering cases requires active preparation. If you can identify and articulate the court's holding, for example, you have learned how to assess the court's language and determine its importance. Simply jotting notes in the margin is too passive to help you master the case. This method helps you only to identify the parts of the case, not to understand them. Therefore, prepare narrative case briefs during your first few terms in law school.

The narrative sample case brief that follows is only a starting point for case briefing. There is no *right* way to brief a case. The proper format for a case brief is whatever helps you to master the court's language.

G. A Sample Case Brief

This sample case brief summarizes, in narrative form, the facts, issue, holding, law, and reasoning in *Santalucia v. County of Broome*, the annotated case on p. 47. To maximize your understanding, reread the case before you study the sample case brief.

Santalucia v. County of Broome

Facts: Plaintiff sued parents for injuries she received when their five-year-old son struck her with his 16-inch bicycle. Plaintiff alleged that defendants negligently entrusted their son with a dangerous instrument—his bike. At the time of the accident, plaintiff was walking on a path in a park. The defendants and their son were biking on the same path. The son became distracted by dogs and collided with plaintiff. The son had been riding a bike since he was three. He had basic bike-riding skills and no history of accidents. The defendants moved for summary judgment dismissing the claim for negligent entrustment of a dangerous instrument (NEDI). The trial court denied the motion. The defendants appealed. The appellate court reversed and granted summary judgment dismissing the claim.

Issue: Did parents negligently entrust a dangerous instrument—a 16-inch bike—to their five-year-old son who had basic bike-riding skills and experience and no history of accidents?

Law: General Rule: Parents cannot be held liable for negligently supervising their children. Exception: A person injured by a child may have a claim for NEDI against the child's parents if the injury occurs because the parents allowed their child to improvidently use a dangerous instrument. A claim for NEDI must establish that

(1) the injury resulted from the child's improvident use of the instrument,
(2) the instrument was dangerous when used by the child,
(3) the parents were aware that their child might not be able to control the instrument without unreasonable risk to third parties, and
(4) the parents could control their child's use of the instrument.

In deciding whether an instrument is dangerous, the courts consider the nature and complexity of the instrument and the age, intelligence, experience, and proficiency of the child.

Holding: No. A 16-inch bike is not a dangerous instrument when operated by a five-year-old who had basic bike-riding skills and experience and no history of accidents.

Reasoning: The court found the son's bike was not a dangerous instrument as a matter of law because a child's bike is not complex. Young children ride bikes without assistance. The son had adequate skills and experience to ride a 16-inch bike. Also, the defendants were not aware that their son might ride his bike carelessly because he had basic skills and no history of irresponsible riding.

Do Exercise 3-C Now, p. 60

EXERCISES

Exercise 3-A

Read the following case. *Identify:*

1. the citation;
2. the name of the case;
3. the court;
4. the date;
5. the editorial summary of the case;
6. the headnotes;
7. the names of the lawyers who represented the parties;
8. the names of the judges who decided the case;
9. the name of the judge who wrote the decision; and
10. the procedural posture of the case.

BARRETT v. STATE] 2

| Cite as 427 S.E.2d 845 (Ga. App. 1993)

Ga. 845

207 Ga. App. 370

BARRETT

v.

The STATE

No. A92A2222

3 [Court of Appeals of Georgia

Feb. 16, 1998.

Defendant appealed conviction for theft by conversion entered by the Jackson State Court, Motes, J. The Court of Appeals, Cooper, J., held that evidence that defendant rented equipment from video rental store and failed to return equipment to store on following Monday as he was required to by rental agreement was not sufficient to support defendant's conviction for theft by conversion.

Reversed.

1. Larceny ⚷ 2

Purpose of theft by conversion statute is to punish fraudulent conversion, not breach of contract. O.C.G.A. § 16-8-4.

2. Larceny ⚷ 63

Evidence that defendant rented equipment from video rental store and failed to return equipment to store on following Monday as he was required to by rental agreement was not sufficient to support defendant's conviction for theft by conversion; there was no evidence as to what happened to equipment, or that defendant knowingly and with fraudulent intent appropriated it for his own use. O.C.G.A. § 16-8-4.

χ [Donna L. Avans, Jefferson, for appellant.
[Donald E. Moore, Sol., for appellee.

4 [COOPER, Judge.] 9

After a bench trial, the trial court found appellant guilty of theft by conversion. In his sole enumeration of error, appellant challenges the sufficiency of the evidence to support this finding.

*   Reprinted from *South Eastern Reporter 2d* with permission of West Group.

Not guilty!

846 Ga.   427 SOUTH EASTERN REPORTER, 2d SERIES

Evidence presented at trial, viewed most favorably to support the verdict, showed that appellant rented equipment from a video rental store on a Friday. Pursuant to the rental agreement, he was to return it to the store the following Monday. He did not return the equipment, and the store was unable to contact him. Even after appellant was served with a criminal warrant, he did not contact the store. The store owner, the State's only witness, acknowledged that she had no idea where the equipment was at the time of trial. Appellant testified that he rented the equipment to use with a neighbor and that the neighbor said he would return it on Monday because the store was on his way to work. Appellant stated that he has not seen the neighbor since and that he was not aware the equipment had not been returned until he was served with the warrant. The trial court disbelieved appellant's testimony and found him guilty by conversion.

[1,2] "A person commits the offense of theft by conversion when, having lawfully obtained . . . property of another . . . under an agreement . . . to make . . . a specified disposition of such property, he knowingly converts the . . . property to his own use in violation of the agreement. . . ." OCGA § 16-8-4. The purpose of this statute is to punish fraudulent conversion, not breach of contract, and it is the requirement that the State prove fraudulent intent that prevents the statute from being unconstitutional. *Smith v. State,* 229 Ga. 727, 194 S.E.2d 82 (1972). "It is the presence of a fraudulent intent . . . that distinguishes theft by conversion from a simple breach of contract. [Cit.]" *Baker v. State,* 148 Ga. App. 302, 303(2), 238 S.E.2d 241 (1977). While acknowledging that he violated his agreement with the store by failing to return the equipment, appellant contends the evidence was insufficient to establish that he knowingly converted the equipment to his own use with fraudulent intent. We agree. The State established only that appellant rented equipment and failed to return it. It presented no evidence regarding what happened to the equipment and failed to show that appellant knowingly and with fraudulent intent appropriated it for his

own use. The State suggests that the required scienter can be inferred from appellant's failure to return the equipment. However, to allow criminal intent to be inferred from nothing more than the fact of the breach would undermine the crucial distinction between fraudulent conversion and breach of contract made in *Smith* and *Baker,* supra, and would possibly render this criminal statute unconstitutional. See *Smith,* supra at 728-729, 194 S.E.2d 82. Because the State failed to prove an essential element of the charged crime, appellant's conviction must be reversed. See *Tchorz v. State,* 197 Ga. App. 185, 397 S.E.2d 619 (1990).

Judgment reversed.

McMURRAY, P.J., and BLACKBURN, J., concur.

① CRIMINAL CONVERSION - prop. obtained legally.
② Agreement something will be done
③

Exercise 3-B

Identify the facts, issue, law, holding, and reasoning in Barrett v. State, *the case in Exercise 3-A above.*

Exercise 3-C

Read the following (edited) case. Write a case brief succinctly summarizing the facts, issue, law, holding, and reasoning. Identify the dictum.

WHELAN

v.

WHELAN

(588 A.2d 251)

Superior Court of Connecticut,

Judicial District of Waterbury.

Jan. 15, 1991.

* * *

BLUE, Judge.

* * *

. . . The facts giving rise to the plaintiff's claims must be taken from her amended complaint. *Kilbride v. Dushkin Publishing Group, Inc.,* 186 Conn. 718, 719, 443 A.2d 922 (1982). The plaintiff claims that on April 6, 1987, while she was married to and living with the defendant, he falsely told her that he had tested positive for acquired immune deficiency syndrome (AIDS). He further told her that he wanted her to take their son to her original home in Canada so that they would not see him suffer and die. She alleges that this false statement, which she relied upon by going to Canada, caused her "severe anxiety and emotional distress and worry about whether she had [contracted] the AIDS virus, about the defendant's own alleged suffering and impending death, and about what the future of her son would be if her son became an orphan." The plaintiff claims that this emotional distress was inflicted intentionally and that the defendant's conduct was "extreme and outrageous." She seeks money and punitive damages.

* * *

The tort of intentional infliction of emotional distress was recognized by the Connecticut Supreme Court in *Petyan v. Ellis,* 200 Conn. 243, 253, 510 A.2d 1337 (1986). . . . [I]n order for the plaintiff to prevail on her claim, she must establish four elements: "(1) that the actor intended to inflict emotional distress; or that he knew or should have know that emotional distress was a likely result of his conduct; (2) that the conduct was extreme and outrageous; (3) that the defendant's conduct was the cause of the plaintiff's distress; and (4) that the emotional distress sustained by the plaintiff was severe." Each of these elements is alleged in the amended complaint. . . .

elements
of em
distre

The defendant was undoubtedly correct when he pointed out at oral argument that virtually all dissolutions of marriage involve the infliction of emotional distress. See *Raftery v. Scott,* 756 F.2d 335, 341 (4th Cir. 1985) (Michael, J., concurring). For the tort of intentional infliction of emotional distress to be established, however, the plaintiff must allege and prove conduct considerably more egregious than that experienced in the rough and tumble of everyday life or, for that matter, the everyday dissolution of marriage. As Prosser and Keeton explain, "[w]hen a citizen who has been called a son of a bitch testifies that the epithet has destroyed his slumber, ruined his digestion, wrecked his nervous system, and permanently impaired his health, other citizens who on occasion have been called the same thing without catastrophic harm may have legitimate doubts that he was really so upset, or that if he were his sufferings could possibly be so reasonable and justified under the circumstances as to be entitled to compensation." W. Prosser & W. Keeton, *supra,* 59. Liability exists only "for conduct exceeding all bounds usually tolerated by decent society, of a nature which is especially calculated to cause, and does cause mental distress of a very serious kind." *Id.* at 60. "[A] line can be drawn between the slight hurts which are the price of a complex society and the severe mental disturbances inflicted by intentional actions wholly lacking in social utility." *Knierim v. Izzo,* 22 Ill. 2d 73, 85, 174 N.E.2d 157 (1961). "Liability has been found only where the conduct has been so outrageous in character, and so extreme in degree, as to go beyond all possible bounds of decency, and to be regarded as atrocious, and utterly intolerable in a civilized community." 1 Restatement (Second) Torts § 46, p. 73, comment (d).

Under this standard, the court is satisfied that the plaintiff has pleaded a recognizable claim. The court does not doubt that insult, indignity and genuine distress are part and parcel of most, if not all, marital breakups, but there is an enormous difference between these unfortunately routine indignities and a false statement to one's spouse that one has AIDS. The former will doubtless cause sadness and grief, but the latter is likely to cause shock and fright of enormous proportions. The former may now be commonplace in our society, but the latter would, nevertheless, in the language of the Restatement, "be regarded as atrocious and utterly intolerable in a civilized community." If a third party, in an apparent position to know, had intentionally and falsely told the plaintiff that her husband had AIDS, she would undoubtedly have a cause of action against that third party for the intentional infliction of emotional distress. That much follows from the seminal case of *Wilkinson v. Downton*, [1897] 2 Q.B.D. 57, holding that a cause of action existed against a defendant who falsely represented to a married woman that her husband had been seriously injured in an accident. The fact that the false speaker is the husband himself should make no legal difference. "When the purposes of the marriage relation have wholly failed by reason of the misconduct of one or both of the parties, there is no reason why the husband or wife should not have the same remedies for injuries inflicted by the other spouse which the courts would give them against other persons." *Brown v. Brown*, 88 Conn. 42, 48-49, 89 A. 889 (1914).

In the context of the present case, the matter is, if anything, aggravated by the fact that the person making the statement is the husband since that fact would enhance the verisimilitude of the statement and intensify its likely impact. Whether the plaintiff's claim can be established in fact remains to be seen, but her claim is one that the law recognizes. The motion to strike directed at the entire complaint is, therefore, denied.

* * *

see- DIA P file Recognizable claim against husband for intentional infliction of emotional distress

CHAPTER 4

Introduction to Legal Proofs

When you master this chapter, you will understand:

1. what a legal proof is;

2. how to structure a legal proof; and

3. why legal proofs are an effective way to organize legal analysis.

A. The Structure of a Legal Proof

As discussed in Chapter 2, you analyze an issue by identifying it, stating a rule derived from the relevant law, and applying that rule to predict how a court would resolve the issue. A legal proof is a way to present your analysis using a logical framework. You structure your analysis in a legal proof to make it logical, accurate, and useful to the reader. A legal proof looks like this:

ISSUE—identify the issue to be analyzed;

RULE—state the applicable rule;

> **RULE SUPPORT**—validate your rule by citing and discussing the "rule cases" (*i.e.*, the cases you based your rule on);

APPLICATION—apply the rule to the facts of your case;

> **CASE COMPARISON**—validate your application by showing that your case is (1) analogous to the rule cases whose holdings match the predicted holding of your case and (2) distinguishable from the rule cases whose holdings do not match your predicted holding; and

CONCLUSION—predict how a court would resolve the issue.

The issue, rule, application, and conclusion sections give the analysis its structure; that is why a legal proof is often referred to by the acronym IRAC. The rule support and case comparison sections support this structure by showing that the analysis is valid, that is, grounded in the law.

B. The Logical Framework of the Legal Proof

Legal proofs are based on a form of reasoning known as the deductive syllogism. A deductive syllogism sets forth three propositions. The first two propositions are called the premises. Together these two premises lead to or *prove* the third proposition, called the conclusion. Here is the classic example:

Example 1: Syllogism

Major Premise: All men are mortal.
Minor Premise: Socrates is a man.
Conclusion: Socrates is mortal.

The conclusion will be valid only if (1) the premises are true and (2) the premises share a common term.

1. The premises must be true

A syllogism with a false premise yields an erroneous conclusion.

Example 2: Faulty Syllogism with a False Premise and an Erroneous Conclusion

Major (False) Premise: All men are gods.
Minor Premise: Socrates is a man.
(Erroneous) Conclusion: Socrates is a god.

2. The premises must share a common term

The common term in the premises forms a link between them, allowing you to reach a logical conclusion about the remaining ideas in the premises. In this example, the common shared term (in SMALL CAPITAL LETTERS) allows you to reach a logical conclusion:

Example 3: Syllogism with Common Term Highlighted

Major Premise: Billie loves all SONGS BY THE BEATLES.
Minor Premise: "Yesterday" is A SONG BY THE BEATLES.
Conclusion: Billie loves the song "Yesterday."

If the shared terms in the premises do not match, the syllogism is faulty (*i.e.*, not logical) and may result in an erroneous conclusion. The following syllogism does not prove its conclusion because the supposedly shared terms (in SMALL CAP-ITAL LETTERS) are not exact matches:

Example 4: Faulty Syllogism with Unmatched Terms and an Erroneous Conclusion

Major Premise: Billie is A GOOD STUDENT.
Minor (Unmatched) Premise: The teacher will give apples to THE STUDENTS WHO BEHAVE WELL.
(Erroneous) Conclusion: The teacher will give an apple to Billie.

This syllogism is faulty because a good student is not necessarily one who behaves well.

The following diagrams illustrate why the syllogism in Example 1 is logical, but the one in Example 4 is not.

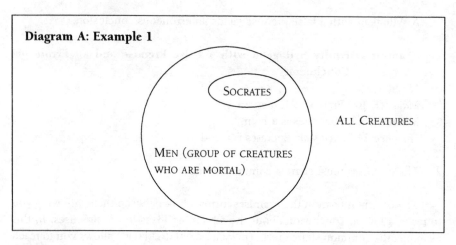

Diagram A: Example 1

Socrates

ALL CREATURES

MEN (GROUP OF CREATURES WHO ARE MORTAL)

Diagram A is a hypothetical grouping of all creatures. One subgroup is "men," all of whom are mortal (contained in the circle). Diagram A makes it clear that since Socrates is a member of the group in the circle (minor premise), all of whose members are mortal (major premise), then it necessarily follows that Socrates is mortal (conclusion).

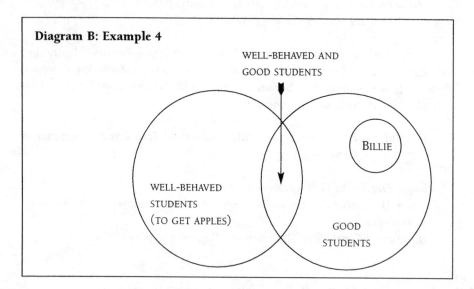

Diagram B: Example 4

WELL-BEHAVED AND GOOD STUDENTS

BILLIE

WELL-BEHAVED STUDENTS (TO GET APPLES)

GOOD STUDENTS

Diagram B shows that unmatched terms may result in an erroneous conclusion. The group of "good students" is not necessarily identical to the group of "well-behaved" ones. Some students might be both good and well-behaved (where the circles overlap), but not all are. If Billie is not in the overlapping part of the circles, then she will not get an apple. Since you do not know from the information in the minor premise whether Billie is well behaved, you cannot be confident of the conclusion that Billie will get an apple.

C. Using the Deductive Syllogism in Legal Proofs

A legal proof is based on the deductive syllogism. You write a legal proof for each issue you have identified. The rule is the syllogism's major premise and the application is the minor premise. Together they prove the conclusion. If you precede the rule with a statement of the issue—the question that the syllogism addresses (*e.g.*, "Is Socrates mortal?")—you have the framework of a legal proof. (If you add rule support and case comparison sections, you have a complete legal proof.)

For example, suppose you represent Cheryl Moss, a model who wants to sue a company for selling a mannequin that looks like her. It has her facial features and body shape, but is sold unclothed and without hair. You determine that Moss may have a claim under Arcadia Civil Rights Law § 51, which gives a person a civil claim for damages against one who "knowingly uses a person's portrait or picture within the State of Arcadia for commercial purposes without the person's written consent." The statute has five elements:

A person violates Arcadia Civil Rights Law § 51 if he
1. knowingly uses
2. another person's portrait or picture
3. within the State of Arcadia
4. for commercial purposes
5. without consent.

To write a legal proof on the second element—the issue of whether the mannequin is a "portrait or picture"—start as follows. (The common terms of the premises are in SMALL CAPITAL LETTERS.)

Example 5: Framework for a Legal Proof

Issue: Is a mannequin that resembles a person a "portrait or picture" of that person under Arcadia Civil Rights Law § 51?

Rule (Major Premise): A "portrait or picture" of a person is ANY TWO OR THREE DIMENSIONAL PHYSICAL REPRESENTATION OF THAT PERSON.

Application (Minor Premise): The mannequin is a THREE-DIMENSIONAL PHYSICAL REPRESENTATION OF CHERYL MOSS.

Conclusion: The mannequin is a "portrait or picture" of Cheryl Moss under Arcadia Civil Rights Law § 51.

Assuming that the premises are true, the syllogism in Example 5 is logical because the common terms in its rule and application match. This match ensures that the conclusion is logical.

Here is an example of a legal proof containing a faulty syllogism with unmatched common terms:

Example 6: Framework of a Legal Proof Containing a Faulty Syllogism

Issue: Is a mannequin that resembles a person a "portrait or picture" of that person under Arcadia Civil Rights Law § 51?

Rule (Major Premise): A "portrait or picture" of a person is ANYTHING THAT VISUALLY PRESENTS THE ESSENTIAL PHYSICAL CHARACTERISTICS OF THAT PERSON.

Application (Minor Premise): The mannequin is a THREE-DIMENSIONAL PHYSICAL REPRESENTATION OF CHERYL MOSS.

Conclusion: The mannequin is a "portrait or picture" of Cheryl Moss under Arcadia Civil Rights Law § 51.

In Example 6, the rule and application premises do not match because the rule speaks of "visually present[ing] the essential physical characteristics of [a] person" and the application speaks of a "three-dimensional physical representation. . . ." Although a three-dimensional representation probably visually presents a person's essential physical characteristics, the syllogism fails logically because it does not prove its conclusion. To make it logical, you must change either the rule or the application so that the shared terms match.

Moreover, the rule and application must also be true. Just as a deductive syllogism that contains a false premise results in an erroneous conclusion, a legal proof that is internally coherent—that is, shares common terms and makes sense—is nonetheless *wrong* if the law is misconstrued or misstated in the rule. For example:

Example 7: Framework of an Internally Coherent Proof with an Inaccurate Rule

Issue: Is a crowbar a deadly weapon?
(Inaccurate) Rule: Only an object that shoots or cuts is a deadly weapon.
(Accurate) Application: A crowbar does not shoot or cut.
(Logical, but Erroneous) Conclusion: A crowbar is not a deadly weapon.

The conclusion in Example 7 is wrong because the rule is wrong: contrary to what is stated, an object that does not shoot or cut may be a deadly weapon under the law.

Similarly, an accurate rule with an inaccurate application also results in an erroneous conclusion.

Example 8: Framework of an Internally Coherent Proof with an Inaccurate Application

Issue: Is a crowbar a deadly weapon?
(Accurate) Rule: An object is a deadly weapon if it is capable of seriously injuring someone who is within the object's effective range.
(Inaccurate) Application: A crowbar is not capable of seriously injuring someone who is within its effective range.
(Erroneous) Conclusion: A crowbar is not a deadly weapon.

The conclusion in Example 8 is wrong because the application is wrong: contrary to what is stated in the application, a crowbar can seriously injure someone who is within its effective range.

When writing a legal proof, follow these guidelines:

- The rule must accurately state the legal concept set forth in the cases and statute (if there is one).

- The facts in the application must be *accurate*. Do not distort the facts to connect them to the rule.

- The rule and application must share a common term. The shared term in the rule and application makes the conclusion logically inevitable.

D. Validating the Analysis: Rule Support and Case Comparison

For each legal proof, you must provide law to support your rule and application. In your rule, you have *asserted* what the law is; in the rule support section, you validate (or *prove*) that the assertion is correct by citing to and discussing the relevant law.

In your application, you assert that the general requirements of the rule are satisfied (or not) in your particular case. The case comparison section supports the assertion made in the application by making factual comparisons between your case and the rule cases. These comparisons show the reader that you are applying your rule correctly, that your application is *consistent with* the holdings of the relevant cases. This consistency enables you to reach a valid conclusion. For example, if in the application you assert that a crowbar is capable of inflicting serious injury, in your case comparison section you must support that assertion with case law, showing that the assertion is consistent with holdings in other similar cases on this issue.

E. An Annotated Legal Proof

This section contains an annotated legal proof, a legal proof that designates each part by name. It is based on the facts described in Section C, p. 67, and the syllogism in Example 5, pp. 67-68.

The issue is whether a mannequin resembling a person is a "portrait or picture" under Arcadia Civil Rights Law § 51, a statute which imposes civil liability for using another's "portrait or picture" without consent. In researching the issue, suppose you find two cases construing the phrase "portrait or picture": *Swoonatra v. Dorsey Doll Co.*, 335 Arc. Rpts. 2d 243 (1999) and *Lombard v. Bears Are Us, Inc.*, 325 Arc. Rpts. 2d 143 (1997). These cases are described in the proof's rule support section.

Here is how an annotated legal proof of this issue might look. Note that the issue is now framed as a statement rather than as a question because the convention in memo writing is to state the issue rather than to pose it as a question.

> *Issue:* The issue is whether a mannequin that resembles Cheryl Moss is a "portrait or picture" of her under Arcadia Civil Rights Law § 51 ("CRL § 51").

[handwritten margin note: Statute + its language →]

> *Rule:* A "portrait or picture" of a person is any two or three dimensional physical representation of that person.

Rule Support: CRL § 51; *Swoonatra v. Dorsey Doll Co.*, 335 Arc. Rpts. 2d 243 (1999); *Lombard v. Bears Are Us, Inc.*, 325 Arc. Rpts. 2d 143 (1997).

In *Swoonatra*, the court held that the plaintiff, the singer Frank Swoonatra, had a claim under CRL § 51 against a doll company for selling a doll that had his body type, face, haircut, and style of dress. The court held that the phrase "portrait or picture" includes any representation that conveys the physical likeness of a person, regardless of whether it is conveyed in a photograph, drawing, statue, or doll.

In *Lombard*, the plaintiff, a famous conductor, sued a manufacturer of toy bears for selling a teddy bear that plaintiff claimed was a "portrait or picture" of him under CRL § 51. The bear had long black hair like the plaintiff's, wore the plaintiff's trademark blue tuxedo, held a conductor's baton, and when squeezed said "Let's play music," a line associated with the plaintiff. The court held that the bear was not a "portrait or picture" because although it was dressed like the plaintiff and spoke words associated with him, physically it resembled a bear, not the plaintiff.

Application: The mannequin is a three-dimensional physical representation of Cheryl Moss.

Case Comparison: Like the doll in *Swoonatra*, which physically resembled the plaintiff, the mannequin captures Moss's physical likeness. Its face and body shape resembles Moss's, just as the doll's body type and face resembled that of the plaintiff in *Swoonatra*.

Although there are some differences between the facts of *Swoonatra* and those in Moss's case, they are probably not critical. Unlike the *Swoonatra* doll, which had the haircut and style of dress of the plaintiff, the mannequin resembling Moss is sold unclothed and without hair. As *Lombard* demonstrates, however, the decisive consideration is physical resemblance, not dress or hairstyle.

Moss's case is distinguishable from *Lombard*. In *Lombard*, the court held that the teddy bear bore no physical resemblance to the plaintiff conductor. The mannequin, however, has a face and body shape like Moss's.

Conclusion: The mannequin is a "portrait or picture" of Cheryl Moss under Arcadia Civil Rights Law § 51.

This legal proof clearly identifies the disputed issue: whether the mannequin is a "portrait or picture" of Moss under the statute. The rule and application have matching terms, thereby insuring the conclusion's validity. The rule support section proves that the rule has a legal basis by citing to the statute and discussing *Swoonatra v. Dorsey Doll Co.* and *Lombard v. Bears Are Us, Inc.*, cases with facts similar to those in Moss's case. The case comparison section proves that the application is consistent with these cases by showing that the mannequin is like the doll in *Swoonatra* (which was held to be a "portrait or picture") and unlike the teddy bear in *Lombard* (which was held not to be a "portrait or picture"). Since the rule support and case comparison sections prove that the rule and application are "true," the conclusion must be valid.

Do Exercises 4-A and 4-B Now, p. 73

Exercise 4-A

Read the following facts, cases, and annotated legal proofs. Decide which annotated legal proof is better. Explain your answer.

Facts

Jessica Cromwell is the granddaughter of Joan Dey. Shortly before her death last July, Dey changed her will and left Shirley Owen, her friend, all of her property. Cromwell wants to contest Dey's will. She believes that Owen unduly influenced Dey to change her will.

Dey met Owen at a book club meeting last December. The two had a lot in common and became close friends. Owen visited Dey several times a week, took her shopping, and ran errands for her. The friendship, as well as Owen's assistance to Dey, continued until Dey's death.

Four weeks before her death, Dey asked Owen to make an appointment for her with Perri Maison, Owen's attorney. Owen made the appointment. A week later, Owen drove Dey to Maison's office. Owen remained in the reception area while Dey met with Maison to discuss, review, and sign her new will. In this will, Dey left her substantial estate entirely to Owen. The new will revoked Dey's 1992 will in which she had left all her assets to Cromwell, her only living relative.

Cases

In re Estate of Herman, 654 Arc. Supp. 345 (1997): Shortly before his death, Harvey Herman made a will in which he left his entire estate to Green, his gardener and friend of many years. The new will revoked Herman's 1997 will in which Walters, Herman's nephew and only living relative, was the sole beneficiary. Walters claims that Green unduly influenced Herman to change his will. The evidence establishes that Green made an appointment for Herman with her own attorney, drove him to the attorney's office, and waited in the office lobby while Herman reviewed and signed his new will. There was no undue influence in this case: Green did not actively participate in the preparation of the will. She did not use coercion or threats to induce Herman to change his will.

In re Estate of Miller, 656 Arc. Supp. 742 (1999): Shortly before her death, Bertha Miller made a will in which she left her entire estate to her former boyfriend Dane. The new will revoked Miller's 1995 will in which Anton, Miller's niece and only living relative, was the sole beneficiary. Anton claims that Dane unduly influenced Miller to change her will. The evidence establishes that Miller ended her relationship with Dane six months before her death. Furious over the breakup, Dane broke into Miller's house late one night and threatened to kill her if she did not provide for him after her death. The next day Dane drove Miller to his attorney and was present when Miller discussed the terms of her new will with the attorney. Miller's will was invalidated on the ground of undue influence: Dane used fear and coercion to induce Miller to change her will and leave her estate to him. He deprived Miller of her free will in disposing of her property.

Annotated Legal Proof A

Issue: The issue is whether Owen unduly influenced Dey, the testator, to change her will.

Rule: To establish undue influence, the plaintiff must prove that the defendant used fear or coercion to deprive the testator of her free will in disposing of her property by threatening to physically harm her or by actively controlling the will-drafting process.

Rule Support: In re Estate of Miller, 656 Arc. Supp. 742 (1999); In re Estate of Herman, 654 Arc. Supp. 345 (1997). In Miller, the court held that the testator's ex-boyfriend used undue influence to induce the testator to change her will: he threatened to kill her if she did not provide for him after her death, drove her to his attorney's office, and was present when she discussed the terms of her will with the attorney. In contrast, the Herman court held that the testator's friend of many years did not use undue influence to induce the testator to change his will because she did not threaten or coerce him. Moreover, although the friend in Herman made an appointment for the testator with her own attorney and drove him to the attorney's office, she did not actively participate in the preparation of the will.

Application: Owen did not use fear or coercion to deprive Dey of her free will in disposing of her property: she did not threaten to physically harm Dey or actively control the will-drafting process.

Case Comparison: Like the friend in *Herman*, Owen made an appointment for the testator with her own attorney and drove the testator to the attorney's office. In addition, Owen, like the friend in *Herman*, was not present when the testator reviewed and signed the will. Unlike the ex-boyfriend in *Miller*, Owen did not threaten to harm the testator and was not present when the testator discussed the terms of the will with the attorney.

Conclusion: Owen did not unduly influence Dey to change her will.

Annotated Legal Proof B

Issue: The issue is whether Owen unduly influenced Dey.

Rule: A testator is unduly influenced if she is deprived of her free will.

Rule Support: *Herman*; *Miller*. In *Miller*, the court held that undue influence was exerted when the ex-boyfriend threatened to kill his former girlfriend. The girlfriend had ended her relationship with him six months before her death. In contrast, the *Herman* court held that the friend did not use undue influence when she made an appointment for the testator with her own attorney and drove him to the attorney's office. She was the testator's friend of many years. While undue influence was found in *Miller*, it was not established in *Herman*.

Application: Owen did not deprive Dey of her free will because she helped Dey and was her good friend.

Case Comparison: Like the friend in *Herman*, Owen made an appointment for the testator with her own attorney and drove the testator to the attorney's office. Moreover, Owen, like the friend in *Herman*, was also close to the testator. Unlike the ex-boyfriend in *Miller*, Owen was not estranged from the testator and did not help prepare the testator's will.

Conclusion: Owen did not unduly influence Dey. Dey likely left Owen her estate because she valued their friendship.

Exercise 4-B

Brendan Shafer has retained your law firm. Read the following facts and cases. Identify the issue raised by applying the case law to the facts. Use the facts and cases to write an annotated legal proof. Remember to include (1) the issue, (2) the rule, (3) rule support, (3) an application, (4) case comparisons, and (5) a conclusion.

Facts

Brendan Shafer is the nephew of Sam Porter. Porter died last August at the age of 85. Shafer would like to contest Porter's will on the ground of lack of testamentary capacity: he claims that the will should be invalidated because Porter was not mentally competent when he made it.

Two months before his death, Porter made a new will in which he left his entire estate to UVX, a shelter for abused and abandoned animals. The new will revoked Porter's 1998 will under which Shafer, Porter's only living relative, was to inherit the entire estate.

Shafer spoke to his uncle two days before the new will was made and found him disoriented. Several times during their conversation, Porter called Shafer "Albert," who was Shafer's deceased father and Porter's deceased brother-in-law. Porter also seemed confused about what he had been doing before Shafer called. The phone call worried Shafer so much that he phoned his uncle the next day to see how he was. When Shafer called, his uncle seemed fine.

Ally Cochran, Porter's attorney, believes that he understood his actions on the day he reviewed and signed his will. Porter told Cochran that his nephew would be very disappointed by the change in the will. He also said that UVX did important work and therefore was a deserving beneficiary of his estate. Porter accurately described the nature and extent of his property to Cochran.

Dr. Martin Welbie, Porter's doctor, saw Porter one week before Porter signed his new will. Although Porter complained of occasional headaches and dizziness, Dr. Welbie found him to be in good health.

Cases

In re Estate of Nathan: Three months before his death, Ernest Nathan made a will in which he left his entire estate to Fenner, a teller at his bank. The new will revoked Nathan's 1996 will in which Joan Freeman, Nathan's sister and only living relative, was the sole beneficiary. Freeman claims that Nathan lacked testamentary capacity to make a new will. When he made the new will, Nathan told his attorney that he was an only child and that Fenner was his son. Moreover, he was confused about whether he owned one apartment or an entire apartment building. These facts established that Nathan lacked testamentary capacity when he made the new will.

In re Estate of Rose: Two months before her death, Charlotte Rose made a will in which she left her entire estate to Young, a neighbor. The new will revoked Rose's 1992 will in which Sally Overton, Rose's niece and only living relative, was the sole beneficiary. Overton claims that Rose lacked testamentary capacity to make a new will. Although Rose suffered from dementia and was unable to care for herself during the year preceding her death, she knew, when she made her new will, what she owned and that she was leaving her estate to Young, her neighbor, and excluding Overton, her niece and only living relative. These facts established that Rose had testamentary capacity.

CHAPTER 5

Analyzing Statutory Issues

When you master this chapter, you will understand:

1. what statutes are;

2. how courts and lawyers determine the meaning of an ambiguous statute; and

3. how to identify and analyze statutory issues.

L awyers analyze statutory issues in very much the same way they analyze common-law issues. For both, the task is to predict how a court will apply general legal concepts to specific facts. Suppose a statute prohibits the sale of liquor to persons who are "visibly intoxicated," and your client, a bar owner, served liquor to a man who he noticed was walking unsteadily and speaking boisterously. Did your client violate the statute? The answer depends on whether the man was *visibly intoxicated* as that term is used in the statute.

Analytically, assessing whether the man's condition satisfies the statutory term *visibly intoxicated* is no different from assessing whether an aunt who lives with her nephew satisfies the *closely-related* element of the common-law claim of negligent infliction of emotional distress. In both cases, you begin by asking how the general term (*visibly intoxicated* or *closely related*) applies to the specific case. And very often you resolve the question by finding or devising a rule to explain the term's meaning and then applying the rule to the particular facts.

Although the method of analyzing statutory issues is the same as that of analyzing common-law issues, many statutes pose a preliminary problem: what does the statute mean? You should therefore first understand what statutes are and how courts and lawyers determine the meaning of an ambiguous statute.

A. Statutes

A statute is a law enacted by a federal or state legislature. Laws passed by local legislatures are called **ordinances**. Statutes and ordinances are either criminal or civil. Criminal (also known as penal) laws declare what acts are crimes, classify them according to their seriousness (such as misdemeanor or felony), and provide penalties for committing them. A related group of statutes—criminal procedure law—spells out the rules for conducting criminal prosecutions.

Civil statutes apply to varied matters: some (such as corporation and partnership laws, employment discrimination laws, and consumer rights laws) regulate business relationships, while others (such as laws on divorce and adoption) regulate personal relationships. Still others regulate government itself: state municipal law directs how cities and towns are created and governed, and state election laws regulate ballots, primaries, and elections. Some civil statutes are enforceable by the government alone, while others create private claims for persons the statute was intended to protect or benefit. For example, many state whistleblower statutes not only provide penalties for employers retaliating against employees who report illegal activities, but also give employees the right to sue employers for such conduct. Finally, civil procedure law sets out the conditions and methods by which civil lawsuits proceed.

Civil statutes often encroach on areas regulated by common law. In many states claims are now regulated by statute that were formerly governed by common-law negligence principles—such as the liability of social hosts (*e.g.*, persons having parties at their home) for injuries caused by someone who became intoxicated at their parties. Similarly, most sales of personal property are no longer governed by common-law contract principles but by the Uniform Commercial Code, a statute enacted in whole or in large part by all fifty states.

B. Statutory Codes

Statutes of a particular jurisdiction are usually published in a set of books called a **code**. A code arranges the statutes by subject. Each subject in the code gets a separate listing called a **title,** which is further divided into sections and subsections. While a code sets out the text of a jurisdiction's statutes, an **annotated code** supplements each section of the code with notes about the section's legislative history, cross-references to other sections, lists of relevant books and articles, and summaries of cases construing the section. The case summaries (sometimes called "Notes of Decisions" or "Case Notes") are a very useful feature of an annotated code because they summarize cases that have applied or construed that section.

C. Determining a Statute's Meaning

1. Legislative history

The most obvious way to determine a statute's meaning is to read it carefully. However, when it is unclear how a generally-worded statute applies in a specific situation, lawyers must turn to other sources for guidance. A lawyer might research a statute's **legislative history** to learn what the legislature intended when it passed the statute. This information may shed light on how the statute should be applied. Legislative history includes reports about the statute reviewed by legislators before they voted on it and transcripts of legislative debates on the statute. However, legislative history is not always available or pertinent. In addition, many courts are reluctant to use legislative history when interpreting unclear statutes because determining intent is often speculative.

2. Administrative regulations

Another way to determine a statute's meaning is to examine administrative **regulations** implementing the statute. Regulations are detailed guidelines that explain and supplement a statute's general provisions. They are usually drafted and adopted by the agency charged with enforcing the statute. For example, the Equal Employment Opportunity Commission, a federal agency, has very detailed guidelines about what constitutes a disability under the Americans with Disabilities Act, a federal statute.

3. Canons of statutory interpretation

Judges trying to determine a statute's meaning sometimes employ **canons of statutory interpretation (or construction)**. A canon is a fundamental principle or general rule. Canons of interpretation are rules that courts sometimes use to make sense of a statute whose wording is unclear or ambiguous. Scholars of statutory interpretation group these canons into three categories. [*See generally*, Kent Greenawalt, *Legislation: Statutory Interpretation: Twenty Questions*, chs. 13 and 15 (Foundation Press, 1999).]

a. *Intrinsic canons* are rules for interpreting the meaning of statutes from the grammar, syntax, and other elements of the text. For example:

> *To express one thing is to exclude another* (a canon often referred to by its Latin name: *expressio unius est exclusio alterius*). Suppose a statute imposes a tax on sales of "automobiles and trucks." Under this canon, sales of buses would not be taxed because only automobiles and trucks are listed (and buses are not).

> *A word's meaning may be determined by referring to the meaning of words associated with it.* Suppose the legislature imposes a tax on the sale of "vehicles, including cars, trucks, motorcycles, airplanes, and boats." You could use this canon to determine whether a bus is subject to the tax. You would look at the words listed after *vehicles* to get some sense of what the legislature meant to tax, and might conclude that a bus would be included.

> *When a general word or phrase follows words of a specific meaning, the general word or phrase will be construed to apply only to the same class of persons or things encompassed by the specific words.* Suppose a statute refers to "passenger cars, sports utility vehicles, panel vans, pickup trucks, and

other means of transportation." A bus would probably be included in the term "other means of transportation" but a bicycle would not since the statutory drafters evidently were referring to large motorized vehicles.

b. *Extrinsic canons* are rules for interpreting the meaning of statutes according to how others have understood the statute. The rule of *stare decisis* (let settled things stand) is an example of an extrinsic canon. The rule of *stare decisis* provides that a case settling a rule of law (including an interpretation of a statute) should be adhered to by later courts. Even if a later court thinks that the earlier case was wrong, it ought not be willing to upset the earlier case without compelling reasons because social expectations and social practices form around announced rules.

c. *Substantive canons* are rules of statutory interpretation dictated by policy considerations. One such canon is that *penal statutes should be strictly construed.* This canon embodies the important policy that a law subjecting people to criminal punishment should be read strictly (that is, narrowly) or else people might not be fairly put on notice of the precise conduct that the statute prohibits. For example, a criminal statute states: "It shall be unlawful for any person to set a fire on a public thoroughfare." Suppose that a person lights a cigarette while walking along a sidewalk and is promptly arrested by the police for setting a fire on a public thoroughfare. Under the canon requiring penal statutes to be strictly construed, the court probably would hold that the statute does not forbid lighting a cigarette. The legislature could have banned smoking on a public thoroughfare by saying so if it had really meant to do so, and it would be unfair to punish someone for a common act without a more explicit warning in the statute.

Because they are general, canons of interpretation, while useful, are rarely dispositive in determining the meaning of a statute.

4. Cases

Other than the statute itself, the most important source of guidance on what statutes mean are cases construing the statute. Often lawsuits involve claims based on statutes. In these lawsuits, courts determine how the statute applies to the situations before them. In doing so, they create law: a court's interpretation of what a statute means is binding authority in that court's jurisdiction.

The remainder of this chapter focuses on how lawyers predict how a statute applies in a situation by using the text of the statute and cases interpreting it.

D. How to Identify and Analyze Statutory Issues

The logical framework for statutory analysis discussed here is the same one discussed in previous chapters on analyzing case law. When you have a question about how a statute applies to a particular set of facts, follow these four steps:

1. Read the applicable statute, break it into its distinct elements, then look for related provisions that define terms used in the statute.

2. Compare the facts of your case with each element in the statute. If the statute's elements clearly match (or clearly do not match) the facts of your case, there is no disputed issue and therefore no need to look further.

3. If it is not clear whether an element of the statute is satisfied, review cases that have construed that element to find case law that is so factually similar or states a rule that is so explicit that it resolves the issue (that is, it tells you whether the element has been satisfied). If you find case law that is factually similar or states an explicit rule that definitely resolves the issue, there is no need to devise a rule.

4. If you do not find case law that expressly resolves the issue, then (a) find or devise a rule based on cases that have construed the element under factually similar situations and (b) apply that rule to predict how a court would resolve the issue.

Step 1. Read the statute carefully, then break it into its distinct elements. Statutory and case law analysis differ in one major, obvious respect: the starting place and the core of statutory analysis are the words of the statute itself. The cases (and any other aids you use to understand the statute) are used to help determine the meaning of the statute's words.

This difference has a practical implication: lawyers and law students must carefully focus on the statutory language to determine whether a legal issue exists. In a common-law claim, you identify issues by carefully comparing the elements of the claim set forth in the case law with the facts of your situation. If the common-law elements do not closely match up with your facts, you have an issue.

In contrast, if your case involves a statute, you must begin by parsing the statute carefully, breaking it into its parts. Doing so not only helps you understand the statute, but also allows you to compare the facts with the statute's language methodically, matching particular elements to particular facts.

For example, under Texas Penal Code § 31.03, a person commits theft if he "unlawfully appropriates property with intent to deprive the owner of property." In addition, the section declares as unlawful, among other things, an appropriation "without the owner's consent." Parsing the statute and the related definition, you could divide theft into these elements:

A person commits theft if he
> 1. *appropriates property* without the *consent* of its *owner*; AND
> 2. *intends* to *deprive* the owner of the property.

Breaking theft into just two elements is not the best strategy, since you can see the first element contains four legal concepts—appropriation, property, consent, and ownership—each of which could raise an issue. The second element adds two more concepts: intent and deprivation. Because you parse the statute to isolate and identify the issues, each element should contain only one legal concept. A better parsing of the statute would separate these concepts:

A person commits theft if he
> 1. (a) APPROPRIATES
>   (b) PROPERTY
>   (c) without the CONSENT
>   (d) of the OWNER
>   AND
> 2. (a) INTENDS
>   (b) to DEPRIVE the owner of it.

Once you have determined the elements of the statute, you should check to see if related provisions define any of the elements. For example, you should look to see if the Texas Penal Code defines unlawful appropriation, property, consent, or intent.

Do Exercise 5-A Now, p. 98

Step 2. Compare the facts of your case with each element in the statute. After carefully parsing the statute, you must determine whether it applies to your case by comparing the facts with the elements of the statute. If it is clear that the statute applies (or that it does not), then you have answered your question. On the other hand, if matching the elements to the law raises a question that cannot be answered without further research, then you must review the relevant case law.

   An example of a clear match. Sometimes matching the facts to an element is an easy task. Suppose, for example, that your client is arrested for shoplifting a diamond ring. The jewelry store's security camera videotaped him slip the ring into his pocket and leave the store. Did he commit theft? You could preliminarily conclude that he did because:

   1. (a) Your client APPROPRIATED the ring.
       (b) The ring is PROPERTY.
       (c) The store did not CONSENT to the appropriation.
       (d) The store was the OWNER of the ring.
            and
   2. (a) Your client INTENDED to take the property out of the store.
       (b) Taking the ring out of the store, he DEPRIVED the owner of the ring.

   You would have to do more research, however, to confirm your conclusion. First, to insure that you understand the theft section of the statute correctly, you would review related provisions of the statute, especially sections that define terms like "intent" and "deprive." These sections may change your understanding of what the statute requires. Also, to confirm that your reading of the statute is consistent with the case law, you would review the Notes of Decisions following the relevant statutory provisions. Finally, to make sure you have all the necessary facts, you would interview your client and review statements and evidence gathered by the police. Assuming these measures confirm your understanding of the law and the facts, you could conclude that your client did indeed commit theft.

Do Exercises 5-B(1) and 5-B(2) Now, p. 98

   Step 3. If it is not clear whether an element of the statute is satisfied, review cases that have construed that element to find case law that is so factually similar or states a rule that is so explicit that it resolves the issue. When you cannot tell whether an element of a statute is satisfied, you must look to case law for guidance. Cases construing statutes often clarify a statute's meaning. The most certain clarification would come from a controlling case. Recall that a case is controlling if it comes from courts to which the decision can be appealed and has the same necessary facts and issue as your case, thereby making it clear that the element is (or is not) satisfied. If you find a controlling case, then you have answered your question. On the other hand, if the case law does not answer the question, you have identified an issue, which you must analyze.

An example of answering the question with a binding case on point. Suppose your client who was arrested for shoplifting the ring was apprehended *before* he left the store. Has he committed robbery under the Texas Penal Code? Matching the elements to these facts, you might ask whether your client actually "appropriated" the ring by putting it in his pocket and walking away from the salesperson. Put another way, does someone "appropriate" property at the moment he takes it or only after he leaves the owner's premises? Since the statute does not address this question, you must look at the case law to see if there are any cases with similar facts. Assume your research uncovers the following case:

Len MASTERS, Appellant,

v.

The STATE of Texas, Appellee.

(437 S.W.2d 868)
Court of Criminal Appeals of Texas.
Jan. 29, 1969.

MORRISON, Judge.

* * *

Appellant's first ground of error is that the evidence is insufficient to support the conviction. The facts showed that appellant was interrupted by the owner of a service station and his employee as appellant was taking money from the station's cash register. When accosted by the owner, appellant "reached in his pockets" and "pulled out a handful of money from each pocket and handed (the money to the owner and his employee) and broke and ran." The amount initially taken from the cash register was approximately $143.00. The amount actually taken by appellant when he fled, after handing some money to the owner and employee, was $16.04.

Appellant contends that only the $16.04 was taken and that a prosecution for theft of over $50.00 is not maintainable. With such contention we do not agree for this Court has many times held that the crime of theft is complete where the article taken is reduced to the possession of the taker. It is not essential that appellant has removed the money from the premises of the service station. In the recent case of *Senter v. State*, Tex. Cr. App., 411 S.W.2d 742, we noted that removal from their accustomed place was sufficient evidence to convict the accused of the theft of hogs. The removal of the money from the cash register by this appellant made the offense complete. [Citations omitted.]

> * * *
>
> Finding no reversible error, the judgment of the trial court is affirmed.

The *Masters* case is on point. Although its facts differ from your case, they are the same in one pertinent respect: in both cases, the alleged thief took the property but did not leave the store with it. *Masters* holds that appropriation takes place as soon as the thief takes possession of the property and that it is not necessary for him to remove it from the owner's premises. Armed with this case (and after updating your research to insure that the case is still good law), you could conclude, without further analysis, that your client appropriated the ring.

Step 4. If you do not find case law that resolves the issue, then (a) find or devise a rule based on cases that have construed the element under factually similar situations and (b) apply that rule to predict how a court would resolve the issue.   Frequently cases that interpret a statute will not resolve the issue because they involve facts that differ substantially from your client's particular situation. When you cannot find a binding case that answers the question, you must analyze the existing cases to predict how a court would resolve the issue.

Suppose your office represents Steve Peters, who was arrested and charged with the crime of "theft from a person" under Texas Penal Code § 31.03(e)(4). A senior partner at your firm asks you to assess whether Peters is likely to be convicted. You review the statements of various witnesses and conclude the following: Peters followed a woman to her car. Before getting into the car, the woman placed a shopping bag and her handbag on the front passenger seat. As she was getting into the car from the driver's side, Peters reached through the open window of the front passenger side and took the handbag, which contained $25 in cash and valuables. The woman realized what had happened and began screaming for help. Peters was immediately apprehended by a store security guard. You must determine whether these facts satisfy all of the elements of the crime of theft from a person. If they do, then Peters will likely be convicted.

First, you would carefully read section 31.03 and divide the crime into its elements. Under subsection (e)(4), a person commits *theft from a person* if (1) he commits theft (*i.e.*, he appropriates the property of another without the consent of the owner and with intent to deprive) and (2) "the property is stolen from the person of another." You would also note that while theft of a handbag containing $25 in cash and valuables is a misdemeanor, theft of that handbag *from a person* is a "state felony," which would subject Peters to a harsher penalty.

Second, compare the facts with these elements. You might quickly conclude that Peters committed a theft because he appropriated the handbag with intent to deprive its owner of it and he did not have her consent to do so. You must then turn to the question whether Peters committed theft *from a person*. The statute is unclear on whether your facts satisfy that additional element, since the woman was not holding or touching the handbag when it was taken.

Third, look at the cases to see if you can find a binding case on point (*i.e.*, a case holding that the defendant was not guilty of theft from a person when he stole property from someone who was not actually touching it at the time of the taking) or one that establishes an applicable rule (*e.g.*, theft from a person does not occur unless the owner is touching the object at the time it is stolen). Unfortunately, you do not find a case that resolves the issue.

Fourth, if you cannot find case law on point or case law that establishes an applicable rule, look for factually similar cases considering the same issue. Suppose you find three relevant cases, which are summarized below:

Sims v. State of Texas, 731 S.W.2d 951
(Tex. Crim. App., Houston 1987)

Defendant entered a store, asked the owner about items for sale, and then dropped or threw change onto the floor behind the counter. Defendant engaged the owner in conversation while the two of them picked up the coins. In the meantime, one of Defendant's two companions took several $10 bills from the unattended, open cash register. Defendant was convicted of theft from a person. The appellate court reversed Defendant's conviction and entered a judgment of acquittal on the ground that theft from an unattended, open cash register does not constitute theft from a person.

Farrell v. State of Texas, 837 S.W.2d 395
(Tex. Crim. App., Dallas 1992)

Defendant approached a woman in a supermarket, engaged her in conversation, and stole the woman's wallet from her unzipped purse. The purse was in the raised portion of the woman's shopping cart. At the time of the theft, the woman was two to three feet away from the shopping cart, facing away from it. She discovered the theft several minutes after Defendant left the scene. Defendant was convicted of theft from a person. The appellate court reversed the conviction and acquitted Defendant.

Theft of a person requires proof of two elements: (1) the defendant unlawfully took property with the intent to permanently deprive the owner of the property; and (2) the defendant took the property from the owner's body, grasp, or immediate possession. The crime of theft from a person is distinguished from ordinary theft because it poses the risk of fright or injury to the victim. The appellate court found that there was insufficient evidence for a rational jury to find beyond a reasonable doubt that Defendant took the wallet from the woman's person, grasp, or immediate possession.

Alfred v. State of Texas, 659 S.W.2d 97
(Tex. Crim. App., Houston 1983)

Defendant snatched a woman's purse from the raised portion of her grocery cart. At the time of the theft, the woman's hand was on the cart near her purse. Defendant was convicted of theft from a person. He appealed his conviction on the ground that the definition of "person" under the statute prohibiting theft from a person was unconstitutionally vague and therefore violative of due process. The appellate court rejected this argument and affirmed his conviction. Applying the ordinary dictionary meaning of the word "person," the appellate court concluded that theft from a person includes taking property from the "presence" of a person as well as taking property in actual contact with the person.

Reviewing these cases, you could conclude that it is still not clear whether Peters committed theft from a person. But *you have identified an issue that must be analyzed.* Remember, the crucial first step in analyzing an issue is to be able to state it. The element at issue is the one requiring the property to be taken "from a person." The necessary facts are that the property was taken from the front passenger side of the car while the person was entering the driver's side. So you could state the issue this way: Did Peters take the victim's handbag from *the person* of the victim when he took it from the front passenger seat of the victim's car while she was entering on the driver's side? Now you are ready to analyze the issue.

First, identify a rule that helps you predict whether a court would convict Peters of theft from a person. The rule could be formulated a number of ways. One way to state it is this: property is taken from "the person" of a victim if there is a risk of fright or injury, because the property is within the victim's grasp, and the victim is aware of the theft as it occurs.

Second, apply the rule. You might conclude that a court would not convict your client because there was little or no risk of fright or injury. You might analogize your case to *Farrell* and *Sims,* noting that your client, like the victims in those cases, did not have the property within her grasp. You could distinguish *Alfred* by noting that the risk of fright or injury was much greater there because the victim could have easily reached for her purse.

On the other hand, you could conclude that a court would convict Peters because the woman was aware of the theft as it occurred (unlike the victims in both *Farrell* and *Sims,* who did not realize their property was taken until after the thefts occurred). Moreover, because she could have quickly reached across the seat to retrieve her handbag, there was indeed a risk of fright or injury, making the woman's case more like *Alfred*.

Each conclusion is reasonable because the facts of your case seem to fall between the two situations represented by *Farrell* and *Sims* (on one side) and *Alfred* (on the other).

Do Exercise 5-C Now, p. 101

E. Identifying the Facts

To identify and analyze statutory issues successfully, lawyers must not only find the relevant law but also identify the necessary facts. In law school, students are often given the pertinent facts and asked to apply the law to them. In actual practice, however, lawyers must identify the necessary facts of their cases. Lawyers cannot understand what facts are necessary to their cases until they know the relevant law. For instance, unless a lawyer knows the case law on theft from a person, she might not appreciate the relevance of facts like the distance between the defendant and the victim and the victim's awareness of the theft. As they research the law, lawyers often note missing facts, which they fill in by talking to their clients or reviewing documents.

Here is another example. The owner of a restaurant with 25 employees asks whether he will violate the state's civil rights statute if he refuses to hire a chef who will not work on Friday nights for religious reasons. The applicable statute provides:

> An employer of ten or more persons may not refuse to hire any individual because of such individual's religion, including any aspect of religious observance and practice, unless the employer demonstrates that he is unable to accommodate the individual's religious observance or practice without undue hardship on the operation of the employer's business.

Here, the answer to your client's question depends on the statute's meaning: how does the statute apply in this particular situation? Must the restaurant owner hire the chef who, for religious reasons, refuses to work on Friday nights?

You should conclude that you do not have enough facts to answer the question. Comparing these facts with the elements of the statute eliminates some issues, however. You know the statute covers the restaurant owner because he has more than 10 employees, and you know the prohibition covers refusals to hire. The reason you cannot answer the question is twofold. First, the statute contains a vague term, *undue hardship*. The statute requires employers to accommodate religious practices unless they can demonstrate that doing so would cause "undue hardship" on their business. What exactly does that phrase mean? You will need to know what it means so that you can tell whether your client's business would suffer one. Second, even if you had a more concrete idea of what undue hardship meant, the facts given above do not provide you with enough information to determine whether or to what extent the restaurant's business would suffer.

To answer the question, you must dig deeper into both the law and the facts. First, you must seek guidance on what "undue hardship" means since the statute itself is not clear. The main source for such guidance is case law construing the statute. Second, you must ask the client for more details about his restaurant and staffing, details that will help you determine if the client will indeed suffer an undue hardship. For example, if other chefs already working in the restaurant could work on Friday nights, the restaurant owner probably would not suffer a hardship by hiring a new chef who could not work on Friday nights. But if all the current employees had religious objections to working on Friday nights, the owner might be legally entitled to find a chef who would work then.

Do Exercise 5-D Now, p. 101

F.   An Example of How Lawyers Research and Analyze Statutory Issues: State v. Dunn

The following is a step-by-step fictional narrative of how a lawyer identifies and resolves statutory issues. The principal characters in the narrative are Blanca Alvarez, an attorney at South Galveston Legal Services, and her client Jane Dunn, who was arrested for aggravated robbery. Michael Benitez, Alvarez's supervisor, asked her to assess whether Dunn is likely to be convicted of aggravated robbery.

This narrative is instructive for several reasons. Up to now, you have been given the facts you needed to understand the examples. But lawyers do not get the facts that way: they have to construct a record through interviewing and reading documents and then sort through the record to separate the necessary facts from the inconsequential ones. Here the facts come from an interview with Dunn.

1. Identifying the issue in the case

a. Getting the facts: an interview with Jane Dunn

Alvarez: Tell me what happened.

Dunn: I admit I robbed the truck. I followed it in my car, a beat up Oldsmobile. When Keyes pulled into the factory yard by the waterfront I figured I was in luck. I'd done a job there before. Those buildings are big. It takes the drivers a while to get in and out. As soon as I saw the driver go through that door, I made my move. It's no big deal breaking into a UPS truck. A crowbar does the trick. Just pop the lock, ruck up the steel gate, and you're in. I knew right away I was gonna make out: the smalls rack was full of packages addressed to a jewelry store. I was grabbing two at a time and lobbing them through the Olds window when I heard the driver yelling at me. I couldn't believe he was back so fast. He scared the daylights outta me. I grabbed the crowbar and spun around. He was walking at me, yellin' his head off, "What the hell you doin' in my truck?" He was mad, I'll tell you. And I guess I panicked. I hefted that crowbar and shook it at him. "Stop right there," I told him, but he didn't. He kept on walking, and by now he was getting real close. I jerked the crowbar at him again and yelled, "Stop right there or you're gonna get hurt." He was only a few feet from me when he decided I meant business and stopped. I grabbed one more package with my free hand, shook the crowbar one more time to keep him in his place, and then I split. Wouldn't you know the drawbridge was open? As soon as I saw all those brake lights I knew I was gonna get busted and the crowbar was right there on the front seat.

b. Finding the law (the statute)

After interviewing Dunn, Alvarez researched the law. She first sought the relevant statute. Since Dunn's case was criminal, Alvarez pulled the three-volume Texas Penal Code off the shelf: *Vernon's Texas Codes Annotated: Penal*. She turned to the index at the back of volume three, looking for aggravated robbery. Whether what Dunn did amounted to aggravated robbery was, after all, the question. The index had separate entries for aggravated assault and battery, aggravated kidnaping, aggravated perjury, and aggravated sexual assault, but no separate entry for aggravated robbery, which Alvarez found under the more general heading "Aggravated Offenses." The index sent her to "Pen 29.03":

§ 29.03. **Aggravated Robbery**

    (a) A person commits an offense if he commits robbery as defined in Section 29.02, and he:

(1) causes serious bodily injury to another; or

(2) uses or exhibits a deadly weapon;

* * *

(b) An offense under this section is a felony of the first degree.

Because section 29.03 referred to section 29.02, Alvarez turned to it next. The definition of aggravated robbery was built on the definition of robbery, a "lesser included offense." That meant that some of the elements of Dunn's offense were set forth in section 29.02:

§ 29.02. **Robbery**

(a) A person commits an offense if, in the course of committing theft as defined in Chapter 31 and with intent to obtain or maintain control of the property, he:

(1) intentionally, knowingly, or recklessly causes bodily injury to another; or

(2) intentionally or knowingly threatens or places another in fear of imminent bodily injury or death.

(b) An offense under this section is a felony of the second degree.

Alvarez made copies of the two Penal Code sections, laid them side by side on the table, and thought about the relationship between the two. Aggravated robbery was robbery with something more. In other words, if you violated section 29.03, you violated section 29.02 too. But the opposite was not true: it was possible that Dunn had committed robbery, but not aggravated robbery. Alvarez reviewed sections 29.02 and 29.03, breaking the provisions down into their elements and thinking about each one: did Dunn's conduct satisfy each element of the crime?

> **Do Exercise 5-E Now, p. 103**

c. **Comparing the facts of Dunn's case with the elements of the statute**

Comparing the facts to robbery. Alvarez started with 29.02, the section on robbery. She talked to herself as she parsed the statute. *"A person."* Well, *no chance of succeeding if we try to argue Dunn's not a person.* "In the course of committing theft as defined in Chapter 31. . . ." Have to look that up. Here it is: Chapter 31. Handy little outline here at the top of the chapter, listing "theft" as being in 31.03. Here it is.

31.03. Theft. Theft is when someone "unlawfully appropriates property with the intent of depriving the owner of property." No question Dunn appropriated the jewelry from the truck, meaning to keep the jeweler from getting it. Unlawfully? Let's see. It was unlawful if she did it without the owner's "effective consent." No way out of that one. We obviously can't argue that the consent was "effective": there wasn't any. Dunn certainly committed theft.

What's the next element of robbery? Back to 29.02, the robbery section: ". . . and with intent to obtain or maintain control of the property . . . ." Yes, she had intent. Now the statute specifies two alternative ways that Dunn could have turned this theft with intent into robbery. The first one, "intentionally, knowingly, or recklessly causes bodily injury to another," doesn't apply. There was no injury, which saves a lot of trouble worrying about what intentionally, knowingly, or recklessly might mean. Number two: "intentionally or knowingly threatens or places another in fear of imminent bodily injury or death." Here's the crux: it's about the threat and the fear. If she committed robbery, here's how she did it. To be guilty of aggravated robbery, Dunn must also have done something more. Time to review aggravated robbery to see if what Dunn did was more than just plain robbery.

Before turning to the Penal Code section on aggravated robbery, Alvarez noted that robbery in Texas is a felony of the second degree, carrying a substantially lighter sentence than that for aggravated robbery.

Comparing the facts to aggravated robbery. Alvarez turned to section 29.03—aggravated robbery. Alvarez worked her way through the section, looking first for elements satisfied by the facts of the case. Since subsection (a)(1): "causes serious bodily injury to another" was not satisfied, Dunn had been charged with subsection (a)(2), which required that she "used or exhibited a deadly weapon."

d. Identifying the issue: deadly weapon

Confident that she had adequately researched and analyzed the elements of the crime, Alvarez turned to the statutory definition of "deadly weapon" in section 1.07(17)(B):

§ 1.07. **Definitions.**

* * *

(17) "Deadly weapon" means:

* * *

(B) anything that in the manner of its use or intended use is capable of causing death or serious bodily injury.

She read the definition carefully and narrowed the question even further: did Dunn use or intend to use the crowbar in a manner capable of causing death or serious injury?

2. Analyzing the issue

a. Researching the case law

To answer the question, Alvarez turned her attention to the case law, starting with the index to the Notes of Decisions that appeared immediately after the statutory definition of "deadly weapon." There she saw cases indexed by the object used: boards, bottles, clubs and bats, firearms, fists or hands, hatchets, knives, nail guns, pistols, pocket knives, scissors, shanks, shotguns, sticks, and tools. No crowbars. Alvarez also found cases listed by the injuries inflicted, the size and manner of their use, and the sufficiency of the evidence.

Reading through the Notes of Decisions, Alvarez gained a very general sense of what she would find once she read the cases. She knew that these Notes condensed a multi-page decision to only a few words; they could therefore hardly capture the complexities and nuances of the actual decision, particularly the reasoning. Nonetheless, the Notes provided some guidance. Alvarez learned, for example, that the statutory definition of "deadly weapon" had survived constitutional challenges for vagueness after courts interpreted "deadly weapon" to include both a dustpan and a floor (in unrelated cases). Although not useful for solving Dunn's problem, it meant that the statutory definition of "deadly weapon" could be quite encompassing. It would be difficult to argue that a crowbar was not a deadly weapon under the statute.

As she went though the Notes of Decisions, Alvarez also noted the kind of evidence juries had when they found defendants guilty of aggravated robbery. She learned that the appellate cases tended to invoke the statutory language over and over, and that the cases held, among other things, that juries did not need evidence of actual injury to find that a defendant intended to use the instrument in a manner capable of causing death or serious injury, and that the state must prove the defendant intended to use it as one.

After reading through the Notes of Decisions in the bound volume, Alvarez turned to the pocket part in the back. The bound volumes had been printed in 1998, according to the publishing information. The pocket part, so called because it is tucked into a pocket in the back cover of the bound volume, was a paperback pamphlet printed every year that updated every part of the annotated codes, including changes made by the legislature to the statute itself, additional reference materials, and recent court decisions relating to the statute. More than one case had been won by meticulously updating research. Alvarez learned that no changes had been made in the statutory language since the hardcover volume was printed, but she discovered many new cases.

b. Reading the case law

Alvarez began her research with every lawyer's constant hope: to find a favorable case, something recent, perhaps something that the District Attorney had overlooked when he charged Dunn. Alvarez needed a successful defendant who used an object the general size and shape of a crowbar, who did not really swing at the victim, who made only mild threats, and who left the scene as soon as possible after the confrontation. Realistically, Alvarez knew the chance of finding such a case was remote.

Alvarez's pessimism turned out to be appropriate: she found no such case. So she began looking for analogous cases, cases like Dunn's in relevant ways. The first case she found was called *Hammons v. State*, involving a robber who brandished a baseball bat. She also chose a case involving a knife because the defendant was found not guilty of aggravated robbery despite having actually cut the victim's hand during the robbery. Alvarez theorized that in common-sense terms a knife is more a deadly weapon than a crowbar; if a knife-wielding robber was not guilty of aggravated robbery, there might be hope for Dunn and her crowbar. Alvarez pulled out the reporters and began to read the cases she had unearthed.

c. Analyzing the cases

After reading the cases, Alvarez confirmed her suspicions: a deadly weapon was not always what one might suppose and was quite often something one did not suspect. The courts seemed to pay as much attention to what people said and did with the object as they did to the object itself. By reviewing what she believed to be the most relevant cases, Alvarez learned the rule that prevailed in the Texas case law: an instrument is deadly if (1) it is objectively capable of causing death or serious injury and (2) the defendant's conduct demonstrated an intent to cause serious injury or death.

d. Predicting whether Dunn is likely to be convicted

Alvarez realized that if Dunn threatened her victim both physically and verbally with any object that under the circumstances could cause death or serious injury, Texas courts would find the object a deadly weapon. Furthermore, the threat did not even have to be both physically and verbally explicit: either was enough. Given Dunn's story, the crowbar was likely a deadly weapon under Texas law. Alvarez would write a memorandum to her supervisor telling him that Dunn would probably be convicted of aggravated robbery.

EXERCISES

Exercise 5-A

Read the following statute. Identify the elements that the prosecution must prove to obtain a conviction under the statute.

> Nirvana Penal Law Section 410: Stalking in the Third Degree
>
> A person is guilty of stalking in the third degree if he intentionally and repeatedly follows, harasses, or threatens another person, causing that person to reasonably fear for his safety or for the safety of his immediate family.

Exercise 5-B(1)

Read the following facts. Apply the elements to the facts that you identified in Exercise 5-A. List issues that may arise from applying the elements of the anti-stalking statute to the facts.

Facts

Donald Lane and Sara Kim casually dated in college. Kim broke off the relationship after they graduated. Lane was distraught. He telephoned Kim several times a week for two months, demanding that she give him another chance. After Kim got an unlisted phone number, Lane started sending her letters. The first three were clever and endearing: Lane wrote poetic notes expressing his deep affection for Kim. Kim did not respond to these letters. Lane then wrote an incoherent fourth letter in which he called Kim "a selfish, uncaring tease who would get what she deserved." In his rambling prose, Lane recounted recent news events which included a report about a young woman who was attacked in a local park.

Exercise 5-B(2)

Read the following statutes and facts. Identify the statutory element(s) at issue in each example.

1. Nirvana Penal Code Section 73(1): Criminal Possession of a Controlled Substance in the Fifth Degree

A person is guilty of criminal possession of a controlled substance in the fifth degree when he, without lawful purpose, knowingly possesses a controlled substance.

Facts

Matthew Thomas missed his bus after work and asked Paige Allen, a co-worker, for a ride home. She agreed, and he got into the front passenger seat of her car. After they had been riding for about fifteen minutes, Thomas noticed a small glassine envelope containing cocaine on the console between the front seats. Just as he observed the envelope, Thomas heard police sirens. Within seconds, Allen was pulled over for speeding. The police officer saw the glassine envelope while he was talking to Allen. He arrested both Allen and Thomas for criminal possession of a controlled substance in the fifth degree. Police laboratory tests confirmed that the white powder in the glassine envelope was cocaine, a controlled substance. Thomas wants to know if he is likely to be convicted.

2. Nirvana Land Use Code Section 25(7): Use of Land in Single-Family Residential Zones

Owners of land in single-family residential zones may not build secondary structures on their land that can be used as dwellings.

Facts

Penelope Wang owns a house in a single-family residential zone. She would like to build a pool cabana in her backyard. The cabana would measure 500 square feet and have plumbing and electricity. Wang plans to use the cabana to prepare and serve poolside snacks. The cabana would also have a bathroom where guests could change. Wang wants to know if she can start construction.

3.   Nirvana Anti-Discrimination Law Section 90(2): Unlawful Discrimination in Employment

It shall be unlawful for an employer with ten or more employees to discriminate in the workplace because of an employee's race, gender, religion, national origin, age, disability, or sexual orientation.

Facts

Robert Watkins claims that he was fired from his job at LKJ because he is African-American. LKJ has five full-time and three part-time employees. The company also employs ten full-time temporary workers every year during its three-month busy season. Watkins wants to know if he can sue LKJ, his former employer, for race discrimination under the Nirvana Anti-Discrimination Law Section 90(2).

4.   Nirvana Penal Code Section 109(4): Forgery in the Fourth Degree

A person is guilty of forgery in the fourth degree if with the intent to deceive another person, he falsely alters a written instrument.

Facts

Jennifer Perkins is a securities trader. She deleted information from a computer database at work so that a client would not know that he lost money on a trade. Perkins was charged with forgery in the fourth degree. Perkins wants to know if she is likely to be convicted.

5. Nirvana Criminal Procedure Code Section 80(3): Speedy trial

A felony charge must be dismissed with prejudice if the state is not ready for trial within four months of the commencement of the criminal action.

Facts

On February 2, 2000, Max Stanley was arrested for the felony crime of burglary in the first degree. The grand jury indicted him on the charge on March 3, 2000. The indictment was filed in court on April 14, 2000. The state was not ready for trial until July 17, 2000. Stanley wants to know if he can file a motion to dismiss the indictment under Nirvana Criminal Procedure Code Section 80(3).

Exercise 5-C

Read the following facts. Apply the elements of theft from a person, Texas Penal Code § 31.03(e)(4), summarized on p. 88, to the facts. Predict whether Roy Davis is likely to be convicted of theft from a person.

Facts

Jane Leung was sitting in the vestibule of a doctor's office. She hung her jacket on the coat stand located about six feet from where she was sitting. Roy Davis removed his sweater from the coat stand and, while doing so, took Leung's wallet from the pocket of her jacket. Although Leung did not see Davis take her wallet, she did see him holding it when he left the office.

Exercise 5-D

Read the following statute, cases, and facts. Answer the questions that follow.

Nirvana Penal Code Section 113(4): Hazing in the Fourth Degree

A person is guilty of hazing in the fourth degree if he is a student in a college, university, or other educational institution, and, in his capacity as a student, intentionally engages in an activity that causes another person physical harm or that creates a substantial likelihood of physical harm to another person.

Cases

State v. Reid: Reid asserts that the indictment charging him with hazing in the fourth degree should be dismissed because he did not engage in an "activity" covered by the statute. Reid's argument is without merit. The term "activity" includes any pastime or recreation which subjects participants to conditions that are substantially likely to cause physical harm. Reid presided over a college fraternity initiation in which he required freshman pledges to drink excessive amounts of alcohol. Although no one suffered actual physical harm, the facts establish that Reid intentionally engaged in an activity that created a substantial likelihood of physical harm, *i.e.*, alcohol poisoning, for participants.

State v. Evans: Evans asserts that the indictment charging her with hazing in the fourth degree should be dismissed because she did not engage in an "activity" covered by the statute. This claim is without merit. The term "activity" includes any pastime or recreation in which a person is struck or otherwise touched in a violent manner. Evans repeatedly struck the nineteen-year-old complainant with a yardstick during a college sorority ritual. The complainant suffered lacerations which required medical treatment. These facts establish that Evans intentionally engaged in an activity that caused physical harm.

Facts: *State v. Arnold*

Our client, Carla Arnold, was arrested and charged with the crime of hazing in the fourth degree. Arnold is a student at Nirvana University and president of CDE Sorority. She requires pledges, as a part of their initiations, to groom the sorority's mascots: four long-haired house cats. Kimberly Prescott, an eighteen-year-old pledge, had a severe asthma attack while she was grooming the cats. She stopped breathing and had to spend several days in the hospital. Prescott's doctor concluded that the cats' fur caused the attack. Arnold claims that she did not know that Prescott was an asthmatic; she does not ask pledges about their medical histories.

Questions

1. List the elements of hazing in the fourth degree.

2. How is the statutory term "activity" defined in the cases? Use the cases to state a rule defining the term.

3. List the necessary facts in *State v. Arnold*.

4. List issues raised by applying the elements of the anti-hazing statute to the facts in *State v. Arnold*.

5. Is a court likely to dismiss the charge against Arnold? Explain how the statute and cases support your answer.

Exercise 5-E

Review Texas Penal Code § 29.02 on p. 94. Parse the statute and isolate the elements the prosecution must prove to convict a defendant of robbery under § 29.02(a)(1) and § 29.02(a)(2).

PART II

Legal Writing and Research

CHAPTER 6

The Legal Memorandum

When you master this chapter, you will understand:

1. why lawyers write legal memoranda;

2. how knowing your reader helps you write a better memo; and

3. how the purpose of a memo affects both its content and form.

A. Why Lawyers Write Legal Memoranda

In the last chapter, the lawyer Blanca Alvarez was faced with the same task that thousands of lawyers face at work every day: explaining in writing the answer she has reached to a legal question. To do so, she must explain her research and demonstrate the steps in her legal reasoning. This lawyerly task is similar to writing a non-legal office memorandum. For example, a non-legal office memo about whether a city water district was using too much water might analyze the question by presenting research on water usage in comparable districts, predicting future usage, and recommending possible solutions.

In the water district example, the writer—who through research and careful thought has become very knowledgeable on the subject—is informing others what a reasonable course of action would be and why. In the Dunn matter, Alvarez's office must decide whether Dunn is likely to be convicted of aggravated robbery. Following her research on the facts and law, Alvarez has become quite knowledgeable about Dunn's case. Her office will therefore rely on her analysis of the question. Her memo explains that analysis in writing.

Alvarez, like any other lawyer, is writing her memo to say, "I have investigated and considered the facts of this matter; I have researched the applicable law; I have identified and analyzed each potential legal issue; and I predict the following outcome if the case goes to court."

B. Helping Your Reader

To help readers understand the question, the law that answers it, and the analysis that supports it, memos follow format conventions. The formal conventions of memo writing help the reader comprehend these things quickly and easily, no matter how complex. The more complex an idea, the more straightforward its explanation must be. Each part of the legal memo's format helps guide the reader through what may be complex or unfamiliar legal terrain. For this reason, each part of the format is self-contained and self-explanatory.

Although they may be called by different names in different offices, most legal memos have the following parts:

- Heading;
- Question(s) Presented;
- Short Answer(s);
- Summary of the Facts;
- Discussion; and
- Conclusion.

Lawyers reading memos bring certain expectations to their reading. One of these expectations is that the Discussion contains the analysis presented in a logical form. This form, known as a legal proof, was introduced in Chapter 4 and will be discussed at length in the next two chapters. Readers also expect the memo to contain an identifying heading, a statement of the issues in the form of a question, a short answer to the question, a summary of the facts, and a conclusion. These parts of the legal memo are discussed in Chapter 9.

In addition to the expectations relating to form and substance, readers always expect professional quality writing. These expectations set standards for legal memo writers in organization, vocabulary, usage, grammar, and punctuation. These standards are discussed in Chapters 10 and 11. This chapter focuses on reader expectations about the purpose and use of the legal memorandum.

C. Knowing Your Reader

To be an effective legal memo writer, you must know your reader. In the Dunn matter (described in Chapter 5, p. 92), Alvarez will be writing a legal memo to her supervisor, who will use the memo to decide how to defend Dunn's aggravated robbery charge without independently gathering the facts, researching the law, or analyzing the issues. In law school, although your reader is actually your writing professor, you will master the skill of memo writing much faster if you view your reader as a practicing lawyer who might use the information contained in your memo.

The usual legal memo reader is a lawyer who

- is busy or impatient (or both);
- does not know or has forgotten the facts;
- does not know or is unsure of the applicable law; and
- may base some further action on your memo.

Readers of legal memos share many common characteristics. Assume that your reader has all of the following attributes, unless you know otherwise:

1. Your reader is a lawyer

Most readers of legal memos are lawyers. That means they know how the American legal system works. They know that legal analysis involves identifying rules in cases and statutes and applying them to the facts. Many novice legal writers make the mistake of including in their memos newly-learned fundamental concepts. Read through your drafts critically to make sure you have acknowl-edged your reader as a lawyer who already understands the fundamentals. Readers expect the legal memo to be a self-contained, self-explanatory, objec-tively-written prediction of the likely answer to a legal question. It must be sup-ported by logically organized and carefully presented analysis. Anything less will fall far below expectations.

2. Your reader is busy or impatient (or both)

In this age of information, few readers in any profession have time to waste. The less time your reader has to spend deciphering your prose, the more suc-cessful your writing will be. Lawyers who *use* memos require those memos to be focused on the subject and easy to read. Writing that is diffuse, disorganized, or ungrammatical makes the reader do the writer's work: assembling information into a comprehensible and useful form. Readers who are asked to do the writer's work often will not do it. This means that the memo is ignored, the hard work is wasted, and, as far as the reader is concerned, the question is unanswered.

It is helpful, therefore, to imagine a reader who is too busy to plow through endless opaque text trying to ferret out information. Imagine also a reader who is too impatient to work at figuring out anything that is not immediately clear from what has been written. It helps to imagine a reader who resents having to reread even a single sentence to understand it and will not bother to read what has been written if it is even slightly confusing.

3. Your reader does not know or has forgotten the facts

Memos are not helpful or useful if necessary information is left out. Lawyers who ask you to analyze a legal question may have only passing familiarity with the facts of the matter. Others may know far more about the facts when they assign a memo. Your job when writing a memo is not just to predict the possible outcome of a situation or to explain how to accomplish a particular objective, but to present all the facts necessary to understanding why you reached your con-clusion.

4. Your reader does not know or is unsure of the applicable law

While your reader, being a lawyer, certainly knows how the law works, she may not know much about the particular law that applies to the client's question. Indeed, why would your reader ask you to write the memo if she were already sure of the law? With the law, as with the facts, you must present your reader with everything needed to understand the matter. If you assume the reader knows the law, you might omit crucial authorities or reasoning, making your memo useless.

Suppose that your reader's area of expertise is far from the subject of your memo. By making your memo self-contained and self-explanatory, you help your reader in two ways. First, your reader will have confidence in your conclusions. Second, your reader will be able to readily answer any question about the matter and know enough to ask additional questions.

Or perhaps your reader is indeed an expert in the subject of your memo, but is quite busy and involved in many similar cases. Working on your memo assignment has made you an expert, and your busy reader is able to rely on you to update the law and apply it to the particular matter at hand. The memo will be useless to your reader if it fails to validate a rule of law with the most current cases, omits a case you think your reader already knows, or skips a case comparison because it is "obvious." For a memo to be effective, *everything* crucial to the matter, both fact and law, must be presented.

5.   Your reader may base some further action on your memo

You should assume that what you write in your memo will serve as the basis for some further action by your reader, even if it is just asking another question. The contents of the memo may be discussed with other members of the office, or with outside counsel, or directly with the client. Your memo will serve its purpose only if it helps the reader and others to remember, understand, and analyze the matter.

D.   Making Predictions

Predicting the outcome of a legal question is one of the most difficult challenges facing the novice legal memo writer. It can be particularly difficult when the writer's budding legal sense is at odds with long-held beliefs or natural sympathies. It is not easy to conclude that a well-liked client has been legally disinherited. It can be distasteful to conclude that someone you consider morally blameworthy is not liable. Under these circumstances, it may seem easier to equivocate than to reach a conclusion.

Although this reluctance to take a legal stand is natural, it must be overcome. Legal memos are useful only if they help their readers. If the writer takes no position, the reader does not know what to think. If the memo writer does not make a prediction and support it with carefully presented legal analysis, the writer might just as well have not written the memo. If a memo offers only a few case citations, some interesting facts from a few relevant precedents, a fact or two from the current matter, or an argument or two that might be made, the writer is asking the reader to do the writer's work. The reader will not. The memo will not be helpful or useful and will probably be ignored, given to someone else to rewrite, or discarded.

E. Being Objective

Many writing texts refer to legal memo writing as "objective" writing. This term may exacerbate the novice writer's initial reluctance to reach legal conclusions. The word "objective" may imply that the writer is not supposed to be definite or take one side or the other. That, however, is not the case. When writing a memo, the writer is obliged to predict the likely outcome and to support the conclusion with a logically organized and carefully presented discussion.

Consider once again the Dunn matter. Blanca Alvarez may sympathize with her client, hoping that she will not be convicted of aggravated robbery. Her research and analysis, however, do not lead her to that conclusion. No matter how sympathetic she is to Dunn, Alvarez must not allow herself to skew the facts, to ignore cases that are not favorable to her client, or to employ a shallow analysis that would conceal the weaknesses of Dunn's position. She must do her best to be objective, even if the likely outcome is distasteful.

Any lawyer who develops an opinion about the likely success or failure of a legal matter based on an objective evaluation of the law and facts is ethically obliged to be honest about that opinion. Think of the consequences of acting otherwise. A memo that equivocates helps no one, least of all your client.

It may help to remember that readers will exercise their own judgment about whether your prediction is sound and adequately supported by your discussion. If your analysis seems unconvincing, your reader may ask you to clear up a point, do additional research, or examine a related question. But your reader should never have to return a memo because it has failed to fulfill its function: to present a reasoned and well-supported prediction of the outcome.

Lawyers are asked for legal advice. Once asked, they are obliged to give it honestly. While you must be objective in assessing the facts and applying the law to the matter, you must answer the question. Your answer need not contain certainties; it may be expressed in degrees of likelihood.

F. Memo Format

Legal memos have a certain look. The audience for a legal memo, whether the original reader or some broader group, is used to a certain format and has developed a psychological comfort in knowing what to expect. For instance, you saw in the chapters on legal analysis that lawyers expect the legal conclusion's validity to be demonstrated. The form of that demonstration is called a legal proof. The Discussion contains the memo's legal proofs and is explained in Chapter 8.

Surrounding the Discussion and providing additional insights into it are a number of other parts: the Heading, Question(s) Presented, Short Answer(s), Summary of the Facts, and Conclusion. Each of these parts (discussed in Chapter 9) has an important function and its own format, but because the legal proof is at the heart of the memo, the next chapter discusses it at length.

Three sample memos are included in the Appendices. The first memo (Appendix A, p. 399) considers whether Jane Dunn, whose case is recounted in Chapter 5, is likely to be convicted of aggravated robbery. The second memo (Appendix B, p. 407) considers whether Nadine Jackson, whose husband was killed in an amusement park accident, has a claim for negligent infliction of emotional distress against the amusement park. The third memo (Appendix C, p. 415), written after Dunn is convicted, assesses whether she can successfully appeal her conviction.

CHAPTER 7

Writing Legal Proofs

When you master this chapter, you will understand:

1. why lawyers and law students write legal proofs; and

2. how to write legal proofs for legal memoranda.

T his chapter focuses on writing legal proofs for legal memoranda using the IRAC structure introduced in Chapter 4. Every legal proof you write should include these IRAC components:

1. **Issue**—a statement of the narrow legal question raised by the facts;

2. **Rule**—a statement of the applicable rule of law, with rule support (citing to and discussing the rule cases and any statutes that validate the rule);

3. **Application**—an application of the rule to the facts of your case, with case comparisons (analogizing your case to and distinguishing your case from the rule cases); and

4. **Conclusion**—a conclusion predicting how a court would resolve the issue.

Remember that while the IRAC structure is useful for logically organizing legal proofs, it is not a mechanical formula. The extent of the analysis—and therefore the length of the proof—depends on the complexity of the issue. You may be able to write a legal proof for a simple, undisputed issue in a single paragraph. On the other hand, the legal proof for a complex, disputed issue may be very lengthy, spanning pages in the memo's Discussion.

A. The Issue

1. Identifying issues

A legal proof must be based on a narrowly-framed issue. An issue is a legal question about how (or whether) the law applies to the facts of your client's case. To identify narrow issues, first identify the claims and defenses (or in a criminal case, crimes and defenses) that might apply to your client's case. Second, for common-law claims and defenses, find a case (or group of cases) delineating their elements; for statutory claims, crimes, and defenses, find the elements in the applicable statute. Third, apply the law to the facts, element by element. *Each element can raise an issue.* Here are two examples:

Example 1: Identifying Common-Law Issues

Step 1. Gather the facts and identify your client's claim.

Your client, Latisha Howard, fell in the lobby of Happy
Travelers Hotel when she caught the heel of her shoe in a broken tile. She suffered permanent injuries to her right ankle.
Howard wants to know if she can sue the hotel to recover damages for her injuries. Your preliminary research reveals that she
may have a common-law claim of negligence against the hotel.

Step 2. Find a case (or group of cases) that sets forth the elements of the claim.

You find the following controlling case:

Kramer v. Tranquility Lodge: In a common-law negligence action
against a hotel, the plaintiff must show that the hotel owed her
a duty of care, that the hotel breached its duty of care, and that
the hotel's breach was the proximate cause of her injury. A claim
for negligence exists if all these elements are satisfied.

Step 3. Use the elements of the claim to identify the issues in your case.

Issue 1: Did the hotel owe Howard a duty of care?
Issue 2: Did the hotel breach its duty of care?
Issue 3: Was the hotel's breach of its duty of care the proximate
cause of Howard's injury?

There are Issues but they'd be written together

Example 2: Identifying Statutory Issues

Step 1. Gather the facts and identify your client's claim.

Your client, Paul Lee, is a chemist at Fountain of Youth Affiliates,
a biotechnology company in the state of Nirvana. He was
recently demoted to a position in which he has little responsibility. Lee claims that he was demoted because he reported to
the Nirvana Biotechnology Oversight Committee what he
believed to be his employer's fraudulent research practices. Your
preliminary research reveals that Lee may have a claim against
his employer under Nirvana's whistleblower statute.

Step 2. Find the statute that sets forth the elements of the claim.

Nirvana Whistleblower Statute Section 726(A)(i) provides:

> An employee has a claim against an employer if
> (a) the employee has an objectively reasonable belief that the employer engaged in a fraudulent practice;
> (b) the employee reports the practice to a government agency; and
> (c) as a result, the employer retaliates against the employee.

Step 3. Use the elements of the statute to identify the issues in your case.

> Issue 1: Did Lee have *an objectively reasonable belief* that his employer engaged in a *fraudulent practice*?
> Issue 2: Did Lee *report* his employer's alleged fraudulent practice *to a government agency*?
> Issue 3: Did the employer *retaliate* against Lee *because* Lee reported the practice?

Notice that in Example 2, the first issue actually raises two narrower **sub-issues**. (Issues that stem from the same element are sometimes called sub-issues.) The two sub-issues are:

> Sub-Issue 1:   Was Lee's belief that his employer was engaged in a fraudulent practice *an objectively reasonable belief*?
> Sub-Issue 2:   Was the employer's practice a *fraudulent practice*?

2.   Moving from the broad legal question to the narrow legal issues

Often lawyers are asked to write legal memoranda in response to broad questions, such as "Can the client successfully appeal her conviction?" or "Can Johnson recover for witnessing her nephew's death?" These questions are not themselves issues. You often must move from the broad question through a series of increasingly narrower ones to identify the legal issues.

For instance, in Chapter 2 you were asked whether Susan Johnson could recover under Arcadia law for witnessing her nephew's death. To get from this broad question to the narrow issue, you had to identify the claim and then apply it, element by element, to your client's case:

The client's question: "Can Johnson recover for witnessing her nephew's death?"

leads to ⇨

The legal question, in broad terms: "Does Johnson have a claim for negligent infliction of emotional distress?"

leads to ⇨

The legal issues, each focused on a particular element of the claim:

Issue 1: "Was Johnson closely related to her nephew?"
Issue 2: "Did Johnson have a sensory and contemporaneous observation of the accident?"
Issue 3: "Did she suffer emotional distress as a result?"

A narrowly-framed issue is essential to a properly-focused analysis. If you state the issue as a broad question, the corresponding rule will be unfocused. For example, the following "issue" is actually a broad legal question, and so the resulting rule provides a poor starting place for an analysis:

Issue: May the client be held liable for common-law fraud?
Rule: A person may be held liable for common-law fraud if she knowingly makes a false statement of material fact to another person who justifiably relies on the statement and suffers damages as a result.

If you adopted this broad legal question as your issue, then your analysis of the issue necessarily would be a very general, unfocused discussion of many issues.

In contrast, when the issue is narrowly-framed (that is, based on an element), the rule that responds to it results in a focused analysis:

Issue: Was Johnson closely related to her nephew Frank?
Rule: An adult is closely related to a child with whom she has a parental relationship. A parental relationship exists if the adult has frequent contact with the child and assumes significant responsibility for his welfare.

3. Identifying disputed and undisputed issues

Some issues are **disputed issues**: you cannot definitively state whether your facts satisfy (or fail to satisfy) an element, so you must predict how a court might resolve them. Others issues are **undisputed issues** because they have answers. That is, your research shows that the element is (or is not) satisfied. For example, one element of a federal age discrimination in employment claim requires proof that the plaintiff is at least 40 years old. Usually this element is satisfied without controversy, and hence is undisputed. However, in such a claim, another element—whether the employer unlawfully discriminated against the plaintiff because of his age—is usually disputed.

To make your analysis logical and complete, cover both disputed and undisputed issues. Since your reader does not have the benefit of your research and understanding, you must identify *each* element of the claim, crime, or defense and explain whether the facts satisfy it and why.

Undisputed elements can be explained in abbreviated legal proofs; sometimes a short paragraph or even a single sentence will suffice. For instance, the thesis in the Dunn memo (Appendix A, p. 399) includes this abbreviated proof: "Dunn committed theft because she unlawfully took property, the packages, with the intent to deprive the owner of the property. Texas Penal Code § 31.03(a)." This proof dispenses with the formal structure for proofs of disputed issues. It begins with the conclusion (Dunn committed theft), not the issue. Moreover, rather than separately stating the rule (theft is unlawful taking of property with the intent to deprive the owner of it) and the application (Dunn took the packages without the owner's consent), the proof combines them into a single clause. And because applied to these facts the rule is unambiguous, it is supported with only a citation to the statute, without quoting or explaining it or discussing cases that have applied it. Of course, proofs of disputed issues must be more structured and developed to explain and support your analysis.

4. Expressing the issue clearly and precisely

When writing a legal proof, make sure that the issue is presented in a focused and precise topic sentence. Use the language of the claim, crime, or defense. Here are examples of issue statements:

- The first issue is whether the hotel owed Jackson a duty of care.
- At issue is whether the employer's research practices are fraudulent under Nirvana's whistleblower statute.

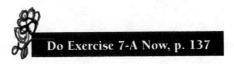

Do Exercise 7-A Now, p. 137

B. The Rule

After you have stated the issue, the next part of a legal proof is to state the rule. A rule is a legal proposition derived from case law or a statute that controls how the issue is resolved.

1. Some rules are expressly stated in case law or statutes

Sometimes a statute or case expressly states a rule. Here are some examples:

Example 1: Rule from a Case Defining an Element of a Common-Law Claim

> *Kline v. Hardy*: In the state of Nirvana, the common-law tort claim of intentional infliction of emotional distress has three elements: (1) the defendant intentionally engaged in extreme and outrageous conduct, (2) the defendant's conduct proximately caused the plaintiff to suffer distress, and (3) the plaintiff's distress was severe. *The rule from Kline defining severe distress*: Distress is severe in cases in which the plaintiff requires medical, psychiatric, or psychological treatment for his distress.

Example 2: Rule from a Statute Defining a Statutory Element

> Nirvana Penal Law § 20(B)(i): Disorderly Conduct in a Residential Neighborhood at Night:
>
> The term Night is the period between twenty minutes after sunset and twenty minutes before sunrise. . . .

Unlike the statute in Example 2, some statutes express the elements of a claim, crime, or defense in broad terms. Litigants often call upon the courts to interpret the meaning of ambiguous statutory terms. The courts must then devise rules that define or explain the unclear statutory elements, as Example 3 illustrates:

Example 3: Rule from Case Law Defining a Statutory Element

> *People v. Joseph*: The State alleges that defendant committed second degree burglary by unlawfully entering the victim's private hospital room and stealing money from her wallet. The defendant maintains that an element of the crime—that the defendant enter a *dwelling*—is not satisfied. The Penal Code defines a dwelling as a building which is generally occupied by a person lodging there at night. *The rule from Joseph defining "dwelling"*: We hold that a private room in a hospital or any extended care facility is a dwelling because it is a room occupied for lodging at night.

2. When rules are not expressly stated, they must be synthesized from holdings in cases

Sometimes rules are not expressly stated in court decisions or statutes. To define a statutory or common-law element in such instances, you must devise the rule by synthesizing the holdings of the relevant cases (rule cases), a technique you were introduced to in Chapters 1 and 2. Use the synthesized rule to answer the legal question posed by the issue. The rule will be valid only if the rule cases and your case involve the same narrow legal issue and have similar necessary facts.

In the Johnson matter, the case law does not precisely define the *closely-related* element of the common-law claim of negligent infliction of emotional distress. Assume that the case law explains the closely-related element this way: "To be closely related, the plaintiff and victim must have a strong emotional bond."

This definition is general enough to cover a wide range of relationships—spouses, lovers, roommates, grandparents, brothers, aunts, and close friends, which means it is not useful as a rule to define closely related. To determine whether Johnson was closely related to the victim (her nephew), the lawyer must find relevant cases, synthesize their holdings, and create a rule that uses details instead of general terms to describe the closely-related element.

a. Chart the cases. Often the first step in synthesizing a rule is to chart the cases. Chapter 2 contains a case chart (see p. 33). There are many different ways to chart cases: your goal is to create a chart that helps you understand the relationship of the law, the necessary facts, and the holdings, thus permitting you to synthesize a rule to predict the holding in your case.

The chart in Chapter 2 showed that in cases addressing whether an adult was closely related to a child, the decisive consideration was whether the adult had a parental relationship with the child. That chart presented the correlation simply, indicating by a "yes" or "no" whether the closely-related element was satisfied and whether a parental relationship existed. Here is how you might go about creating a chart like that. (The chart in this chapter is a more advanced version of the chart in Chapter 2, providing details about the facts of each case.)

(1) Start by sorting your cases into two groups by their holdings. For example, the first group would be cases holding that the plaintiffs were closely related to the victims and the other group would be cases holding that they were not.

(2) Create a chart with three columns, one column labeled "Case," the second "Necessary Facts" (make this the largest column), and the last "Holdings." Recall that necessary facts are the facts that determine the outcome of the case.

(3) Complete the chart. The Necessary Facts column should include specific details. Include *all* the pertinent facts on the issue. Describe the holdings by the result only ("Yes" or "No"). For example, in the Johnson matter, "Closely related—yes" and "Closely related—no" would be a good way to describe the holdings.

A chart of the holdings of the three cases on the issue might look like this:

ISSUE: WAS THE AUNT CLOSELY RELATED TO HER NEPHEW?

CASE	NECESSARY FACTS	HOLDINGS
Mills v. Donaldson	Uncle exercised parental responsibilities (disciplined, taught, attended parent-teacher meetings); financially supported child; was not primary caregiver.	Closely related? Yes
Smith v. Jones	Uncle visited child almost daily (read to and played with child); had child overnight at his house twice a week; went on numerous outings with him during year; was not primary caregiver.	Closely related? Yes
Patrick v. Michaels	Aunt did not take care of child (no bathing, babysitting, or diaper-changing); was not primary caregiver.	Closely related? No

b. Generalize the facts of the rule cases, but only to the extent necessary to reconcile them into one rule. Once you have charted the cases, the next step is to derive a rule from the information on your chart. Divide the cases into groups based on their holdings. Study the facts and the holdings of the cases and figure out why the court held that the plaintiff was closely related to the victim in *Mills* and *Smith* but not in *Patrick*. Then try to describe *factually* what separates one group of cases from the other, explaining why the cases sorted out the way they did. You might formulate this rule:

Example 1. Narrow rule on the closely-related element

An adult and child who are related but not immediate family are closely-related if the adult has frequent contact with the child and assumes significant responsibility for his welfare.

In contrast, the following rule is too broad because the writer generalized the facts more than is necessary:

Example 2. Broad rule on closely-related element

An adult and child who are related but not immediate family are closely related if the child has a close relationship with the adult.

Unlike Example 1, Example 2 does not provide a concrete way to determine if the adult and child are closely related. This rule is not specific enough to guide the lawyer in predicting an outcome.

3. When synthesizing a rule derived from cases with dissimilar facts, make the rule broad enough to cover the cases

Although narrowly-framed rules are preferable, sometimes the rule must be broad. A rule derived from factually disparate cases must be broader than one derived from cases with similar facts. This distinction makes sense: you must generalize to bring diverse facts under one rule.

For example, Chapter 4 presented a legal proof on the issue of whether a mannequin was a "portrait or picture" under a privacy statute. Three annotated legal proofs of this issue are included in Section I, p. 133. The first proof is based on a controlling case, the second on factually analogous cases, and the third on factually dissimilar cases. The rule based on the controlling case is factually specific:

Example 3. Rule based on a controlling case

> Rule: A "portrait or picture" of a person is any carved or mold-
> ed representation of that person.

The second proof is based on factually analogous cases. (It is premised on the assumption that no on-point case exists.) The rule in that proof is broader than the rule in the first proof:

Example 4. Rule based on factually analogous cases

> Rule: A "portrait or picture" of a person is any two- or three-
> dimensional physical representation of that person.

The third proof is based on cases with facts that are not similar to the facts of your case. (It is premised on the assumption that no factually analogous cases exist.) Because it is derived from cases that considered the term "portrait or pic-ture" in diverse contexts, the rule is broad:

Example 5. Rule based on factually dissimilar cases

> Rule: A "portrait or picture" is any visual representation of a
> person's likeness.

Generalize only to the extent necessary to derive a rule that *accurately* reflects the holdings of the rule cases. Realize that the broader the rule, the more difficult it will be to support and apply.

4. Write a clear, precise rule statement for every legal issue

The rule statement in a legal proof must accurately present the law that applies to the issue. When writing a legal proof, you must make sure that the rule is presented clearly and precisely. The length of the rule statement depends on the complexity of the legal proposition it explains. Here is an example of an effec-tive rule statement:

> A defendant willfully detains a person if he restrains her move-
> ment by violence, threats, or other means. *Randall's Food
> Market v. Johnson*, 891 S.W.2d 640, 644 (Tex. 1995). When a
> person asserts that a threat was made to restrain her, she must
> establish that the threat caused her to suffer a just fear of injury

to her reputation, person, or property. *Id.* Even if the threatened person does not resist the detention, she still may establish willful detention if the circumstances were oppressive and she had a particular vulnerability that made her susceptible to the defendant's intimidation. *Fojtik v. Charter Medical Corp.*, 985 S.W.2d 625, 628 (Tex. App. 1999).

Do Exercises 7-B(1), 7-B(2), and 7-C Now, p. 138

C. Rule Support

The purpose of rule support is to show that the rule has a legal basis. Assume that the reader has challenged the rule, maintaining that it is not grounded in the law. In the rule support section, you respond to the challenge, demonstrating that it is.

Some rules are easy to support. A rule expressly stated in a case or statute can be supported by quoting or explaining the rule and citing the source:

> In a prosecution for burglary in the second degree, a dwelling is a building that is usually occupied by a person at night. *State v. Brubecker*, 245 Orion Rpts. 2d 888 (1989).

If your rule is a synthesized one, you must show that you correctly derived it from the rule cases. Usually you can show this by citing the rule cases and describing their facts, holdings, and reasoning. Suppose you are writing a memo on whether a person has a claim for negligent infliction of emotional distress. Your rule on one of the claim's elements might be:

> A plaintiff has a sensory and contemporaneous observance if she (1) sees the victim immediately before the accident, (2) sees or hears the accident, and (3) sees the victim immediately after the accident. *See Bliss v. Allentown Library*, 497 F. Supp. 487, 489 (E.D. Pa. 1980); *Neff v. Lasso*, 555 A.2d 1304, 1313-1314 (Pa. Super. 1989). Such a plaintiff qualifies as a "percipient witness" whose awareness of the accident caused her shock. *See Neff*, 555 A.2d at 1313. Conversely, a plaintiff does not have a sensory and contemporaneous observance of the accident if she learns about it from a third party after its occurrence and therefore has time to brace her emotions. *Mazzagatti v.*

Everingham, 516 A.2d 672, 679 (Pa. 1986). In this situation, the plaintiff's prior knowledge of the accident is considered to be a buffer that shields her from the full emotional impact of observing the accident's aftermath. *Id.*

Having stated the rule, you would then show its legal basis by discussing cases in which it was applied:

The sensory and contemporaneous observance requirement was satisfied in *Neff* and *Bliss*. In *Neff*, the plaintiff, standing at her kitchen window, saw her husband's pickup being followed by a speeding car, heard a collision, and then ran out of the house to find her husband lying unconscious on their front lawn. *Neff*, 555 A.2d at 1313. In *Bliss*, the plaintiff, from a distance of about twenty-five feet, saw her daughter right before a statue fell, heard a crashing sound, and immediately looked up to see the statue lying on the injured child. 497 F. Supp. at 488-489. These plaintiffs were found to be percipient witnesses; their awareness of the accidents caused their emotional shock. *Neff*, 555 A.2d at 1313; *Bliss*, 497 F. Supp. at 488-489.

In contrast to the plaintiffs in *Neff* and *Bliss*, the plaintiff in *Mazzagatti* was not a percipient witness because she did not know that an accident had occurred until she received a telephone call informing her about it. *Mazzagatti*, 516 A.2d at 678-679. At the time of the accident, the plaintiff was at work, about one mile away from the accident scene. *Id.* at 673-74. She received a telephone call informing her that her daughter had been injured in an automobile collision. The plaintiff then drove to the scene and arrived there a few minutes after the accident. The court held that the plaintiff did not have a sensory and contemporaneous observance of the accident, reasoning that she did not know about the accident until after it occurred and that the telephone call buffered her from the full emotional impact of observing her daughter's injury. *Id.* at 679.

Broad rules often need more extensive rule support than narrow, concrete ones because the connection between the general rule and the specific holding of the cases may not be apparent to the reader. For instance, the preceding section gave three different rules (Examples 3, 4, and 5) on the issue of whether a mannequin was a "portrait or picture" under Arcadia's privacy statute. The more diverse the rule cases were, the more general the rule was. If you review the rule support sections of these legal proofs in Section I, beginning on p. 133, you can see how the extent of rule support varies with the level of generality of the rule:

- Analysis A is a proof of an undisputed issue. The rule is based on a controlling case and definitively resolves the issue, so you can support it by briefly describing the statute that created the privacy claim and briefly summarizing the holding of the case.

- In Analysis B, however, the issue is a disputed issue and the rule must be synthesized from analogous cases. To support that rule, you must provide a more detailed explanation of the holdings of the rule cases than you did in Analysis A.

- Analysis C is based on factually dissimilar cases and therefore requires the most support. The issue is a disputed issue. Moreover, since the rule is very general, the connection between it and the rule cases is not self-evident. You must therefore not only review the holdings of the rule cases but also explain how the policy underlying these holdings justifies your rule.

D. Application, Case Comparison, and Alternative Arguments

1. Application

Once you have identified the issue and the rule, and supported the rule by citing or explaining the rule cases, you must apply the rule. The application is a statement of whether the rule is met. The application, therefore, should use the language in the rule. Here are some examples of rules and applications:

> *Rule:* An object is a dangerous instrument if its physical characteristics make it capable of causing serious injury when wielded within effective range of the victim. *Ellington v. Shaw*, 405 Arc. Rpts. 2d 78 (1991).
> *Application:* In Coltrane's case, the shovel was a dangerous instrument because its physical characteristics made it capable of causing serious injury when Coltrane wielded it within striking distance of Fitzgerald.

> *Rule:* The phrase "portrait or picture" in Arcadia's privacy statute is not limited to photographs, but can include any representation, whether by

photograph, drawing, or sculpture, that conveys the likeness of the individual. *Monroe v. Starlight Cinema*, 325 Arc. Rpts. 2d 57 (1997).
Application: Here, the mannequin used by the defendant in its advertising campaign is a "portrait or picture" under Arcadia's privacy statute because it is a sculpture that conveyed plaintiff's likeness.

2.   Case comparison

The assertion in the application is supported by the case comparison section of the proof. This section demonstrates that the application is consistent with the holdings of the rule cases. The principle of *stare decisis* requires this consistency: cases should have the same result if they involve the same legal issue and are factually analogous.

The factual comparisons between your case and the rule support cases must be based on *necessary* facts—those facts that determine the outcome of the cases. Point out the factual *similarities* between your case and the rule support cases with holdings that are *consistent* with your conclusion. Distinguish the factual *differences* between your case and the rule support cases with holdings *contrary* to your conclusion. For example, suppose you are writing a memo on whether a housekeeper was falsely imprisoned by her employer. You might make the following case comparisons:

> Taylor, like the plaintiff in *Black*, was particularly vulnerable to her employer's threat to have her arrested for theft. Although she has more education than did the plaintiff in *Black*, Taylor, age 25, also is relatively young and lacking in business experience—she had not worked outside the home during her marriage. Moreover, as a single parent, Taylor was especially vulnerable to a threat, such as the one made by the Clarks, that could injure her reputation in the community and result in her incarceration.
>
> This matter is distinguishable from *Fotjik* and *Johnson*, cases were there was no willful detention. Taylor is unlike the plaintiff in *Fotjik*, a mature businessman who was not susceptible to intimidation. And because the Clarks actually threatened Taylor, her situation is also different from that of the plaintiff in *Johnson*, who was not threatened by her employer. Furthermore, in contrast to the plaintiffs in both *Johnson* and *Fojtik*, Taylor never left the place of her alleged confinement. Although she could have left—there was no lock on the door, no one was guarding her, and she knew how to get out of the

house—she was afraid to do so. In fact, she remained in the
same chair for three hours.

All legal proofs require case comparisons, but the extent of these comparisons can vary. Develop the section as much as is needed to show how the assertion in the application is consistent with the specific holdings of the rule cases.

Compare the three analyses in Section I of this chapter. The case comparison
section in Analysis A, p. 133—a proof of an undisputed issue based on a controlling case—achieves its purpose with minimal discussion. In the case comparison section, the writer briefly demonstrates that the cast in the rule case,
which was considered a "portrait or picture," is similar to the mannequin of
Moss, thereby making a straightforward connection between the application and
the single, controlling rule case.

Analysis B, p. 134, requires a more developed case comparison section than
Analysis A for two reasons. First, the connection between the assertion in the
application and the holdings of the rule cases is not self-evident. Therefore, you
must make that connection for the reader with a more developed case comparison section, showing how your assertion that the mannequin is a "portrait or picture" is consistent with the holdings of the rule cases. Second, Analysis B is based
on *two* rule cases, not one, which necessarily results in a lengthier case discussion since you must discuss both of them.

Analysis C, p. 135, requires a different kind of case comparison section. The
assertion in Analysis C's application is that the mannequin is a visual representation of Moss. To validate this assertion, you must show that your case is consistent with the holdings of the rule cases. Because the rule cases—involving a
celebrity look-alike and a vocal imitation—are factually distinct from Moss's situation, the factual analogies and distinctions are buttressed by policy comparisons, showing that the policy underlying the holdings of the rule cases—to
prevent exploitation of a person's image—also justifies the asserted application in
Moss's situation.

Do Exercise 7-D Now, p. 140

3.　Alternative arguments

A thorough analysis should include alternative arguments that are reasonably suggested by the case law. If you conclude that the matter is likely to be
resolved in your client's favor, the alternative arguments are likely to be those the
opposing party might advance in support of his position. On the other hand, if

you determine that your client's position is weak, the alternative arguments might be the points that are favorable to your client.

Often the alternative arguments can be integrated into the case comparison section. For example, by explaining why a particular case is distinguishable from your matter, you may effectively raise and refute a possible alternative argument. In some instances, however, you may decide to include a separate section on alternative arguments after the case comparison section. The complexity of the facts, issues, and law will determine how you organize and present alternative arguments.

Present and evaluate the merits of alternative arguments succinctly and coherently. Do not digress from the issue or strain to create an alternative argument when the case law clearly favors a particular position. There are instances when there are no credible alternative arguments.

E. Conclusion

The conclusion completes the legal proof. Once you have identified the issue, stated and supported the rule, applied your rule to the particular facts, and demonstrated the validity of your application by including case comparisons, a valid conclusion that predicts the outcome should be inescapable. The conclusion for the legal proof in the Moss case might state:

> Therefore, the mannequin is a "portrait or picture" of
> Cheryl Moss under Arcadia Civil Rights Law § 51.

Do Exercises 7-E(1) and 7-E(2) Now, p. 141

F. Legal Proofs of Statutory Issues

Often a legal issue arises from interpreting a statute. When you construct a legal proof of a statutory issue, follow the same organizational pattern described in this chapter, bearing in mind the advice in Chapter 5 on statutory analysis.

Appendices A and C in this book contain legal memos that analyze statutory issues. Review these memos to learn how legal proofs of statutory issues are constructed.

G. Analyzing Issues Involving Factor Analysis or Balancing of Interests

Generally, the legal issues in this and preceding chapters focused on whether a particular set of facts satisfies the elements of a claim, crime, or defense. Not all legal issues relate to elements, however. Some legal issues pivot on **factors**. Unlike elements, which are conditions for establishing a claim, crime, or defense, factors are guidelines for decision-making, lists of relevant matters for a court to consider when resolving issues. Factors are created by statute and by common law. Statutes, for example, may list factors that courts must consider when sentencing defendants, or when deciding which parent should have custody of his child. Common-law claims and defenses often hinge on factors. For instance, in determining whether an infant may avoid a contract, courts consider factors such as the business experience and maturity of the infant, the contract's fairness, and the term of the contract.

Compared to elements, factors give the decision-maker more flexibility in deciding a case because no one factor is determinative. Rather, the court bases its decision on an evaluation of all the factors.

Balancing of the interest tests are similar to factor analysis. In a balancing test, the court weighs competing interests. For instance, in deciding whether the state may fire one of its employees for speaking his mind on the job, the court weighs (or balances) the employee's interest in freely discussing matters of public concern against the state's interest as an employer in running an efficient workplace.

A more detailed discussion of issues involving factor analysis and balancing of the interest tests appears in Chapter 15.

H. Legal Proofs Are the Core of the Discussion Section

Writing a good legal proof takes time. You must actively read the cases, identify or synthesize a useful rule, apply it logically, and validate your analysis by citing to and explaining the applicable law. Moreover, you must write your proof in clear, precise language, so that the reader can assess it. Once you have completed a legal proof on the issue (or issues) you intend to cover in a legal memorandum, you are ready to start writing the memo's Discussion. The Discussion is the focus of the next chapter.

I. Three Legal Proofs of the Same Issue

The following are examples of three legal proofs on the issue of whether a mannequin is a picture or portrait under a privacy statute. The first proof is based on a controlling case, the second on factually analogous cases, and the third on factually dissimilar cases.

Analysis A: An Annotated Legal Proof
Based on a Controlling Case

Issue: The issue is whether a mannequin that resembles a person is a "portrait or picture" of that person under Arcadia Civil Rights Law § 51 ("CRL § 51").

Rule: A "portrait or picture" of a person includes any carved or molded representation of that person.

Rule Support: CRL § 51; *Cara v. Hollywood Faces, Inc.*, 340 Arc. Rpts. 2d 343 (2000). In *Cara*, a plaster cast of the plaintiff's face was held to be a "portrait or picture" because the cast conveyed the plaintiff's likeness. The court held that "any carved or molded representation of a person constitutes a 'portrait or picture' of him under CRL § 51." 340 Arc. Rpts. 2d at 345.

Application: The mannequin is a molded representation of Cheryl Moss.

Case Comparison: The mannequin falls within the general rule announced in *Cara* because it is a "carved or molded representation." Moreover, the case is factually controlling: both the cast in *Cara* and the mannequin here convey a physical likeness not by a photograph, painting or drawing, but by a molded likeness of the person's physical features.

Conclusion: The mannequin is a "portrait or picture" of Cheryl Moss under Arcadia CRL § 51.

Analysis B: An Annotated Legal Proof
Based on Analogous Cases
(Assumes that a controlling case does not exist.)

Issue: The issue is whether a mannequin that resembles a person is a "portrait or picture" of that person under Arcadia Civil Rights Law § 51 ("CRL § 51").

Rule: A "portrait or picture" of a person is any two- or three-dimensional physical representation of that person.

Rule Support: CRL § 51; *Swoonatra v. Dorsey Doll Co.,* 335 Arc. Rpts. 2d 243 (1999); *Lombard v. Bears Are Us, Inc.,* 325 Arc. Rpts. 2d 143 (1997).

Cases construing CRL § 51 have held that the phrase "portrait or picture" is not limited to two-dimensional photographs and drawings, but includes three-dimensional representations (such as dolls) that convey a person's physical likeness.

In *Swoonatra,* the court held that the plaintiff, the singer Frank Swoonatra, had a claim under CRL § 51 against a doll company for selling a doll that had his body type, face, haircut, and style of dress. The court held that the phrase "portrait or picture" includes any representation that conveys the physical likeness of a person, regardless of whether conveyed in a photograph, drawing, statue, or doll. *Swoonatra,* 335 Arc. Rpts. 2d at 247.

In *Lombard,* the plaintiff, a famous conductor, sued a manufacturer of toy bears for selling a teddy bear that the plaintiff claimed was a "portrait or picture" of him under CRL § 51. The bear had long black hair like the plaintiff's, wore the plaintiff's trademark blue tuxedo, held a conductor's baton, and when squeezed said "Let's play music," a line associated with the plaintiff. The court held that the bear was not a "portrait or picture" because although it was dressed like the plaintiff and spoke words associated with him, physically it resembled a bear, not the plaintiff. *Lombard,* 325 Arc. Rpts. 2d at 148.

Application: The mannequin is a three-dimensional physical representation of Cheryl Moss.

Case Comparison: Like the doll in *Swoonatra*, which was held to be a portrait or picture of the plaintiff singer, the mannequin captures Moss's physical likeness. Its face and body shape resembles Moss's, just as the doll had the shape and face of the plaintiff in *Swoonatra*.

Although there are some differences between the facts of *Swoonatra* and those in Moss's case, they are probably not critical. Unlike the *Swoonatra* doll, which had the haircut and style of dress like the plaintiff singer, the mannequin of Moss is sold undressed and without hair. As *Lombard* demonstrates, however, the decisive consideration is physical resemblance, not dress or hairstyle.

Moss's case is distinguishable from *Lombard*. In *Lombard*, the court held that the teddy bear was not a portrait or picture because it bore no physical resemblance to the plaintiff conductor. The Moss mannequin, however, has a face and body like Moss's.

Conclusion: The mannequin is a "portrait or picture" of Cheryl Moss under CRL § 51.

Analysis C: An Annotated Legal Proof Based on Factually Dissimilar Cases
*(assumes that neither a controlling case nor
factually analogous cases exist)*

Issue: The issue is whether a mannequin that resembles a person is a "portrait or picture" of that person under Arcadia Civil Rights Law § 51 ("CRL § 51").

Rule: A "portrait or picture" is any visual representation of a person's likeness.

Rule Support: CRL § 51; *McIntyre v Timbelwon Sports Company*, 297 Arc. Rpts. 1002 (1994); *Wilbur v. 60-Second Sell, LLC*, 326 Arc. Rpts. 23 (1997). Courts applying CRL § 51 have construed the phrase "portrait or picture" broadly, holding it to include not only photographs and drawn likenesses but visual representations in other media as well.

In *McIntyre*, a former professional tennis player sued a sports equipment manufacturer for promoting its products at tennis matches with live performances between games by an actor dressed in tennis gear who bore a "strong physical resemblance to the plaintiff" and who spoke like him. 297 Arc. Rpts. at 1005. The court rejected the defendant's contention that the performance was not a "portrait or picture" of the plaintiff, holding that CRL § 51 applied to live commercial performances by look-alikes. In reaching its decision, the court noted that the purpose of the section was to "prevent the exploitation of a person's image for commercial purposes in any form." 297 Arc. Rpts. at 1010.

In contrast, in *Wilbur*, a television commercial featuring a talking pig whose voice matched the plaintiff's distinctive vocal style was held not to be actionable under CRL § 51. The court distinguished *McIntyre*, noting that "unlike the situation in *McIntyre*, plaintiff's voice, not his physical appearance, was imitated. Section 51 was not intended to cover vocal, as opposed to visual, representations of a person." 326 Arc. Rpts. at 32.

Application: The mannequin is a visual representation of Cheryl Moss.

Case Comparison: Moss's case is comparable to *McIntyre*. Like the look-alike in *McIntyre*, the mannequin in Moss's case involves a visual representation that is non-pictorial. The rationale of that case—to protect against commercial exploitation of another's appearance—applies equally to Moss's case. Furthermore, Moss's case is easily distinguishable from *Wilbur*. That case involved a vocal, not a visual, representation.

Conclusion: The mannequin is a "portrait or picture" of Cheryl Moss under Arcadia CRL § 51.

EXERCISES

Exercise 7-A

Read the following Client File Summaries. Decide which legal question is the most specific in each. Explain how you would identify the narrow issue(s) in each.

Client File Summary: Yolanda Moore

Our client, Yolanda Moore, a sales agent, plans to resign from her job at EFG, a computer software company in Olympus, and open a competing company. She wants to know if she can use her employer's client list to solicit business for her company. In Olympus, a client list may qualify as trade secret information if certain criteria are met. The law in Olympus prohibits an employee from appropriating her employer's trade secret information for her own use.

1. Can Moore use her employer's client list in her own company?

2. Can EFG sue Moore if she uses its client list in a new business?

3. Is EFG's client list trade secret information?

Client File Summary 2: David Wolf

Our client, David Wolf, got into an argument with his son's baseball coach, Jake Carr, at a recent game. Wolf complained after his son was benched for several innings. He claims that Carr then called him a "loud-mouthed lunatic and liar" in front of a group of parents. Wolf wants to know if he can sue Carr. In Olympus, Carr's statement about Wolf may be slanderous.

1. Does Carr have to pay Wolf money damages?

 2. Is Carr's statement in which he called Wolf a "loud-mouthed lunatic and liar" slanderous?

3. Can Wolf sue Carr for making critical comments about
    him?

Exercise 7-B(1)

*Read the following case. Decide which statement best expresses the rule on puni-
tive damages. Explain how the case supports your answer.*

Buckley v. Henry: While driving intoxicated, Henry crashed into
Buckley, who was jogging on the sidewalk. Buckley suffered a
spinal cord injury and may never be able to walk again. Henry
asserts that Buckley's claim for punitive damages should not be
submitted to the jury. In Olympus, punitive damages may be
awarded if there is evidence that the tortfeasor engaged in willful, wanton conduct. Here, there is sufficient evidence that
Henry embarked on a course of conduct that put the lives of
others in jeopardy. Because there is sufficient evidence that
Henry engaged in willful, wanton conduct, Buckley's claim for
punitive damages will be submitted to the jury.

1. Punitive damages may be awarded in cases in which the
    plaintiff suffers serious physical injury.

2. Punitive damages may be awarded when there is sufficient
    evidence that the tortfeasor engaged in willful, wanton
    conduct that put the lives of others in jeopardy.

3. The jury must decide whether to award punitive damages.

Exercise 7-B(2)

*Read the following case. Decide which statement best expresses the rule on qual-
ified privilege. Explain how the case supports your answer.*

Giovanni v. Hart: Giovanni and Hart are co-workers at MJH
Industries. Hart wrote Chow, his supervisor, a memorandum
alleging that Giovanni engaged in fraudulent billing practices.
Giovanni claims that the allegations are false. He sued Hart for
libel. Hart asserts that the libel claim must be dismissed because

his statement about Giovanni was protected by a qualified privilege. In Olympus, the defense of <u>qualified privilege applies if the speaker and listener share a bona fide common interest in or duty with respect to the subject matter of the statement.</u> The statement in this matter was protected by a qualified privilege: Hart had a duty to report information concerning alleged illegal employee conduct to his supervisor Chow, a person with a corresponding duty to investigate such allegations. The libel claim is therefore dismissed.

1. A defendant in a libel action may assert the defense of qualified privilege to avoid liability for any statement if he (a) had a bona fide interest in or duty regarding the subject matter of the statement and (b) published the statement to a person with a corresponding interest or duty.

2. A qualified privilege defense entitles a defendant to avoid a libel claim if he was interested in the statement.

not enough

3. The defense of qualified privilege applies if the speaker and listener share a common interest in the statement.

Exercise 7-C

Study the following case chart that summarizes the necessary facts and holdings on the element of physical injury in three criminal assault cases in Olympus. Use the chart to synthesize a rule on physical injury.

Case	Necessary Facts	Holding: Physical Injury?
State v. Davis	Davis punched the victim in the face and fractured his jaw. The victim required medical treatment for six months.	Yes
State v. Edwards	Edwards slapped the victim in the face. Although the victim experienced mild pain for a day and had a bruise on his cheek, he did not need medical treatment.	No

[Chart continued on next page] *physical injury: intentional physical contact, resulting in requiring medical treatment due t[o] substantial pain.*

State v. Wade	Wade kicked the victim in the stomach. The victim was in substantial pain for a week. Her doctor gave her painkillers and told her that she would be fine.	Yes

Exercise 7-D

Read the following facts, case, and case comparisons. Decide which case comparison is better. Explain your answer.

Facts

Our client, Francesca Lombardi, a police officer in Nirvana, believes that she was subjected to a sexually hostile work environment. Lombardi claims that several male officers told sexually offensive jokes and referred to her as a "bimbo." She states that this conduct occurred frequently (several times a month) over a two-year period.

Case

Grisweld v. MNO Industries: To state a claim for hostile work environment sexual harassment in Nirvana, a plaintiff, as a threshold matter, must establish that the complained-of conduct was <u>severe</u> and <u>pervasive</u>. Grisweld proved that her supervisor, on almost a daily basis over a year-long period, made sexually provocative comments about her clothing and e-mailed her copies of sexually offensive <u>jokes</u>. This evidence establishes severe and pervasive conduct.

Case Comparison 1: Like the plaintiff in *Grisweld*, Lombardi was subjected to gender-biased conduct over a prolonged period of time. The plaintiff in *Grisweld* established that her supervisor made sexually provocative comments and sent her copies of sexually offensive jokes; this conduct occurred almost daily for a year. Similarly, over a two-year period, Lombardi's co-workers, at least several times every month, called her a "bimbo" and told sexually offensive jokes. The facts in this matter, like those in *Grisweld*, are sufficient to establish that the complained-of conduct was severe and pervasive, a threshold element of hostile work environment sexual harassment.

This comparison is More detailed + specific about the actual similarities in the case

Case Comparison 2: Lombardi's case is similar to the plaintiff's in *Grisweld*. Both women endured sexual harassment in the workplace on a frequent basis. Therefore, the severe and pervasive conduct element is satisfied. Relying on *Grisweld*, Lombardi should be able to recover for hostile work environment sexual harassment.

Exercise 7-E(1)

The Workplace Equality Commission ("WEC") recently brought a sex discrimination action against XYZ Corp. XYZ Corp. has retained your law firm. Your senior partner would like to know whether XYZ Corp. can successfully move to have the complaint dismissed by asserting the defense of laches. Read the following facts and cases. Prepare a chart that identifies the necessary facts and holding of each case. Then answer the questions that follow.

Facts

On September 27, 1993, Marla Marberry filed a charge with WEC alleging that her employer, XYZ Corp., unlawfully discriminated against her because of her sex. Marberry asserted that she was denied a promotion and raise because she refused to submit to the sexual advances of her supervisor, Harold Baxendale.

Burdened with a backlog of cases in 1993, WEC did not notify XYZ Corp. of Marberry's charge until March 7, 1994. The company denied the allegations in their entirety and fully cooperated with WEC's request for documents. WEC's investigation of the matter was not completed until the summer of 2000. On September 28, 2000, WEC filed a formal complaint against XYZ Corp. asserting that the company had subjected Marberry to unlawful sex discrimination in 1993.

WEC claims that the seven-year delay in the proceedings was attributable to a heavy caseload, a shortage of personnel, and settlement negotiations between the parties that continued for six months. XYZ Corp. claims that the extraordinary delay has prejudiced its defense. Baxendale, the alleged harasser, was fired and has moved out of the country. In addition, Patricia Palsgraf, the other supervisor who participated in the promotion decision at issue, died in 1996.

Cases

WEC v. Jones: WEC filed a complaint against Jones, an employer, six years after receiving a charge of sex discrimination. The employer now moves to dismiss the complaint claiming laches. The employer asserts that it cannot defend the charge because several key witnesses have died and the memories of others have faded with the passage of time. WEC argues that the delay was attributable to a backlog of investigations in the office. The employer's motion to dismiss the complaint is granted. In Olympus, no express statute of limitations applies to proceedings commenced by WEC. The equitable doctrine of laches may, however, bar an action if WEC's delay in filing the complaint was inexcusable and the delay results in undue prejudice to the employer.

WEC v. Smith: WEC filed a complaint against Smith, an employer, three years after receiving a charge of sex discrimination. The employer now moves to dismiss the complaint, claiming laches. WEC contends that any arguable delay was caused by the employer's refusal to provide documents and a year-long period of settlement negotiations between the parties. The employer's motion to dismiss the complaint is denied. Employers who obstruct discovery proceedings cannot assert the defense of laches. Moreover, time spent in settlement negotiations does not constitute inexcusable delay.

WEC v. Rogers: WEC filed a complaint against Rogers, an employer, five years after receiving a charge of sex discrimination involving eight female employees. The employer now moves to dismiss the complaint claiming laches. WEC maintains that it had to interview many witnesses and review thousands of documents and therefore any arguable delay was excusable. The employer's motion to dismiss the complaint is denied. To establish a defense of laches, the employer must show more than the mere passage of time. There must be proof that the delay was inexcusable.

WEC v. Wells: WEC filed a complaint against Wells, an employer, ten years after receiving a charge of sex discrimination. The employer now moves to dismiss the complaint claiming laches.

The employer asserts that it cannot defend the charge because documents critical to its defense were destroyed in a fire. WEC maintains that it was understaffed and therefore any arguable delay was excusable. The employer's motion to dismiss the complaint is granted. The longer WEC delays, the more likely the employer is to suffer undue prejudice. It would be manifestly unfair to require an employer to defend stale claims.

Questions

1. What is the claim, crime, or defense?

2. List the elements of laches.

3. What are the legal issues in *WEC v. XYZ Corp.*?

4. What rules of law are established in the cases? Use the cases to synthesize the rules.

5. List the necessary facts in *WEC v. XYZ Corp.*

6. Is a court likely to dismiss the complaint against XYZ Corp.? Explain how the cases support your answer.

Exercise 7-E(2)

Write an annotated legal proof analyzing whether XYZ Corp. can establish inexcusable delay by WEC. Remember to include (1) the issue, (2) the rule, (3) rule support, (4) an application of the law to the facts supported by case comparisons, and (5) a conclusion.

CHAPTER 8

The Legal Memorandum: The Discussion Section

When you master this chapter, you will understand:

1. the purpose and structure of the Discussion in a legal memo;

2. how to begin the Discussion with a thesis that effectively prepares the reader for the legal analysis to follow; and

3. how to incorporate complete legal proofs into the Discussion.

C hapter 6 introduced the legal office memorandum. In a legal memo the writer *predicts* the outcome of a legal question in the context of particular circumstances and *demonstrates* the soundness of that prediction. Chapter 7 explained how to make and demonstrate these predictions in legal proofs.

This chapter focuses on the Discussion, the main component of the legal memo that contains the legal proofs. Although the Discussion comes *after* the Question(s) Presented, Short Answer(s), and Summary of the Facts, you will study it first. These preceding sections prepare the reader for the Discussion's comprehensive legal analysis. So it makes sense to learn how to write the Discussion before learning to write these other sections. The remaining sections of the legal memorandum, including the Conclusion which follows the Discussion, are discussed in Chapter 9.

A. Consider Your Reader

Good writing is always reader-oriented. Think of the reader of your memo as someone who is looking to you for information and guidance, the busy (or impatient) lawyer you read about in Chapter 6. Do not assume that your reader already knows the facts, the law, or the issues.

Do not write the Discussion as if your writing professor is the intended audience. If you do, you may unconsciously attribute to your reader your professor's understanding of the law and the issues. Consequently, you will neglect the crucial tasks of educating the reader on the law and clearly and logically guiding him through your analysis.

Worse than imagining your professor as your reader is not imagining anyone at all. Then you probably will write a Discussion that makes sense only to you. So when you write and review your Discussion, stand in your reader's shoes. Ask yourself, "Will my reader be able to understand this analysis, or am I assuming he knows something that I haven't told him?"

B. The Format of the Discussion Section

The Discussion section has two parts:

1. **Thesis.** Begin by preparing the reader for your analysis by outlining what you will cover in it.

2. **Analysis.** Then present a complete legal proof *for each issue* following the format described in Chapters 4 and 7.

1. The thesis

The thesis is the first part of the Discussion. It succinctly states the issues and predicts an outcome without analyzing the law. The thesis serves as a road map for the analysis. Here is a format for a thesis:

a. identify the subject of the memo (*e.g.*, the claim, crime, or defense) and summarize it;

b. explain how matching the law to the facts raises the issues considered in the analysis (include abbreviated proofs of undisputed issues, if appropriate);

c. predict how the issues might be resolved and briefly explain the reasoning behind your prediction; and

d. predict the outcome (*e.g.*, whether the client has a negligence claim, whether the defendant will be convicted of murder, or whether an employer must pay back wages).

Even legal memos that analyze just one issue should have a thesis. Otherwise you run the risk of confusing the reader by launching into a legal proof without giving the requisite background information.

Sometimes the thesis is referred to as the thesis *paragraph*, but that term is misleading. A thesis has no correct number of paragraphs. Its length depends on the intricacy of the subject and the number and complexity of the issues to be discussed in the analysis. A thesis must be as long as it needs to be to achieve its purpose of focusing the reader on the issues, educating him on the law, and advising him of your predictions and the general reasoning behind them.

Keep in mind that the thesis format presented here is well-suited to legal questions that are fact-sensitive and claims, crimes, or defenses that have elements or parts. You will likely have to modify the format when writing about purely legal questions (*e.g.*, the constitutionality of a statute) or issues that require a balancing of the interests or factor analysis.

2. Writing the thesis

a. Identify the subject of the memo (e.g., claim, crime, or defense) and summarize it

To put the legal issues in context, you must first identify the subject of the memo and summarize it. This information will enable the reader to understand the origin of the issues.

Often the subject is a claim. In that case, you must identify it and set forth its elements. Here is an example from the Jackson memo (Appendix B, p. 407):

> Under Pennsylvania law, a plaintiff has a claim for negligent infliction of emotional distress against a defendant who injures or kills another person if the plaintiff can show that the defendant had reason to foresee her distress. To demonstrate foreseeability, the plaintiff must establish that (1) she was closely related to the victim, (2) she was near the scene of the accident, and (3) she had a sensory and contemporaneous observance of the accident which caused her to suffer a direct emotional shock. *Sinn v. Burd*, 404 A.2d 672, 685 (Pa. 1979).

Alternatively, you could give the same information by personalizing the facts in the summary:

> Under Pennsylvania law, Jackson has a claim for negligent infliction of emotional distress against Hi-Five if she can establish that Hi-Five had reason to foresee her distress. To demonstrate foreseeability, Jackson must establish three elements: (1) she was closely related to the victim; (2) she was near the scene of the accident, and (3) she had a sensory and contemporaneous observance of the accident which caused her to suffer a direct emotional shock. *Sinn v. Burd*, 404 A.2d 672, 677 (Pa. 1979).

The next example from the Dunn memo (Appendix A, p. 399) illustrates how you might introduce a crime and its elements in the thesis:

> In Texas, a person may be found guilty of the crime of aggravated robbery if the prosecution proves three elements beyond a reasonable doubt. *See Lockett v. State*, 874 S.W.2d 810, 813-814 (Tex. Crim. App. 1994). First, the person must commit theft by unlawfully taking property with the intent to deprive the owner

of the property. Texas Penal Code Ann. § 31.03(a) (West 1994). Second, while committing the theft, the person, with the intent to obtain or retain the property, must intentionally or knowingly threaten or place another person in fear of imminent bodily injury or death. Texas Penal Code Ann. § 29.02(a)(2). Third, the person must use or exhibit a deadly weapon. Texas Penal Code Ann. § 29.03(a)(2). The first two elements establish the crime of robbery; the addition of the third element elevates the crime to aggravated robbery. *Lockett*, 874 S.W.2d at 814.

b. Explain how matching the law to the facts raises the issues considered in the analysis

In the Jackson memo, the subject is negligent infliction of emotional distress, a claim with three elements. By matching the law to the facts, you determine that the first two elements of the claim are easily satisfied. You must explain your conclusions on these elements in abbreviated legal proofs. These proofs can be included in the thesis or in the analysis part of the Discussion. In the next example, the proofs of the two undisputed elements of the claim are included in the thesis (the first and second sentences) because of their simplicity and brevity.

In the Jackson matter, the third element of the claim is in dispute. Consequently, the issue that will be considered in the analysis is whether Jackson had a sensory and contemporaneous observance which caused her to suffer a direct emotional shock. You might continue your thesis this way:

> Here, Jackson was closely related to the victim because he was her husband. *Neff v. Lasso*, 555 A.2d 1304, 1308 (Pa. Super. 1989) (holding that the victim's wife was closely related to him). Moreover, standing no more than ten feet from the entrance to the ride, Jackson was near the scene of the accident. *Bliss v. Allentown Public Library*, 497 F. Supp. 487 (E.D. Pa. 1980) (holding that the plaintiff, who was about 25 feet from the accident, was near the scene). The disputed issue is whether Jackson had a sensory and contemporaneous observance of the accident that caused her to suffer a direct emotional shock.

In the Dunn matter, the subject is aggravated robbery, a crime with three elements. By matching the law to the facts, you determine that the first two elements of the crime are satisfied. The third element, however, is disputed. Consequently, the issue that will be considered in the analysis is whether Dunn used or exhibited the crowbar as a deadly weapon:

The prosecution can probably prove the first two elements. Dunn committed theft because she unlawfully took property, the packages, with the intent to deprive the owner of the property. Texas Penal Code Ann. § 31.03(a). Furthermore, to obtain the packages, she threatened Keyes with imminent bodily injury. Texas Penal Code Ann. § 29.02(a)(2). In dispute is the third element: whether Dunn used or exhibited a deadly weapon, the crowbar.

c.   **Predict how the issues might be resolved and briefly explain the reasoning behind your prediction**

In this part of the thesis in the Jackson memo, you might state:

A court is likely to hold that she did because her emotional shock directly resulted from her visual awareness of the setting, her auditory perception of the accident, and her immediate observation of its aftermath.

In the Dunn matter, you might summarize your conclusion on the issue like this:

The prosecution is likely to prove this element because the crowbar had the objective capacity to cause serious injury, and Dunn's conduct demonstrated her intent to use it to seriously injure Keyes.

d.   **Predict the outcome**

The final step in drafting the thesis is to predict the outcome. The Jackson memo might conclude:

Therefore, Jackson probably has a claim against Hi-Five for negligent infliction of emotional distress.

Similarly, the thesis in the Dunn memo might conclude this way:

Therefore, Dunn is likely to be convicted of aggravated robbery.

After reading the thesis, the reader should:

- understand the subject;
- know what issues are disputed;
- know your conclusions on the issues and have a general idea why you reached them; and
- know your prediction on the outcome.

Do Exercises 8-A, 8-B, and 8-C(1) Now, p. 155

C. The Analysis

The analysis part of the Discussion contains the legal proofs, one complete legal proof for each disputed issue identified in the thesis. You should also include in the analysis abbreviated legal proofs for the undisputed issues if you did not include them in the thesis.

The organization of the analysis should mirror the organization of the thesis: the legal proofs in the analysis should follow the order in which the issues are introduced in the thesis. Your goal is to make the Discussion easy for the reader to understand on a first reading. To succeed, the analysis must follow the roadmap outlined in the thesis.

As explained in Chapter 7, each legal proof in the analysis should be structured in the IRAC format:

1. Begin every legal proof with a concise topic sentence stating the **Issue**.

2. State the applicable **Rule** of law from the controlling case law and/or statute.

3. Support the rule by citing to case law or statutes and by discussing the facts, holdings, and reasoning in the key cases—the "rule cases"—to show the reader how courts apply the rule.

4. **Apply** the rule to the facts of your case and compare and contrast your case to the rule cases. The Application and Case Comparison sections of the legal proof should demonstrate that your conclusion on the issue is sound. In addition, present alternative arguments reasonably suggested by the case law.

5.   End with a **Conclusion** on the issue.

Remember that the IRAC format is the starting point for a legal proof. As you learned in Chapter 7, the length and scope of a legal proof are determined by the complexity and nature of the issue and the law.

If the analysis in your Discussion contains more than one legal proof, you must make sure that the legal proofs are smoothly connected by logical transitions. Use enumeration, substantive connections, and/or transitional words or phrases to coherently link one paragraph to another. (These techniques are discussed in Chapter 10.) The legal proofs in the Analysis should fit together substantively and structurally like interlocking pieces of a jigsaw puzzle.

Do Exercises 8-C(2) and 8-D Now, p. 158

D. An Annotated Thesis for a Legal Memorandum in the Jackson Matter

Identification of the claim and summary of its elements.	Under Pennsylvania law, a plaintiff has a claim for negligent infliction of emotional distress against a defendant who injures or kills another person if the plaintiff can show that the defendant had reason to foresee her distress. To demonstrate foreseeability, the plaintiff must establish that (1) she was closely related to the victim, (2) she was near the scene of the accident, and (3) she had a sensory and contemporaneous observance of the accident which caused her to suffer a direct emotional shock. *Sinn v. Burd*, 404 A.2d 672, 685 (Pa. 1979).
Explanation of how matching the elements to the facts raises the issues.	Here, Jackson was closely related to the victim because he was her husband. *Neff v. Lasso*, 555 A.2d 1304, 1308 (Pa. Super. 1989) (holding that the wife of the victim was closely related to him). Moreover, standing no more than ten feet from the entrance to the ride, Jackson was near the scene of the accident. *Bliss v. Allentown Public Library*, 497 F.

Supp. 487 (E.D. Pa. 1980) (holding that the plaintiff, who was about 25 feet from the accident, was near the scene).

Prediction of how the disputed issue might be resolved and why.

The disputed issue is whether Jackson had a sensory and contemporaneous observance of the accident that caused her to suffer a direct emotional shock. A court is likely to hold that she did because her emotional shock resulted from her visual awareness of the setting, her auditory perception of the accident, and her immediate observation of its aftermath. Therefore, Jackson probably has a claim against Hi-Five for negligent infliction of emotional distress.

Prediction of the outcome.

E. An Annotated Thesis for a Legal Memorandum in the Dunn Matter

Identification of the crime and summary of its elements.

In Texas, a person may be found guilty of aggravated robbery if the prosecution proves three elements beyond a reasonable doubt. See *Lockett v. State*, 874 S.W.2d 810, 813-814 (Tex. Crim. App. 1994). First, the person must commit theft. Texas Penal Code Ann. § 31.03(a) (West 1994). Second, while committing theft, the person, with the intent to obtain or retain the property, must intentionally or knowingly threaten or place another person in fear of imminent bodily injury or death. Texas Penal Code Ann. § 29.02(a)(2). Third, the person must use or exhibit a deadly weapon. Texas Penal Code Ann. § 29.03(a)(2). The first two elements establish the crime of robbery; the third element elevates the crime to aggravated robbery. *Lockett*, 874 S.W.2d at 814.

Explanation of how matching the elements to the facts raises the issues.

The prosecution can probably prove the first two elements. Dunn committed theft because she unlawfully took property, the packages, with the intent to deprive the owner of them. Texas Penal Code Ann. § 31.03(a). Furthermore, to obtain the packages, she threatened Keyes with imminent bodily injury. Texas Penal Code Ann. § 29.02(a)(2).

Prediction of how the disputed issue might be resolved and why.

In dispute is the third element: whether Dunn used or exhibited a deadly weapon, the crowbar. The prosecution is likely to prove this element because the crowbar has the capacity to cause serious injury, and Dunn's conduct demonstrated her intent to use it to seriously injure Keyes. Therefore, Dunn is likely to be convicted of aggravated robbery.

Prediction of the outcome.

EXERCISES

Exercise 8-A

laches—
common law of limitations—
statute Contracts—2
Torts—2

Organize the sentences in A through D into a thesis for the Discussion in a memo on whether a court is likely to dismiss a sexual harassment complaint against XYZ Corp. on the ground of laches, a defense. The facts are in Exercise 7-E(1), p. 141. Match the sentences to the parts of this outline.

1. identification of the defense and summary of its elements

2. explanation of how matching the elements to the facts raises the issues considered in the analysis

3. prediction of how the issues might be resolved and a brief explanation of the reasoning behind the prediction

4. prediction of the outcome

2 A. XYZ Corp. will be able to establish undue prejudice because it cannot adequately defend the charge of sexual discrimination: one key witness moved out of the country and another died. *See id.* At issue is whether XYZ Corp. can prove that WEC inexcusably delayed filing the complaint.

1 B. To establish the defense of laches, the employer must prove that (1) the Workplace Equality Commission ("WEC") inexcusably delayed filing the complaint, and (2) the delay caused the employer to suffer undue prejudice. *WEC v. Jones*, 67 Nirv. 2d 83, 87 (1989).

4 C. Therefore, the complaint against XYZ Corp. will probably be dismissed on the ground of laches.

3 D. A court is likely to find inexcusable delay because WEC's dilatory conduct was caused by understaffing and a backlog of cases. *Jones*, 67 Nirv. 2d at 89.

Exercise 8-B

You represent Michael Phillips, who was arrested and charged with the crime of theft from a person, a violation of Texas Penal Code § 31.03(e)(4). Read the following Client File Summary and applicable statute. Write a thesis for the Discussion in a memo on whether the prosecution will be able to prove that Phillips is guilty of the crime. (Texas cases relating to the crime of theft from a person [Sims v. State, Farrell v. State, and Alfred v. State] are summarized in Chapter 5, p. 89-90.) Make sure your thesis includes:

1.   identification of the crime and summary of its elements or parts

2.   explanation of how matching the elements to the facts raises the disputed issue considered in the analysis

3.   prediction of how the disputed issue might be resolved and a brief explanation of the reasoning behind the prediction

4.   prediction of the outcome

Client File Summary: Michael Phillips

Ted Weinstein is a student at PQR University. He took off his gold watch while he was in the library and placed it on the table where he was studying. Michael Phillips, another student, came over to the table and asked Weinstein a question. During the conversation, Phillips knocked over Weinstein's notebook. As Weinstein bent down to pick up his notebook, he saw Philips take his watch. Weinstein was about two feet away from the watch when it was taken. Security responded when Weinstein started shouting at Philips. Philips was arrested and charged with theft from a person under Texas Penal Code § 31.03(e)(4).

Applicable Statute

A person violates Texas Penal Code § 31.03(e)(4) if (1) he commits theft (i.e., he appropriates property without the owner's consent with the intent to deprive the owner of the property) and (2) "the property is stolen from the person of another."

Exercise 8-C(1)

Your senior partner has asked whether sixteen-year-old Emanuel Gilbert can state a claim of negligent hiring against QRS Tennis Academy. Gilbert, a student at the Academy, was assaulted by John Doer, a tennis instructor employed by the Academy. Read the following theses. Decide which one is better and explain why.

Thesis A

In Nirvana, a person injured by an employee has a claim against the employer for negligent hiring if he can prove that (1) the employer had reason to know of its employee's unfitness or incompetence, (2) the employer could have reasonably foreseen that such characteristics created a risk of harm to third parties, and (3) the employee's unfitness or incompetence proximately caused the injury. *George v. Bell*, 96 Nirv. 2d 64 (1998). Gilbert can satisfy the first and second elements: the Academy had reason to know that Doer had been twice convicted of armed robbery and therefore could have reasonably foreseen that he posed a risk of harm to children enrolled in the Academy. At issue is the third element: whether Doer's unfitness proximately caused Gilbert's injury. A court is likely to hold that Doer's violent disposition was the proximate cause of the attack. Therefore, Gilbert probably has a claim of negligent hiring against the Academy.

[handwritten: the formula is better.]

Thesis B

[handwritten: makes reader think theres more elements]

Negligent hiring includes the following elements: (1) the employer had reason to know of its employee's unfitness or incompetence, (2) the employer could have reasonably foreseen that such characteristics created a risk of harm to third parties, and (3) the employee's unfitness or incompetence proximately caused the injury. *George v. Bell*, 96 Nirv. 2d 64, 67 (1998). At issue is whether John Doer's unfitness proximately caused Gilbert's injury. Gilbert can satisfy the first and second elements: the QRS Tennis Academy knew that Doer had been twice convicted of armed robbery and could have predicted that he posed a risk of harm. A court would likely hold that Doer's unfitness was the proximate cause of the attack on Gilbert. Therefore, Gilbert probably has a claim of negligent hiring.

Exercise 8-C(2)

Organize sentences A through F into a legal proof on whether Emanuel Gilbert can establish the first element of negligent hiring: that QRS Tennis Academy had reason to know of John Doer's unfitness. Match the sentences to the parts of this outline.

1. statement of the issue

2. statement of the rule

3. rule support

4. application of the rule to the facts

5. comparison between the facts of the client's case and the precedent case

6. conclusion on the issue

A. Gilbert therefore should be able to establish that the Academy had reason to know of Doer's unfitness to work with children.

B. For example, the court in *Levine* held that the employer had reason to know of its employee's unfitness to work as a camp counselor because a pre-hiring criminal background check would have revealed his prior rape conviction. *Levine*, 110 Nirv. 2d at 60.

C. The first element Gilbert must establish is that the Academy had reason to know of Doer's unfitness to work with children.

D. An employer has reason to know of an employee's unfitness if a thorough pre-hiring background check would have uncovered information demonstrating that the employee was unsuitable for the job. *See Levine v. Edmonds*, 110 Nirv. 2d 55, 59 (1997).

E. Like the defendant in *Levine*, the Academy had reason to know of its employee's unfitness: a pre-hiring criminal background check would have revealed Doer's prior armed robbery convictions.

F. Here, the Academy would have learned that Doer was unsuitable for the job if it had checked his background before hiring him.

Exercise 8-D

Use the facts and cases in Exercise 7-E(1), p. 141, to write an annotated legal proof analyzing whether XYZ Corp. can establish undue prejudice. Remember to include (1) the issue, (2) the rule, (3) rule support, (4) an application of the law to the facts supported by case comparisons, and (5) a conclusion.

CHAPTER 9

The Legal Memorandum: Beyond the Discussion

When you master this chapter, you will understand:

1. the purpose of the Heading, Question Presented, Short Answer, Summary of the Facts, and Conclusion in a legal memo; and

2. how to write each of these parts.

L
egal memos serve many functions. Sometimes memos are used to advise clients make decisions about a course of action, update the law, or educate the reader about a complicated transaction or procedure. The best memos are made up of self-contained and self-explanatory components. Memos that achieve this goal are easy to read and useful to the reader.

In every office, legal memos take on an idiosyncratic format developed over time. For that reason, a legal memo written in one office may look different from a memo written in another. However, all legal memos have common characteristics. If you understand the purpose of each part of the memo, you can easily adapt to the variations encountered in practice.

Chapter 8 examined the Discussion section of the legal memo: the legal proofs, introduced by a thesis that summarizes your legal analysis. It may help to think of your Discussion as the central act of your legal problem-solving drama. This chapter examines the remaining parts of the memo. The parts that precede the Discussion—the Heading, Question Presented, Short Answer, and Summary of the Facts—serve as a prologue, setting the scene, summarizing the action so far, and giving the reader a preview of what is to come. The Conclusion, which follows the Discussion, provides closure to the memo: it reiterates the prediction on the outcome and recaps the conclusions on the issues.

A. The Heading

The standard legal office memorandum contains a heading that looks like this:

To:
From:
Date:
Re:

While the first three lines require little more than filling in the blanks, the fourth line requires the writer to think about the memo's function.

The word "Re" derives from Latin and today is used to mean "about." Some people think of it as a shortened version of "Regarding." The "Re" line tells the reader what the memo is about. Consider the potential usefulness to the reader of the following "Re" lines Nadine Jackson's attorney could use in his memo about Dwight Jackson's accident on an amusement park ride:

1. Re: Nadine Jackson
2. Re: Jackson's Claim
3. Re: Negligent Infliction of Emotional Distress
4. Re: Jackson's Question about Negligent Infliction of Emotional Distress
5. Re: Nadine Jackson's Potential Claim for Negligent Infliction of Emotional Distress

Most useful

Clearly, some of these headings are more useful than others. The memo headed simply "Nadine Jackson," for instance, tells the reader nothing about the nature of the case. The reader is forced to read further just to determine if this is a memo about whether she has a claim for negligent infliction of emotional distress. Therefore, number 5—"Re: Nadine Jackson's Potential Claim for Negligent Infliction of Emotional Distress"—is the most useful because it is the most complete. Although these examples may seem trivial, the point is important. Even in writing the "Re" line, the careful writer must think about the reader.

Beyond being self-contained and self-explanatory, each part of a legal memo must be complete, clear, and correct. To construct a good heading, the "Re" line should contain the following:

- the name of the client or potential client,
- the nature of the matter or claim (*e.g.*, slander, aggravated robbery),
- the procedural status of the matter (*e.g.*, appeal of conviction, settlement, motion for summary judgment), if any.

B. The Question Presented

The Question Presented is a guide to the legal memorandum. You should have a separate Question Presented for each disputed issue discussed in the analysis. While there are many different ways to write a Question Presented, the following style will help the novice legal writer draft one that is clear and complete:

1. Identify the claim, crime, or defense and the element that gives rise to the disputed issue that will be discussed in the analysis part of the Discussion.

2. Summarize the necessary facts relating to the disputed issue.

3. Conclude with a question that identifies the disputed issue.

For example, attorney Alvarez could have written the following Question Presented in her memo on the Dunn matter:

> Under Texas Penal Code § 29.03(a)(2), a person may be convicted of aggravated robbery if she uses or exhibits a deadly weapon during a robbery. Jane Dunn brandished a crowbar at the driver of a UPS truck and threatened to hit him with it during the robbery of his truck. Did Dunn use or exhibit a deadly weapon?

Notice how this Question Presented is put together:

1. *The crime and the element that is in dispute:*
   Under Texas Penal Code § 29.03(a)(2), a person may be convicted of aggravated robbery if she uses or exhibits a deadly weapon during a robbery.

2. *The necessary facts relating to the disputed issue:*
   Jane Dunn brandished a crowbar at the driver of a UPS truck and threatened to hit him with it during the robbery of his truck.

3. *The issue:*
   Did Dunn use or exhibit a deadly weapon?

These additional examples use the same format:

A Contested Will
A will is not valid in Arkansas if it was procured by undue influence. Joan Dey made a new will in favor of a friend, Rhonda Wilson, who chose a lawyer for her and drove her to the lawyer's office to sign the will. Did Wilson unduly influence Dey to change her will?

A Climbing Accident
In Orion, a participant in a sporting event is reckless if he knowingly disregards a risk of danger. Cole Kerry turned to speak to a park ranger and allowed a rock-climbing rope supporting his partner to slip. Did Kerry knowingly disregard a risk of danger?

An Amusement Park Death
In Pennsylvania, a plaintiff claiming negligent infliction of emotional distress must establish that she suffered a direct emotional shock from a "sensory and contemporaneous observance" of an accident. Nadine

Jackson saw her husband get on an amusement park ride, heard but did not see the ride crash, and moments later, saw him lying dead on the ground. Did Jackson suffer a direct emotional shock from a sensory and contemporaneous observance of the accident?

Since lawyers cannot resolve most legal questions without regard to the facts that underlie them, the Question Presented must summarize these necessary facts. In the Question Presented you cannot recite *all* of the necessary facts. A short summary of the facts that determine the resolution of the disputed issue is all that is required.

These necessary facts may be written in many different ways, as long as the statement is concise and accurate. For example, the necessary facts for the Question Presented in the Dunn matter could be written as follows:

- The defendant shook a crowbar at the driver and threatened to harm him.
- Dunn physically and verbally threatened the driver with a crowbar.
- Dunn raised a crowbar and prevented the driver from interfering, by both word and action.
- Dunn both gestured with a crowbar and made verbal threats to the driver.
- Dunn shook a crowbar at the driver's head and threatened to hit him with it.

The purpose of the Question Presented is to alert the reader to the law, necessary facts, and issue. It describes the nature and scope of what follows.

Do Exercise 9-A Now, p. 173

C. The Short Answer

The Short Answer section of the legal memorandum responds to the Question Presented. It is a concise summary of the writer's conclusion on the issue. You should have a Short Answer for each Question Presented. Like the other parts of a legal memo, the Short Answer must be self-contained and self-explanatory. It should not, however, contain citations to authority or legal analysis. Consider once more the Question Presented in the Jackson amusement park accident matter:

Question Presented: In Pennsylvania, a plaintiff claiming negligent infliction of emotional distress must establish that she suffered a direct emotional shock from a "sensory and contemporaneous observance" of an accident. Nadine Jackson saw her husband get on an amusement park ride, heard but did not see the ride crash, and moments later, saw him lying dead on the ground. Did Jackson suffer a direct and emotional shock from a sensory and contemporaneous observance of the accident?

If the legal outcome is certain, this question can be answered in one word—either yes or no. If the law is less clear, the answer may be expressed in degrees of likelihood. Because analysis is an art, not a science, some lesser degree of certainty is often appropriate. For example, Jackson's attorney could have written the following Short Answer in the matter:

Short Answer: Probably. Jackson's visual awareness of the setting, simultaneous auditory perception of the accident, and her immediate observation of its aftermath most likely constitute a sensory and contemporaneous observance that caused her to suffer a direct emotional shock.

Here are some further examples of Short Answers to Questions Presented:

A Contested Will

Question Presented: A will is not valid in Arkansas if it was procured by undue influence. Joan Dey made a new will in favor of a friend, Rhonda Wilson, who chose a lawyer for her and drove her to the lawyer's office to sign the will. Did Wilson unduly influence Dey to change her will?

Short Answer: Probably not. Wilson's actions did not unduly influence Joan Dey's judgment sufficiently to invalidate her will.

A Climbing Accident

Question Presented: In Orion, a participant in a sporting event is reckless if he knowingly disregards a risk of danger. Cole Kerry turned to a park ranger and allowed a rock-climbing rope supporting his partner to slip. Did Kerry knowingly disregard a risk of danger?

Short Answer: Probably. Kerry ignored the usual practices and standards of the sport by letting the safety rope go slack and therefore knowingly disregarded a risk of danger.

These Short Answers have several characteristics in common.

- They are succinct.
- They answer the Question Presented.
- They include a brief explanation of the answer.

Do Exercise 9-B Now, p. 173

D. The Summary of the Facts

The Summary of the Facts, like all the other parts of the legal memorandum, must be self-contained and self-explanatory. The purpose of this section is to tell the reader what happened in an accurate and objective way. To be objective, you must include both favorable and unfavorable facts and identify unknown facts. Deciding which facts to include is the main challenge when writing a Summary of the Facts. You must include enough information so that someone unfamiliar with the case can understand what happened. But all facts are not equally important. Some facts are necessary to your analysis because they help you predict how the court might rule. Some facts support the necessary facts by providing background. Other facts are simply inconsequential. You should include only the facts necessary to your analysis and the supporting facts that help your reader understand those necessary facts.

The Summary of the Facts includes

- a context statement, including the procedural posture, and
- the necessary and pertinent supporting facts.

1. The context statement

The Summary of the Facts should begin with a context statement explaining who the parties are, what the claim, crime, or defense is, and why the writer is writing the memo. A brief mention of the procedural posture of the matter should also be included. Here are some examples:

- Joan Dey's granddaughters have asked whether they will be able to invalidate her will on the ground of undue influence.

- Kevin Jordan has asked whether he will be able to overturn the summary judgment against him in his negligence action against the driver who injured him in a car accident.

2.   Identifying the facts

The Summary of the Facts must include the facts necessary to your legal analysis and should include supporting facts to provide your reader with the context to understand the necessary facts. Your understanding of which facts to include in the memo will evolve as you do your research and determine the rules of law that apply. However, even then, deciding which facts to include is not an exact science. You will learn by experience and common sense what to include.

Necessary facts are those facts that enable you to predict how a court would rule on your issue. When you have researched the law and can identify and articulate the elements and disputed issue, you will be ready to identify the necessary facts. These are the facts that a court considers conclusive. If those facts appeared again in a different situation, you could reasonably predict that the court would rule the same way. If the facts were different or did not exist, then the court would reach a different decision.

Necessary facts are not absolutes, however. They depend on the law for their importance. If you have the same transaction, occurrence, or event but a different legal claim, the necessary facts might change because the courts look at different facts to determine the outcome of different legal claims. For example, suppose your client has been fired. She is convinced that she has been terminated because of her age. She also has an employment contract that contains a clause that permits her termination only "for cause." She sues her employer for unlawful termination on two grounds: (1) violation of the Age Discrimination in Employment Act ("ADEA"), a statutory claim derived from the federal statute that prohibits discrimination in employment (including termination) based on an employee's age, and (2) breach of her employment contract, a common-law contract claim. While both of these claims arise from the same occurrence—your client's termination—the rules of law that apply are quite different. For instance, the facts that prove the existence of a valid employment contract are not necessary for proving that her employer violated the ADEA.

If you read a decision carefully, you can often identify the necessary facts by the way the court characterizes them. Sometimes courts will label facts "determinative" or "important." Or, if a court refers to or analyzes certain facts in other cases, the court is signaling it thinks those facts are necessary. For example, in *Mazzagatti v. Everingham*, 516 A.2d 672, 679 (Pa. 1986), the court identified the requirement that a close relative be present at the scene of an accident as a necessary fact in a negligent infliction of emotional distress action when it said, "We believe that where the close relative is not present at the scene of the accident, but instead learns of the accident from a third party, the close relative's prior knowledge of the injury to the victim serves as a buffer against the full impact of observing the accident scene."

Supporting facts are not necessary to the outcome of the case, but assist the reader in understanding what happened. They can provide background, a context for the necessary facts, or emotion to the story. While all necessary facts must be included in the Summary of the Facts, only pertinent supporting facts should be included. Keep in mind that details that do not relate in any significant way to necessary facts do not belong in the Summary.

Inconsequential facts are details that are not crucial to the outcome of the case or particularly helpful to its understanding. Do not include inconsequential facts in the Summary of the Facts.

Inferences are *not* facts; they are *conclusions* derived from facts. A fact is an actual occurrence, event, or circumstance. Facts are things *known* through observation. In contrast, inferences are value-laden *characterizations*, such as "intentional," "reckless," "reasonable," or "malicious." Inferences do not belong in the Summary of the Facts. For example:

> *Fact:*   Alex hit Rebecca with a rock while screaming "That'll show you!"
>
> *Inference (derived from the fact):* Alex intended to injure Rebecca.

Nonoccurrences are things that did *not* happen. Sometimes nonoccurrences can be necessary facts. In the ADEA-breach of contract example above, assume that your client had failed to sign her employment contract. Her failure to execute the contract properly would be a necessary fact since it affects the outcome of the breach-of-contract claim. In the Dunn matter, Dunn did *not* hit Keyes with the crowbar even though she had the opportunity and the ability to do so. If Dunn had hit Keyes with the crowbar, Keyes would have been seriously injured, defeating the argument that the crowbar was not a deadly weapon. That Dunn had the opportunity but did not use it, while not rising to the level of a necessary fact, may still be important. Make sure you identify important nonoccurrences and include them in the Summary of the Facts.

Crucial unknown facts are things that you do not know but need to know because they might affect the outcome of the case. In the ADEA-breach of contract example above, you will need to know many statistics—the ages of employees in jobs similar to that of your client and the ages of all employees who have been terminated—to determine whether the statutory ADEA claim can be made. These important unknown facts should be identified in the Summary of the Facts.

3. Organization

One of the memo writer's more important tasks is to impose order on the facts, selecting and arranging them in a way that helps the reader quickly and easily understand what happened. The Summary of the Facts is usually organized in one of three ways: topically, chronologically, or mixed. The purpose of the memorandum and the nature of the issues often suggest the most appropriate organization.

If a legal memo involves multiple claims or issues, the topical organizational scheme works best. Facts are grouped by issue, element, crime, or claim to help the reader understand how they fit together.

A chronological scheme that presents the facts in the order of their occurrence helps the reader to understand the story or "big picture." If you use a chronological scheme to organize the Summary of the Facts, do not make the mistake of including inconsequential facts—extraneous details—which can complicate and obfuscate rather than clarify the necessary facts.

A mixed organizational scheme is a bit more complicated to draft. Facts are organized by topic and then, within the topic, chronologically. This type of organization works best for issues that involve a series of events or transactions. For example, if the case involves a number of property financings, you would organize your facts first by topic—each financing—and then within each topic, chronologically—the events in the order that they occurred describing each financing.

Simply adopting the facts as they come to you will not produce a coherent Summary of the Facts. First you must identify the purpose of the memo and the issues you will analyze and discuss. Then you can determine the most appropriate organizational scheme. Not only may the facts be confusingly out of order, they may come to you in the first person (from interviews or transcripts), or in the idioms of common speech, which are not appropriate to the formal writing style required in a legal memo. The memo writer frequently, therefore, must also rewrite the facts to put them in a consistent and appropriate style and tone.

4.   Conforming the facts

Every fact you mention in your Discussion must be in the Summary of the Facts. After you have written the first draft of your memo, you must conform the document: read through the completed Discussion section carefully, noting each fact that has been used in the analysis. Make sure that all the facts that appear in the analysis are also included in the Summary of the Facts.

5.   A sample Summary of the Facts

The following is a sample Summary of the Facts. Identify the parts of the context statement and the organizational scheme.

Summary of the Facts

Krista and Michael Hathaway have asked whether they will likely succeed in an appeal of a verdict finding that they negligently entrusted a dangerous instrument, their jet ski, to their son. On August 23, 2000, the Hathaways' son Tyler, who was then twelve years old, fatally injured George Kline in a jet ski accident on Lake Serenity in upstate Nirvana. Kline's estate sued the Hathaways for the tort of negligent entrustment of a dangerous instrument. On March 8, 2001, the jury returned a verdict for the Kline estate and awarded it $12 million in damages.

The Hathaways have lived in the Lake Serenity community since 1985. Most of the recreational activities in the community involve water sports. Tyler has been swimming since he was a year old. When he was five, Tyler started jet skiing with his father. The Hathaways have owned a Sea Whiz jet ski for years. It weighs 550 pounds and is 106 inches long, 46 inches wide, and 37 inches high. It can travel up to 45 mph.

In June 1999, when Tyler turned eleven, his parents allowed him to use the jet ski alone. Although the Hathaways did not require Tyler to take jet ski lessons, they did set rules for its use. Tyler was to ask permission before he used the jet ski, could not ride faster than 20 mph, and could not race.

The Hathaways discovered that Tyler had been racing the jet ski with his friends twice during the summer of 1999. They grounded Tyler for a week each time. In June 2000, the Lake Police brought Tyler back to the Hathaways' home when they caught him speeding on the jet ski. The Hathaways grounded Tyler for two weeks and warned him that he would not be permitted to use the jet ski again if he was caught speeding one more time. While they never caught him speeding again, in late July they learned that Tyler had been using the jet ski without permission. Tyler admitted that it was very hard to resist using the jet ski since both his parents worked and the keys hung on a peg in the kitchen. He promised not to take it again without permission.

On August 23, 2000, Tyler decided to go jet skiing on Lake Serenity. He did not have permission to use the jet ski. While he was riding the jet ski, Tyler waved to his friends on the shore. Because he was distracted, Tyler did not see Kline in his kayak.

By the time he did see Kline, it was too late. Tyler was going about 40 mph and was too close to Kline to slow down in time. Kline's kayak turned over as soon as Tyler's jet ski hit him, killing him instantly.

Do Exercises 9-C and 9-D Now, p. 174

E. The Conclusion

The Conclusion provides closure to the Discussion: it succinctly recaps your conclusions on the issues and reiterates your prediction on the outcome in the matter. The Conclusion should be direct and concise. Do not re-analyze case law or the facts of your case. Remember that the Conclusion does not impart new information but rather wraps up the Discussion. Here is an example of a Conclusion from the Jackson memo:

Jackson probably has a claim against Hi-Five for negligent infliction of emotional distress. She was closely related to the victim, stood near the scene of the accident, and had a sensory and contemporaneous observance of the accident which caused her to suffer a direct emotional shock.

EXERCISES

Exercise 9-A

Use the statute and facts in Exercise 8-B on p. 156 to write a Question Presented for a legal memo on whether Michael Phillips is likely to be convicted of the crime of theft from a person. Remember to include (1) the claim, crime, or defense and the element that gives rise to the disputed issue; (2) the necessary facts relating to the disputed issue; and (3) a question that identifies the disputed issue.

Exercise 9-B

Review the material on common-law fraud in Exercises 2-B(1) and 2-B(2) on pp. 35-36 and the material on common-law battery in Exercises 2-C(1) and 2-C(2) on pp. 36-37. Read the following Questions Presented and Short Answers. Decide which Question Presented and Short Answer is best in each example. Explain your answers.

Example A

1. ***Question Presented:*** In Olympus, a plaintiff states a common-law fraud claim if she proves the defendant made a false statement. Arthur Endicott sold a house to Margaret Wang that was adjacent to an abandoned industrial landfill. Did Endicott make a false statement of material fact to Wang?

   Short Answer: Yes. Endicott misrepresented the condition of the surrounding neighborhood.

2. ***Question Presented:*** In Olympus, one of the elements a plaintiff claiming common-law fraud must prove is that the defendant was dishonest. Arthur Endicott told Margaret Wang that her house was not near an industrial landfill. Was Endicott dishonest?

   Short Answer: Yes. Endicott's statement to Wang was false.

3. ***Question Presented:*** In Olympus, one of the elements a plaintiff claiming common-law fraud must prove is that the defendant made a false statement of material fact to her. Arthur Endicott sold a house to Margaret Wang and told her that the adjacent property had never been used for industrial purposes. Did Endicott make a false statement of material fact to Wang?

disputed element

Short Answer: Yes. At the time he sold the house to Wang and told her that the adjacent property had never been used for industrial purposes, Endicott knew that the adjacent property had been used as an industrial landfill and that this prior use might affect the value of Wang's house.

Example B

1. *Question Presented:* In Olympus, one of the elements a plaintiff claiming common-law battery must prove is that the defendant touched him in a harmful or offensive manner. Turner slapped Sakamura in the face during a business meeting, causing Sakamura to suffer mild pain and great humiliation. Did Turner touch Sakamura in a harmful or offensive manner?

   Short Answer: Yes. The contact was both harmful and offensive because when Turner slapped Sakamura, he caused him to suffer pain and also offended his personal dignity.

2. *Question Presented:* In Olympus, a plaintiff who suffers pain has a claim of common-law battery. Sakamura suffered pain as a result of Turner's conduct. Does Sakamura have a claim of common-law battery?

   Short Answer: Yes. Sakamura suffered pain when Turner slapped him.

3. *Question Presented:* In Olympus, one of the elements a plaintiff claiming common-law battery must prove is that the defendant contacted him in a harmful or offensive manner. Turner caused Sakamura to suffer mild pain and great humiliation. Did Turner contact Sakamura in a harmful or offensive manner?

   Short Answer: Yes. Turner contacted Sakamura in a harmful and offensive manner.

Exercise 9-C

Read the following case and Summary of the Facts. Identify the context statement and necessary and supporting facts in the Summary of the Facts. Identify the organizational structure used in the Summary of the Facts.

Case

Kincaid v. Frugality Inns: In Nirvana, a hotel may be held liable for injuries sustained by a hotel guest who is a victim of a crime on its premises. To state a negligence claim against a hotel, a guest injured as a result of a criminal attack on the hotel's premises must establish that (1) the hotel had a duty of care to protect its guests from such an attack, (2) the hotel breached its duty of care by failing to provide adequate security, and (3) the breach proximately caused the injury. A duty of care to protect guests from criminal attack exists only if the attack is foreseeable. A criminal attack is foreseeable if substantially similar crimes recently occurred on the hotel's premises.

Summary of the Facts

You asked whether Charles Parker has a negligence claim against the Welford Plaza Hotel. Parker, while a guest at the hotel, was attacked in one of the hotel's lobbies by Roy Jenkins, who was neither a guest nor an employee of the hotel.

The Welford Plaza Hotel, owned by Leonard Harris, is a five-star luxury property located in New Town, Nirvana. It has 350 guest rooms and three lobbies. Three security guards are on duty at all times: one in the main lobby and two floaters. The floaters patrol the common areas and respond to emergency calls. There are no surveillance cameras on the premises.

The hotel has experienced increased criminal activity in recent years. About five years ago, an intruder broke into a guest's room and stole her wallet. No one was harmed. Three years ago, there were several attempted thefts of cars in the hotel's parking lot. The hotel's security guards were able to scare off the thieves. Last year, a guest was robbed while waiting for the atrium-lobby elevator. He was not, however, physically harmed. Other than a few arguments between guests using the health club, there have been no problems on the lower-level of the hotel.

On September 2, 2000, Parker, a financial analyst from New York City, checked into the Welford Plaza Hotel for a business trip. Jenkins attacked Parker that evening in the dimly lit lower-level lobby located adjacent to the hotel's health club. He brandished a knife and demanded Parker's money. Jenkins

[handwritten margin note: context statement]

became enraged when Parker announced that he had no money. He then slashed Parker twice in the stomach. The police arrested Jenkins in the neighborhood later that evening.

Parker was operated on to repair internal injuries from the stab wounds. Although he has recovered physically, he still suffers from extreme anxiety and depression because of the attack.

Exercise 9-D

Use the facts and cases in Exercise 7-E(1) on pp. 141-143 to write a Summary of the Facts for a legal memo on behalf of XYZ Corp. Remember to include (1) a context statement, (2) necessary facts, and (3) pertinent supporting facts.

CHAPTER 10

Writing for Readability

When you master this chapter, you will understand:

1. why readability is the key to good writing;

2. what readability means; and

3. how to make your writing readable.

A. Thought and Its Expression

Thought and its expression are inextricably intertwined. You communicate your thoughts by putting them into words. The particular words you choose and how you arrange them will determine how well your readers will understand what you are trying to say. The most subtle and penetrating idea is useless if it is not conveyed in understandable prose; the most beautiful arrangement of words is pointless if it does not convey any idea.

A single thought may be expressed in many different ways. Consider these famous lines from the Declaration of Independence:

> We hold these truths to be self-evident, that all Men are created equal, that they are endowed by their Creator with certain unalienable Rights, that among these are Life, Liberty, and the Pursuit of Happiness . . . .

Suppose, instead, Thomas Jefferson had written:

> It seems perfectly obvious to us, everything considered, that all the various and different people on the earth are deserving of equality with respect to important aspects of their lives, that by virtue of their being human beings created in the image of God they are entitled to make certain claims of right, which nobody can take away from them, that will entitle them to live their lives free from arbitrary restraints and to devise life plans to secure their preferences for happiness. (Version 1)

Or suppose an editor who was unhappy at the length of Version 1 had boiled it down to this sentence:

> Obviously, everybody's equal, with the right to live, act freely, and seek to be happy. (Version 2)

You do not need much of an eye or an ear to see immediately that something is very wrong with the way the idea is expressed in these alternative versions. Version 1 is too long; Version 2 is too short. Nor is that all that is wrong. Version 1 is too long because it is wordy: the clutter of unnecessary words leads not to precision but to fuzziness; the sharp, almost poetic style of the original is lost. In contrast, the very brevity of Version 2 distorts the original's meaning and robs it of the beauty of Jefferson's prose.

Composing readable thought is the craft of writing. The craft cannot be captured by a single formula: what is best for one reader on one occasion is not best for another reader on another occasion. Although there are no formulas, there are simple and effective principles that can help you put your thoughts into clear, concise, and coherent prose—writing that is *readable*.

B. Readability

A document is readable if the reader can understand it on a *single* reading. The more often the reader must reread what you have written, the more likely it is that the reader will either misunderstand or abandon your writing altogether. Sometimes a document is unclear because the writer does not really know what he wants to say. The problem, in other words, may lie in the thought (or lack of thought) itself. But even when the writer has a point to make and knows what it is, the writing may still be difficult to comprehend. Unreadable writing of this sort is caused by one or more of the following:

- *Imprecise vocabulary:* using the wrong word for the intended meaning;
- *Improper word order:* placing words or phrases in the wrong place;
- *Lack of orientation:* omitting appropriate background information;
- *Lack of organization:* failing to present thoughts in a coherent way;
- *Verbosity:* using unnecessary words;
- *Unnecessary complexity:* putting too many thoughts in a single sentence or paragraph;
- *Mistakes in grammar, syntax, and usage:* deviating from the rules for constructing well-ordered sentences; and
- *Incorrect punctuation:* using punctuation that misleads the reader or keeps the reader from understanding intended connections between thoughts.

It is the writer's job to make his writing readable. The writer cannot rely on the reader to work hard at interpreting a difficult document. Moreover, a readable document is almost always shorter than an unreadable one. In the legal profession, brevity is important. More and more, courts and governmental agencies are imposing word or page limits on documents they receive. Even when there is no limit, the reader inevitably will have too much to read and will prefer the short document to the long one. The lawyer-writer must insure that clients do not waste their money on documents that try readers' patience and risk their misunderstanding.

The single most important criterion of readable writing is to *pay attention to your readers*. You are writing for a purpose: to provide information to readers, to give them a point of view, to enable them to see matters in a new light, or to persuade them to take some course of action. Unless you think about who your readers are, what they know, what they want to know, and why they want to know it, you cannot do your job as a lawyer-writer.

Avoiding all potential traps and mistakes is not easy. Professional writers spend years perfecting their writing. Because lawyers are professional writers, it is essential to begin now to cultivate good writing habits that will repay your efforts with rich dividends in the years to come. This and the next chapter are designed to provide you with a solid foundation in the most basic principles of good writing. This chapter reviews the forms of the standard sentence and paragraph. The next chapter examines readers' expectations about the work as a whole.

C. Fifteen Basic Principles for Making Your Writing Readable

Here are 15 principles for writing that, if practiced diligently, will make your writing readable so that your readers understand, in a single reading, what you have written.

1. Arrange sentence components properly

a.   The basic components of a sentence and their arrangement

The sentence is the basic unit of thought. Readers expect a standard sentence to have (1) a subject, (2) a verb, and sometimes (3) an object. The subject is what the sentence is about. Ordinarily, the subject performs the action that is expressed in the verb. Many standard sentences also have objects, the thing to which the action of the sentence is done (*e.g.*, Thomas researched the *law*.), although a sentence need not always have an object to be grammatically correct (*e.g.*, Lauren argued.).

Sentence 1: The lawyer drafted the contract.

In Sentence 1, the subject is *lawyer*, the action is expressed in the verb *drafted*, and the object, *contract*, is the thing to which the action is done. A sentence without a subject or verb is a fragment. Formal writing should not contain fragments.

Readers also expect to find the subject, verb, and object closely connected. In Sentence 2, the writer strays from this expectation:

Sentence 2: The lawyer, who was feeling sick and had not been to the office in several days, drafted, without the benefit of the proper statutory material or the pertinent cases, the memo.

In this sentence, the writer interrupts the flow of the sentence from subject to verb to object with side thoughts. The reader may be confused when encountering the verb so far away from the subject and the object at the end of the sentence far from the verb. Revised Sentence 2 is much more coherent:

Revised Sentence 2: Sick and absent from the office for several days, the lawyer drafted the memo, even though he did not have the proper statutory material or the pertinent cases.

Do Exercise 10-A Now, p. 210

Subject, verb, and object are the main components of the sentence. Other components—introductory phrases, subordinate clauses, prepositional phrases, and the like—have an important function in many sentences. These ancillary components will aid your reader's comprehension, but they must be properly connected to one of the main components to be understandable and grammatically correct. One troubling problem is the *dangling modifier,* as in the next example:

Sentence 3: Before addressing your specific complaints, *some general comments* are in order.

In this sentence, the first phrase ("Before addressing your specific complaints") is dangling because it is not connected to the person to whom the action of the phrase refers. Who will address the complaints? The sentence suggests that "some general comments" will address the complaints. That of course makes no sense. It is *the lawyer* who intends to address the client's complaints. Attach the phrase to an appropriate subject:

Revised Sentence 3: Before addressing your specific complaints, *the Assistant District Attorney* will offer some general comments.

Another modifier that often plagues careless writers is the word *only*. Different placements of *only* in a single sentence can change the meaning. Consider three places in which *only* might appear in the following sentence:

> **Sentence 4:** The lawyer *only* [1] drafted *only* [2] the contract *only* [3] yesterday.

In position 1, the writer is saying that the only thing the lawyer did was draft the contract; he did not do anything else. In position 2, the writer is saying that the lawyer drafted just the contract, not any other document. In position 3, the writer is saying that the lawyer drafted the contract yesterday, not earlier. To insure the accuracy of your writing, pay close attention to the placement of the word *only* in sentences.

Do Exercise 10-B Now, p. 210

b.   The substantive arrangement of a sentence

Beyond the grammatical form of a sentence, readers expect substantive information to be in a particular sequence, according to two general principles:

- Old or less important information should come before new or more important information.
- Short information should come before long information.

1.   *Information that is familiar or prepares the reader for new or more important information should be put at the beginning of the sentence.* How do you know whether your reader is familiar with certain information? You might already have made the point expressly, or you might reasonably assume the reader has the necessary background information. Old or less important information is subsidiary to the main point of the sentence. New or more important information should be put at the end of the sentence. This arrangement of old to new and less important to more important prepares the reader to accept new and more important information and facilitates the transitions between sentences, helping them to flow. Consider the placement of information in the following sentence:

> **Sentence 5:** The defendant was found guilty by the jury after several hours of deliberation.

In Sentence 5, the reader probably already understands that the jury determines the defendant's fate. The deliberation of the jury is therefore old or less important information than what the jury actually determined—the defendant's guilt. Moreover, the information that the jury took several hours to deliberate is probably less important than that it finally arrived at a guilty verdict. Revise the sentence, therefore, as follows:

> **Revised Sentence 5:** After deliberating for several hours, the jury found the defendant guilty.

2. *Short comes before long in a sentence.* This arrangement enhances sentence clarity. If you have two related and equally important points to make in a sentence, and one point can be expressed in fewer words than the other, put the shorter one first. Consider the arrangement of the words in the next example:

> **Sentence 6:** The lawyer drafted the contract containing the price, the quantity of products to be sold, and the due dates, and a letter to the client.

In Sentence 6, the writer has used a compound object: a contract and a letter were both drafted. But the description of the contract overwhelms that of the letter, which seems an afterthought. Transpose the two objects, however, and the sentence is clearer:

> **Revised Sentence 6:** The lawyer drafted a letter to the client and a contract containing the price, the quantity of products to be sold, and the due dates.

The same rule applies to other long parts of a sentence. A very long sentence can keep the reader from getting to the verb, and the uncertainty prompted by the delay will make the sentence less readable.

> **Sentence 7:** Contracts that are clearly drafted, that use precise language, that are not longer than they need to be to achieve their purpose are what we want.

In Sentence 7 the writer takes much too long to get to the verb (and is otherwise wordy). Compare to the revised version:

> **Revised Sentence 7a:** We want contracts that are clearly drafted, that use precise language, and that are not longer than they need to be to achieve their purpose.

Revised Sentence 7a can be revised again to eliminate wordiness:

> **Revised Sentence 7b:** We want contracts that are clear, precise, and concise.

☞ **2.   Keep sentences short**

Put one main thought in each sentence. That thought does not have to be simple-minded; it can be sophisticated and complex. But a sentence that includes too many thoughts makes it difficult to follow the point, as in the next example:

> **Sentence 8:** Sick and absent from the office for several days, the lawyer drafted the contract, which concerned the sale of his client's company's chips, which were now being made in a modernized factory capable of producing 10,000 per day, compared to a paltry 1,000 per day before the modernization, allowing the company to cut costs and therefore offer better terms, even though he did not have the statute or the pertinent cases.

Rewriting leads to several sentences, making the point easier to understand:

> **Revised Sentence 8:** Recuperating from an illness, the lawyer drafted the new sales contract from home, even though he did not have the statute or pertinent cases. The new contract was necessary because after the client modernized its factory, it produced 10,000 rather than a paltry 1,000 chips per day. This greater efficiency has lowered production costs and permits the client to offer better sale terms.

☞ **3.   Make connections parallel**

Many sentences internally connect a series of elements. A sentence might have a compound subject (The *lawyer* and her *paralegal* drafted the contract.), verb (The lawyer *researched* the law, *drafted* the contract, and *wrote* the letter.), object (The lawyer drafted *a contract and a letter*.), or modifier (The lawyer made an *emotional* and *persuasive* plea for the defendant's release.). When connecting the elements in a series, each should be of the same grammatical type: nouns, adjectives, verbs, and clauses. When the elements are of the same type, the sentence construction is parallel.

When using *and*, *or*, and other connectives in a sentence, make sure that the elements connected by them are of the same type. Do *not* say:

> **Sentence 9:** When writing prospective employers, you should provide personal information *and* why you want to work for them.

The *and* in Sentence 9 signals that a compound object is about to follow. Instead, the writer follows with a clause "why you want to work for them." Make the sentence parallel either by adding a verb, altering the verb to make the objects parallel, or turning the "why" clause into an object as in the next three revisions:

> **Revised Sentence 9a:** When writing prospective employers, you should *provide* personal information and *explain* why you want to work for them. *or*
> **Revised Sentence 9b:** When writing prospective employers, you should say *who you are* and *why you want* to work for them. *or*
> **Revised Sentence 9c:** When writing prospective employers, you should provide personal information and the reason for your application.

In the following example, the writer has included a verb form ("bound to be") in a string of adjectives ("irrelevant," "immaterial"):

> **Sentence 10:** The judge excluded the evidence because she thought it was irrelevant, immaterial, and *bound to be* prejudicial.

Find a word that will substitute for the thought expressed in the verb (for example, the adverb "clearly"), as follows:

> **Revised Sentence 10a:** The judge excluded the evidence because she thought it was irrelevant, immaterial, and clearly prejudicial.

This revision is itself not quite parallel, since only one of the adjectives in the string is qualified by an adverb. Rewrite the sentence to make it fully parallel:

> **Revised Sentence 10b:** The judge excluded the evidence because she thought it was completely irrelevant, wholly immaterial, and clearly prejudicial.

The resulting sentence is parallel, but it is now wordy and inflated. Words like "irrelevant" and "immaterial" do not need qualification: something either is or is not relevant or material. A better revision, therefore, is this one:

> **Revised Sentence 10c:** The judge excluded the evidence, holding it irrelevant, immaterial, and prejudicial.

Inexperienced writers frequently link adjectives and nouns, usually leaving a wordy, awkward construction:

> **Sentence 11:** The adversaries were *knowledgeable* and *people of intelligence*.

In this sentence, the writer has incorrectly linked an adjective ("knowledgeable") and noun phrase ("people of intelligence"). Rewrite, substituting an adjective for the noun phrase:

> **Revised Sentence 11:** The adversaries were *knowledgeable and intelligent* people.

Even when the words in a list are of the same grammatical type, they must be in the same form.

> **Sentence 12:** The detective proposed a plan *to raid* the drug dealer's office and *arresting* all his workers.

The *and* in Sentence 12 signals a connection between "to raid" and "arresting." But because these verbs are not in the same form, the sentence is difficult to follow. Make the sentence readable by changing one of the verb forms to parallel the other, as in the next two revisions:

> **Revised Sentence 12a:** The detective proposed a plan *to raid* the drug dealer's office and *to arrest* all his workers.

> **Revised Sentence 12b:** The detective proposed *raiding* the drug dealer's office and *arresting* all his workers.

Another common example of faulty parallelism is the omission of a second "that" in a sentence combining or comparing two relative clauses, the first of which begins with "that."

> **Sentence 13:** The weary young lawyer hoped *that* her boss would leave and the phone would stop ringing.

This sentence connects the clause "that her boss would leave" to a noun ("the phone"). Although the writer's meaning comes through in this sentence, you should get in the habit of introducing both clauses with the same term.

> **Revised Sentence 13:** The weary young lawyer hoped *that* her boss would leave and *that* the phone would stop ringing.

Parallelism is especially important when using paired conjunctions, such as *either . . . or, both . . . and, not only . . . but also.* The reader expects the same type of elements to follow each of the conjunctions in the pair. Failing to make them parallel interferes with readability. For example:

> **Sentence 14:** The lawyer *not only* drafted the contract *but also* the letter.

In Sentence 14, the reader expects to see that the lawyer took *two* actions: she *drafted* the contract and did something else—for example, faxed the letter. The end of the sentence tells a different story: the lawyer did not do two different things after all. Rather, she did one thing—drafted—to two objects. Rewrite:

> **Revised Sentence 14:** The lawyer <u>not only</u> *drafted* the contract <u>but also</u> *faxed* it to the client. *or*
> **Alternate Revised Sentence 14:** The lawyer drafted <u>not only</u> *the contract* <u>but also</u> *the letter.*

In Revised Sentence 14, the writer makes the verbs parallel, showing the lawyer doing two things, *drafting* and *faxing*. In Alternate Revised Sentence 14, the writer has moved *not only* after the verb so that it connects two objects, the *contract* and the *letter*.

Do Exercise 10-C Now, p. 210

---

4. **Focus each paragraph on one thought, organize it around a topic sentence, and connect the sentences that follow**

Like the sentence, the paragraph is a unit of thought that has a standard form. The standard paragraph begins with a *topic sentence*—a sentence that presents the main point. The rest of the sentences in the paragraph describe, comment on, add to, or otherwise explain the point introduced in the topic sentence. A paragraph is readable when the sentences are arranged in a logical sequence. The writer who follows the basic rules for forming sentences will find that the paragraphs that emerge are generally well-formed as well. If you move from old to new information within your sentences, then each succeeding sentence will begin with a reference or connection to what has gone before (the old). Moving from old to new within a sentence promotes a similar progression within a paragraph. A paragraph that contains sentences that do *not* move from old to new confuses the reader. For example:

> ***Paragraph 1:*** The child was financially supported by an uncle who lived in the same house in the *Mills* case. The aunt did not provide for the child, but she lived in the same apartment in the *Patrick* case. The uncle did not live in the same house, but he lived on the block and took care of the child in the *Smith* case. Susan Johnson lived in the basement of the home where her nephew Frank Taylor lived. Her living quarters were separate. If you reside on a daily basis in the same house or apartment then you are living in the same household. Johnson was living in the same household as Taylor, the courts would probably hold. There were no locks on the door between Johnson's basement quarters and Taylor's upstairs space.

This paragraph is quite jumbled. It does not begin with a topic sentence, so the reader is bewildered after the first few sentences. What point is the writer trying to make? Who cares whether a child was supported by an uncle or not supported by an aunt who happened to live in the same house or on the same block? Why is it important to know that Johnson lived in the basement? Not until much later in the paragraph does the reader learn that the writer has something to say about the rule for determining whether an aunt lives in the "same household" as her nephew. Even then, the writer does not make clear the connection between that rule and the absence of locks. Moreover, the sentences do not present old and less important information first. As a consequence, the sentences do not connect well. Here are the same thoughts rearranged following the old to new information principle:

> ***Revised Paragraph 1:*** The question is whether Susan Johnson lived in the same household as her nephew Frank Taylor [S1]. Living in the same household means residing in the same house or apartment on a daily basis [S2]. In *Mills*, the uncle lived in the same house [S3]. In *Patrick*, the aunt lived in the same apartment [S4]. In *Smith*, the court held that an uncle who lived on the same block and kept the child overnight twice a week did not live in the same household [S5]. Although Johnson had separate living quarters in the basement of the Taylor home, they were accessible from the main floor through a door without locks [S6]. A court, therefore, would probably hold that she and Frank Taylor were living in the same household [S7].

In Revised Paragraph 1, the writer begins with a topic sentence [S1], stating the main point that the paragraph discusses. S2 follows up with a statement of the rule. Note that the first part of S2 contains the older information about "living in the same household," a phrase already presented in S1. S2 goes on to the new information defining the phrase. S3-S5 describe other cases, beginning with less important information (the names of the cases) and structured in the same way to permit the reader to absorb the information more readily. S6 moves from old information (the location of the living quarters) to a new type of information that may make the difference (no locks to keep her out). S7 provides the reader with a conclusion that follows from the information already presented, again opening with the less important information (it is the court doing the holding) and ending with the more important information (what that holding is likely to be).

☞ **5.   Use transition words properly and sparingly**

Transitions are words and phrases that link sentences and paragraphs. Transition words can:

- *sequence* (first, next, finally),
- *oppose* (but, however, nevertheless, although),
- *compare* (in contrast, conversely, similarly, likewise),
- *amplify* (furthermore, moreover, in addition),
- *stress* (indeed, even, in fact),
- *illustrate* (for example, to illustrate), and
- *show logical relation* (therefore, so, as a result, consequently).

Although transitions are extremely useful in showing connections between thoughts, not every pair of sentences needs one, since the internal sense of the sentences may be a sufficient connection. When you do use transitions, use them properly. Transition words have meanings. Using the wrong transition leads to misunderstanding. *Finally,* using an unnecessary one is pedantic and wordy (in this sentence, the word "finally" is superfluous, because the paragraph does not list anything for which "finally" would be a useful conclusion). And avoid transition phrases that are more verbal clutter than functional transitions—for instance, "it is interesting to note that" or "the next item of importance is . . . ."

☞ **6.   Put the action of the sentence in the verb**

a.   Remove the action from nouns

The action of a sentence should be expressed in the verb. All too often, however, lawyers put the action in nouns. The overuse of nouns in this way is called *nominalization* (*naming* the action, rather than *showing* it). Nominalizing often makes your sentences longer and less concrete because it forces the writer to use more clauses and weak, general verbs. For example:

Sentence 15: The police conducted an investigation of the crime.

In this sentence, the true action is not in the weak verb (*conducted*), but rather what is buried in the object (*investigation*). By using the nominalization, the writer was forced to use the prepositional phrase "of the crime." Rewritten to eliminate the nominalization—that is, expressing the real action in a more active verb—results in a shorter and more direct sentence.

Revised Sentence 15: The police investigated the crime.

Lawyers frequently use these nominalizations, all of which can be turned into simple, active verbs:

> determination ⇨ determine
> commencement ⇨ commence (or even better, begin)
> investigation ⇨ investigate
> reliance ⇨ rely
> failure ⇨ fail
> formulation ⇨ formulate
> submission ⇨ submit
> application ⇨ apply
> violation ⇨ violate
> analysis ⇨ analyze
> agreement ⇨ agree
> settlement ⇨ settle.

Sentence 16: The handwriting expert *did an analysis of* the letter.
Revised Sentence 16: The handwriting expert *analyzed* the letter.

Sentence 17: Our *submission* is *in support of* our petition.
Revised Sentence 17: We *submit* this affidavit *to support* our petition.

b.   Remove the action from adjectives

Sometimes the writer puts the action of a sentence or clause into an adjective rather than a noun. The same principle applies: the action should be in the verb.

Sentence 18: He was *supportive* of her efforts.
Revised Sentence 18: He *supported* her efforts.

c. Use strong verbs

Strong verbs express action in their very meaning. Relying too frequently on weak verbs like *is, has,* or *was* robs your writing of vitality. We could have said: "Relying too frequently on *is, has,* or *was* keeps your writing from being vital." The verb "keep" is dull; it has few, if any connotations. The verb *rob,* with its metaphoric richness, more aptly makes the point.

Sentence 19: Two cars were *involved* in the accident at the intersection.

Words like *involve, have, make, do,* and *seem* are weak. They pack little verbal punch. In Sentence 19, what kind of accident was it? The reader cannot tell. The writer should have found a strong verb to express the specific point.

Revised Sentence 19: Two cars *crashed* at the intersection.

There are some writers who rely heavily on weak phrases such as *there is* and *there were,* as in this sentence. Look at your own writing to see if you are guilty of overusing these phrases. Find a way to avoid them. In the sentence above, for example, say: "Some writers rely heavily . . . ," thereby shortening the sentence and beginning more directly.

Do Exercise 10-D Now, p. 211

7. Prefer the active to the passive voice

Active sentences are preferable to passive ones because they are more direct, usually shorter, and therefore easier to read. The passive voice is a verb form that disguises who has done the action expressed in the verb. When a sentence is written in the passive, the subject of the sentence is not doing the action in the verb, but is receiving the action. The passive voice can always be spotted by finding (1) the main verb coupled with a form of the verb *to be* (be, being, been, am, is, are, was, were, has been, will be, etc.) and (2) a prepositional phrase beginning with *by,* either actually or implicitly, in the sentence. For example:

Sentence 20: The contract *was drafted by* the lawyer. (Passive)

Revised Sentence 20: The lawyer *drafted* the contract. (Active)

Notice how in Revised Sentence 20 the subject (the lawyer) is now doing the action (drafting).

Here is an example of the passive construction in which the main verb (seen) is coupled with a form of the verb to be (was). This example contains an *actual* prepositional phrase beginning with *by*:

Sentence 21: The arsonist was seen *by the officer* near the building that burned.

To make this sentence active, eliminate the *to be* verb form and change the object of the preposition *by* into the subject of the sentence:

Revised Sentence 21: The officer *saw* the arsonist near the building that burned.

Here is an example of the passive construction in which the main verb (*seen*) is coupled with a form of the verb *to be* (*was*). In this sentence the prepositional phrase is implicit: the reader must guess who observed the arsonist:

Sentence 22: The arsonist *was seen* near the building that burned.

In Sentence 22, the writer tells us something about the arsonist but not about who spotted him. To make the sentence active, you will need to identify who saw the arsonist:

Revised Sentence 22: The *officer* saw the arsonist near the building that burned.

Despite its overuse, the passive voice is a perfectly grammatical device, and it has important functions. The problem with the passive voice is its misuse and overuse, not its use as such. If you find that you write in the passive voice without any clear understanding that you are doing so and without any good reason, then you should edit your sentences to make them active. But if you use the passive voice because the agent is unimportant, or you choose to comment on the object throughout the paragraph, or you wish to link two thoughts from one sentence to the other, then the passive voice may be quite appropriate. Consider the following sentence:

Sentence 23: The passive voice can always be spotted by finding two syntactical constructions.

Sentence 23 was written in the passive voice (just as this sentence is being written) for two reasons. First, the subject of the verb—that is, the person doing the spotting—is obviously "you," the reader. The sentence could have begun: "You can always spot the passive voice by finding . . . ." But writing the sentence that way emphasizes the reader rather than the thing to which the writer wishes to call the reader's attention, namely, the passive voice itself. Second, the rest of the paragraph is about the passive voice. Focusing the topic sentence on the object makes tighter the connection between each of the sentences in the paragraph. Since you will often choose to comment on the object (that is, the thing to which the action is done) rather than the subject (the agent or person or thing doing the action), you should learn when it is appropriate to use the passive voice.

Sentence 24: More than 50 arsonists were convicted in this city last year.

Criminal defendants are convicted by juries or judges. But the reader of Sentence 24 does not need to focus on the identity of the fact-finders, since it is obvious that if the arsonists were convicted they were convicted by judges or juries. The writer has chosen to focus the reader's attention instead on the object of the convictions, namely, the arsonists themselves. Otherwise, the sentence would read:

Revised Sentence 24a: Juries convicted more than 50 arsonists in this city last year.

This revision is grammatical and clear, but it changes the focus from arsonists to juries. If that is the focus that you want, the revision makes sense; but if your true focus is on the arsonists, then the passive construction of Sentence 24 is appropriate. Moreover, if the writer wishes to be accurate, and some of the arsonists were convicted by juries and some by judges, this would be the resulting sentence:

Revised Sentence 24b: Juries and some judges convicted more than 50 arsonists in this city last year.

This sentence contains more information than is useful, again assuming that the real point is to discuss the number of convictions. The seeming precision of the phrase "juries and some judges" forces the reader's attention to a different point.

The passive voice is useful in linking sentences while applying the principle that older information should come before newer information in each sentence.

Sentences 25 and 26: DNA tests can often identify rapists and murderers. DNA testing *is taught* to forensic scientists in laboratories in all major urban jurisdictions.

The passive voice can also help the writer avoid a top-heavy sentence in which, for example, the subject is extended and the reader must travel a long distance before finding the verb (the subject in the following sentence is in brackets):

Sentence 27: [Baseball players, umpires, managers, coaches, scouts, and even the fans themselves] know the problem.
Revised Sentence 27: The problem *is known* to baseball players, umpires, managers, coaches, scouts, and even the fans themselves.

In the revision, the passive voice permits the writer to put into the object of the sentence the extended list of people who know the problem, thereby connecting the subject, verb, and object much more closely than in the original sentence.

Do Exercise 10-E Now, p. 211

8.   Write concisely: eliminate verbosity and redundancy

Using too many words impairs readability simply because a short document is easier to read than a long one. You have already learned that certain habits— nominalizing and using the passive voice—can make a sentence longer. But the most common reason for the overly long sentence is word clutter. Word clutter comes in different forms: verbosity (unnecessary phrases or expressions and multi-word phrases substituting for a single word) and redundancies (repetitive words and phrases).

a.   Verbosity

Sentence 28: We will discuss my recommendation *with regard to* sentencing *in the event that* you are convicted.

Many lawyers use multi-word phrases when single, everyday words will do. *With regard to* and *concerning the matter of* easily translate into *about. In the event that* and *under circumstances in which* are inflated ways of saying *if*.

Revised Sentence 28a: We will discuss my recommendation about sentencing if you are convicted. Or, even better:
Revised Sentence 28b: We will discuss my sentencing recommendation if you are convicted.

Other inflated phrases include:

- *there is a need for* or *it is important that*: use **must** or **should** [*It is important that* we be there on time. ⇨ We **must** be there on time.];
- *is able to* or *has the ability to*: use **can** [He *is able to* appeal. ⇨ He **can** appeal.];
- *it is possible that*: use **might** or **may** or **can** or **could** [*It is possible that* he will be acquitted. ⇨ He **might** be acquitted.];
- *under circumstances in which*: use **when** [Defendants might be acquitted *under circumstances in which* eyewitnesses have poor vision. ⇨ Defendants might be acquitted **when** eyewitnesses have poor vision.];
- *on the grounds that* or *for the reason that*: use **because** [He was convicted *for the reason that* he lied. ⇨ He was convicted **because** he lied.]
- *prior to* or *subsequent to*: use **before** [*Prior to* the end of the trial, the defendant confessed. ⇨ **Before** the end of the trial, the defendant confessed.] or **after** [*Subsequent to* the end of the trial, the defendant confessed. ⇨ **After** the trial, the defendant confessed.]
- *the fact that*: use **although**, **even though**, or **because** [He missed the trial *due to the fact that* he was late. ⇨ He missed the trial **because** he was late.]

Sometimes verbal clutter arises from the writer's false attempt at precision. The result is an extra word or phrase that can be removed without any loss of meaning.

Sentence 29: The police failed to discover the *existence of* the conspiracy between the arsonist and the building owner.

In Sentence 29, the writer believes that he is being precise by specifying that the police were after the conspiracy's very existence, but the phrase is verbose and unnecessary. To uncover a conspiracy is the same as uncovering its existence.

Revised Sentence 29a: The police failed to discover the conspiracy between the arsonist and the building owner.

You could further revise Sentence 29 by removing the nominalization *conspiracy* to make the sentence even more direct:

> **Revised Sentence 29b:** The police failed to discover that the arsonist and the owner conspired to burn down the building.

Another common verbosity is the phrase "the course of":

> **Sentence 30:** He revealed the secret during *the course of* our phone conversation.

Conversations always have a course or duration so the phrase is unnecessary and should be omitted:

> **Revised Sentence 30:** He revealed the secret during our phone conversation.

In terms of is another overworked phrase in the lawyer's vocabulary and should be avoided:

> **Sentence 31:** It was a favorable case *in terms of* precedent.
> **Revised Sentence 31:** The case was a favorable precedent.

A related kind of clutter is the throat-clearing expression that writers sometimes use to introduce a topic or thought. Expressions such as *it is interesting to note that*, *it is important to point out that*, and *needless to say*, are rarely, if ever, necessary. Let the thought itself carry its own interest or importance: if the point is truly interesting or important, let the reader find it so by how you express it.

b.   Redundancy

Another type of wordiness is redundancy. Redundant words and phrases are those that repeat what has just been said. A simple example is "the officer's uniform is blue in color." Blue is a color, so it is enough to say "the officer's uniform is blue." Other common redundancies are found in paired words, such as *future plans*, *consensus of opinion*, *terrible tragedy*, *each and every*, and *period of time*. Why speak of your "*future plans* for getting a job," when plans necessarily point to the future? *Consensus* means the opinion of most people within the group, so *of opinion* is redundant. And if something is a tragedy, how can it not be terrible? Learn to spot and eliminate these types of redundancies.

> **Sentence 32:** The lawyers joined *together* in the appeal.
> **Revised Sentence 32:** The lawyers joined in the appeal.

Do Exercise 10-F Now, p. 212

☞ **9. Write in the affirmative, not the negative**

Probably because it sounds elegant or complex, some writers habitually use double negatives (such as *not without*) to express an affirmative proposition. For example:

> **Sentence 33:** The defendant's argument is *not without* support under the case law.

The statement is confusing. Does the writer mean that case law does support the argument? Or does the argument have some but not an overwhelming amount of support? Using a double negative is always confusing, almost always ambiguous, and almost always unnecessary. Do not make the reader mull over your possible meanings.

> **Revised Sentence 33a:** The defendant's argument is supported by the case law.

Or, even better, eliminate the passive construction:

> **Revised Sentence 33b:** Case law supports the defendant's argument.

Negative statements can also take a simpler form and be eliminated by carefully choosing the right words. For example:

> **Sentence 34:** The victim could *not recall* the color of the car that hit him.
> **Revised Sentence 34:** The victim *forgot* the color of the car that hit him.

The next time you are tempted to write: "Not many people . . . " write "Few people . . . " instead.

Do Exercise 10-G Now, p. 212

☞ 10. Use precise vocabulary

Because the English language has borrowed from almost every language in the world, it has a rich store of synonyms, and by carefully choosing them, the writer can create quite nuanced prose. Suppose you wish to describe the gait of a severely intoxicated defendant. You might simply say he *walked unsteadily*, or *walked like a drunkard*. But consider these alternatives: lurched, wobbled, staggered, swayed, pitched, listed, tilted, stumbled, reeled, rolled, veered, swerved, and careened.

To keep these nuances straight, you must use a dictionary. Adept use of the dictionary will keep you from any number of verbal blunders. Consider, for example, the problem of prepositions, those short words that connect parts of sentences (in, on, under, around, through, by, of, to, etc.). The wrong preposition can dramatically change the meaning of your sentence.

> **Here is a list of the prepositions that attach to the simple word *look*:** look about, look after, look around, look at, look back, look down, look down on, look for, look forward to, look in, look in on, look into, look on, look out, look out for, look over, look to, look up, look up to, and look upon. *Each phrase has a different meaning.*

Avoid the much overused preposition *as to*; substitute the proper idiomatic preposition instead.

Sentence 35: The debate *as to* the defendant's identity took two days.
Revised Sentence 35: The debate *over* [or *about*] the defendant's identity took two days.

When you use words in a sentence, make sure the words fit together logically. Another common lack of precision comes from the inexact matching of nouns and verbs. For example, in this sentence, the subject and verb do not match:

Sentence 36: The *factors analyze* whether the relationship is parental.

Factors do not analyze, courts and lawyers do. Here is a more precise way to express the thought:

Revised Sentence 36: Courts apply the factors to determine whether the relationship is parental.

Similarly, here the writer fails to precisely relate the phrase "Dismissing plaintiff's claim" with the verb "interpreted":

Sentence 37: *Dismissing plaintiff's claim interpreted* the statute too narrowly.

The sentence's subject (the phrase "Dismissing plaintiff's claim") cannot interpret a statute. What the writer probably means to say is either this:

Revised Sentence 37a: The court interpreted the statute too narrowly when it dismissed plaintiff's claim. *Or this:*
Revised Sentence 37b: The court's dismissal of plaintiff's claim was based on an overly narrow interpretation of the statute.

Here is another sentence that sloppily connects concepts, in this case mismatching the sentence's verb and object:

Sentence 38: The company discriminated against Mr. Smith's religious beliefs.

Civil rights laws prohibit discrimination against people, not things. The company did not discriminate against the *beliefs*; it discriminated against *Mr. Smith* for his beliefs. Revise to link the proper object with the verb:

Revised Sentence 38: The company discriminated against Mr. Smith because of his religious beliefs.

☞ 11. Avoid legalese: Latinisms, pomposities, and bureaucratese

From the first day of law school, you have been learning some bad writing habits quite unintentionally. You have been reading cases and other legal documents, and many of these cases and documents are poorly written. But that writing may seem to you the model that you should follow. Happily, since some time in the 1980s, the old convoluted, pompous, Latinate prose style of the lawyer has been under sustained attack, and many judges and lawyers have begun to write in a more readable style. But much of the old writing style still endures, some of it in older cases that law students must read and some of it produced by lawyers who have not learned their lessons.

A classic instance of legalese run amok is the following passage from an 1842 English case:

> The declaration stated, that the plaintiff theretofore, and at the time of the committing of the grievance thereinafter mentioned, to wit, on, etc., was lawfully possessed of a certain donkey, which said donkey of the plaintiff was then lawfully in a certain highway; and the defendant was then possessed of a certain wagon and of certain horses drawing the same, which said wagon and horses of the defendant were then under the care, government, and direction of a certain then servant of the defendant, in and along the said highway; nevertheless the defendant . . . then ran and struck with great violence against the said donkey of the plaintiff, and thereby then wounded, crushed, and killed the same. [*Davis v. Mann*, 10 M. & W. 546, 152 Eng. Rep. 588 (Exch. 1842), *quoted in* Brian A. Garner, *A Dictionary of Modern Legal Usage* (New York: Oxford University Press, 1987), p. 516.]

This passage illustrates the twin evils of legalese: (1) It makes the writing wordy, trying readers' patience with empty words and phrases. (2) It makes the writing murky, confusing the reader, even though it is intended to clarify.

Although such extended passages today are no longer the norm, the use of unnecessary legal words persists. This does not include the *genuine* **term of art**, the word or phrase that has an exact meaning within the legal system, like "petition for certiorari" or "parol evidence rule." Rather, much legal writing continues to be overrun with terms such as "theretofore," "said," and "hereinafter."

In his well-known *Plain English for Lawyers*, Professor Richard C. Wydick says of legalese: "Lawyerisms are words like *aforementioned, whereas, res gestae,* and *hereinafter.* They give writing a legal smell, but they carry little or no legal substance. When they are used in writing addressed to nonlawyers, they baffle and annoy. When used in other legal writing, they give a false sense of precision and sometimes obscure a dangerous gap in analysis." [Richard C. Wydick, *Plain English for Lawyers* (Carolina Academic Press, 4th ed., 1998) p. 61.]

Another kind of legalese is more subtle and widespread and should be avoided for the same reasons.

Sentence 39: *Pursuant to* his request, the witness arrived at noon.
Revised Sentence 39: As he requested, the witness arrived at noon.

One mark of an insecure writer is the presence of "big" words when simpler words will do. Saying "the trial commenced" instead of "the trial began" makes the writing stuffy, not elegant. Ordinarily you should eschew the polysyllabic (shun large words). Likewise, you should desist from (avoid) pompousities that often are committed to paper (written) as bureaucrat-speak.

Sentence 40: The police *apprehended the perpetrator* at the scene of the arson.
Revised Sentence 40: The police *arrested the arsonist* at the scene.

☞ **12. Avoid hedge words and fillers**

Lawyers often hedge for no reason other than a fear of committing themselves to a position. The hesitation is expressed in qualifiers such as *almost, seemingly,* and *possibly,* which take away the force of a statement. Use these words sparingly, and then only when the qualification is necessary.

Many lawyers also suffer from a verbal caution that adds nothing to their point:

Sentence 41: It would seem that you should tell the truth at trial.

Why be afraid to say point blank that a witness should tell the truth? *It would seem* minimizes the underlying point or even suggests that the opposite might on some occasions be a better choice.

Revised Sentence 41: You should tell the truth at trial.

At the opposite extreme is the reckless writer, who blithely sprinkles his prose with words such as *clearly, undoubtedly, obviously, necessarily, as can be plainly seen,* and *certainly,* as if adding these words will convince the reader that the statements they support are true. If a point is really clear, write a sentence or paragraph that shows it to be so. Do not suppose you have proved your point merely by saying it must be *clearly* so.

Some writers throw in fillers, words that mean little, hoping to make the point more precise. Examples of fillers are *basically, generally, definitely, practically, actually, virtually, given, various,* and *different.* Learn to avoid these words.

Sentence 42: The witness *pretty much* conceded that he did not see the cars crash.

What does this qualifier add to the point of the sentence? Nothing but fill. Write instead:

Revised Sentence 42: The witness conceded that he did not see the cars crash.

☞ 13. Use an appropriate tone

Tone is the manner or mood that the writing sets. When lawyers think about the tone of their writing, they usually are weighing its formality. Consider the following three sentences from a lawyer's letter to a client:

> **Sentence 43**: I am enclosing the contract.
> **Sentence 44**: The contract is enclosed.
> **Sentence 45**: Enclosed herewith please find the contract.

The tone of Sentence 43 is informal, the way one person would talk to another. Sentence 44 is more formal, impersonal, businesslike. Sentence 45 is inflated, pompous, self-important. Setting the appropriate tone depends on the nature of the document you are writing. An informal tone is usually appropriate in writing a letter, unless it is intended as a formal opinion letter. A brief to a court or government agency always should be written in a formal tone. Although many lawyers write in the pompous tone of Sentence 45, you should learn to avoid it. Strive for a quiet, confident tone that does not call attention to itself, as the bombastic, pretentious style always does.

In a brief or formal memorandum, omit references to yourself as the writer. Do not use *I, we, us,* or *our*:

> **Sentence 46**: *I* wish to point out that the law of this jurisdiction requires *our* client, the defendant, to . . .
> **Revised Sentence 46**: The law of this jurisdiction requires the defendant to . . .

Whichever tone you adopt in a particular document, use it consistently. Readers can adapt to your tone, whatever it is, but will have difficulty adjusting to shifts in tone. If you are addressing the recipient of a letter as *you*, do not suddenly refer to him as *the recipient*.

> **Sentence 47**: During *our* afternoon meeting, the applicability of the law became known to *the attendees*.

The first part of the sentence is informal, since it refers to *our* meeting; the second part lapses into a highly formalized and dense description of what happened. Among others attending the meeting were obviously you and I (otherwise, why refer to *our* meeting?), but the writer refers to us, collectively, as *attendees*.

Revised Sentence 47: During *our* afternoon meeting, *we* learned that the law was applicable.

☞ 14. Be grammatical and observe the important rules of usage

Every law student is presumed to have a solid grounding in grammar. But since a few grammatical problems are so widespread, the most serious infractions are reviewed here.

a.   Subject-verb agreement

Sentence 48: The *complexity* of the tax issues and the potential *liability* of a large number of non-debtor affiliates *militates* towards abstention by the bankruptcy court.

Here is a (poorly-written) sentence that might be found in a legal memo. The writer has not noticed that the subject of the sentence is compound—"complexity" *and* "liability"—and therefore requires a plural verb to agree:

Revised Sentence 48: The *complexity* of the tax issues and the potential *liability* of a large number of non-debtor affiliates *militate* towards abstention by the bankruptcy court.

Do Exercise 10-H Now, p. 212

b.   Objects of prepositions

Sentence 49: This matter is highly confidential, so let's keep what we've discussed just *between you and I*.

This expression is one of the most frequently heard mistakes. The word *between* is a preposition and always requires the pronouns that are its objects to be in the objective case.

Revised Sentence 49: This matter is highly confidential, so let's keep what we've discussed just *between you and me*.

Also write *between you and her* not *you and she*.

c. Who-Whom

The distinctions between *who* and *whom* seem to puzzle many people who otherwise know the difference between *she* and *her. Who* is a subject; *whom* is an object. Mistakes often arise because the sentence obscures whether *who* or *whom* is being used as subject or object.

Sentence 50: The jury acquitted the defendant, *whom* everyone thought was guilty.

A simple trick is to substitute *she* for *who* or *her* for *whom*. You can see instantly that you would not say "everyone thought *her* was guilty." Another simple trick is to eliminate the subject and verb that immediately follow who or whom, and if the sentence still makes sense (even if the meaning is changed), then the pronoun should be *who*:

Revised Sentence 50: The jury acquitted the defendant, *who* was guilty.

Because the phrase *everyone thought* can be eliminated (even though the meaning has changed), the proper pronoun is *who*.

d. Proper usage

Usage is simply the *right way* of using words and phrases. Because the language is constantly changing, grammarians and usage experts are never unanimous. But for many contested words and phrases there is a consensus. Good writing requires proper usage. That is why a good usage reference book is as important as a dictionary.

Sentence 51: The penalty for violating the law *is comprised of* three parts.

Although *is comprised of* is often used in spoken language, it is not proper written usage. *Comprise* means to include or contain, not to constitute or compose. You would not say "is contained of," and you should not use *comprise* in that way either.

Revised Sentence 51: The penalty for violating the law *comprises* three parts.

Another common usage error is the phrase *based on*, all too often used as a dangling modifier:

Sentence 52: *Based on* a close reading of the statute, he concluded that his client could make the deal.

This sentence states that "he" is *based on* a reading of the statute. But obviously, he is not *based on* what he read. The writer meant to say that the lawyer's *conclusion* was based on his reading of the law. But in the sentence as written, the phrase "based on . . ." attempts to modify the verb and in so doing winds up making a nonsensical comment about the subject.

Revised Sentence 52a: His conclusion that his client could make the deal was based on a close reading of the statute.
Revised Sentence 52b: He based his conclusion that his client could make the deal on a close reading of the statute.

Another very common usage mistake is the misuse of "where" for "when":

Sentence 53: Students must read assignments nightly, or *where* this is impossible, at least every other night.

The word *where* refers to location, geographic space. The writer used it to refer to time or to a conditional possibility, for which the proper word is *when*.

Revised Sentence 53: Students must read assignments nightly, or *when* this is impossible, at least weekly.

Still another common usage mistake is the omission of a necessary word in a coordinating phrase:

Sentence 54: This case is just *as or more important than* the other case you cited.

The writer is asserting two comparisons between the cases: The one is either equal in importance to the other or it is more important than the other. As written, the sentence seems to be saying about the first comparison that the one case is "as important than." That is improper usage. The proper phrase is "as important as."

Revised Sentence 54: This case is just *as important as or more important than* the other case.

e.   Gender-neutral language

In spoken English, the plural pronouns *they, their,* and *them* are commonly used when referring to a singular noun or pronoun (*everyone, anybody, law school graduate*), as in Sentence 55:

> **Sentence 55:** *Every* law school *graduate* has until June 1 to submit *their* application to take the bar.

In writing, a singular noun or pronoun requires a singular reference: *anyone . . . he; everyone . . . she.* However, applying this rule forces the grammatical writer into using sexist expressions:

> **Revised Sentence 55a:** *Every* law school *graduate* has until June 1 to submit *his* application to take the bar.

English unfortunately does not have a singular, ungendered pronoun to match *everyone, anyone,* etc. To avoid using sexist pronouns, omit the pronoun reference or use the plural.

> **Revised Sentence 55b:** *Every* law school *graduate* has until June 1 to submit *an* application to take the bar. (Pronoun omitted)
> **Revised Sentence 55c:** *All* law school *graduates have* until June 1 to submit *their* applications to take the bar. (Plural)

☞ 15. Use proper punctuation

Punctuation is a crucial ingredient in written work. Proper punctuation makes connections clear. Improper punctuation can obscure or alter the meaning of a sentence. Here are some common punctuation problems:

a.   Apostrophes

Apostrophes indicate either possession or the combination of two words and the omission of a letter or letters in a contraction. Since contractions should not be used in professional writing, the apostrophe usually indicates possession: the *lawyer's* office, the *women's* vote. Words not ending in "s" rarely pose a problem; singular nouns ending in "s" sometimes prove troublesome. Purists require an apostrophe followed by a final "s": *James's* car. Plural nouns take the apostrophe after the final "s": *readers'* eyes. Perhaps the greatest confusion arises between *its* and *it's.*

Sentence 56: The security guard reported that the office door had *it's* lock picked; "*its* wide open," he said.

Both words are incorrectly used in Sentence 56. Referring to the door's locks, the pronoun required is the possessive *its*, without the apostrophe, just as you would say of a person's wallet: *his* or *her* wallet. When the security guard speaks about the door, he means to say that "it is wide open"; *it's* is a contraction for *it is* and takes an apostrophe to indicate the missing letter "i."

Revised Sentence 56: The security guard reported that the office door had *its* lock picked; "*it's* wide open," he said.

Do Exercise 10-I Now, p. 213

b. Commas

Commas pose many problems for the unwary: the omission of one comma when a pair is required, the misuse of the comma surrounding the word *however*, and the substitution of the comma for other punctuation in run-on sentences.

Sentence 57: The *team* of lawyers, working all night *managed* to draft the contract before the office opened.

The phrase *working all night* is an aside, a comment about the team of lawyers. It requires a second comma to set it apart. Not finding it makes the reader lose the connection between the subject, *team*, and the sentence verb, *managed*.

Revised Sentence 57: The *team* of lawyers, working all night, *managed* to draft the contract before the office opened.

Including or omitting a pair of commas can change the meaning of a sentence. Pay attention to the way in which commas tell the reader how the phrase applies to the meaning of the noun that the phrase modifies.

Sentence 58: Lawyers who work all the time are chronically depressed.
Sentence 59: Lawyers, who work all the time, are chronically depressed.

Sentence 58, without the commas, says that only certain lawyers, those who work all the time, are chronically depressed. But Sentence 59 says something quite different: it asserts that *all* lawyers are chronically depressed. The phrase "who work all the time" is a side comment about lawyers in general.

> ***Sentence 60:*** The client managed to find the crucial documents, however, he did not find them until after the lawyer went home.

Sentence 60 is an example of a run-on sentence (sometimes called a *comma splice*, because two separate sentences are incorrectly connected by a comma). When using the word *however* in this sense, you must separate the first sentence from the second with either a period or a semi-colon.

> ***Revised Sentence 60a:*** The client managed to find the crucial documents. However, he did not find them until after the lawyer went home.
> ***Revised Sentence 60b:*** The client managed to find the crucial documents; however, he did not find them until after the lawyer went home.

Although *however* often seems to lead to comma splices, sentences can be run-on in many other ways.

> ***Sentence 61:*** The lawyer was exhausted, he had been working for 36 hours straight.

These are two separate thoughts, each with a subject and verb, and they cannot be joined by a comma. Use a connecting word, a semi-colon, or a period.

> ***Revised Sentence 61a:*** The lawyer was exhausted *because* he had been working for 36 hours straight.
> ***Revised Sentence 61b:*** The lawyer was exhausted; he had been working for 36 hours straight.
> ***Revised Sentence 61c:*** The lawyer was exhausted. He had been working for 36 hours straight.

When beginning a sentence with a connecting word (*and, but, or, because, yet*, etc.), do *not* follow with a comma:

> ***Sentence 62:*** The lawyer told her client that everything would work out. But she was not so sure.

Incidentally, despite what someone may have told you years ago, there is no rule against beginning a sentence with any one of these words.

Do Exercise 10-J Now, p. 213

Much more could, of course, be said about principles of sentence construction, grammar, and usage. The *Merriam-Webster Dictionary of Usage*, for example, is 978 pages long. But the writer who studies and masters the 15 basic principles illustrated in this chapter will avoid the worst mistakes and produce sentences that are guaranteed to be readable.

Exercise 10-A

Correct the following sentence fragments.

1. The inmate asked to use the prison law library. To research the grounds for his appeal.

2. Although the employer knew that sexual harassment in the workplace is illegal. She made sexually disparaging remarks to her male employees.

3. The doctor asked his new partner to sign a restrictive covenant. To prevent unfair competition if the partnership terminated.

Exercise 10-B

Rewrite the following sentences so that the modifiers refer to the correct word(s).

1. Only Trial Advocacy is offered in the third year of law school.

2. Well-written and readable, the lawyer drafted a brief.

3. The evidence, a scarf, was introduced by the prosecutor checkered and torn.

4. The student appealed to the teacher trying to raise his grade.

5. The defendant was distraught because the judge, sentenced to fifteen years in prison, showed no mercy.

6. The court reasoned, at the time the purse was taken, that the defendant acted with felonious intent.

Exercise 10-C

Rewrite the following sentences so that they have parallel structures.

1. When writing a legal memo, you should analyze the relevant case law and why certain facts are important.

2. The court admitted the lineup identification, suppressed the confession, and the severance motion was denied.

3. The first-year student hoped that the workload would diminish and the tests would be easy.

4. The attorney interviewed the client, researched the claims, and the facts were investigated.

5. The law review editor reviewed the chronology of the string citations and that the quotations were accurate.

Exercise 10-D

Rewrite the following sentences to place the action in the verb.

1. The detective's failure to uncover sufficient evidence created despair in the assistant district attorney.

2. The chemist made a determination that the white powder was cocaine.

3. The employer did an analysis of the productivity of its workers.

4. The victim was the owner of the jewels.

5. The debtor made an application for an extension of the term of her loan.

Exercise 10-E

The following sentences are written in the passive voice. Rewrite them in the active voice.

1. A counterclaim for misappropriation of trade secret information was filed by Sam Becker, a defendant in a breach of contract case.

2. The brief, addressing the constitutionality of Nirvana's anti-stalking statute, was written by the moot court team.

3. A severance agreement was executed by Jane Williams and EFG Company.

4. The failure to inspect the tires was realized by the mechanic on duty.

Exercise 10-F

Rewrite the following sentences to make them more concise.

1. The employer could have reasonably concluded and therefore foreseen that the employee was unfit and had something in his background that rendered him dangerous to third parties.

2. Our client, whose name is Jordan Wilson, was engaged in the course of drinking in the company of a friend at a local bar.

3. With respect to the issue of intent, the court admitted the said evidence heretofore offered by the plaintiff.

Exercise 10-G

Rewrite the following sentences in the affirmative.

1. The litigant's argument is not unlike that in the precedent case.

2. The divorce decree will not become invalid unless it was procured by fraud.

3. Not very many of the employees were entitled to a three-week vacation.

Exercise 10-H

Correct the following sentences to make the verbs agree with the subjects.

1. One of the assistant district attorneys in the Office of the District Attorney for Arcadia County are charged with witness tampering.

2. Either the plaintiff or defendant are filing a motion.

3. Neither the nurse nor the medical assistants is able to perform the procedure.

4. Neither the father nor the aunt are competent to care for the child.

5. The jury, after deliberating for two weeks, are ready to render a verdict.

Exercise 10-I

Insert necessary apostrophes and delete unnecessary apostrophes in the following sentences.

1. The law firm invited its' summer associates to a black-tie fund raiser for it's *pro bono* program.

2. The Hathaways fifteen-year-old son was arrested for vehicular homicide.

3. The publisher gave a list of it's new books to the law school.

4. Its very difficult to master legal analysis in the first semester of law school.

5. The court dismissed the co-defendants counterclaims.

Exercise 10-J

Insert necessary commas, delete unnecessary commas, and correct run-on sentences and comma splices in the following sentences.

1. The lawyer retained a handwriting expert Carter Harris to analyze the documents.

2. The check vouchers however did not incriminate the politician.

3. The student was an excellent writer but she did not proofread her brief before submitting it to a prospective employer.

4. The landlord installed smoke detectors and, repaired the broken door locks.

5. She prepared, for the oral argument, by reviewing the trial transcripts and briefs.

6. The lawyer was late for the hearing. But, he had an excuse.

7. The defendant wanted to represent herself at trial, she thought her attorney was incompetent.

8. Jones filed a negligence claim against the supermarket when she was shopping there she slipped on a banana peel and broke her ankle.

9. The parents complained about the dangerous conditions in their children's school, they wanted metal detectors installed at the entrances to the building.

10. Madison's business is incorporated in Delaware he wants Florida law to apply to the contract.

CHAPTER 11

Revising for Effectiveness and Editing for Readability

When you master this chapter, you will understand why every document must be

1. revised and edited;

2. properly structured; and

3. edited in discrete steps.

A. The First Draft Is Only the Beginning

A first draft is only that—a draft, a beginning. It should never be the final product. When presented with a legal question, the lawyer writes his way toward an answer. The first draft may be nothing more than a "brain dump" which memorializes facts, research, and theories. Through the act of composing, the lawyer gropes for the answer. When the answer comes, it is invariably on the paper in bits and pieces, not in a coherent, organized whole. Only when the whole answer is grasped can the lawyer arrange the paper in a way that will best communicate the solution to the reader. This is the task of revising and editing.

Every legal document must be revised and edited for three reasons:

1. To insure that the paper is properly structured—organized to help the reader understand the writer's points and lead the reader to the writer's conclusion.
2. To insure that the facts and the law are relayed accurately and completely.
3. To insure that the sentences and paragraphs conform to the basic principles of writing in Chapter 10.

This chapter demonstrates how to revise for effectiveness and edit for readability, and recommends an editing sequence for all of your writing.

B. Readers' Expectations

Readers have two general sets of expectations when they read a legal document. One set, covered in Chapter 10, consists of expectations about sentence and paragraph arrangement. The other, covered in this chapter, is a set of expectations about the substance of the writing:

• that the writer will provide the reader with whatever information the reader needs to understand what is being written and why, and
• that the writer will enable the reader to understand, on the *first* reading, what is being written and why.

C. Revising for Effectiveness

Revising focuses on the overall *effectiveness* of the document. After writing your first draft, you must reread it, reviewing it for content and organization.

Determine whether it is factually and analytically correct. Ask yourself whether what you have written will make sense to an uninformed reader. Make sure that you have included all of the information the reader needs to understand the document. This is the time to add missing information and explanations, and to delete redundant and unnecessary or irrelevant discussions.

In the second draft, you look at the document to identify its deficiencies and revise it to improve its overall effectiveness. In the next draft, you look at the document to sharpen its clarity and to improve its readability.

D. Editing for Readability

Editing focuses on the *readability* of the document. After writing your first draft and revising it for effectiveness, you are ready to edit for readability. Now is the time to determine whether the reader will be able to easily understand, on the first reading, what you want to say. Remember, the good writer helps the reader achieve the writer's level of understanding with minimal effort. This is readability and can only be accomplished by examining and editing all parts of the document.

1. Formal structure

The formal structure of a document comprises the particular parts required by the type of document you are writing. A common format of a legal memorandum, for example, calls for five parts: Question(s) Presented, Short Answer(s), Summary of the Facts, Discussion, and Conclusion, in that order. Other formal parts may be required for a brief—for example, a Table of Authorities and a Summary of the Argument. These parts will not necessarily aid a reader's understanding; they are simply potentially useful. Office convention or court rules govern the formal structure of legal documents.

But using the conventional formal structure of a document does not guarantee that your reader will understand what you have written. To reach your reader, you must provide a *necessary structure*.

2. Necessary structure

Every paper has a necessary structure—a beginning, middle, and end that, properly written, will inform the reader. The necessary structure is not arbitrary; it is not just *any* beginning, middle, or end that will work. To be readable, your writing must comport with readers' expectations of how a story is told. First, you must furnish readers with a road map to the document, setting out what you intend to accomplish. Second, you must deliver what you promise, supplying the reader with the information that you outlined in your road map. Third, you must draw a conclusion that follows from the information you provide.

a.   The road map: Your thesis

Imagine that a friend calls you up and says at the beginning of the conversation: "Hello. You'll see a supermarket on your right. That's how you'll know you're getting close." Would you have any idea what she is talking about? Start the conversation again. She invites you to spend the weekend at her house. Now the line about the supermarket has taken on context: it was part of the directions to her house. Even so, when giving directions to your home, you do not begin by saying: "Let me tell you first about a really interesting landmark you'll see somewhere near the middle." When you give directions you first say why you are providing them and then, beginning at the beginning, you literally provide a verbal road map: "Here's how you go from here to there."

Every memorandum and other document you write should have a clear and logical beginning. You must provide a road map for the analysis that follows. In the final version of your memo, the reader must encounter at the very beginning of the Discussion the *thesis* that sets the stage and makes clear to the reader what the document will do and why. Refer to Chapter 8 for a detailed discussion of the thesis of an office memo.

In providing an overview, the thesis accomplishes an important objective for both writer and reader. The thesis *focuses* the reader's attention on the legal issues and tells the reader to be on the lookout for a specific story. Thus alerted, the reader will understand the significance of the discussion that follows.

The writer, too, benefits from revising the thesis, for now she must strive to insure that the reader's expectations will be met. In other words, the proper thesis is a road map not just for the reader but for the writer. It tells the writer about to edit a draft what the focus of the discussion must be, highlighting the major points and helping the writer think about the connections among the facts, the law, and the desired outcome.

b.   The Discussion

Following the thesis, the balance of the Discussion of the memo contains the analysis of the legal issues in the form of legal proofs. In editing the draft, the writer should strive to insure that the central part of the paper follows the outline of the thesis.

c. Conclusion

Although you will have highlighted your conclusion in the thesis, you should reiterate your conclusion after the Discussion to provide closure to the memo. Since you want your readers to agree with you and to come away from the document believing in what you have written, the last words should be the point toward which the document has been driving.

E. The Ten-Step Editing Sequence

Editing is the technique by which the writer transforms a raw draft into a readable final document. It is not a random or haphazard process. The writer knows what he wants to say, and that knowledge is communicated to the reader through the words on the page. If those words do not in themselves make sense, the reader will not understand the writer's point.

All writers have had the experience of being puzzled when rereading something they wrote earlier. No doubt they thought at the time they wrote the sentence that it made sense, but as they later read it they were confounded: what could they have been trying to say? During the time between the initial writing and the rereading, the writer's mind has been transformed: the writer no longer remembers exactly what he was thinking when he wrote the sentence. The intention behind the words has either vanished or become opaque. The writer, in other words, is now reading as the reader will. Only then, when the writer becomes the reader and reads as his intended audience will read, is it possible to edit the document to make it readable.

The first thing you must do, therefore, is to let some time elapse between writing the draft and reading it. Waiting until the last minute to write the first draft defeats the purpose. Get in the habit of writing to a "false" deadline. The false deadline will allow you to wait a day or two between writing and editing. Returning to the paper after the delay will enable you to reread it as a potential reader rather than as the actual author.

Of necessity, you must reread the paper more than once, for you will be editing in stages. Approach the editing task as a continuum: begin with large-scale structure and move along to fine detail. The reason for this sequence is obvious: In restructuring the paper you will necessarily be altering sentences and paragraphs. If you begin by editing sentences you will be forced to re-edit them once you get to the large-scale change. In an era of computerized word processing, rearranging and editing sentences and paragraphs (and even moving major portions of the paper) are quick and easy to do. If you are editing on screen you may well find yourself fixing minor errors as you encounter them. Nevertheless, the editing sequence described below is the most efficient and comprehensive method for editing for readability.

---

10 Steps to Editing for Readability

1. Reread for the big picture.
2. Consider your audience.
3. Rewrite the thesis.
4. Use the new thesis to check structure and organization.
5. Check for formal structure.
6. Test topic sentences and the coherence of each paragraph.
7. Review sentence structure.
8. Put the paper away and read it again later.
9. Check length, format, and citation form.
10. Proofread the final hard copy.

---

1. Reread for the big picture

Reread the paper to insure that you have indeed resolved the issues or answered the question completely. You may have convinced yourself late at night that you had done so, but in the cold light of day you may discover that you have not succeeded. If not, keep working until you do.

2. Consider your audience

Once satisfied that you have thoroughly analyzed the issue, you must consider the matter from the perspective of your audience. Who are your readers? What are they likely to know or to have forgotten? Imagine yourself in their place and ask what information should be included to make your point understandable. For example, if you are writing to a partner in your law firm who is extremely familiar with the facts and law in your case, you can omit much of the detail that you would otherwise be required to include if you were writing to someone less familiar with the matter. Ask yourself not only what the reader knows about the law, but also what she knows about the particular matter. Consider also why she will be reading what you write, so you can tailor the writing to your reader's needs.

3. Rewrite the thesis

The thesis of the *finished* document may bear little resemblance to that in the *original* draft. Think about what you have accomplished in the paper you have just reread and write a thesis that sets the stage and provides a road map to the revised document.

4. Use the new thesis to check structure and organization

Using the new thesis to guide you, go through the rest of the paper to check the structure of your analysis. Does it follow the road map in your thesis? Are the main and subsidiary points logically organized, or do the sentences and paragraphs wander? One quick way to check the tightness of your organization is to construct an outline from what you have actually written. Do the topics of each paragraph and section fit into a logical outline, or do you come back later to matters you had covered earlier? If you find bits and pieces of Section I in Sections III and IV, you will need to reorganize. Rearrange until the paper conforms to an orderly outline.

5. Check for formal structure

When you are satisfied that the paper is coherent and properly organized, make sure that the required parts of the document are all present and in their appropriate places.

6. Test topic sentences and the coherence of each paragraph

You are now midway through the editing continuum. At this point you should check to see whether every paragraph has a topic sentence and whether the balance of the paragraph supports that sentence. Also check for the flow of paragraphs and transitions between them: will the reader understand why one paragraph follows the next? Invariably, in editing paragraphs you may find yourself working on sentences themselves, not merely moving them around, because the flow of information depends heavily on the internal structure of sentences. But your major task at this point is to insure that the paragraphs as a whole are properly placed and organized.

7. Review sentence structure

You are now ready to review sentence structure. Your task will be greatly simplified if you go through your entire paper several times, checking each time for different problems. Since the largest obstacles to clear writing are unnecessary nominalizations, passive voice, and interruptions between the standard components of the sentence, you should begin by checking for each of these. Denominalize first. When you do so, you will often find that you necessarily change the passive to the active voice and reconnect parts of the sentence that belong together. But just in case, go through the paper again looking for passive constructions and interruptions between subject and verb and verb and object. Then check to see whether the internal structure of the sentence is as it should be: are you beginning with the less important and older information and moving to the more important and newer? Next, turn to smaller elements of the sentence. Look for verbosity: cluttered phrases and redundancies. Consider your word choice: are you relying on inflated, pompous, Latinate words? Of course, along the way you might spot grammatical difficulties and other sorts of problems that are worth fixing as you encounter them. But if you know you have a particular weakness (pronoun antecedents, subject-verb agreement, or whatever else), read through the paper another time looking just for those errors. Wind up, after all other changes have been made, by checking for proper punctuation.

8.   Put the paper away and read it again later

Make the time to put the paper away to let your editing changes "cool." The same principle that applied to your first rereading of the paper applies to the edited version. You need time to let your mind, which has been actively thinking about what needed to be done, forget why you made the changes you did. You need to read the paper at least one final time from the perspective of your reader, asking yourself again the general question: is what I have written understandable and readable? Do I stumble over a sentence? Do I understand why each of the issues is discussed where it appears in the paper? Have I provided enough background information for the reader to grasp what is at stake and how the issues have been resolved?

9.   Check length, format, and citation form

When you have at last completed your substantive changes and now have the paper the way you want it, check to insure that the citation form is correct. Then see how long the paper is. Many courts, agencies, and offices impose length limitations, either word or page limits, on legal documents. Do not dismiss these limitations as unimportant. Many courts and agencies will reject documents that violate these rules. Also make sure that the paper conforms to whatever formatting rules apply: margin, line spacing, footnoting, and the like. While you are at it, examine how the final document will look: does the top line on a page have only a word or two (what proofreaders call a "widow")? Does a page end with a heading? Revise to give the final paper a polished look.

10. Proofread the final hard copy

If you can satisfactorily answer the questions posed under Step 9, you now must proofread the document in its final form—on paper. Are all the words spelled correctly? Is the punctuation that you added at the last moment properly incorporated in this final draft? You may believe it is unnecessary to read the paper copy because you used your word processor to spell check it. Do not be lulled into a false sense of security. Spell checkers are quirky and full of internal errors. They do not contain many words particular to your document. Moreover, they cannot spot incorrectly used homonyms (for instance, *their* instead of *there*) or simple typos (*that* instead of *than*). Also, what you see on the screen is not always what you get on the printed page. Computer glitches sometimes incorrectly send information to the printer, and the result can be gibberish on the hard copy. Or the paper may not have been placed straight in the printer and the result is a page with uneven or missing lines. Finally, use page numbers and check the order of the pages in the completed paper. You may have taken them out of the printer and stapled them in the wrong order. Once you have completed these steps, you can submit the paper confident that it is correct, concise, coherent, readable, and polished.

CHAPTER 12

Using the Appropriate Law for Your Case

When you master this chapter, you will understand:

1. where laws come from;

2. how the court system is structured; and

3. how to use the appropriate law for your case.

A. Sources of Law

Lawyers look for pertinent legal rules—the law that applies to their cases—in constitutions, statutes, ordinances, administrative regulations, and judicial decisions. To know which law is applicable when analyzing legal questions, you first must have a basic understanding of where law comes from. In Chapter 2, you were introduced to the structure of our legal system and the three branches of government: the legislature, the executive, and the judiciary. In civics classes you learned that the legislature makes law, the executive branch enforces it, and the courts interpret it. As Chapter 2 explained, this description, while accurate, oversimplifies the process of law-making: in reality, all three branches of government play active roles in the making of law.

1.   Law established by the legislature

Legislatures write and amend their constitutions, an important source of law. The United States and all 50 states have constitutions, which create and structure the the relationships among the branches of government, and provide individual rights, such as free speech and a fair trial, against the exercise of government power. In addition, the federal constitution divides powers between federal and state governments.

Federal, state, and local legislatures enact civil and criminal statutes. Laws enacted by a subdivision of a state (county, town, etc.) are called ordinances. As explained in Chapter 5, statutes and ordinances regulate many aspects of inter-personal relationships, business, and government.

2.   Law established by the executive branch

Both the United States and the states have charged a large variety of diverse agencies with the responsibilities of running the government. These agencies promulgate administrative regulations to fill in gaps in the laws passed by the legislatures. Administrative regulations help determine what a statute means and how it should be applied, and they often establish legal rules outside the text of the statute. In other words, administrative regulations can have independent legal authority.

3.   Law established by the courts

Judicial decisions, embodied in the written opinions of decided cases, are called case law or precedent. As noted in Chapter 2, courts write decisions establishing rules of law in areas in which the legislature has not acted, a body of law that collectively is known as the common law. State common law is extensive; federal common law is much more limited. Legislatures may enact statutes to change or even abolish common-law rules that they find to be antiquated, unworkable, or inconsistent with public policy.

Courts also write decisions in cases interpreting the scope and applicability of constitutional provisions, statutes, ordinances, and administrative regulations. Litigants frequently call upon the courts to explain the meaning of legislative and executive law and previous judicial decisions.

4. The hierarchy of law

All laws are not created equal. Laws are hierarchical: some legal rules are more important than others. A constitutional rule "trumps" a conflicting statute, just as a statute trumps conflicting administrative regulations and common-law rules. On the other hand, a court decision interpreting a constitution has the legal effect of establishing the meaning of the constitutional provision and how it will be applied to the facts of the case before the court. A court's interpretation of the constitution can be overturned only by a higher court or by a constitutional amendment.

Not only are the types of laws arranged in a hierarchy, but so also are the types of courts that hear cases interpreting and applying the laws. To understand how to use the appropriate law in a case, you must master the hierarchy of laws and courts.

B. Overview of the Court System

The American judicial system has two parallel court systems: the federal and state judiciaries. Federal courts have jurisdiction—i.e., authority—to hear cases in which

- one of the legal claims arises from the federal constitution, a treaty, or a federal law;
- the parties are from different states and the amount in controversy exceeds $75,000 (this is called **diversity of citizenship** jurisdiction or often, simply, **diversity jurisdiction**);
- the United States is a party; or
- the controversy is between two states.

States courts have jurisdiction when one of the claims arises from a state consti-tution, state statute, or state common law. Often, federal and state courts have **concurrent jurisdiction**; that is, both a federal and a state court have authority to hear the same claim (although only one court may in fact hear the case). For example, an automobile accident claim in which the parties are from different states may be heard in federal court under its diversity jurisdiction (if the amount in controversy exceeds $75,000) or in the state court in the state in which the accident occurred.

1.   Structure of the federal court system

The federal court system has three tiers (see Chart 1, p. 237): (i) United States District Courts (federal district courts); (ii) United States Courts of Appeals (federal courts of appeals); and (iii) the United States Supreme Court. The federal court system also has specialty courts of limited jurisdiction with authority to hear only particular types of claims. For example, the United States Tax Court hears certain types of federal tax disputes, and the United States Court of Federal Claims resolves disputes involving money claims against the federal government.

United States District Courts are trial courts of **general jurisdiction** because they may try most types of federal cases. Most federal cases begin in the United States District Courts. There are 94 federal districts with a combined total of sev-eral hundred federal district judges. Every state has at least one federal district court, and some have several. Both New York and California have four federal district courts, each covering a designated geographic part of the state. Ordinarily, a single judge will hear a case brought to a federal district court.

A litigant who believes a federal district court erred in deciding his case usu-ally may appeal to a federal court of appeals, the intermediate level of the federal court system. There are thirteen federal courts of appeals (see Chart 2, p. 238). Eleven are identified by number. These eleven courts have jurisdiction over appeals from federal district courts in designated contiguous states and, in some instances, territories of the United States. The United States Court of Appeals for the First Circuit, for example, hears appeals from federal district courts in Maine, New Hampshire, Massachusetts, Puerto Rico, and the Virgin Islands. Cases appealed to a federal court of appeals are heard by a panel of three circuit judges, although in rare instances the entire bench—all the judges of the circuit—may hear a case.

In addition to the eleven numbered circuits, there are two other federal courts of appeals: the United States Court of Appeals for the District of Columbia and the United States Court of Appeals for the Federal Circuit. The United States Court of Appeals for the District of Columbia hears cases from the District Court for the District of Columbia and from many of the federal administrative agencies. The United States Court of Appeals for the Federal Circuit has jurisdiction over certain specialized types of cases, including those involving patents, trademarks, international trade, and government contracts. These cases are tried initially in federal specialty courts like the United States Court of International Trade and the United States Court of Federal Claims.

The highest court in the federal court system is the United States Supreme Court. It has jurisdiction over cases from the United States Courts of Appeals and, when particular issues are involved, the United States District Courts and the highest state courts. The United States Supreme Court has almost complete discretion to choose which cases on appeal to hear. The Supreme Court never sits in panels; appeals are heard by the Chief Justice and the eight Associate Justices sitting together.

2. Structure of the state court systems

Like the federal court system, most state court systems also have three tiers: (i) state trial courts; (ii) state appellate courts; and (iii) state supreme courts (see Chart 3, p. 239). While the highest state courts are usually called "supreme courts," some states use other designations. For instance, the highest state court in New York is called the New York Court of Appeals. Ten states do not have intermediate appellate courts. Others have several intermediate appellate courts of equal authority that hear appeals from particular geographic regions within the state.

Within the state court systems, some trial courts have authority to hear only certain types of cases. These trial courts are often referred to as courts of inferior jurisdiction. Some of these courts have jurisdiction over cases in which the scope of civil or criminal liability is limited by statute. They may hear, among other things, misdemeanor cases and civil disputes in which the alleged monetary damages do not exceed a specified amount. Other state courts of inferior jurisdiction are specialty courts. These courts hear only particular types of cases, such as those involving housing, matrimonial, juvenile, or probate matters.

Other cases involving state law claims begin in the state trial courts of general jurisdiction. State appellate courts generally hear appeals from decisions rendered in state trial courts. State supreme courts have the authority to review the decisions of the state appellate courts and, in some cases, state trial courts. When certain federal questions are involved, the United States Supreme Court may hear appeals from the highest courts in the state systems.

C. Using the Appropriate Law for Your Case

1. Locate the law that applies to your case: state, federal, or both

When a client or a professor presents you with a legal question, you first must determine what law applies—state, federal, or both. You will then know where to start your legal research: state sources, federal sources, or a combination of the two.

To get a sense of what law applies, you may have to undertake some preliminary factual investigation or preliminary legal research. Try to answer these questions:

- Where do the parties live?
- Does the claim involve parties from different states?
- Where did the event giving rise to the legal question occur?
- Is the matter civil or criminal?
- In civil matters, did the parties execute a contract or other document specifying what law would apply in the event of litigation?
- In civil matters, what is the amount in controversy?
- Does the question involve a claim under the federal constitution or a federal statute?
- Does the question involve a claim under a state constitution, a state statute, or state common law?

Consider the following situations:

- Your client was married in Connecticut, has lived there with her husband for all ten years of their marriage, and now wants a divorce. Preliminary research shows that a cause of action for divorce is a state law claim and that Connecticut law applies because the parties reside in the state as husband and wife.

- Your client is a lobbyist who is being investigated by a United States Attorney for federal campaign fund-raising improprieties. This information would lead you to conclude that federal law applies because your client is being investigated by an arm of the federal government for possible violations of federal law.

- Your client, who works in New York, is denied a promotion after she refuses her supervisor's sexual advances. After preliminary research you would learn that both New York state and federal law may apply. Your

client may have claims for sex discrimination under both New York state
and federal anti-discrimination statutes.

Once you initially have determined what law applies—state, federal, or
both—you must begin in-depth legal research on the legal question. Your initial
determination of what law applies may change after you intensify your research
efforts. You may find, for instance, that a legal question which at first glance
appeared to raise only state law issues may also implicate federal law issues.

2. Determine the controlling legal authority in your case

Most legal issues have a legal rule or set of rules that is controlling—that is,
a rule that determines how to resolve it. You must research your legal question to
locate the controlling legal authority. Determining the controlling legal authority
requires not merely finding applicable statutes or legal rules but also understanding the hierarchy of legal rules. The controlling legal authority might be a
statute, a common-law rule, a municipal ordinance, an administrative regulation,
or even a constitutional provision. In the absence of a rule embodied in the federal or a state constitution, the highest legal authority is a statute. *If a statute
applies, it is the controlling legal authority in your case. The court must apply the
statute to answer the legal question.* When the statute does not provide a definitive
answer (which it often does not), the court then must apply controlling case law
interpreting the statute to arrive at an answer. If no statute applies to your legal
question, the question likely derives from common law. If it is necessary to look
to judicial precedent (as it often will be), you must determine which precedents
are applicable.

3. Find the precedent that applies to your case

As you now know, courts use case law to analyze both statutory and common-law legal issues (as well as legal issues arising under the constitution or
administrative regulations). But not just any court case is a controlling precedent.
Common sense suggests that the principle of *stare decisis* does not require a court
in California to follow a legal rule announced by a court in Maine. To determine
which cases must be treated as precedent, you must understand the distinction
between binding authority and persuasive authority.

Stare decisis applies only if a prior judicial opinion is binding authority. A
prior opinion is binding authority—a true precedent—if it comes from a *higher
court in the same jurisdiction* and is on point. A case is on point if it involves a
similar set of facts raising the same legal issues. If a higher court in a state holds
that a particular rule applies to a particular set of circumstances, courts whose

decisions can be appealed to that higher court must follow the higher court's rules when faced with similar circumstances in a later case.

A court always has the authority to overrule its own decisions—that is, it can decide that a prior legal rule it established is no longer valid unless a higher court in the meantime has confirmed it. Moreover, a higher court can always overrule a lower court's decision. So a state court of appeals can set precedent for trial courts in the state, and a state supreme court can set precedent for its courts of appeals. The U.S. Supreme Court can set precedent for both federal appeals courts and state supreme courts and thus for all the courts in the country.

Persuasive authority, in contrast, is a prior case that is *not binding* on the court but nonetheless is instructive because it involves a legal issue that is identical or similar to the one before the court. A case is not binding on a court when it was decided by a lower court in the same jurisdiction, by a sister court in the same jurisdiction (for example, one trial court may look to decisions of another trial court in the same state), or by courts in other jurisdictions. Often, when there is no binding authority on a particular legal issue, the court will look to persuasive authority to see how other courts have decided the same or similar issues.

a.   Weight of authority in the federal court system

On questions of federal law, federal courts must follow the precedent established by all higher federal courts. These are the basic rules:

(1) A United States District Court is bound by the decisions of the United States Court of Appeals which has jurisdiction over it and by the decisions of the United States Supreme Court. Example: The United States District Court for the District of New Jersey must follow decisions of the United States Court of Appeals for the Third Circuit and of the United States Supreme Court.

(2) A United States Court of Appeals is bound by decisions of the United States Supreme Court. The United States Courts of Appeals for each circuit must follow decisions of the United States Supreme Court.

(3) A United States Court of Appeals is not bound by decisions of other United States Courts of Appeals. Example: The United States Court of Appeals for the Fifth Circuit need not follow decisions of the United States Court of Appeals for the Sixth Circuit.

(4) When there is no binding authority on a question of federal law, a federal court may look to persuasive authority—precedent from lower federal courts or from other jurisdictions (state or federal)—to answer the question. Example: Suppose the United States Court of Appeals for the Ninth Circuit must decide a question which neither it nor the United States Supreme Court has addressed. Since no binding precedent exists, the court can refer to decisions from the

United States District Courts, other United States Courts of Appeals, or state courts for guidance on the question, but it is not bound by them.

Sometimes, state law claims are litigated in federal court. For example, in a federal action based on an alleged violation of the Family and Medical Leave Act, a federal statute, the *federal court* has the authority to hear **pendent** *state* law **claims**—other legal claims deriving from the same incident. In such a case, the federal court must follow state law on all state law questions. Likewise, when a federal court hears a case based on diversity of citizenship it must decide state law claims under the applicable state law, and prior state cases will therefore be binding precedent. (You will study these types of questions in much more detail in courses in Civil Procedure, Federal Courts, and Conflicts of Laws.)

b. Weight of authority in the state court system

On questions of state law, state courts must follow the precedent established by all higher courts in the state and the United States Supreme Court. These are the basic rules:

(1) A state trial court is bound by decisions of the state's highest court and the state's intermediate appellate court if one exists. Example: The New Jersey Superior Court, Law Division, a state trial court, must follow decisions of the New Jersey Superior Court, Appellate Division, the intermediate state appellate court in New Jersey, and the New Jersey Supreme Court, the highest court in New Jersey.

(2) If more than one intermediate appellate court exists in a state, the state trial court is bound by the decisions of the intermediate appellate court in its jurisdiction. Example: The New York Civil Court, Queens County, a state trial court, must follow decisions of the New York Supreme Court, Appellate Term, Second Department and the New York Supreme Court, Appellate Division, Second Department, the intermediate appellate courts that have jurisdiction over it.

(3) An intermediate appellate court is not bound by the decisions of another intermediate appellate court within the state because the courts are of equal jurisdiction. Example: The New York Supreme Court, Appellate Division, First Department is not bound by decisions of the New York Supreme Court, Appellate Division, Second Department.

(4) A state intermediate appellate court is bound by decisions of the highest court in the state. Example: The New Jersey Superior Court, Appellate Division must follow decisions of the New Jersey Supreme Court. Example: The New York Supreme Court, Appellate Division, Second Department must follow decisions of the New York Court of Appeals, the highest state court in New York.

(5) All state courts are bound by United States Supreme Court decisions on issues that control or supersede state law. Example: State courts must follow decisions of the United States Supreme Court on the federal constitutionality of state statutes.

(6) When there is no binding authority on a question of state law, a state court may use persuasive authority—precedent from lower state courts or from other jurisdictions (state or federal)—to answer the question. Example: Suppose the New Jersey Superior Court, Appellate Division, must decide a question which neither it nor the New Jersey Supreme Court has addressed. Since no binding precedent exists, the court may refer to decisions from the New Jersey Superior Court, Law Division, a lower state court, or from other state or federal courts to rule on the question, but it is not bound by them.

Do the Exercise on p. 235 Now

EXERCISE

Choose the correct answer(s) for each question and explain why.

1. You represent a client in a case pending in the Connecticut Appellate Court. The legal question is whether your client has a state common-law claim for intentional infliction of emotional distress. Which of the following might be binding precedent?
   (a) a decision from the Connecticut Supreme Court on the issue of intentional infliction of emotional distress.
   (b) a decision from the state trial court in the town where your client lives on the issue of intentional infliction of emotional distress.
   (c) a decision from the United States District Court for the District of Connecticut on the issue of intentional infliction of emotional distress under Connecticut law.

2. You represent a client in a case pending in the Florida Circuit Court, a state trial court. The legal question is whether your client violated a state election statute. Which of the following might be binding precedent?
   (a) a decision from the United States Supreme Court interpreting a federal election statute.
   (b) a decision from the Florida District Court of Appeal (a state intermediate appellate court with jurisdiction over the court in which the case is pending) interpreting the state election statute.
   (c) a decision from the Florida Supreme Court interpreting the state election statute.

3. You represent a client in a case pending in the United States District Court for the Southern District of New York. The legal question is whether your client has a claim for race discrimination under a federal anti-discrimination statute. Which of the following might be binding precedent?
   (a) a decision from the United States Court of Appeals for the Second Circuit interpreting the federal anti-discrimination statute.
   (b) a decision from the United States Court of Appeals for the Eleventh Circuit interpreting the federal anti-discrimination statute.
   (c) a decision from the United States Supreme Court interpreting the federal anti-discrimination statute.

4. You represent a client in a case pending in the United States District Court for the District of New Jersey. The legal question is whether your client, under New Jersey law, has a common-law claim for breach of contract. Which of the following might be binding precedent?
   (a) a decision from the United States Court of Appeals for the Third Circuit interpreting a federal statute on government contracts.
   (b) a decision from the New Jersey Supreme Court on the issue of breach of contract.
   (c) a decision from the Delaware Supreme Court on the issue of breach of contract under New Jersey common law.

5. Why might the decisions from the courts you selected in answer to Questions 1–4 above not be binding precedent?

Chart 1
The Federal Court System

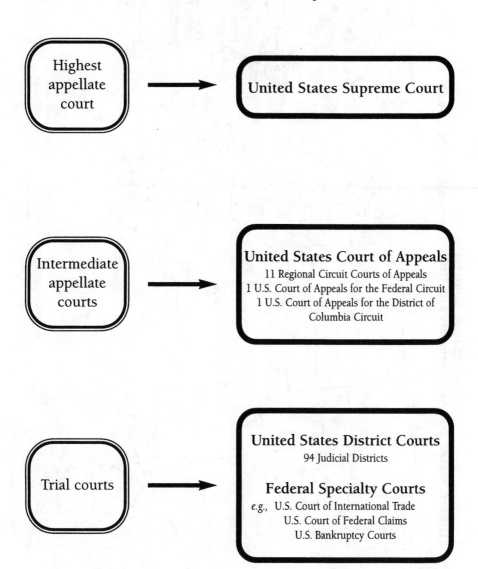

Highest appellate court → **United States Supreme Court**

Intermediate appellate courts → **United States Court of Appeals**
11 Regional Circuit Courts of Appeals
1 U.S. Court of Appeals for the Federal Circuit
1 U.S. Court of Appeals for the District of Columbia Circuit

Trial courts → **United States District Courts**
94 Judicial Districts

Federal Specialty Courts
e.g., U.S. Court of International Trade
U.S. Court of Federal Claims
U.S. Bankruptcy Courts

Chart 2

Geographical Boundaries of
United States Courts of Appeals and United States District Courts

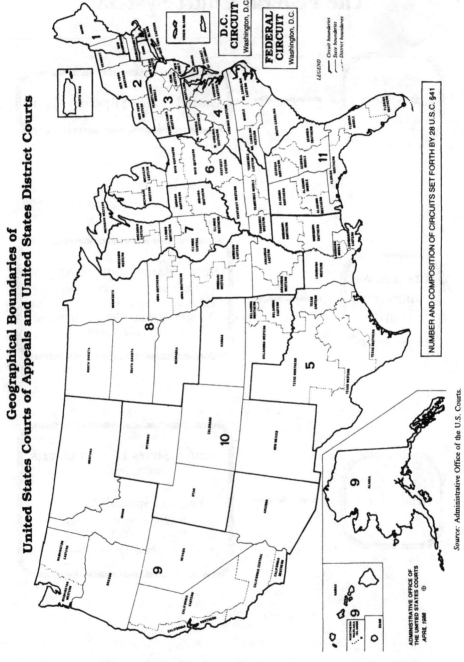

Source: Administrative Office of the U.S. Courts.

Reprinted with permission from BNA's Directory of State and Federal Courts, Judges, and Clerks (2001 ed., compiled by Catherine A. Kitchell, Washington, D.C.) p. xx.

Chart 3 *
N.Y.S. Court System

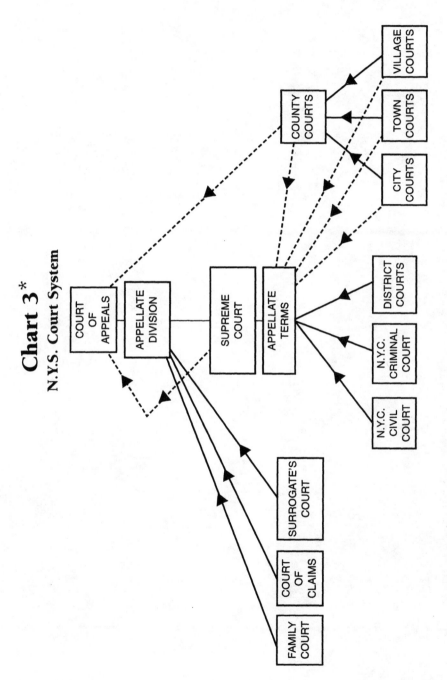

*   Reprinted from *Siegel's Hornbook on New York Practice, 3d*, with permission of David D. Siegel and West Group.

CHAPTER 13

Research Sources and Strategies

When you master this chapter, you will understand:

1. how research, fact gathering, and analysis fit together;

2. what the major sources of research material are; and

3. some strategies for researching legal memos.

I n previous chapters, you learned to analyze issues under controlled conditions. You were given a concise summary of the facts. You were also given the law. If your issue involved a common-law claim or defense, you were given related cases. If the issue was statutory, you were given the statute and some cases construing it. Until now, your task was to identify issues by applying given law to stated facts and then to analyze those issues.

In practice, however, *lawyers* must identify the necessary facts and relevant law. Clients rarely pose focused legal questions, such as whether a particular employment practice constitutes unlawful discrimination under Title VII of the Civil Rights Act, or whether a person has satisfied a specific element of the claim of negligent infliction of emotional distress. Usually clients just tell their stories and explain their concerns. Lawyers gather the facts by interviewing their clients and anybody else who might have relevant information, and by reviewing letters, agreements, documents, and other evidence. Clients depend on their lawyers to determine whether their concerns involve federal, state, or local law, and to understand the controlling law. Finally, clients depend on their lawyers to identify and analyze any issues that result from applying the relevant law to the facts.

This chapter is an overview of how lawyers find and evaluate the relevant law, and how they gradually refine their analysis as they do their research. It is not an exhaustive description of research sources and strategies. Rather, it offers practical advice on how to think about and approach a research project.

A. Research, Fact-Gathering, and Analysis: A Combined Endeavor

Legal research, fact gathering, and analysis are integrally related. To answer a legal question properly, you must understand how these tasks relate to each other. You might think that research precedes analysis: legal issues are identified when you apply the law to the facts, and you cannot apply law that you do not know. So you must research the law before you can apply it. However, research and analysis are intertwined, because while it is true that you cannot analyze an issue unless you know the applicable law, it is also true that you cannot know— or, at least appreciate the significance of—the applicable law until you know the issue.

Your understanding of the facts that relate to an issue develops as you research and analyze the issue. You cannot appreciate a fact's importance until you know the relevant law, but you cannot find the relevant law without knowing the facts. The solution, again, is to recognize that gathering the necessary facts, finding the applicable law, and deepening your legal analysis, are not three separate steps, but one multi-faceted task.

Suppose you represent Susan Johnson, the woman whose nephew was struck and killed by a reckless driver. As you may recall, the issue was whether the woman was *closely related* to the boy, a required element of the claim of negligent infliction of emotional distress. Unless you knew the applicable law well, you probably would not immediately realize that the closely-related element was a disputed issue. Instead, you might approach the problem this way:

- **Fact gathering:** you conduct an initial interview with your client.

- **Research:** you do some preliminary research to determine what the claim might be and to educate yourself generally on its elements.

- **Analysis:** you apply the law to your client's particular situation to determine whether all the elements of the claim are satisfied. After doing so, you might realize that you do not have enough information. Perhaps you did not adequately explore the nature of the relationship between your client and her nephew in your initial interview.

- **Fact gathering:** you speak to your client again to gather specific facts about their relationship, facts that your research suggested you need to uncover.

- **Research:** having obtained additional facts about the relationship, you research for factually similar cases that consider the closely-related element of the claim. After doing so, you might find that facts you thought were unimportant—such as the amount of time the aunt spent with her nephew—are important after all.

- **Fact gathering:** you speak to your client again, asking for specific information about living arrangements.

- **Research:** fully aware of the necessary facts and focused on the identified issue, you continue your research, looking for factually similar cases and reevaluating the relevance of cases you have already reviewed.

- **Update:** once you find the relevant cases, you must determine that they are still good law.

- **Analysis:** you are ready to formulate a rule (based on the cases you determine are relevant) and apply it to your client's particular situation.

The process of researching, fact gathering, and legal analysis will vary greatly from question to question since your knowledge of the facts and applicable law will vary with each question. So you must be flexible in your approach to this task.

B. Research Sources and Formats

Research materials are categorized as either primary or secondary authority. **Primary authorities** reproduce the *actual text of the law*. Primary authority includes federal and state constitutions, statutes, cases, and administrative regulations. **Secondary authorities** help you understand and/or find primary authority. Secondary authority includes (a) *digests,* which are organized by subject and summarize or "digest" the holdings of cases; (b) *narrative secondary authorities,* which discuss or explain primary authority; and (c) *citation services*, which help you find cases and statutes and update the law.

A particular source may function both as primary and secondary authority. For example, annotated codes contain not only the statutes themselves but also commentaries on the law and summaries of cases construing the statutes.

Research materials are available in print and online formats. Since books have been around much longer than computers, many sources (especially older ones) are available only in print. As time goes on, many sources surely will be available only online. For this reason, you cannot rely on only one tool when conducting your research.

Online search tools often provide an alternative to print sources when locating primary and secondary authority. Although many databases on the Internet contain some of these authorities, the most comprehensive search engines and databases are on Westlaw and Lexis-Nexis. It is important to learn how to conduct online searches productively and efficiently because, outside of law school, time spent conducting online searches costs money. Therefore, before going online, you should familiarize yourself with researching techniques on Westlaw and Lexis-Nexis and get hands-on instruction.

1. Primary authority

a. Statutes

Statutes are published in two basic forms: by chronology (in the order they were enacted) and by subject. Statutes passed during a particular legislative session are called **session laws**. Session laws are arranged and published chronologically. The official chronological record of federal laws is *Statutes At Large*.

States also publish their statutes in chronological (or session law) form. When a law is enacted by the legislature, it is first published in a chronological source. So if you were trying to locate recently-enacted legislation, you might start with a chronological source. Chronological sources are also good for finding laws that have been repealed if you know when they were enacted.

Federal and state laws are also arranged and published by subject. These subject compilations are called **codes**. Codes are very useful for statutory research because it is easier to find and review law arranged by subject. Codes are published in official (*i.e.*, by the government) and unofficial form. Many lawyers prefer unofficial codes to the official ones because unofficial codes are more frequently updated than the official codes and because they are annotated.

b. Cases

Reporters (sometimes called *reports*) are sets of books that publish court and administrative decisions. There are separate reporters for federal and state court decisions. Often a particular reporter publishes only the decisions of a single court. *United States Reports* is a single-court reporter, containing the decisions of the United States Supreme Court. So is *California Reports*, the official reporter for California Supreme Court cases. Other reporters publish decisions of a group of courts. For example, the *Federal Supplement* reporter publishes select decisions of all the federal district courts, while *New York Miscellaneous Reports* contains, among other things, select decisions of the New York trial courts.

Not all reporters are organized by court or court system. Instead, some reporters are dedicated to cases in a particular area of law. The *Bankruptcy Reporter* publishes cases that interpret and apply federal bankruptcy law. Because the cases in this reporter are determined by subject, not by court, a typical volume of *Bankruptcy Reporter* includes decisions of United States Bankruptcy Courts as well as decisions of federal district courts, courts of appeals, and the United States Supreme Court. Similarly, in *Federal Rules Decisions*, you will find decisions of various federal courts, all construing federal rules of civil and criminal procedure.

A court's decisions may be published in more than one reporter. For instance, United States Supreme Court decisions are published as collections in three different reporters:

- *United States Reports* (published by the United States government);
- *Supreme Court Reporter* (published by West Publishing Co.); and
- *United States Supreme Court Reports, Lawyers' Edition* (published by Lexis Publishing Co.).

Reporters can be official or unofficial. An official reporter is published or approved by the court or court system. An unofficial reporter is privately published. *United States Reports* is the official reporter of U.S. Supreme Court cases. The other two principal reporters are unofficial. Because the unofficial reporters are annotated and cross-referenced, researchers may find them more useful than the official reporters.

The principal publisher of unofficial reporters is West Publishing Co. West publishes decisions of federal and state courts in all 50 states. West refers to its various federal and state court reporters as the National Reporter System.

Decisions in West reporters are usually preceded by headnotes. Each headnote summarizes a rule of law announced in a decision. Here is a sample headnote from the *Santalucia* opinion published in full in Chapter 3:

> **4. Parent and Child 13(1)**
> Bicycle ridden by five-year-old child was not a "dangerous instrument" for purposes of imposing duty on parents to supervise a child who struck pedestrian; undisputed evidence established that child had been riding bicycle two years prior to the accident, and that he possessed basic skills to ride it and had never had a prior accident.

This one-sentence summary is not the court's holding on this issue. Rather, it is merely a *summary* of a rule of law in this opinion. *Headnotes are written by West Publishing Co. and are not part of the court's opinion.* Although headnotes are not primary authority, they can help you determine if a particular case is on point. Moreover, they are an especially useful tool for finding other cases.

West creates a headnote for each rule of law. A two-page opinion might generate two or three headnotes; a thirty-page opinion 40 or 50. The title that precedes the headnote—"4. Parent and Child"—tells you two things. The "4" means that this headnote is the fourth headnote for *this* opinion. The remaining information in the title is the **topic** and **key number** for that headnote. In the example, the topic is "Parent and Child"and the key number is "13(1)." West divides the law into about 400 topics. Topics are further subdivided into more narrow numbered categories called key numbers. West assigns topic and key number references to headnotes to facilitate research through its Key Number Digests (discussed below) and through Westlaw.

2. Secondary authority

Secondary authorities are books, articles, and annotations that summarize, explain, and help you update the law. Secondary authorities play an important role in research. They provide background information if you are unfamiliar with an area of law and can help you gain enough familiarity with the issue or area of law to begin more detailed research in primary sources or digests. In addition, these secondary authorities may provide you with a valuable citation to a case or a statute, allowing you to move directly to reporters or annotated codes.

a. Digests

A **digest** is a set of books that summarizes (or digests) the holdings of cases in a particular jurisdiction. Digests are comprehensive secondary authorities: they summarize *every* case in a particular jurisdiction or subject. The most widely used case digests—known as West's Key Number Digests—are published by West Publishing Co.

West's Key Number Digests help you find court holdings about specific rules of law. A West Digest gathers the headnotes for the decisions of a particular jurisdiction—the same headnotes that precede these decisions in West reporters— and arranges them by subject. Although West has different digests for different reporters and reporter groups, key numbers are universal—the same key number outline is used in every digest and remains the same across jurisdictions. For example, if you were looking for California cases on duress in the making of a contract, you would find headnotes on this point in West's California Digest under "Contracts 95." "Contracts" is one of more than 400 broad topics into which West has divided the law, "95" is the key number or sub-category within that topic. The title of that sub-category is "Duress." If you were researching this issue under Florida law, you would find Florida cases on duress under the same topic and key number in West's Florida Digest. If you were looking for persuasive authority outside your state, you could consult West's Decennial Digest. The Decennial Digest contains headnotes from all jurisdictions, federal as well as state.

Often West includes a headnote in more than one key number because the rule of law relates to more than one area of law. The headnote is included in multiple topics and/or key numbers to make it easier for you to find the headnote when you are researching an issue.

Digests are useful research aids. Once you get to the key number in the digest that relates to your legal issue, you can review the case summaries in that key number to find cases that appear to be relevant. Of course, since annotations and headnotes are not primary authority, you must read the full text of the decision to determine whether a case that seems relevant really is.

b.   Narrative secondary authorities

Narrative secondary authorities are more narrowly focused than digests. Narrative secondary authorities generally give you an overview of the law, citing only important or representative cases, and are not updated as frequently as digests, if at all. As a result, they are best used for background information and issue identification.

Legal encyclopedias, like *Corpus Juris Secundum* and *American Jurisprudence*, are narrative secondary authorities that offer background information about particular areas of law. To find an entry in a legal encyclopedia, use its index. If you know the appropriate entry, you can use the index at the end of the entry to find the relevant section. In addition, you can access *American Jurisprudence* online.

Hornbooks and treatises are narrative secondary authorities that cover a broad area of law, such as torts, contracts, employment discrimination, or constitutional law. These books are especially useful if you know the area of law that relates to your client's problem but have not focused on the specific claim or issues. You can review the book's index or table of contents and skim relevant chapters. For instance, if your client's problem related to slander, and you knew slander was a tort, you could review the chapter on slander in a torts treatise to familiarize yourself generally with the claim and its defenses.

Other narrative secondary authorities are more focused and should be consulted after you understand your issue. *Law review articles* often focus on discrete, narrow issues and provide a good survey of the case law related to the issue. Similarly, *American Law Reports* ("A.L.R.") focuses on extremely narrow issues and discusses and summarizes relevant cases on the issue. A.L.R. articles are regularly updated to include the most recent cases. Many recent law review articles, as well as *American Law Reports* articles, are available online too.

c.   Citation services

Legal research often involves a search for relevant statutes or cases. But when you find a relevant case or statute, you must first determine that it is still good law (that is, still in force and not repealed or overruled) before you can rely on it. Citation services help you determine that your case is still good law. They recite the case or statute's treatment history: whether your case has been affirmed or reversed on appeal, or limited, modified, or overruled in a subsequent litigation. The two main citation services are Shepards (available in print, CD-ROM, and online on Lexis) and KeyCite (available on Westlaw).

Moreover, citation services are also excellent case-finding tools. They help you find additional statutes or relevant cases since they contain citations to all jurisdictions. You can also find other cases that have cited your case. Then you can review these other cases to see if they consider the same legal issue and are relevant to your search.

Citation services list not only statutes and cases, but certain secondary authorities, including *American Law Reports* and selected law reviews. So a lawyer researching an issue also might use Shepards or KeyCite to find a law review article or an *A.L.R.* article dealing with the issue he is researching.

C. Strategies for Researching Legal Memos

Finding the law requires a flexible research strategy. As you research, you must constantly review the facts and refine your analysis. You must continue to question whether you understand the issues, and you must choose research sources that are most suitable for your level of understanding at the moment. Research in stages, thinking carefully and creatively at each step. Here are some guidelines for researching a legal memo:

1. Determine the relevant law by doing preliminary background research

Many students plunge into their research by going online, or by reviewing immense collections of case summaries in annotated codes or digests, before they have identified their issue. As a result, they squander their time reading cases that will ultimately prove irrelevant. The reason these students waste so much time is that they have not done preliminary background research in secondary authorities.

Your threshold inquiries are whether your question is controlled by federal or state law, and whether the controlling law is constitutional, statutory, or common law. Determine the relevant law by consulting secondary authorities that offer background information about particular areas of law. Find a hornbook or treatise or an encyclopedia article that discusses the area of the law relevant to your question. Use them not only to identify the relevant law but also to understand the general structure and purpose of the law. All issues arise in a context. If you have a particular issue relating to libel, it is unwise to zero in on your issue without first knowing the elements of a claim for libel and the defenses to it. You can find this information in secondary authorities.

2. Identify and refine the issue

When you have done your preliminary research, determine which principles of law relate to the question. *Apply these principles to the facts of your case.* For instance, once you determine that the crime of aggravated robbery has elements, determine whether these elements are satisfied. You do this by matching each element to the necessary facts in your question. When you cannot match an element or it is unclear whether the element is matched, you have identified an issue that must be analyzed. Remember, closing in on the issue is a gradual process. At each stage of your research, actively apply the law to the facts to identify and refine your issue.

3. Keep the question in mind

As your understanding of the law develops, so should your understanding of the issue. Reread the instructions in the assignment, and understand the question you must answer. Identify the necessary facts. You may find that facts you disregarded initially are now important. Keep going back to the question and the facts.

4. Design a research strategy

When you have completed your background research and identified the issue, you must devise a comprehensive note-taking strategy that works for you. Taking good notes is essential to doing thorough research. Develop a consistent method for taking notes. Remember to use quotation marks and note specific page numbers to avoid inadvertent plagiarism. If you think you have found a relevant case, brief it, and then update it to insure that it is still good law. Note the case's relevant headnote numbers (if you are using a case in a West reporter or Westlaw) and its subsequent history. To avoid duplicating your efforts later, keep a central list of all of the sources you consulted, including those you did not find useful. Jot down your ideas about the issues, possible arguments, and additional areas to investigate as you research. Keep all of your notes in one place and take them with you whenever you do research.

5. Stop researching when you keep finding the same cases

When you understand your issue and your research is not uncovering any new cases, stop researching and concentrate on writing your memo. Give yourself sufficient time to write and rewrite your memo.

6. Continue to update the law

When you decide what cases are relevant, you must update them (using Shepards or KeyCite) to be certain they are still good law. You must continue to update the law periodically to insure that it has not changed (or that you have not missed anything new) since you did your original research. Also, when you update a case, make sure to note all subsequent history (such as an affirmance or a recent denial of certiorari) because certain subsequent history notes must be included in the citations in your memos.

D. Sample Research Strategies

You must also have a research strategy in mind when you begin your research in comprehensive sources. While there are many ways to get to the same law, if you start with one of the following research paths, you will find what you are looking for. Here are two examples of research strategies, one for common-law issues and the other for statutory issues.

1. Research strategy for common-law issues

Step 1A. If your background research yielded a relevant case, then

    a.   read the full text of the case in a West reporter or online;

    b.   note the key numbers of the relevant headnotes; and

    c.   do one of the following:
        (1) review entries under those key numbers in the appropriate West Digest;
        (2) do a Key Number Search in Westlaw, searching for those key numbers in the appropriate federal or state database; or
        (3) use a citation service to find other relevant cases and secondary authorities.

Step 1B. If your background research did not yield a relevant case, then

    a.   find cases in the appropriate West Digest, starting with the Descriptive Word Index; or

    b.   search for relevant words or phrases in Westlaw or Lexis.

Step 2. Read the full text of the cases in a reporter or online. If a case is not relevant, note it to insure that you do not consider it again. If a case is relevant, brief it, and note the key numbers of the relevant headnotes.

Step 3. Find additional cases two ways:

  a.   If you noted any relevant key numbers in step 2 above, then
      (1) review entries under those key numbers in the appropriate West Digest; or
      (2) do a Key Number Search in Westlaw, searching for those key numbers in the appropriate federal or state database.

  b.   Update the most promising cases using Shepards or KeyCite. Using a citation service may lead to other, relevant cases, law review articles, A.L.R. articles, and other secondary sources. If the case has multiple headnotes, update only the relevant headnotes.

2.   Research strategy for statutory issues

Step 1. Find the relevant statutory sections by using the statutory code's Index or Popular Name Table, or search for relevant words or phrases in an online version of the code.

Step 2. Review the relevant statutory provisions and all pertinent definitional provisions in an annotated code.

Step 3. Read the case annotations, looking for relevant cases. Make a list of cases to read.

Step 4. Read the full text of the cases. If a case is not relevant, note it to insure that you do not consider it again. If a case is relevant, brief it, and note the key numbers of the relevant headnotes.

Step 5. Find additional cases three ways:

  a.   If you noted any relevant key numbers in step 4 above, then
      (1) review entries under those key numbers in the appropriate West Digest; or
      (2) do a Key Number Search in Westlaw, searching for those key numbers in the appropriate federal or state database.

  b.   Update the most promising cases using Shepards or KeyCite. Using a citation service may lead to other, relevant cases, law review articles, A.L.R. articles, and other secondary sources. If the case has multiple headnotes, update only the relevant headnotes.

c. Annotated codes have cross-references to secondary authorities. Review the cross references to find relevant law review articles and *A.L.R.* articles.

Do not hesitate to abandon dead ends.

Step-by-step research strategies oversimplify the research process. Have a research strategy, but keep it flexible. Move to more comprehensive sources as your appreciation of the issue develops. Return to secondary authorities if you become confused or lose the "big picture." Be realistic. Recognize when a particular research path is not working and switch to another. There are many research paths to the same law.

Mastering the techniques of research requires lots of practice. New and easier to use research tools are being developed with increasing frequency. This chapter is an overview of basic research sources and strategies. It is not a substitute for a course in legal research.

CHAPTER 14

Citation

When you master this chapter, you will understand:

1. why lawyers must cite authority when writing legal memos and other legal documents; and

2. what citation manuals are and how to use them.

W hen writing office memoranda, briefs, and other legal documents, lawyers must cite authorities (*e.g.*, cases, statutes, law review articles) for the legal statements they make. One reason you must cite authorities is to show the reader that the legal statements in your document are supported by the law or secondary materials. These statements become more credible (and therefore more persuasive) when supported by citations to cases, statutes, or scholarly works in secondary sources. For example, in matters of constitutional law, your opinion does not support a discussion on constitutional principles. So if a legal statement in your writing is based on a U.S. Supreme Court case, you must cite that case to give the statement support and authority.

Another reason to cite authorities is to avoid **plagiarism**. Plagiarism—using another's ideas, facts, or language without correct use of quotation marks, citation, or other attribution—is grounds for disciplinary action, including expulsion, in law school.

A citation also provides information that enables the reader to identify and locate the authority. A citation to a case, therefore, generally includes the case name, the volume and page of the reporter in which it appears, the particular page(s) of the decision that provide support, the court that decided the case, and the date of the decision. Using this information, the reader can retrieve the case and determine whether it is binding or persuasive authority in the matter and whether you have accurately cited it as such.

When citing sources in documents to be submitted in court, lawyers must follow the citation rules of the appropriate court. Cases and statutes often can be found in several sources, and court rules usually specify which source to cite. In addition, lawyers and law students often must comply with rules in **citation manuals**. Citation manuals are reference books that specify the substance and format of citations. Two well-known citation manuals are the *ALWD Citation Manual* ("*ALWD*") by the Association of Legal Writing Directors and Darby Dickerson and *The Bluebook: A Uniform System of Citation* (the "*Bluebook*") by the Columbia, Harvard, University of Pennsylvania, and Yale law reviews.

A. Citation Manuals

You may be required to use a citation manual (most likely either *ALWD* or the *Bluebook*) for your first-year writing assignments, upper-class writing projects such as moot court briefs, course papers, and journal articles, and in practice.

Although you need not memorize your citation manual's rules, you should become familiar with its structure so you can efficiently use it to construct citations. Like most citation manuals, *ALWD* and the *Bluebook* have rules that generally apply to all types of sources—cases, statutes, books, CD-ROMs, trial transcripts, etc.—and rules that separately treat these specific sources. To cite a specific source, you must consult both the general rules and the specific rules relating to that source.

ALWD has fifty rules. Of these, eighteen concern matters common to all citations, such as typeface, abbreviations, and quotation. The other rules are source-specific, separately treating different print sources—ranging from frequently-cited sources like cases, statutes, and secondary sources, to less-cited materials such as interviews, sound recordings, and unpublished works—and on-line sources, including Westlaw, Lexis, and World Wide Web sites.

The *Bluebook* is similarly structured. It has twenty rules, the first ten concerning citation generally and the last ten explaining how to cite specific sources. The *Bluebook* also has a special set of rules at the beginning of the book called "Practitioners' Notes." These rules simplify some of the *Bluebook*'s other rules. The Practitioners' Notes apply to legal memoranda and briefs (*even when prepared in law school*), but not to papers and journal articles.

In addition, both manuals have appendices, providing detailed information about primary sources, local court rules, and acceptable abbreviations.

Familiarize yourself with your citation manual's structure and organization by reviewing its detailed table of contents. (In *ALWD*, you should also familiarize yourself with the "Locator" charts on the inside front and back covers of the book. These charts will help you locate specific rules for the most common sources.) Use your citation manual's detailed index to find rules that you cannot locate using the table of contents.

B. When to Cite

When writing a legal document, you must provide a citation for *every* statement that relies on a source. For example, if you state that a plaintiff in a false imprisonment case must prove the elements of that claim, then you must cite an authority that supports that statement:

Example 1

A plaintiff in a false imprisonment case must prove that the defendant willfully detained her without consent and without authority of law. *Black v. Kroger*, 527 S.W.2d 794, 796 (Tex. Civ. App. 1975).

Moreover, if different clauses in a single sentence draw support from different authorities, your citations must be placed so that they indicate which clause is supported by which authority:

Example 2

Although a defendant willfully detains another if he restrains her movement by threats, *Randall's Food Market v. Johnson*, 891 S.W.2d 640, 645-46 (Tex. 1995), a mere threat of arrest is in itself insufficient to effect a willful detention, *Fojtik v. Charter Medical Corp.*, 985 S.W.2d 625, 629 (Tex. Crim. App. 1999).

According to some citation manuals, if you rely on the same part of the same authority to support several sentences in the same paragraph, you may cite to the authority once at the end of the paragraph:

Example 3

A plaintiff has a sensory and contemporaneous observance of an accident if she (1) sees the victim immediately before the accident, (2) sees or hears the accident, and (3) sees the victim immediately after the accident. Such a plaintiff qualifies as a "percipient witness" whose awareness of the accident caused her shock. *Neff v. Lasso*, 555 A.2d 1304, 1313 (Pa. Super. 1989).

C. Citing Cases

1.   The basic components of a full citation

Like all citations, case citations have two main forms: full citation format and short citation format. As the name suggests, a full citation to a case provides more information about the case than a short citation. When citing a source for the first time, you must provide its full citation. Thereafter, to save space and avoid redundancy, use a short citation. All the above examples are in full citation format. Here is an annotated example of a full case citation:

Example 4

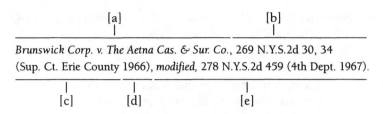

a. *The name of the case.* This part lists the parties to the lawsuit. Case names are often long and unwieldy. For example, a case may have numerous defendants, or a party's name might be very long. Shortening the case name makes it much easier to read and to use as a reference. If you read the case cited in Example 4 in a reporter, its caption would read as follows:

BRUNSWICK CORPORATION, Plaintiff, v. The AETNA CASU-
ALTY AND INSURANCE COMPANY, et. al., Defendants.

It was shortened to *Brunswick Corp. v. The Aetna Cas. & Sur. Co.* using ALWD's rules for shortening case names. The *Bluebook* would use the same case name except that the word "The" would be omitted.

b. *Reporter information.* This part of the citation tells the reader where to find the case, as well as the particular part of the case that is being used to support the statement. You would find *Brunswick* in volume 269 of the *New York Supplement* (*second series*), beginning on page 30. The particular language of the case that supports the statement appears on page 34. A citation to a particular page of a case is called a **pinpoint citation**. Use pinpoint citations whenever possible.

Since cases are often published in more than one reporter, you often have to decide which one(s) to cite to. For example, U.S. Supreme Court decisions are published in three reporters: *United States Reports, Supreme Court Reporter*, and *United States Supreme Court Reports, Lawyer's Edition*. Similarly, the case in Example 4 was published in both the *Miscellaneous Reporter* and *New York Supplement*. Your citation manual specifies which reporters to include in your cite. Example 4 cites to *New York Supplement*, a West reporter, in accordance with *ALWD* and *Bluebook* rules.

In some situations, a court rule or citation manual will require or recommend parallel citations to cases. A parallel citation includes citations to the principal reporters in which the same case appears. A parallel citation for *Brunswick* would look like this:

Example 5

Brunswick Corp. v. The Aetna Cas. & Sur. Co., 49 Misc. 2d 1018,
1022, 269 N.Y.S.2d 30, 34 (Sup. Ct. Erie County 1966), *modi-fied*, 27 A.D.2d 182, 278 N.Y.S.2d 459 (4th Dept. 1967).

Example 5 differs from Example 4 in that it cites not only *New York Supplement* but also *Miscellaneous Reports* (for the case) and *Appellate Division Reports* (for the order modifying the case).

Very often a case is available on Westlaw, Lexis, and the internet. Under both *ALWD* and the *Bluebook*, cite on-line sources only if the case is not available in a reporter. A citation to an on-line case looks like this:

Example 6

U.S. v. Barrett, 1996 WL 636001 at *3 (S.D.N.Y. Nov. 4, 1996).

In Example 6, "1996 WL 636001" is Westlaw's identifier number for that document, and "at *3" is a pinpoint reference. The deciding court and the date of the decision are in parentheses.

c.`Court. This part of the citation identifies the court that decided the case. In Example 5, "Sup. Ct. Erie County" indicates that the case was decided by New York's Supreme Court, Erie County. New York is not specified because the reporter reference—*New York Supplement*—already conveys this information.

d. Date. This part of the citation identifies the date of the decision: 1966. Identifying the year alone suffices when citing to a reporter, but the exact date must be indicated for citations located in other sources, including Westlaw (as in Example 6) and Lexis.

e. Prior and subsequent history. This part of the citation lists other decisions relating to the same case, such as a modification, affirmance, or reversal on appeal. In Example 4, the parenthetical indicates that the cited case was modified and that the modification appears in volume 278 of the *New York Supplement* (*second series*), beginning on page 459.

2.   Constructing a full citation to a case

The best way to write a full citation is to put it together part by part, following the "components list" in Example 4. Consult your citation manual for the rules for the case name, reporter information, court, date, and prior and subsequent history.

3.   Placing a full citation in a sentence

Usually citations to cases follow sentences (as in Example 1) or parts of sentences that they support (as in Example 2). However, citations to a case are sometimes placed in the text of the sentence even when they support the whole sentence:

Example 7

In *Fojtik v. Charter Medical Corp.*, 985 S.W.2d 625, 629 (Tex. Crim. App. 1999), the court held that a mere threat of arrest is in itself insufficient to effect a willful detention.

Citing a case in the text of a sentence makes it harder to read by breaking its flow, so it is best to keep the citation out of the text, as in Example 1.

4.   Short-form case citations

Once a case is cited in full format, the shorter form may be used in the rest of the document. For instance, if you had already cited the *Brunswick* case in full, you could subsequently cite it this way:

Example 8

Generally, material prepared by an attorney for trial is not discoverable by other parties. *Brunswick Corp. v. The Aetna Cas. & Sur. Co.*, 269 N.Y.S.2d at 33.

The short-form citation in Example 8 includes just enough information to enable the reader to locate the support (the case name, volume of the reporter, and page number). It leaves out information already contained in the full citation (Example 4), specifically the beginning page of the decision, the court that decided the case, the date of the decision, and it subsequent history (*i.e.*, that it was modified on appeal).

If you have already cited a case and want to mention it in a sentence, use just the name of one of the parties:

Example 9

In *Brunswick*, the court held that an investigative report prepared for a law firm was material prepared for trial.

After referring to a case by its name, a short-form pinpoint citation is included. When this pinpoint citation is added, Example 9 looks like this:

Example 10

In *Brunswick*, the court held that an investigative report prepared for a law firm was material prepared for trial. 269 N.Y.S.2d at 34-35.

Notice that in Example 10, the pinpoint citation omits the case name. This is an acceptable citation format because the name of the case is already mentioned in the sentence.

5. Typeface

Citations should be in ordinary type. Certain parts of citations, however, must be *italicized* (or alternatively, underlined), including (1) introductory signals, (2) the case name, and (3) phrases indicating subsequent history. These three parts are italicized in the following example:

Example 11

<u>1</u>   <u>2</u>   <u>3</u>
See Priest v. Hennessy, 427 N.Y.S.2d 110 (4th Dept. 1980), *aff'd*, 431 N.Y.S.2d 511 (N.Y. 1980).

6. Abbreviations and spacing

Both *ALWD* and the *Bluebook* offer guidance on abbreviating and spacing. Most of the rules are about what words to abbreviate and how to abbreviate them. These rules are often cross-referenced to lists of abbreviations contained in the appendices in the back of the book. The manuals also specify when to insert spaces in abbreviations.

D. Citing Statutes

When citing a statute that is currently in force and published in a code, the statutory citation must include the following information: the name of the code, the relevant title and section, and the publication date of the particular code volume in which the section appears. A citation to the *United States Code*, an official code, is in this format:

Example 12

11 U.S.C. § 724 (1994).

In Example 12, the number preceding "U.S.C." is the title number, and the number following it is the section number. (The symbol "§" means section.). The date gives the year the volume of the United States Code was published, *not* the date the statute was passed.

If the section you are citing does not appear in the *United States Code* (it may not because the code is infrequently updated), cite to an unofficial code and identify the publisher. A citation to *United States Code Annotated*, an unofficial code published by West Publishing Co., is in this format:

Example 13

42 U.S.C.A. § 2000e (West 1999).

The format for citing state statutes varies. In some states, the relevant code title is indicated by its name, not its number:

Example 14

N.Y. Gen. Oblig. Law § 5-501 (McKinney 1996).

Example 14 identifies the state (New York), the particular title of New York's code in which the section is found (General Obligations Law), the section number (5-501) in that title, the publisher of the code (McKinney), and the publication year of the volume in which the section appears (1996).

Citation manuals have specific rules for citing each state's statutes, as well as rules on citing statutes in short form, referring to statutes in text sentences, and citing newly-enacted statutes that have not yet been published in a code.

E. Miscellaneous Matters

1.   Citing authorities other than cases and statutes

Citation manuals contain specific rules not just on citing cases and statutes, but also on citing a wide range of sources, including law review articles, movies, treaties, speeches, and web sites. To cite these sources and others, find the pertinent rule using the table of contents or index (or in *ALWD*, the Fast Format Locator on the inside front cover) and follow the rule for the citation format regarding that source.

2.   Using signals

Writers cite an authority for various reasons: to identify the source of a quotation, to support a statement, to give an example, to provide background information, or to illustrate a conflict in the law. Signals explain to the reader why the source is being cited. Some common signals are: *E.g.* (cited authority is an example); *See* (cited authority supports the statements); *But see* (cited authority contradicts the statements); and *See generally* (cited authority is helpful background information). In Example 15, the signal *See generally* indicates that the authority is cited to provide helpful background information:

> **Example 15**
>
> You can learn to write an effective brief by thoughtfully organizing, composing, and editing your work. *See generally* Bryan A. Garner, *The Winning Brief* (Oxford U. Press, 1999).

The absence of a signal is significant too: in most citation manuals, omitting a signal means that the cited authority provides direct support for the statement.

3.   Using *Id.*

If you wanted to cite a case in a citation sentence or clause, and have just cited that authority (that is, you have not cited to any other authorities in the interim), then you can use "*id.*" instead of repeating the citation. For instance, if the last citation was to page 34 of the *Brunswick* case (as in Example 4), a subsequent citation to that same case and page would look like this:

Example 16

Unlike the situation in our case, the report in *Brunswick* was sent directly to the attorneys in charge of the investigation. *Id.*

A citation to a page in *Brunswick* different from that of the previous citation would look like this:

Example 17

Unlike the situation in our case, the report in *Brunswick* was sent directly to the attorneys in charge of the investigation. *Id.* at 34.

Do not confuse *id.* with *supra*. Use *supra* to refer to a prior page or part of the document you are writing, not the authority you are citing. For instance, in law review articles, *supra* is often used to refer to a prior footnote in that article. The opposite of *supra* is *infra*: it directs the reader to a later page or part of the same document.

4. Parenthetical information

Sometimes writers include substantive information about an authority in the citation itself. An explanatory parenthetical gives the reader just enough information to understand why the authority is pertinent. This information is given in parentheses following the citation. For example, an explanatory parenthetical about the *Brunswick* case might look this way:

Example 18

Generally, material prepared by an attorney for trial is not discoverable by other parties. *Brunswick Corp. v. The Aetna Cas. & Sur. Co.*, 269 N.Y.S.2d 30, 34 (Sup. Ct. Erie County 1966) (holding that a report prepared by fire investigators for the plaintiff's attorneys was not discoverable by the defendant), *modified,* 278 N.Y.S.2d 459 (4th Dept. 1967).

Parenthetical information may be included in all types of citations—full or short form citations and citations to cases, statutes, books, etc. However, reading textual information in the citation itself is difficult because it is hidden in the citation and written in incomplete sentences. Use explanatory parentheticals only when a fuller discussion of the information in the text would divert the reader's attention from your point or when space is limited.

5.   Quotations

Both manuals have useful rules on quotations, specifying when you should block quote (*i.e.*, separate the quoted material from the text in an indented block) and how to indicate changes and omissions to a quoted text, including when to use ellipses (. . .).

> *Citing legal authority is a required tool of your trade. You must learn how to do it correctly and follow the rules consistently and thoroughly at all times.*

CHAPTER 15

Complex Memoranda

When you master this chapter, you will understand:

1. how procedural and evidentiary considerations affect your analysis;

2. how to analyze and organize a multi-issue discussion; and

3. how to analyze and organize an issue involving factors or balancing tests.

A. Integrating Procedural Considerations Into an Analysis

Previous chapters have focused on substantive law. You learned to identify and use rules to predict how law applied to your case. But courts' decisions are influenced not only by the applicable substantive law—the elements of claims, crimes, and defenses—but also by procedural considerations. Because these procedural considerations influence courts' decisions, your analyses—your predictions on how courts might resolve issues—must account for them. In this section, you will learn how to integrate these considerations into your analysis.

Specifically, this section examines the following procedural considerations:

- **Burdens of proof:** The burden of proof determines which party must prove particular facts.

- **Standard of proof:** The standard of proof is the amount or degree of proof a party must produce to prevail.

- **Procedural posture:** The procedural posture of a case is the stage of the proceeding at which a legal issue is raised. Procedural posture dictates how closely courts scrutinize necessary facts at a particular stage of a lawsuit.

- **Standards of review:** Standards of review dictate how closely appellate courts examine trial court decisions. In other words, they control the degree to which the appellate court may substitute its judgment for that of the trial court. The standard of review depends on the nature of the trial court decision.

To assess how these procedural considerations affect analysis, you must understand the roles of the trial judge, jury, and appellate courts.

1. How the power to decide is allocated among the trial judge, the jury, and the appellate court

a. The jury

The jury is the trial court's principal trier of fact. It examines the evidence at trials (and in criminal cases, at indictment proceedings too) and from the evidence, finds facts. When a jury "finds" facts, it is deciding **questions of fact**. A question of fact is a question about what happened. Here are examples of questions of fact:

Julia Carlin
Gretchen Jenkins
Brian Daitzman

In a criminal action: Was the defendant the man seen leaving the crime scene?

In a civil action for slander: Did the defendant tell the plaintiff's employer that the plaintiff was a crook and should be fired?

Notice that these questions are independent of the law in the case. The answer turns solely on whether the evidence establishes that the event actually happened.

Usually, the jury not only finds facts, but also applies the law to the facts. When the jury applies the law to the facts, it decides a **mixed question of law and fact**—that is, the jury determines whether the facts establish requirements set out in the law. In a criminal case, whether a defendant's actions constituted intentional murder is a mixed question of law and fact. Similarly, in a civil case, whether a supervisor's comments amounted to sexual harassment is also a mixed question of law and fact. Juries rarely announce purely factual findings; usually they render their decisions in verdicts ("guilty," "not guilty," "the defendant libeled the plaintiff," etc.), which are ultimate answers to mixed questions of law and fact.

b. The trial judge

The trial judge's decisions fall into three general categories. These categories are not a complete list of the types of decisions a trial judge makes, and many trial judges' decisions fall into more than one category. The categories do, however, reflect the types of questions that trial judges frequently resolve.

(1) The trial judge decides **questions of law**. The trial judge interprets the substantive law applicable to a case. A question of law is a question about what the law means. For example, Title VII of the federal Civil Rights Act expressly prohibits employment discrimination based on sex. But does that prohibition include sexual harassment? If it does include sexual harassment, does the prohibition extend to same-sex harassment? Both of these questions are questions of law, questions about what Title VII means.

(2) In overseeing the progress of cases assigned to her, the trial judge makes a variety of decisions that can be broadly categorized as case management decisions. She decides, for instance, whether a plaintiff can amend his complaint, whether a party is entitled to examine documents in possession of another party, and whether a party may postpone the trial date. Case-management decisions often raise issues requiring a broad understanding of civil and criminal procedure and evidence.

(3) The trial judge sometimes acts as a **trier of fact**. Although the jury is the principal trier of fact, the judge assumes that role:

- in civil and criminal trials, when the parties have waived or are not entitled to a trial by jury;

- in pre-trial decisions in civil and criminal cases, when the decision requires fact-finding, such as whether the defendant was properly served, or whether a confession was improperly obtained;

- before, during, or after a jury trial, when the trial judge believes that the evidence is so one-sided that any reasonable jury should render a particular verdict.

c.   The appellate court

Appellate courts review decisions made by trial judges and juries. On appeal, the parties cannot (subject to certain limited exceptions) submit new evidence to the appellate court. Rather, the appellate court reviews only the testimony (in transcript form) and evidence that was admitted into the record at the trial level. While some trial-level decisions cannot be appealed until a final judgment is rendered, many rulings can be appealed while the lawsuit is still in progress at the trial level. Appeals taken prior to the entry of a final judgment are called **interlocutory appeals**. The job of the appellate court is to determine whether the lower court committed legal errors. Only under certain limited circumstances may an appellate court review the factual determinations made by a jury or trial judge.

2.   The burden and standard of proof

a.   The burden of proof at trial

The burden of proof determines which party must prove a particular fact. In civil actions, plaintiffs generally have the burden of proving their claims, and defendants have the burden of proving their defenses. Conversely, defendants must prove **counterclaims** (claims asserted by defendants against plaintiffs), and plaintiffs must prove their defenses to counterclaims.

b. The standard of proof at trial

Typically, in civil actions, the party who bears the burden of proof must establish each element of his claim, counterclaim, or defense by a **preponderance of the evidence**. That is, the party with the burden of proving an element must convince the trier of fact that his contention is more probable than not. If the evidence on both sides is equal, the trier of fact must decide against the party with the burden. In some civil proceedings, the standard is higher: the party with the burden must prove his case with "clear and convincing evidence."

In criminal actions, the government has a higher burden of proof. Because a criminal defendant is entitled to a presumption of innocence, the government must prove each element of the crime **beyond a reasonable doubt**.

c. How the burden and standard of proof affect your analysis

When analyzing an issue based on disputed facts, you must take the burden and standard of proof into account. Make sure you know which party has the burden of proof. Review relevant cases to confirm who has the burden and what standard of proof must be met.

Often, you must integrate the burden and standard of proof into your analysis. In particular, the thesis in the Discussion of a legal memo should include who has the burden of proof on each claim and defense. It also should include the applicable standards of proof when pertinent.

Suppose you represent a village—the Village of Kelsey—in a dispute between the village fire department and Harriet Daniels, a woman who suffered severe burns in a house fire. You have been told that the woman was trapped inside her upstairs bedroom when the firefighters arrived, and that after they arrived, the fire spread to her bedroom, severely burning her. Joseph Daniels, Harriet's husband, claims that the firefighters ignored his pleas to rescue his wife and stopped him from running back into the house to do so. If you were writing a memorandum assessing Ms. Daniels's chances of recovering against the village, you should include the parties' burdens of proof, as well as the standards of proof, in your Discussion's thesis:

> To prevail in a negligence action against our client, the Village of Kelsey, *Ms. Daniels must prove by a preponderance of the evidence* that (1) a special relationship existed between her and the village, thereby creating a specific duty to protect her; (2) the village (through the firefighters who responded to the fire) breached that duty by negligently failing to rescue her; and (3) Ms. Daniels's injuries were proximately caused by the village's

breach of its duty of care. Even if Ms. Daniels establishes the village's negligence, the village may nonetheless avoid liability by proving that Ms. Daniels's own negligence contributed to her injuries. In Arcadia, contributory negligence is an affirmative defense, and therefore, *the village has the burden of proving it by a preponderance of the evidence.*

In many cases, it is enough simply to describe the burden and standard of proof in the thesis, without further analysis of these concepts in the legal proofs for particular issues. For instance, it would be premature to assess whether the burden of proof can be met at trial if the matter is in a preliminary stage, and the evidence has not yet been collected. However, when you have evidence at hand, you may need to discuss how the burden and standard of proof affect your assessment of the strength of the parties' claims and defenses.

3.   Procedural posture

The procedural context in which a decision is made greatly affects the decision itself. When a court makes a decision, it must consider the stage of the proceedings and the procedural relief requested by the parties. The degree to which the court scrutinizes the necessary facts is affected by the procedural posture of the case.

In a motion to dismiss, for instance, a party in a civil case asks the trial judge to dismiss another party's claim or defense. Parties allege their claims in **pleadings**. Pleadings outline and explain the parties' claims and defenses. Every civil case begins with at least two pleadings: the complaint and the answer. The gist of a motion to dismiss is that the other party's claim or defense is without legal merit, even if all of the factual allegations in the pleadings are true. Therefore, the motion focuses on what the other party has alleged on paper, not on what that party can actually prove. A defendant making a motion to dismiss for failure to state a claim is in effect telling the court: "Plaintiff has no case. Even if for the sake of argument every fact alleged in the complaint were true, those facts would not satisfy the elements of plaintiff's claim."

In deciding a motion to dismiss, therefore, the court is required to presume, for the purpose of the request, that the other party's version of the facts is true. Suppose, for instance, the plaintiff claims the defendant promised to buy her a car and that the defendant changed his mind and reneged on his promise. The defendant could move to dismiss claiming that a mere promise is not legally enforceable—in other words, the plaintiff, in her complaint, has not stated a legally sufficient claim. For purposes of deciding the motion to dismiss, the court would accept as true the plaintiff's claim that the defendant promised to buy her a car. But since that fact alone is not enough to amount to a contract or any other legally enforceable obligation on the defendant's part, the court would grant the motion and dismiss the case. It would never be necessary to actually prove (*i.e.*, offer evidence) that the defendant made the promise.

Here is an example of how the procedural posture of a motion to dismiss affects legal analysis: Consider the Daniels case again and assume that Ms. Daniels has sued the village. To be legally sufficient, her complaint must describe the facts that support each element of her negligence claim against the village. If you were asked to write a memo assessing whether the village could move to dismiss Ms. Daniels's claim, your analysis would be based exclusively on the allegations in the complaint. At this stage of the case, you would not consider whether Ms. Daniels could meet her burden of proof at trial because, for the purposes of the motion, simply alleging a fact in the complaint makes it true.

Since the court deciding the village's motion will assume that the allegations in the complaint are true and will read those facts in the light most favorable to the plaintiff, so must you. The Summary of the Facts in your memo would recite the allegations in the complaint, regardless of whether the village has denied (or plans to deny) those allegations in its answer. The Discussion must reflect and analyze the procedural issue too. For instance, a memo to the village on the feasibility of dismissing the complaint might contain the following thesis:

> To obtain a dismissal of the Daniels's complaint, *the village must convince the court that the allegations in the complaint do not satisfy the elements of the negligence claim.* Generally, municipalities have no duty to protect their citizens from danger. Therefore, to state a claim against the village, Ms. Daniels's complaint must allege the following elements: (1) there was a special relationship between herself and the village (thereby creating a duty to protect her), (2) the village breached that duty of care, and (3) the village's breach of its duty of care proximately caused her injuries.
>
> A court should not dismiss the complaint for failing to sufficiently allege the second and third elements of the claim. In her complaint, Ms. Daniels alleges that the village acted "negligently, by, among other things, failing to rescue plaintiff and restraining plaintiff's husband from rescuing her." This allegation, if proven, provides a reasonable basis for a jury finding of negligence. Similarly, the complaint alleges that she suffered severe burns and other injuries from the fire as a direct result of defendant's negligence. Again, if proven, this allegation establishes the third element of her claim.

The village might succeed, however, in having the complaint dismissed on the ground that it fails to establish the first element: that a special relationship existed between the village and Ms. Daniels. To satisfy the special relationship element, Ms. Daniels must allege facts satisfying the following sub-elements (1) the village affirmatively undertook to protect Ms. Daniels; (2) the village had direct contact with Ms. Daniels; and (3) Ms. Daniels relied on the village's affirmative undertaking to protect her. Although the complaint alleges facts satisfying the first sub-element, it fails to allege facts satisfying the second and third ones. Specifically, the complaint does not allege that Ms. Daniels had any contact with the firefighters who were attempting to rescue her. Furthermore, although it alleges that the firefighters promised to rescue her, it does not allege that she relied on—or was even aware of—that promise. Therefore, a court might dismiss her complaint on the ground that it fails to state a claim.

4. Standards of Review

When reviewing a trial-level decision, the appellate court is bound by the standard of review. The standard determines how closely the appellate court will examine the trial-level decision.

Different types of decisions are reviewed under different standards. Generally, the standard of review depends on whether the appellate court is reviewing factual determinations (i.e., questions of fact) or legal ones (i.e., questions of law). Because fact-finding often involves judgments about credibility, appellate courts defer to determinations by trial courts (whether made by a judge or jury) on questions of fact, not reversing them unless they are **clearly erroneous**. Since the appellate court is limited to reading the trial transcript and viewing the evidence admitted at trial, appellate judges generally defer to the impressions and judgments of the triers of fact who viewed the testimony first-hand. On the other hand, since appellate courts have legal authority superior to trial courts, appellate courts review questions of law under a **de novo standard** (also called a **plenary standard**), the least deferential standard of review. In a de novo review, the appellate court can freely substitute its judgment for that of the trial court.

The standard of review for mixed questions of law and fact depends on the jurisdiction and the nature of the question. Generally, mixed questions that involve concepts easily accessible to non-lawyers are subject to the clearly erroneous standard. Most negligence cases are reviewed under this standard. An appellate court would not set aside a jury verdict or a trial judge's decision that the defendant was (or was not) negligent unless it could conclude that the fact-finder at the trial level clearly misjudged the evidence. If, on the other hand, the law is particularly complex, then a court is more likely to apply a *de novo* standard.

Like procedural rules, the standard of review affects how you analyze a legal question. For example, your analysis of whether an appellate court will set aside a jury verdict against your client must take the applicable standard of review into account. This standard of review generally requires the appellate court to affirm the jury's verdict unless the jury acted unreasonably.

Assume that *Daniels v. Village of Kelsey* went to trial, and that the jury rendered a verdict against the village. If the village wanted to appeal the verdict, it must consider the available grounds for appeal. If the judge's instructions to the jury were incorrect (and the village had objected to them at the trial level), it could appeal on that basis. Or if the village had objected to an evidentiary ruling at trial, the village could appeal that ruling. Or if the village believed the verdict reached by the jury was against the weight of the evidence, the village could appeal on that ground.

In each of these situations, your assessment of whether the village could successfully appeal would be affected by the applicable standard of review. So your first step would be to find the appropriate standard for each ground for appeal. You would discover that issues about jury instructions and evidentiary rulings are questions of law and are therefore subject to *de novo* review, but that review of jury verdicts are subject to the clearly erroneous standard. Your assessment of whether an appeal would be successful on any of these grounds must take the applicable standard into account.

Appendix C (p. 415) is an example of a legal memorandum that incorporates procedural considerations. Prior chapters analyzed whether Jane Dunn was likely to be convicted of aggravated robbery (see Appendix A, p. 399). Suppose, however, that Dunn went to trial, was convicted by a jury, and wanted to appeal the jury verdict. The question is no longer whether a jury is likely to convict Dunn (that has been definitively answered), but whether an appellate court is likely to overturn that verdict. A legal memorandum on this question appears in Appendix C.

The two memos both focus on the "deadly weapon" element of aggravated robbery. Note how the content and focus of the Dunn memo in Appendix C reflect the applicable standard of review. The Summary of the Facts includes only facts derived from the testimony and evidence introduced at trial. The Question Presented, while focused on the legal issue (whether a crowbar as used by Dunn was a deadly weapon), reflects the appellate posture of the case. And the Discussion's thesis identifies and explains the standard of review.

Legal issues cannot be analyzed in isolation.

Researching substantive law is only part of your inquiry. You must consider procedural law as well. Understand the procedural posture of your case, and learn how the burden and standard of proof or the standard of review will affect your analysis. Only then will your analysis be complete.

B. Discussing Multiple Issues

Sometimes a legal memorandum analyzes more than one issue. The Discussion Section of a multiple-issue memo contains a series of legal proofs—one proof for each issue. Each proof follows the IRAC structure discussed in Chapter 7. To present these legal proofs effectively, you must put them in a logical order. To effectively communicate the structure of your presentation to the reader, you must, at various points in the memo, provide the reader with roadmaps (in the form of thesis sections) and signposts (in the form of headings).

1.   Putting your legal proofs in the right order

When determining the order of legal proofs in a Discussion of a multiple-issue memo, follow these guidelines:

a.   Start with threshold issues

For example, if in a breach-of-contract action there is an issue whether the court has personal jurisdiction over the defendant, discuss the jurisdictional issue before discussing the breach-of-contract issues. If the breach-of-contract claim raises issues about whether a contract exists and—assuming it exists—whether the defendant breached it, analyze the threshold issue of the contract's existence before the breach issue.

b.   Organize issues by claim, crime, or defense

For example, if you are discussing whether an employee has claims for intentional infliction of emotional distress and racial harassment, put the issues relating to the distress claim together and the issues relating to the harassment claim together.

c. Discuss issues relating to defenses after discussing the claim or crime to which the defense is raised

For example, if you are discussing a libel claim and a defense to that claim (such as privilege), first discuss issues relating to the elements of libel and then discuss issues relating to the defense of privilege.

d. Organize issues within each claim, crime, or defense logically

After discussing threshold issues, order issues within each claim, crime, or defense in a logical way that enhances the readability of the memo.

> *(1) Discuss elements in their traditional order.* If the elements of a claim have a traditional order (for instance, the elements of a negligence claim are typically listed as duty, breach, causation, and damage), then present them in that order.

> *(2) Discuss simple issues before complex ones.* If some issues differ in complexity, consider analyzing simple issues before complex ones. If two elements of a claim are disputed, then deal with the simplest issue first, even if this is not the traditional order in which the elements are considered. If one of the disputed elements raises sub-issues and the other a single issue, then start with the single-issue element.

Once you decide the right order for the issues and sub-issues in the Discussion, make sure your Questions Presented conform to this order.

2. Give the reader roadmaps and signposts

After choosing how to organize the legal proofs in the Discussion, you must determine how to signal your organization to the reader. As explained in Chapter 8, every Discussion should begin with a thesis that outlines what is covered in the analysis and ends with a conclusion that answers the questions that prompted the memo.

Multiple-issue memos, however, often require subsidiary thesis sections, providing a road map for particular sections of the memo. Draft subsidiary thesis sections for each major section of your memo. If you are discussing more than one claim, crime, or defense, consider each one in a separate section, and begin each section with a subsidiary thesis.

For instance, suppose you are writing a memo about a personal injury lawsuit against an out-of-state toy manufacturer that raised these questions:

1.   Does the court have personal jurisdiction over the defendant?

2.   Is the defendant liable for the plaintiff's injuries?

These two questions might prompt numerous issues. The first question might raise multiple issues because there are different grounds for giving a court jurisdiction over an out-of-state manufacturer. The second question would likely raise more issues because the plaintiff may have different claims against the manufacturer (such as negligence, breach of implied warranty, breach of contract, and strict products liability), and each of the claims may raise additional issues.

A memo analyzing the issues raised by these questions needs more than just an opening thesis. It should have an opening thesis that introduces the reader to all of the issues, one subsidiary thesis for the part of the memo dealing with the jurisdictional issues and another for the substantive ones. Each thesis section would guide the reader through that part of the memo, preparing her to understand and accept the memo's legal proofs.

In multiple-issue memos, it is helpful to insert headings (*e.g.*: <u>Breach of Contract Claim</u>) at the beginning of each major section of the Discussion. If a section is long, you should insert headings for the sub-sections too. Allow your reader to distinguish between section and subsection headings by designating them differently (*e.g.*: "1," "2," "3" for sections and "A," "B," "C" for subsections) or by giving them different typeface (*e.g.*: SMALL CAPITALS for sections versus Initial Capitals for subsections; or **bold** for sections and *italics* for subsections).

The memo assessing Dunn's chances of successfully appealing her conviction for aggravated robbery is an example of how to organize a multi-issue memorandum (Appendix C, p. 415). The principal issue—whether Dunn exhibited a deadly weapon—raises two sub-issues: whether the evidence sufficiently proved that (1) the crowbar was deadly and (2) Dunn used the crowbar in an assertive manner demonstrating an intent to use it.

The memo's Discussion begins with a thesis section that

- summarizes the law relevant to the broad question (Can Dunn successfully appeal?);
- shows how applying the law to the facts raises the issue and sub-issues; and
- predicts how a court might resolve the issue and sub-issues, briefly explaining the reasoning behind the prediction.

The thesis is followed by two complete legal proofs, one for each sub-issue. Short headings at the beginning of each proof provide signposts to the reader. Follow the Discussion with a Conclusion on the outcome in the matter that answers the general question posed at the beginning.

There is no one pattern or formula for organizing a multiple-issue memo. When creating a structure for your memo, consider the reader's lack of familiarity with the questions and issues covered in it, and structure your Discussion to guide the reader through the issues with a minimum of confusion.

C. Analyzing Issues Involving Factors or Balancing Tests

1. Factor analysis and balancing of interest tests

Because most claims, crimes, and defenses are defined by elements, the issues considered in prior chapters centered on applying elements to facts. Not all legal rules are based on elements, however. Statutes, administrative rules, and cases often list factors to be considered or create balancing tests to resolve legal issues.

Sometimes a legal rule is based on a list of relevant factors that the decision-maker must consider. For instance, some documents (such as letters between an attorney and client) are privileged and therefore need not be disclosed in a lawsuit. The privilege, however, may be waived. To determine whether an inadvertent disclosure of a privileged document waives the privilege, some courts consider

- whether the party asserting the privilege took reasonable precautions to prevent the disclosure of the privileged documents;
- whether the party asserting the privilege promptly objected to the disclosure after discovering it; and
- whether the party claiming waiver will be prejudiced in the lawsuit if the document is not disclosed.

To determine whether an inadvertent disclosure was a waiver, the court would consider the facts of the case in light of these factors. It then would determine whether these factors, *taken together*, favor a holding for or against waiver.

In a balancing test, the decision-maker must weigh competing interests, or considerations. For instance, under some zoning statutes, zoning boards, before granting a variance, must balance these competing interests

- the benefit to the applicant if the variance is granted against

- the detriment to the health, safety, and welfare of the community that might result from its being granted.

Factor analysis and balancing tests give the decision-maker more flexibility than elements. If a statute defines a crime by required elements, then to convict a defendant of that crime, the decision-maker must determine that each element is satisfied. In contrast, in a factor analysis or a balancing test, no one factor is determinative. Rather, the decision-maker assesses the *relative* importance of various factors.

2.   How to analyze issues arising from factors or a balancing test

When analyzing issues resolved by a factor analysis or a balancing test, structure your legal proof like any other IRAC proof:

Issue—a statement of the narrow legal question raised by the facts;

Rule—a description of the applicable factors or balancing test, with rule support (citing to and discussing the statute or case that established the test, as well as any pertinent cases that have applied it);

Application—an application of the test to the facts of your case with case comparisons (comparing your case to and distinguishing your case from the rule cases); and

Conclusion—a conclusion predicting how a court would resolve the issue.

Consider how you would apply a factor analysis for inadvertent disclosure of privileged documents to these facts: the plaintiff serves a request for documents on the defendant. The defendant's attorney does not personally review the documents to be disclosed to the plaintiff but instead delegates this task to his paralegal, who mistakenly gives the plaintiff privileged material. Three months later, the defendant's attorney realizes the error, and two weeks after that files a motion in court to prohibit the plaintiff from using the privileged material at trial. During the three and a half months, the plaintiff decided not to take pre-trial testimony of two employees of the defendant because he believed that the privileged documents he obtained were sufficient to prove his case at trial. Here is how you might structure the analysis:

a. Issue. Like any issue statement, the issue statement in a factor analysis or a balancing-test analysis should be narrowly-framed. However, it need not refer to the factors to be considered under the test.

> At issue is whether the defendant waived the attorney-client privilege on the report he prepared for his attorney when the plaintiff was inadvertently sent a copy of it.

b. Rule. State the test. Since the rule is an established test (as opposed to a synthesized rule), your rule support section need not include an extensive discussion of the facts and holdings of cases applying it. You should, however, describe pertinent cases to establish the test.

> In determining whether a party has waived the attorney-client privilege, courts consider whether the party asserting the privilege took reasonable precautions to prevent the disclosure of privileged documents, whether the party asserting the privilege promptly objected to the disclosure after discovering it, and whether the party claiming waiver will be prejudiced in the lawsuit if the document is not disclosed. *Leland v. Lawyers' Bank & Trust Co.*, 327 Arc. Rpts. 2d 234 (1997); *Simons v. Handy*, 345 Arc. Rpts. 2d 4 (1999).
>
> In *Leland*, the defendant bank mistakenly delivered protected documents to the plaintiff, even though its in-house attorneys had reviewed them. The five privileged documents were in a file containing over 2,000 documents. Five months later, it realized its mistake and initiated proceedings to have them returned. The court stated, "The bank had well-developed screening procedures and moved to correct its erroneous delivery of the report one week after discovering it. We conclude that it did not intend to waive the privilege." 327 Arc. Rpts. 2d at 236. In contrast, in *Simons*, the plaintiff objected to the disclosure of privileged documents fifteen months after realizing its mistake, and the court considered the delay "inordinately long," especially since the defendant had, during this period, used the documents in questioning witnesses and preparing for his case. *Id.* (The *Simons* opinion does not consider whether the plaintiff took reasonable precautions to protect against disclosure.)

c. Application. Assess the importance and strength of each factor separately, comparing or distinguishing your case.

> In our case, a court might find that the defendant failed to take reasonable precautions to protect against disclosure. The defendant delegated to his paralegal the task of determining whether documents were privileged. Certainly this procedure is much less rigorous than the "well-developed" screening process found acceptable in *Leland*.
>
> On the other hand, it appears likely that a court would consider the defendant's objection to be prompt. The defendant objected to the disclosure two weeks after discovering it. This period is not much longer than the one-week delay in *Leland* and is certainly distinguishable from the fifteen-month delay found unacceptable in *Simons*.
>
> Unlike the situation in *Leland*, the plaintiff in our case arguably will suffer prejudice if prohibited from using the privileged document. Like the defendant in *Simons*, the plaintiff's preparation for trial was influenced by his assumption that he would be able to use the privileged material at trial. Although our case is distinguishable from *Simons* on this factor— arguably a fifteen-month delay is more prejudicial than a three-and-a-half month one—this factor nonetheless weighs against the defendant.

d. Conclusion. After assessing each factor separately, assess the relative strength of the factors, indicating whether the factors, taken together, favor one result or another. Remember, however, that because factor and balancing tests are subjective, it is often difficult to predict how a court might apply them. Accordingly, your conclusion may be more tentative than in an elements analysis.

> Although the defendant promptly objected to the disclosure once it was discovered, the defendant's failure to take adequate precaution, coupled with the prejudice that the plaintiff may suffer, makes it more likely than not that a court will hold that the defendant waived the attorney-client privilege for these documents.

In certain situations, it may be impractical to consider factors separately. For instance, in divorce proceedings, courts often consider numerous factors when dividing marital assets and awarding alimony or maintenance. Some of these factors may not apply to the client's financial situation, and others may only be marginally relevant. In that situation, the best approach might be to group relevant factors together—those that favor your client and those that do not—and assess the relative strengths of these two groups.

Deciding whether to separately assess factors in a factor or balancing test calls for judgment. Attempt to assess factors separately, but if this approach becomes cumbersome or confusing, try the grouping-of-factors approach. In any event, make sure you accomplish the goal of the application section, which is to demonstrate how the test is likely to be applied in your case.

Do the Exercise on p. 284 Now

Octavian Kerrov, a restauranteur, has consulted your law firm. He asserts that Dimitri Childes, his former employee, stole his secret soup recipes. Read the facts and summary of law that follows. Outline the Discussion for a legal memo on whether Kerrov's soup recipes are trade secrets.

Facts

Octavian Kerrov owns Jones Street, a fashionable and highly successful restaurant located in New City, Orion. Diplomats, artists, and financiers frequent Jones Street. Kerrov, who grew up in Romania amidst political and social turmoil, is understandably proud of his accomplishments. A master chef in his native Romania, Kerrov serves only dishes that he has personally developed over the years. He is particularly well-known for his robust and fragrant soups. The most popular include beet vodka, potato leek, and sweet and sour cabbage soups.

Employees of Jones Street are advised when they begin employment that all recipes are confidential. Although employees are not required to sign proprietary agreements, the Jones Street handbook, which is distributed to the entire workforce, contains a provision stating that the ingredients used in the dishes and the methods of cooking constitute confidential, trade secret information which is not to be divulged to third parties. Kerrov keeps a booklet of his recipes in a safe at his penthouse apartment. He tells new chefs how to prepare the recipes on the menu.

In recent years, Jones Street has received much media attention. The charming and witty Kerrov has been interviewed by the local news media. He also had a cameo role as a idiosyncratic chef in a popular television sitcom. Despite a longstanding policy of not permitting visitors into the kitchen at Jones Street, Kerrov did allow a select group of food critics and reporters to conduct interviews with his chef in this restricted area. This group was not, however, permitted to bring cameras into the kitchen.

Capitalizing on his acclaim, Kerrov wrote an article for *Cuisine Magazine* in which he described his cooking techniques. This article discussed various ingredients used in several of the soups on the menu at Jones Street. No specific recipes were provided.

Dimitri Childes, the head chef at Jones Street for seven years, resigned in January 2001 because he was dissatisfied with his compensation package. Childes opened a café in New City. This café already boasts a sophisticated and steady clientele. Kerrov was enraged when he recently learned that his two most popular soups—beet vodka and potato leek—are featured items on Childes's menu. Business at Jones Street dramatically declined after Childes opened his café.

Summary of the Law

A trade secret includes information a person uses in his business to gain an advantage over his competitors. Factors a court may evaluate in determining whether information a person uses in his business constitute a trade secret are

"1. the extent to which the information is known outside his business;

2. the extent to which it is known by employees and others involved in his business;

3. the extent of measures taken by him to guard the secrecy of the information;

4. the value of the information to him and to his competitors;

5. the amount of effort or money expended by him in developing the information;

6. the ease or difficulty with which the information could be properly acquired or duplicated by others." [Restatement of Torts 2d § 757, Comment b].

CHAPTER 16

Oral Reports: Talking About Research Results

When you master this chapter, you will understand:

1. why lawyers orally report on research results;

2. how to prepare for an oral report; and

3. what makes a successful oral presentation.

T alking about research results is different from writing about them. When you *write* about your research results, you usually do so in a legal memorandum. The memo may be read by many different readers at different times. The person who asked for the memo will surely be a reader, but the memo may also be read by other attorneys or your client. In addition, since the written memo becomes a part of the case file, it may be read at a later time by other lawyers in your office or firm. In short, the written memo's true audience can be anticipated, but not completely identified. This uncertainty requires you to prepare a formal, comprehensive written document. The writer must insure that all readers know all of the necessary facts, rules of law, and possible interpretations and applications. As a result, the document cannot always be fine-tuned to the needs of known, specific readers.

Talking about research results is much more informal and interactive. When you are asked to *talk* about your research results, you know who your audience is. You can adjust your presentation to their needs. You can answer questions, go into more detail, or even skip over parts of your presentation. Because an oral report is interactive, it provides a flexibility that written memos do not have. However, oral reports do not memorialize the facts, rules of law, or your analysis the way written memos do. The message of an oral report is more holistic—the audience is left with broader impressions and opinions than in a written memo and is less likely to come away with detailed information.

An effective presentation of research results requires you to be well prepared and highly organized. To be successful, you must provide your audience with the right information and create the right impression.

A. The Purpose of an Oral Report

Lawyers are asked to report orally on research results for several, often overlapping, reasons. Often they are asked to answer a question or to solve a problem, as in "Will Jane Dunn be convicted of aggravated robbery?" Sometimes the assignment is narrower—a report on the status of the law or facts (or both), as in "Where do we stand on the Franklin real estate matter?" Sometimes the assignment is broader—to suggest a course of action or to propose a strategic plan, as in "Our client's husband wants custody of the kids and possession of the house. What can we do to prevent this?" Or, "How do we structure this transaction to pay minimal taxes?" Whatever the actual assignment, the expectation is that the oral report will be responsive and informative. Exhaustive preparation is the key to fulfilling these expectations.

B. Preparing for an Oral Report

The key to a successful oral presentation is preparation. Before you can prepare the actual *substance* of the presentation, know the answers to these questions:

1. What is the specific question you have been asked to report on?

Make sure you understand the assignment. Ask for clarification if the initial question is not clear. When you are asked to talk about a question or problem, you must be responsive. Talking about extraneous matters not only may confuse your listener, but also may give the impression that you are confused or disorganized.

2. Who is the audience?

Find out who is expected to attend your presentation. What do they know about the subject, issue, facts, and general area of the law? If you do not know, try to find out. Determine whether your audience has particular questions or concerns they want you to cover. You will save yourself lots of work if you can identify your audience and determine how much they already know before you begin your legal research.

3. What are your time constraints?

When is the oral report to be given? Find out how much time you have to prepare. How much time will you be given to make your presentation? You will have a better idea of what is expected if you find that you have been scheduled for 15 minutes or two hours.

4. What do you already know?

Review the files and your notes, and summarize for yourself the relevant information. Identify gaps in your knowledge and areas to be researched.

5. What do you need to know before you can present your oral report?

Here is where your research begins. Seek out the additional facts you think may be helpful in understanding the law. Research the law exhaustively. Study the law until you are conversant with it. You must understand the law so well that you could explain it clearly and coherently to a non-lawyer.

When you can answer these questions, you are ready to prepare the *substance* of your oral report. Begin by compiling a *detailed outline.* Include the following:

1. Introduction
   a. *Present the specific question or issue.* Identify the purpose of the report.
   b. *Orient the audience with the necessary background information.* Include a brief summary of how the question arose. Explain terms of art, trade practices, statutory schemes, and historical background. The length and breadth of this section is determined by the audience's knowledge. So make sure you know who your audience is and what they know. The more they know, the less you need to say.
   c. *Briefly answer the question.* Tell the audience your conclusion at the beginning of your presentation. Doing so helps to orient your listeners and puts the discussion in context.

2. Discussion
   a. *Explain the applicable law succinctly.* In your presentation, you should not spend much time developing the rules of law. Oral reports do not require the same kind of support as written memos. While your research and analysis must be equally exhaustive, the conversational nature of the oral report precludes lengthy development of legal rules. Explain the law in easy to follow terms. Since the audience can interrupt with questions at any time, you only need to describe the rule. If the audience wants more support or clarification, you will be asked to provide it.
   b. *Review the necessary facts.* Highlight the necessary facts so that your audience will understand why you have applied the law to those facts to reach your conclusion.
   c. *Apply the rules to the facts.* As in a written memo, this part of the discussion is the anchor of your analysis. Compare similar cases or situations, distinguish different cases or situations. Use the law and the facts to show your audience why the conclusions you have reached are inescapable.
   d. *Evaluate your conclusions.* Review possible solutions, courses of action, or strategies. Predict their likelihood.

3. Conclusion
   a. *Summarize the probable outcome.* Here is your ultimate conclusion, stripped of all the disclaimers and hedge words. If you have done a

thorough job in your discussion, your conclusion should be self-evident. If your analysis yields alternative outcomes, do not despair. Present the pros and cons of the alternatives as objectively as possible. Your audience will take it from there.

b. *Recommend a course of action.* Tell the audience what *you* think is the best way to proceed and why. Make sure you let your audience know that you are giving *your opinion* by explicitly stating that you are.

c. *Ask for questions.* Check that your audience is still with you. Did they understand you? Did you miscalculate how much they know? Here is your opportunity to clear up any misunderstandings or add support to your analysis.

Once you have prepared a detailed outline, you are ready to *rehearse* your oral report. Make sure you know both the information in your outline and the information that supports it so well that you do not need it any more. The outline is just a tool to help you organize your thoughts and the presentation.

If you think it would be helpful, prepare a short, one-page outline of your presentation to take with you as a memory prompt. It may help to remind you of the important areas you want to cover and the points you want to make. Practice presenting your report in front of the mirror until you feel comfortable. You should be able to speak about everything important in the proper order without looking at your notes.

C. The Presentation

You have done your research, organized your presentation, and practiced until you can answer any question that comes your way. Now it is time to think about your delivery. Follow these pointers and you should be ready for anything:

1. An oral report is not read; it is *spoken.* Do not read your notes or a written memo.

2. Maintain eye contact and a comfortable, but alert, body posture.

3. The tone of an oral report is *conversational.* You probably will be in an office or small conference room with one, two, or a few people. While the appropriate language is not as formal as the language you would use in an oral argument in court, you still are giving a formal report. Avoid slang, jargon, colloquialisms, and inappropriate humor.

4. Ask how much time you have to make your presentation, and adjust accordingly. If you have more material than time, ask what you should talk about first. Keep your eye on the clock and pace yourself.

5. Be forthright. Use simple, precise, and objective language. Do not try to impress with legalisms, big words, or long sentences. Let your knowledge speak for itself.

6. Be courteous and respectful. Listen carefully and respond appropriately. Do not interrupt others or disagree in a confrontational way.

7. Be responsive. Remember, the purpose of an oral report is to educate your audience, not to show how much you know. Answer questions fully when they are asked, even if they take you off the subject. When you finish answering a question, pick up where you left off. Take notes when follow-up is required. Then make sure you follow up in a timely way.

8. Read body language. Is your audience bored, impatient, lost? If they are not listening or understanding, you are doing something wrong. Adjust your style, pace, or the level of discussion.

9. If the material calls for it, prepare a handout for distribution. Referring to a chart, graph, time line, or tangible article (such as a picture of the crime scene, a complicated statutory provision, or a corporation's by-laws) may save everyone a lot of time and confusion. But do not hand out unnecessary materials just to impress your audience. Audiences know what is superfluous; they will not be impressed.

10. Bring information you might need to answer questions (such as files or statutes) to the presentation so that you do not have to interrupt the report to get something. On the other hand, do not cart in the whole file cabinet "just in case." Be realistic and keep aids to a reasonable minimum.

Now that you understand the purpose of an oral report on research results, and how to prepare for and present one, you should recognize the importance of your role as presenter. A well-prepared, logically organized, and effective presentation can help decision-makers determine their course of action. Your report can help shape their decisions.

CHAPTER 17

Preparing for and Writing the Law School Exam

When you master this chapter, you will understand:

1. the purpose of law school examinations;

2. how to study for law school examinations; and

3. how to organize and write your answers.

A. The Purpose of an Examination

Most professors would say that the purpose of a law school examination is to test a student's ability (a) to spot issues buried in factual situations, (b) to apply legal doctrine to the facts posed, and (c) to present a concise, coherent analysis in an organized and well-written manner.

Some practical considerations also apply: professors want to motivate students to learn the material and, given the realities of school, need to distinguish among students by grading. Remember that it is the *exam book* that is being graded, not you. Your professor grades *what you write down*, not what you know. Your task is to demonstrate by what you say and how you say it that you have mastered the material. To earn credit, you must demonstrate your knowledge clearly and coherently so that your professor can easily understand what you have written.

B. Preparing for an Examination

1. Outline actively

When studying, your goal should be to *master* the material, to be able to say to yourself (and ultimately, of course, to demonstrate to your professor) that

- you understand what was taught in the course,

- you understand the doctrines in the texts, and

- you can apply those doctrines to real-world situations.

You can master the material by preparing *actively*. Do not simply reread the cases, memorize key words, and suppose that you now know the course. Active preparation entails writing an outline or summary of the course, combining what is in your text with the notes you have made in class that clarify the reading and class discussion. Your outline should include the following:

- *The major doctrinal areas you studied.* For example, in torts you might have considered intentional acts, negligence, and strict liability. Study the Table of Contents in your text. The topics listed there will almost certainly tell you the major doctrinal areas of study.

- *The major subtopics within those areas.* For example, under the heading of intentional torts you might have considered assault and battery, false imprisonment, and intentional infliction of emotional distress. Again, many of these subtopics can be found and grouped in a sensible way by studying the Table of Contents in detail.

- *The factual issues.* You must understand what kinds of factual problems arise in the areas you have studied. For example, you will need to know that assault and battery cases can occur not only on the street by a mugger but also in a hospital if the proper consent has not been obtained.

- *The important cases.* Few professors, if any, will require you to memorize the names of cases, although the student who demonstrates mastery of the cases, including their names, is quite likely to get more credit for the same answer. At a minimum, you should strive to know the holdings, reasoning, and the necessary facts of the important cases—those that announce new doctrine or changes in old doctrine.

Do not rely on commercial outlines. Relying on commercial outlines is not productive. They may not be accurate. Their emphasis may be quite different from that of your professor. More importantly, if you rely too heavily on a commercial outline you may be tempted to avoid or skimp on preparing your own. It is the *act of preparation* that is crucial to mastering the material. By preparing the outline *yourself*, you are reviewing the material, assessing its relative importance, and learning how the information fits together. Merely reading a canned outline will not help you develop mastery.

2.   Boil down your outline

To be an effective study aid, your outline should be concise and well-organized. Your initial outline may be quite detailed and sprawling. The next step is to outline your outline, boiling down your initial effort. Do this two or three more times, until you have a concise statement of the law, facts, holdings, and reasoning of the important cases, and policy considerations.

3.   Take practice exams

A paper outline will do you no good at exam time if you are not permitted to bring the notes into the exam room. You should prepare for every exam, therefore, as if books and notes were prohibited in the exam. Many professors file old exams in the library or will give you one if you ask. Take one or more of these exams under closed-book and timed conditions. After taking a practice exam, let it sit for a day. Then go back to it with your outline and book open, read through it, and see how you could improve not only your answer, but your outline.

C. Exam-Taking Strategies

Unlike college exams, in which you were usually asked to recount facts or theories that you absorbed from your reading, almost all law school examinations require you to analyze problems and predict probable outcomes. To develop successful exam-taking strategies, you must consider what kinds of problems your professor is likely to pose and why. You will be called on to *use* the information that you have studied, to show that you have learned to use the law to analyze the problem posed. Understanding this difference should help you see why conventional strategies for writing answers on college exams generally fail on law school exams:

- The "mind dump" strategy: You pour onto a page the contents of your mind, hoping that somewhere in the running verbiage a version of the correct answer will emerge.

- The outline strategy: You jot down point headings, hoping that the organizational scheme will show your professor that you have thought through the law.

- The fuzzy strategy: Maybe this, maybe that. The law is not clear, you figure, so why should your answer be?

- The "look how smart I am" strategy: "Oh, by the way, Professor, I know some other things too."

These strategies waste your time and your reader's time:

- You may never get to the point.

- You may run out of time.

- You risk inviting your reader to conclude that you do not know what was asked or what is relevant.

- You probably will not answer the question.

> *The correct strategy for taking a law school exam is to demonstrate as concisely as possible that you can spot the legal issues and predict the probable outcomes with the facts at hand.*

How can you demonstrate your knowledge on an exam, given a limited amount of time? Here is a systematic way to approach the law school essay examination:

1. *Read through the entire exam quickly.* Get a sense of what you are being asked to answer. Sometimes a second question will shed light on what the professor might be asking about in a first question. Decide which major areas or doctrines are being tested. Do this by comparing the questions with the mental outline you prepared before the examination.

2. *Plan your time.* Determine the weight of each question and make yourself a schedule for writing the answers. If one question is worth twice the weight of another, assume that it has twice as many issues or that your professor considers it twice as important. Spend twice as much time on it.

3. *Read each question carefully.* Read it more than once. Do *not* rush to scribble down thoughts. Ask yourself:

- What am I being asked to answer?
- What are the necessary facts?
- What body of law or doctrine does this question require me to know?
- What legal test or law applies?
- What role am I being asked to play? (Your approach to the answer should be significantly different if you are answering as the plaintiff's lawyer, the judge, or counsel to a legislative committee.)

4. *As you spot issues, jot them down.* Remember that it is the question that creates issues. If the question is whether the plaintiff and defendant have entered into an enforceable contract, you need not consider whether the contract will benefit unrelated parties. Relate the facts to the legal issues you are spotting. Ask yourself how the facts given present or solve the problem. If you are told that the defendant who breached the contract was fifteen years old, you have been told that the defendant was a minor, and therefore the contract may be unenforceable. As these thoughts occur, jot down key words or phrases from which you will assemble an outline. In jotting down issues, consider the significance of each word and phrase. If a question about the enforceability of a contract tells you that the contract concerned a wager and that one of the parties was a fifteen-year-old,

do not talk exclusively about the problem of illegality and ignore the issue of minority. This is the time to jot down *each point* that you are going to discuss. If you omit points here, the odds are high that you will forget to write about them in your answer.

5. *Go back and read through the question again.* This time, check the question against the appropriate section of your mental doctrinal outline to see what is missing. For example, if the question is whether the defendant committed larceny, look to see whether you are presented with facts that satisfy each element of larceny—recalling the elements of the crime will allow you to identify some of the necessary facts that you might have missed on your first reading. If facts about one element are absent, ask yourself whether it is relevant that they are missing and whether you need to make an assumption about their absence.

6. *Outline your answer.* You can now create an organized, sequenced outline from which you will draft your answer. This outline can be quickly assembled from the points you have already written down. Your task is to arrange the points of your answer into a logical, coherent discussion. Once you have an organized outline, you may then proceed to write your answer by expanding the outline in complete, literate, short sentences.

D. Writing Your Answer

A successful answer responds to the question clearly and coherently. Here are some helpful hints for drafting exam answers:

1. *Answer the question asked.* Do not write an essay showing all that you know about the particular area of law involved. If you are asked whether a valid contract has been formed, do not write a historical essay on the development of contract law, or outline the nature of the remedies that might be available if the contract is breached. Just answer the question posed.

2. *Use the facts.* Do not repeat the facts or the question. Use the facts as necessary parts of your answer, but do not provide a lengthy preamble restating what you have been asked. Doing so takes up valuable time and space. Your professor already knows the facts. Assume, however, that your professor does not know the law and that you must explain it, showing how facts in the situation presented require your conclusion under the applicable legal principles.

Suppose you are given these facts: "A has always hated B and for years has been looking for a way to eliminate him. He knows that B will attend a concert on Monday evening. Positioning himself in front of the theater, A waits until B appears and shoots him. B dies." Do not say this: "This is a case involving A, who has long hated B, and who has looked for ways of getting rid of him, who shoots him, which is illegal." Instead, say this: "In shooting B without justification, A is guilty of murder. Murder is the unlawful killing of someone with malice afore-thought. A's knowledge of B's whereabouts and his stalking of B in front of the theater with gun in hand show that A killed B with premeditation."

3. *Make sure your answer is plausible.* You will not get credit for spotting issues that are far-fetched or non-existent, or for arguing a position that is unten-able. Keep your answers grounded in reality.

4. *Begin by stating your conclusion.* By stating your conclusion first, you give your reader a context for understanding your discussion. Otherwise, it is very difficult for your reader to interpret the explanation that follows. Begin this way: "The plaintiff will prevail in her lawsuit because . . ." or "The court should ren-der judgment for . . . ." Make sure your reader knows your conclusion. "The defendant is guilty of murder" or "the contract is not supported by sufficient con-sideration." Sometimes definitive answers can be given; part of the purpose of the examination is to determine whether you can recognize when a factual situation compels a particular legal result. But often, of course, there will be no clear answer, either because the issues are unsettled or because the test applied is not a formula that mathematically determines the outcome. In unclear situations, point out that the law supports alternative conclusions.

5. *Next, explain separately each issue and its related rule.* Omit a long intro-duction. Do not say: "This question involves several legal issues, especially in the area of *mens rea, scienter,* criminal intent, and knowledge of the defendant." Get right to the issue and applicable rule of law: "The question is whether in giving the victim the poison the defendant had the criminal intent to kill her. Murder requires . . . ."

6. *Then, apply the rule to the facts to support your conclusion.* State the rule of law succinctly and then apply it to the facts. Suppose you are asked about a defendant's claim to ownership of property by adverse possession. Do not merely restate the rule: "This property has been adversely possessed because the defen-dant acted in an open and notorious way." This is a conclusion that is not explained or supported in any way. Use the facts to show how the rule is (or is not) met: "The defendant is entitled to claim title by adverse possession because

when he built a garage that encroached on his neighbor's property, he did so openly and in such a way that the construction did not escape his neighbor's attention."

a. Discuss all aspects thoroughly. Consider and respond to each alternative; do not suppose that if under one alternative the defendant should be acquitted of the crime, you need not consider other alternatives, since you might be wrong about the first one. If your answer moots several other potential points, do not ignore those points. Suppose you conclude that the court lacks subject matter jurisdiction. In the real world, if that answer were correct, the court would not need to reach the merits; having no power to hear the case, it would have to dismiss it. But a lawyer would never stop at that point because he might be wrong and the court would then reach the merits.

b. Do not ignore the status of the law. While a lawyer in practice may argue that the holding in a particular case should be overruled, you should not do that on an exam. For example, you will not get points by asserting that the parol evidence rule is wrong and should never be given effect. Only in rare instances might you have a strong reason to argue that the law should (or will) be changed. Stick to the current state of the law. Demonstrate that you know what the law is now.

c. Assume facts only when it is necessary to fill in a gap that might turn the issue one way or the other. Make sure you label your assumptions. Suppose you are told that A gave B aspirin, and because B was allergic to aspirin, he died. You are asked whether A is guilty of B's murder. On these facts, you cannot be sure. You could point out that if A knew about B's allergy, A likely is guilty of murder, but if A had no knowledge of the allergy he did not have the requisite criminal intent.

d. Be objective. Evaluate all sides of the argument. If you are asked whether the facts establish that the defendant was guilty of murder, do not analyze the question entirely from the perspective of the prosecutor or the defendant. Remember that the other side will undoubtedly have an opposing argument. Your task is to present both sides and assess the *strength* of the competing positions, just as in practice a lawyer must anticipate and respond to an adversary's arguments. Show how the facts help support and oppose competing arguments.

7. End your analysis by repeating your conclusion. By the time you get to the end of your answer, your conclusion should be self-evident. Do not miss the opportunity to tie it all together by restating your conclusion.

E. Exam Composition

1. Formal requirements

Proper syntax, grammar, spelling and coherent expression count. Frequent misspellings and grammatical lapses will generally remove any benefit of the doubt your professor might otherwise have given to a dubious statement, weak analysis, or lapse in logic. Remember to follow all format rules, including page or word limits. Do not lose points because you failed to heed the instructions.

2. Sentences

a. *Use complete sentences.* Fragments of thought, transferred from your outline, are hard to read and interpret and never gain full credit. Frequently they may cost you all credit. "Murder: premeditation + intention = o.k." is not a sentence your professor will understand or can give you points for.

b. *Keep your sentences short.* Do not try to pack too many ideas into a single sentence. You will get lost, and so will your reader.

3. Verbiage

You do not have much time, and you have very little space. Make your point once and do not repeat it. Avoid unnecessary phrases: "I believe that . . ." or "It seems to me . . ." or "in light of the fact that" (write "because") or "in the event that" (write "if"), etc.

4. Write legibly

If you have a messy, sloppy, generally unreadable handwriting, slow down. Print if necessary. You will not get credit if your professor cannot read your answer.

5. Abbreviations

You may use common abbreviations, if you first say what the abbreviation is. If you say: "The plaintiff (P) argues . . ." and use P thereafter, your reader will know what P means. But do not use private shorthand, even if you explain what it is, because it is confusing. Avoid carrying your abbreviations over from one answer to the next. Your professor may not read exam questions sequentially, and so in reading may not know that you defined an abbreviation in an earlier answer.

6.   Tone

Use a conversational tone. Use simple, clear language. Avoid slang and jargon. Do not joke or use sarcasm.

F.   At the End

1.   What to do when you are running out of time

If you see that you are running out of time, write a note in your exam book. Then attempt to answer every question, even if you must resort to very short answers. It is better to respond to every question however briefly, than risk losing points by leaving a question out entirely.

2.   When the exam is finished, move on

Do not replay the exam, brood about it, or discuss it with friends. You gain nothing by ruminating about it for what may turn out to be an imaginary mistake. Instead, concentrate on the next exam.

G.   Sample Property Exam Question and Annotated Answer

Question

In 1993, Samantha Semler lived with her family in a house on Westside Blvd. in Putnam. Although Semler, an art teacher, had little money to spend, she collected folk art sculptures of Uncle Sam.

On July 4, 1993, a brush fire broke out in the hills around Putnam. It was soon out of control. Semler packed up her favorite sculptures, loaded them into a trailer coupled to her car, and locked the trailer. Unfortunately, as she pulled the trailer onto the street, the coupling broke and the trailer rolled down the Westside Boulevard hill, where it came to a halt. Before Semler could unload the sculptures into her car, a police officer announced the area was being evacuated and ordered her and her family to leave immediately. She left the trailer where it was at the foot of Westside Boulevard.

Semler was not permitted to return to her home until July 11. The house was still standing, but it had been looted. Semler found the trailer where she had left it, but there were no sculptures inside. The lock on the trailer had been broken. She immediately reported the missing items to the police and gave them snapshots of the missing sculptures. The missing items were not recovered.

In 1997, Semler and her family were on vacation in Gracie Square. They stopped at the local art museum, which was displaying a new folk art exhibit. To her surprise, two of the Uncle Sam sculptures that had been packed in her trailer were featured in the exhibit. Both sculptures were labeled "On loan from the private collection of Emilie Barnet." Semler immediately notified the museum's curator that the sculptures belonged to her and that she wanted them back. The curator informed Semler that the museum had only temporary custody of the art work and could not release them to anyone but Barnet.

Barnet can prove that she purchased the sculptures in 1994 for a total of $4,500 from the Hoffman Gallery in New York City. The Gallery is a well-known and respected folk art gallery. The Gallery can prove that it bought the sculptures from Jay Fribish in December 1993. Fribish claims that he owned the sculptures, having found them abandoned on the side of a road in Putnam during the summer of 1993.

Semler hopes to recover the two sculptures. You are an associate in the law firm she has hired to advise her. Please explain whether Semler will be able to recover the sculptures and why.

Answer

(*Words in brackets are the authors' annotations and do not belong in an exam answer.*)

Samantha Semler will be able to recover the two Uncle Sam sculptures from Barnet [Conclusion] if she can prove that Barnet did not acquire good title to them. [Issue] Even a good faith or *bona fide* purchaser for value (BFPV) cannot acquire good title from a thief. So the only way that good title to the sculptures could be passed is if they were abandoned. [Rule]

Fribish claims that he found the sculptures abandoned on the side of the road in the summer of 1993. We don't know if he is telling the truth about this since Semler returned on July 11, 1993 to find the trailer empty, with a broken lock, and the sculptures gone. If Fribish is lying, then he stole the sculptures from the locked trailer and therefore could not have passed good title. [Application]

Even if the sculptures were stolen from the trailer by someone other than Fribish and dropped on the side of the road as he says, Fribish still could not claim that the property was *abandoned* by Semler, its true owner, since courts look at the intent of the true owner in determining whether property is abandoned. The facts clearly indicate that Semler never intended to abandon the sculptures. She was prevented from retrieving them because of a police order in an emergency. She returned to claim them as soon as she was permitted to do so and filed a police report seeking their return. As soon as she saw them in the museum, she again sought their return. [*Application continued*]

Since the crime of theft requires the element of mental culpability, a court could find that someone seeing the trailer alone at the bottom of the hill might believe that it and its contents were abandoned, and therefore not stolen. After all, the trailer was standing at the foot of Westside Blvd., not in the Semler driveway or in front of the house. But this result seems unlikely since the trailer, which originally was locked, was found just one week later with a broken lock. Nonetheless, even if the sculptures were not stolen, they were not abandoned either. Therefore, Barnet could not have received good title even though she is a BFPV. [*Application continued*]

Since Samantha Semler can probably prove that the two Uncle Sam sculptures were stolen and not abandoned, she is likely to be able to recover them from Barnet. [*Conclusion repeated*]

PART III

Appellate Advocacy

CHAPTER 18

Appellate Advocacy: An Overview

When you master this chapter, you will understand:

1. what an appeal is;

2. how appellate courts differ from trial courts;

3. how to find a basis for an appeal;

4. what standards of review may apply on appeal; and

5. how an appeal proceeds.

A. What is an Appeal?

An **appeal** is a proceeding in which a party to a lawsuit requests an appellate court to reverse or modify an adverse decision by a lower court in the case. In some appeals, the party may also request that the case be remanded (returned) to the lower court for further proceedings. The power to appeal an adverse judicial decision is a cornerstone of our legal system. Appellate review helps ensure the soundness, integrity, and uniformity of the adversary system.

A litigant who disagrees with a decision of the trial court in his case may appeal to the appropriate appellate court in the jurisdiction. The party appealing is the **appellant**, sometimes called the **petitioner**. The party seeking the affirmance of the lower court's decision is the **appellee**, sometimes called the **respondent**.

A judge or jury's *final* judgment on the merits of a case is usually appealable as a matter of right. For example, a criminal defendant who is convicted of murder or a civil defendant who is found negligent can appeal because such findings are final judgments on the merits. An appeal from a decision made before a final judgment, called an interlocutory appeal, is usually discretionary; the appellate court has the authority to determine whether or not to hear the appeal. For example, a trial court's ruling granting one party's request to discover financial documents possessed by the other party in a breach of contract action may be the subject of an interlocutory appeal. Such a ruling during a lawsuit does not adjudicate the merits of the case.

Trial court decisions are not the only appealable decisions. Decisions of a state appellate court are often subject to review by the highest court in the state. Similarly, many federal appellate court decisions and certain decisions of the highest state courts are reviewable by the United States Supreme Court.

B. How Appellate Courts Differ From Trial Courts

Appellate courts differ from trial courts in several significant respects. One of the most striking distinctions is the identity of the trial and appellate decision-makers. As you learned in Chapter 15, a case litigated to verdict in a trial court is usually presented to a trial judge and a jury, composed of citizens from the community. On appeal, a panel of appellate judges hears the case; appellate courts do not use juries.

The roles of the jury and trial judge and that of the appellate court are also very different. In a jury trial, the jury decides questions of fact (*e.g.*, the defendant killed the victim) and the trial judge decides questions of law (*e.g.*, which murder and manslaughter statutes are applicable). The jury applies the law, as defined by the trial judge, to the facts (*e.g.*, the jury verdict finding that the defendant, who stabbed and killed the victim, committed murder). Although the jury is the principal trier of fact, the trial judge assumes that role when (1) the parties have waived or are not entitled to a jury trial, (2) pretrial decisions require fact-finding, or (3) the evidence is so one-sided that a reasonable jury could only reach a certain verdict. An appellate court reviews the decisions made by the jury and trial judge, but it is not empowered to make independent findings of fact.

And unlike the trial court, the appellate court may not consider new evidence (with certain narrow exceptions). The record on appeal may include only the testimony, other evidence (*e.g.*, documents and affidavits), and relevant legal filings (*e.g.*, the complaint, answer, motions papers, and briefs) accepted by the lower court. In contrast, litigants at the trial level develop the record by presenting evidence to the trial court.

Finally, in an appellate court, the permissible scope of legal argument is much narrower than it is in a trial court. At the trial level, lawyers may advance any legal argument supported by the facts and the applicable law. Legal argument on appeal is more circumscribed; the parties to an appeal generally are limited to arguing legal points raised in the lower court.

C. Finding a Basis for an Appeal

In deciding whether to appeal a lower court's decision, the lawyer first must understand his client's procedural objective (*e.g.*, reversal of a summary judgment or reduction of a damages award). He must then review the trial record, identify possible legal errors (which are grounds for an appeal), and assess whether an appellate court is likely to grant his client's relief on those grounds. If the client has a fair chance of succeeding on one or more grounds, he should appeal.

A variety of issues may be raised on appeal. Challenges to a trial court's factual findings, legal conclusions, and determinations on mixed questions of law and fact may form the basis of an appeal. Here are examples of issues that may be appealed:

- *Appellate challenge to a factual finding*: Whether the evidence supported the finding that a member of a hospital board of trustees publicly called a surgeon an "incompetent butcher."

- *Appellate challenge to a legal conclusion*: Whether the trial judge correctly determined that the tax law precludes deductions for home office expenses.

- *Appellate challenge to a determination on a mixed question of law and fact*: Whether the evidence supported the finding that the defendant, the owner of an ice-skating rink, negligently maintained the premises.

Because appellate courts accord great deference to purely factual findings and rarely set them aside, appellants often dispute the correctness of the legal conclusions and determinations on mixed questions of law and fact made in the lower courts.

D. Standards of Appellate Review

Chapter 15 explained that an appellate court is bound by the applicable standard of review. The standard determines how closely the appellate court will examine the lower court's decision. Remember that it is the appellant who has the task of overcoming the decision against him in the lower court.

The laws of the jurisdiction in which the appeal is pending usually delineate the standard of review for different types of decisions. The standard depends on whether the appellate court is reviewing a factual or legal determination. In most cases the appellate court is limited to a review of the trial court record and cannot judge the credibility of witnesses or make independent findings of fact. Rather, it usually defers to the judgments of the triers of fact who viewed the testimony and evidence firsthand. Therefore, an appellate court generally will not set aside a factual decision by a trial court (whether made by the judge or jury) unless it is clearly erroneous—that is, unless no rational trier of fact could have reached such a conclusion. In contrast, appellate courts have legal authority superior to trial courts. Appellate courts review legal conclusions under a *de novo* standard (also known as a plenary standard), the least deferential standard of review. In a *de novo* review, the appellate court may freely substitute its judgment for that of the trial court.

The standard of review for decisions on mixed questions of law and fact depends on the jurisdiction and the nature of the question. Generally, mixed questions involving law that is easily accessible to non-lawyers, such as negligence, are reviewed under the clearly erroneous standard. However, if the law is very complex, the appellate court may apply a *de novo* standard.

E. Procedural Requirements on Appeal

Most jurisdictions have detailed rules prescribing the procedural requirements to pursue an appeal. Generally, litigants may challenge on appeal only those decisions they formally objected to at the trial-level. Hence, the groundwork for an appeal—preserving the right to appeal particular decisions—is established in the trial court by way of timely motions and **objections** to decisions.

A litigant who wants to appeal an adverse decision against him by a lower court must file what many jurisdictions call a notice of appeal. Notices of appeal identify (1) the parties to the appeal, (2) the judgment or order being challenged, and (3) the issues that will be raised on appeal. The appellant, or in some jurisdictions the appellant and appellee jointly, must submit to the appellate court the record for the appeal.

The heart of an appeal is the appellate brief—a formal legal document that persuasively argues a party's factual and legal position. The appellant and appellee submit appellate briefs according to a schedule established by the applicable court rules. In most jurisdictions, the appellant files the initial brief; the appellee may file an answering (or responding) brief; and the appellant may file a reply to the appellee's answering brief.

After all the briefs are filed, the appellate court might hear oral arguments. Generally, oral argument is granted at the discretion of the appellate court. A litigant who wants an oral argument usually has to make a timely written request for it.

F. Appellate Briefs and Oral Argument

Unlike trial advocacy, which entails live testimony, a panoply of motions, and battles over the admission of evidence, appellate advocacy has two basic components: the appellate brief and oral argument. The appellate brief is the lawyer's main vehicle for persuading the appellate court to grant the requested relief. The lawyer's challenge is to craft a well-researched document that conveys with passion the legal merit and equity of his client's position. Oral argument is the lawyer's final opportunity to discredit his adversary's arguments and convince the appellate court that the relief his client seeks is supported by the facts, the law, and public policy. The techniques of persuasion and the purpose, structure, and style of the appellate brief are covered in Chapters 19 through 23. Chapter 24 discusses oral argument.

Do the Exercise on p. 312 Now

EXERCISE

Answer each question. Explain your answers.

1. A trial judge sitting without a jury convicted Benita Smith of perjury and extortion. Smith wants to appeal her conviction.
    (a) Smith may appeal her conviction if she has grounds to do so.
    (b) Smith's appeal is discretionary because it is interlocutory.
    (c) Smith may not appeal.

2. A jury found Dionne Wilson liable for false imprisonment. Wilson wants to appeal the verdict on the ground that the trial judge gave the jury legally incorrect instructions on the elements of false imprisonment.
    (a) On appeal, Wilson probably may submit new jury instructions to the appellate court.
    (b) On appeal, Wilson probably may assert that the jury instructions were legally flawed if her attorney objected to them at trial.
    (c) The propriety of jury instructions is not appealable.

3. A jury convicted Walter Hayes of murder. Hayes chose not to testify at trial because he believed the prosecution's case against him was weak. Hayes wants to appeal his conviction.
    (a) Hayes may submit to the appellate court a sworn statement in which he presents his defense to the charge of murder and explains why he did not testify at trial.
    (b) Hayes cannot submit to the appellate court evidence that he chose not to present to the jury.
    (c) Hayes probably can appeal his conviction.
    (d) Both b and c.

4. A trial judge found that a statute prohibiting loitering was unconstitutionally vague.
    (a) An appellate court is likely to review the finding under the clearly erroneous standard.
    (b) An appellate court is likely to review the finding under the *de novo* standard.
    (c) An appellate court will never review a trial court's decision on the constitutionality of a statute.

CHAPTER 19

Introduction to Persuasion and the Appellate Brief

When you master this chapter, you will understand:

1. the nature of persuasion;

2. the purpose of an appellate brief;

3. the structure of an appellate brief;

4. basic principles to follow when crafting an appellate brief; and

5. how to make your appellate brief persuasive.

A s you learned in Chapter 18, an appellate brief is a formal legal document that advocates a party's position in an appeal. It is the main vehicle a lawyer uses to persuade the appellate court to reverse, affirm, modify, or remand the lower court's decision. This chapter explores the nature of persuasion and the craft of writing an effective appellate brief.

A. Persuasion is an Everyday Activity

You learn from an early age the need to persuade. Wanting someone to agree with you, to assist you, to participate in an activity, to act, or to refrain from acting is an everyday occurrence. With experience, you also learn which method of persuasion works best in a particular situation. Think of the last time you persuaded a friend to go to a movie. You might have appealed to your friend's sense of fairness ("We went to your choice last time"); to his willingness to bargain ("We'll go to see your choice next time"); to his interest ("It's your favorite type of film"); to his desire to please you ("I really, really want to see it"); or even to his needs ("What do you care which movie? It will do you good to take a break from studying").

In its broadest sense, "persuasion" means to induce, influence, or impel someone to agree with you. So Mario Puzo's famous line from *The Godfather* that "I'll make him an offer he can't refuse" has become a modern euphemism for a convincing threat. Threats and acts of harm as a means of persuasion are, of course, unlawful. So are several other forms of inducement—bribery, for example. The lawyer necessarily must define persuasion in narrower terms. In the law, persuasion is not simply any inducement but an argument that appeals to reason, understanding, belief, or interest.

To succeed in writing persuasively you must consider your audience, your objective, the impact of your words and arguments on your readers, and the types of logical errors that will cause your readers to doubt your claims and conclusions.

B. Know Your Audience

Knowing your audience is essential to persuasion. You must always keep in mind that the person you are trying to convince is the reader, not yourself. Just as the best present for a friend is the present your friend would like, not one you like, the most persuasive arguments are those that will appeal to your audience.

The audience for much of the persuasive writing that lawyers undertake is other lawyers—most particularly, judges and counsel for their clients' adversaries. They are sophisticated readers and thinkers who are not likely to be persuaded by blatant appeals to emotion, verbal pyrotechnics, or misleading suggestions.

1. Learn what your reader knows

Any story can be told with varying degrees of detail. For economy's sake, we always take for granted certain background information. For example, consider how you would explain an Internet website, on the one hand, to a friend who frequently goes online and, on the other, to your grandmother who has no idea what "URL" means. To persuade your readers, then, you must strive to understand what your readers know and think about the assumptions they will make as they read your argument.

A common trap for the inexperienced lawyer is to assume that the court knows the facts of the case, who the parties are, and how they are connected. To persuade the court that your argument makes sense, you must provide it with all the pertinent information on which anyone, coming to the issues for the first time, can form a reliable judgment. Without all the necessary facts, the story you tell will be difficult to follow; if the story makes little sense, your argument about it will make even less.

2. Take into account your reader's common sense

Just as every reader has a stock of background information, every reader also has a set of background assumptions, or common sense, about the way the world works. Common sense tells us that when the sky suddenly darkens it is likely to rain soon. Likewise, common sense might tell us that when someone sees a police officer and turns and runs away, he has something to hide. Unfortunately, common sense is not always true. The darkening sky might be the result of a solar eclipse. The fleeing individual might fear the police officer.

You must always take into account the court's common sense, not to prove it right or wrong, but to know enough about it to use it or counter it as necessary to make your case. To make a persuasive case, you must provide information that will help confirm (or overcome) the court's assumptions.

C. The Appellate Brief

The primary purpose of an appellate brief is to *persuade* the appellate court that the relief requested is mandated by law and the facts of the case, and is consistent with public policy. It also serves to *inform* the appellate court of the relevant facts, procedure, and law. When writing an appellate brief, make sure you accomplish the following:

1. Inform the appellate court of the facts and procedural history of the case

The appellate judges who will be reading your appellate brief have no independent knowledge of the facts or procedural history of the case. You must introduce the parties and explain the events or transactions that are the basis of the lawsuit in the light most favorable to your client. (Chapter 21 explains how to do this.)

In addition to the facts, the appellate court must be apprised of the procedural history. Summarize the legal and factual allegations in the pleadings to familiarize the appellate court with the parties' claims and defenses. Present other procedural information relevant to the appeal, including the substance of any judgments, rulings, orders, or decisions being appealed.

2. Inform the appellate court of the relief your client is seeking

In clear and simple terms, state the nature of the procedural relief your client desires (e.g., reversal, affirmance, or modification of the trial court's judgment). Does your client want the appellate court to set aside a verdict finding him liable for fraudulent misrepresentation or does he want the appellate court to reduce the damages award? The appellate court needs to know precisely what it is being asked to do.

3. Inform the appellate court of the controlling law

The starting point for any legal argument is a presentation of the controlling law. Appellate judges expect and appreciate a comprehensive, yet succinct, exposition of the laws being relied on or challenged by the parties, even the basic legal principles. And remember that although appellate judges are well-versed in many areas of law, they may have limited knowledge of certain legal subjects, especially those that are novel or highly specialized. So in some cases, your brief may introduce the appellate court to a particular area of law. Always strive to present the law in a manner that reinforces the validity of your client's position.

4. Persuade the appellate court that the requested relief is mandated by the facts and controlling law and is consistent with public policy

The challenge of writing an appellate brief is persuading the appellate court that the facts, controlling law, and, when applicable, public policy compel a decision for your client. You must explain how the law favorably applies to the facts as you view them. In addition, you must analogize your case to favorable precedent, distinguish adverse precedent, and, in many cases, discredit opposing arguments. Your objective is to convince the appellate court that a decision in your client's favor is correct and just.

D. The Parts of an Appellate Brief

An appellate brief has a formal structure that is prescribed by the court rules of the jurisdiction where the appeal is pending. The structure acquaints the appellate court with unfamiliar information (e.g., procedural history and facts). It also presents the court with the legal arguments and requests for relief in a uniform format that facilitates the comparison of opposing briefs.

Although they may be called different names in different jurisdictions, most appellate briefs have the following parts:

- Title Page
- Table of Contents
- Table of Authorities
- Question(s) Presented
- Statement of the Case
  - Procedural History
  - Statement of Facts
- Summary of the Argument
- Argument
- Conclusion
- Signature
- Appendix (if required)

Each part of the appellate brief is unique and serves a distinct purpose. The parts will be discussed in detail in Chapters 20, 21, and 22.

E. Crafting an Effective Appellate Brief

A lawyer succeeds in persuading the appellate court largely on the strength of her client's factual and legal position. Certainly, writing a convincing argument is easier when the law overwhelmingly supports your client's position than when, for example, you are asking the appellate court to carve out an exception to a rule. Regardless of the merits of the case, the lawyer must craft an appellate brief that provides the appellate court with viable reasons to rule in her client's favor. Here are some basic principles which, if followed, will enhance every argument.

1. Use the facts to tell a compelling story

Devise a theme, a unifying "story" presenting the facts in a manner that advances your legal argument. Identify the facts that you must emphasize to prevail on the legal arguments. The theme should stress the favorable facts and also explain away or minimize the unfavorable aspects of your case. It is often conceived during lower court proceedings and then further developed and argued on appeal.

Facts and characterizations flowing from facts are far more persuasive than conclusory statements because they are, or appear to be, independent of the self-interest of the lawyer and client. To make the case that a person is unsavory, you are unlikely to succeed simply by labeling him "nasty" or a "lowlife." But if you can show that once in a fit of rage he beat up his mother, you will provide the court with a factual basis on which it can agree with your conclusion.

Arousing sympathy for your client (or antipathy for your adversary) is almost always useful, but doing so is often difficult to accomplish. Mere characterization is rarely useful, so simply referring to your client as "deserving of respect" or "suffering" (or to your adversary as an "undeserving crook") is unlikely to evoke compassion for you client or loathing for the opposing party. For that reason, the following is likely to backfire:

> Like all of the rest of his assertions, the appellant's claim is preposterous. Although we have come to expect from the appellant's attorney an endless stream of malicious distortions and exaggerations, the Court should not take this waste of its time lying down but should give absolutely no credence to his muddle-headed and laughable insistence that he knows what the law requires.

This pronouncement is extremely heavy-handed. In branding the appellant and his attorney stupid and venal, the brief may lead the court to question what has led the writer to such shrillness. The language highlights the writer's antagonism instead of focusing the court on the law and facts.

Although blatant emotional appeals are rarely persuasive, you can use the *facts* to present your position in a favorable light:

> In three previous briefs to this Court, the appellant has asserted the same interpretation of the rule at issue. Each time, this Court has rejected that interpretation. Undeterred, the appellant persists in this fourth attempt, trying the patience of the appellee, if not the Court, consuming four months and requiring twelve hearings without offering any new theory.

Now the appellant has been put in his place with facts that should persuade the court to agree with the appellee.

In the next example, the attorney's objective is to show that her client has endured cruel and unusual punishment in prison. Merely declaring that prison conditions are "barbaric" is unlikely to persuade the appellate court to release him. Generalizations are empty and unpersuasive:

> The appellant has been treated barbarically. The conditions at the prison are inhumane. The supervision is wholly inadequate.

The attorney will more likely succeed by offering information that supports her characterizations:

> The conditions at the prison are barbaric and inhumane. For 23 hours every day, the appellant is confined to a cell six feet long by four feet wide, barely enough space for the single cot with broken springs, a cracked toilet, and a leaking sink that constitute virtually his entire universe. Although state regulations prescribe a daily shower, the chronically understaffed prison— for the last two years, only 40 percent of the required number of guards have been available—has reduced each prisoner's shower privileges to one a week.

A court encountering these facts will be open to further arguments designed to elicit the conclusion that such conditions are indeed cruel and unusual. To provide a persuasive rebuttal, the lawyer for the prison cannot, as in the next example, offer mere conclusory statements:

> The appellant has been treated well. The prison is safe and com-
> fortable.

Rather he must counter facts with facts:

> The appellant has not been mistreated. Although his cell is
> smaller than the appellant would like, he is not required to
> share his space with other inmates. Moreover, his cell is larger
> than the per capita space allocated to inmates in 60 percent of
> the state prisons. The sink and toilet may be unaesthetic, but
> each works, and when the sink broke six months earlier, it was
> fixed the same day. The sink is sufficiently large, and ample
> soap is provided, to permit the appellant to clean himself as
> often as he likes in the absence of a daily shower.

2.   Capture the appellate court's attention

Appellate judges read thousands of pages of legal argument every year. To
distinguish your case from the others, you have to muster all of your analytical
ability and creativity to write an eloquent, engaging appellate brief. Make your
theme come alive by using the active voice, strong nouns, active verbs, and when
appropriate, descriptive adjectives and adverbs. Choosing the proper words can
make your writing clearer and improve its readability. But word choice can do
more than that. Using the right word can make your writing more persuasive.
Mark Twain put the point in a well-known line: "The difference between the
almost-right word and the *right* word is really a large matter—it's the difference
between the lightning bug and the lightning." [From a Mark Twain letter to
George Bainton, October 15, 1888, *quoted in* John Bartlett, *Familiar Quotations*,
Justin Kaplan, general ed. (Little Brown, 16th ed. 1992), p. 527.]

Careless writers think that they can dress up their writing by scattering synonyms throughout their paragraphs, heedless of the possibility that the words
they think are the same in fact mean something different. The careful writer must
also be aware that words have connotations—secondary meanings or resonances
that can subtly influence how people will respond. Here is a simple collection of
related words: say, declare, admit, concede. At the scene of an accident, the
driver, is quoted as speaking these words: "I'm not sure what happened." Now
consider the following sentences in a brief:

> Sentence 1: "I'm not sure what happened," the driver said.
> Sentence 2: "I'm not sure what happened," the driver declared.
> Sentence 3: "I'm not sure what happened," the driver admitted.

Sentence 4: "I'm not sure what happened," the driver conceded.

Sentence 1 is a straightforward narrative of what happened. It is neutral about the import of the driver's statement. Sentence 2 will suggest to at least some readers that the driver was making a statement, not merely talking. The connotation changes considerably in Sentence 3, because the word "admit" suggests that the driver might have been at fault and was pressed to speak against his own interest. Sentence 4 makes it sound even worse for the driver, for now he may be perceived not merely as having said something against his interest but as having been forced to change his story. Not everyone, to be sure, will react in the same way to these proposed nuances in the different verbs, but many people will. The lawyer who wants to persuade the appellate court to his point of view must weigh carefully the meaning of words and their background significance, so that he can control the nuances imparted.

3. Maintain credibility

A lawyer has an ethical duty to represent the law and facts accurately in all court proceedings and legal filings. Furthermore, the ultimate goal of persuasion will be achieved only if the appellate court has confidence in the credibility of your arguments. A beautifully written appellate brief will fail in its objective if it is predicated upon misstatements of law or fact. Even a single unintentional misstatement may destroy the appellate court's confidence in the integrity of your client's position. And your adversary will, in all likelihood, gleefully point out that your argument, if premised on misstatements, is disingenuous and analytically flawed. A lack of precision may also undermine your client's position and jeopardize your professional reputation. Carefully review your appellate brief to insure that statements of law and fact are accurate and that any characterizations are supported by the record.

4. Pitch the argument at the least vulnerable level

It is a lucky lawyer who represents a client with a claim supported by facts that fall squarely within the law's entitlement. For example, your client is suing to recover damages in a breach-of-contract suit in which it is clear that the defendant has willfully breached the contract and is refusing to pay. Lawyers are rarely lucky in this way, for disputes that are so legally clear rarely end up in court. Most of the time, the law or facts can be interpreted in different ways. How do you persuade the court to rule for your client when the law is or facts are against you?

Most legal issues can be understood, and most legal arguments can be carried out, at different levels of abstraction, from the level of a very particular set of facts ("This is a case about a dog named Spot that bit Mary Jane Smolenski, my client, causing her injury"), to the level of the law ("This case concerns an interpretation of the state common-law rule governing injuries by animals"), to the level of issue and policy ("This case raises the issue of whether the common-law rule governing injuries by animals is causing an intolerable strain on the court system and hence should be revised"). The skillful advocate will pitch the argument at the least vulnerable point.

If you represent the dog owner, you would not suggest that the victim is lying about being bitten if all the evidence showed that the dog attacked her. Instead, you might fashion an argument from other facts (perhaps Spot had not bitten anyone before). Or, if Spot had bitten someone before, you might argue instead that the rule should be that the owner must know about the first bite and that he had no such knowledge in your case. Failing that, you might try to persuade the court by arguing that the rule is too restrictive and should be rejected and that the court should adopt a first-bite rule. If you must go this far to pitch the argument, you will need to give the court a compelling reason for changing the law: perhaps because other states have such a rule; or without such a rule the number of cases will overtax judicial resources; or without such a rule dog ownership in the state will decline to the great detriment of a rich tradition and family comfort. The lawyer must pitch his argument at the level of abstraction that is the least vulnerable to attack, but is still supported by the facts, law, and logic. In other words, make it easy for the appellate court to decide the case in your client's favor. Convince the court that the requested relief is not only correct in your particular case but will also serve as good precedent for future cases.

F. Constructing a Sound Argument: Logical Devices

In constructing a persuasive argument, the lawyer may use various rhetorical strategies. Which one to choose depends on the nature of your case, your objective, and the available evidence that supports your position. This section describes the major types of logical devices.

1. Cause and effect

The success of a causal argument depends on the reader's belief that a particular condition or event will cause a particular result or that an event or condition must have had a certain cause. One common cause and effect argument is the basis of the common-law rule *res ipsa loquitur:* "the thing speaks for itself." The rule permits a judge or jury to infer from the fact of an accident that it must have been caused by the defendant's negligence: if the fire in the building was started by a cigarette, it *must have been caused by* someone's negligence in not put-ting the cigarette out. To succeed in an argument based on cause and effect, you must either rely on the reader's well-founded belief in the causal connection between an earlier event and a later one, or else show the connection.

2. Circumstance

Sometimes the law excuses acts (or failures to act) because of particular cir-cumstances. For example, a rule of contract law excuses the failure to perform an agreement if it has become impossible to carry out. Suppose your client hires a painter to scrape and paint the outside of her house. Before the painter can start, the house burns down. The homeowner is excused from paying the painter because the contract can no longer be performed. Using circumstance success-fully as a persuasive strategy requires that you show why the circumstance is of a type that should excuse the act or omission.

3. Definition

A common rhetorical strategy is to show that one thing belongs (or does not belong) to a class of things to which the law applies. In effect, you seek to per-suade your reader that *by definition* the answer to the question whether the law applies follows from properly understanding the basis of the legal dispute. For example, in the Dunn matter, the question was whether a crowbar is a deadly weapon. To succeed at persuading the court, lawyers for both the defendant and the prosecution have a definitional task: to demonstrate that the crowbar Dunn brandished while committing the robbery is (or is not) like other types of objects the courts have defined as "deadly weapons."

4. Similarity

Similarity is like definition, except that you are not arguing that one thing is identical to the other. You are asserting, rather, that one thing is similar or anal-ogous to something else and that it should therefore be treated by the law in a similar manner. For example, the law in most states says that a jilted fiancé may not sue for damages if the marriage does not take place. Suppose the defendant has promised to attend a party at which his engagement to the plaintiff was to be announced, but at the last minute he backs out and the engagement is canceled. May the plaintiff sue? The defendant's lawyer could argue that although the rule against suits for "alienation of affection" applies to marriages, engagements are sufficiently similar that the rule should apply to them as well.

5. Comparison

An argument based on comparison asserts that a claim must be upheld because it is a *stronger* claim than one that would be upheld under the rule. This argument is often signaled by the Latin words *a fortiori*, meaning "all the more" or "all the stronger." Suppose you represent a parent whose 13-year-old child signed a contract to buy an expensive bicycle and who has refused to pay. The cycle store has filed suit. You find a case holding that a 15-year-old child may not be legally bound by a contract he signs. It must necessarily follow that if a 15-year-old is not bound, neither is someone younger.

6. Contraries

To argue from contraries is to assert that a benefit would flow to a client from the opposite of the situation in which the client is being injured. For example, your client's neighbor raises chickens in his backyard. Your client understandably fears that the chickens create a health hazard, and he seeks relief from the risk. You argue to the court that an injunction barring his neighbor from raising chickens will provide the necessary protection, the benefit.

7. Authority

To argue from authority is to assert that something is true (or false) because an authority on the subject says that it is. Should an environmental agency destroy mushrooms growing in the woods because they are deadly? A naturalist might protest and insist that the agency should not act unless harm occurs— someone eats them and dies. The law obviously does not require such a drastic condition before action is taken. The courts would probably accept as persuasive a well-regarded authority (a renowned botanist, for example) who attests that the mushrooms are indeed fatal if eaten.

8. Evidence

When the facts themselves are disputed, the reader can only be persuaded about what actually happened by credible evidence. Did the driver run the red light? No amount of abstract argumentation will settle the issue: evidence is required. There are, of course, different forms of evidence, and some types are inherently less persuasive than others. The most persuasive evidence would be testimony from unbiased witnesses who saw what happened. The crucial question is whether the evidence is credible. If it is, it is likely to be persuasive to the degree that it establishes (or defeats) the claim.

G. Attacking an Argument: Logical Fallacies

Just as you can construct a persuasive argument using the logical devices described above, you can attack a weak argument by identifying it's logical fallacies. Once you have learned to identify common errors in logic, you will be able to recognize them when they appear in your adversary's arguments and persuade the court just how faulty the logic is.

1. Begging the question

To beg the question is circular reasoning. It assumes the truth of the conclusion that you are attempting to prove. It is question begging for the defendant in the dog bite case to argue that the plaintiff could not have been injured since his dog "really is friendly." Learning to spot question begging is a useful skill: it will put you on guard against committing the error and help you to refute the arguments of adversaries who engage in it.

2. Non sequitur

A *non sequitur* is a conclusion that does not follow from the premises of the argument. A good example is the claim that because a student worked hard on his assignment, he is entitled to a good grade. The conclusion is a *non sequitur* because it assumes (falsely) that the degree of effort dictates the grade to be received. It would be a *non sequitur* for Dunn to argue that the crowbar was not a deadly weapon because it did not seriously injure or kill anyone.

3. Arguments ad hominem

The *ad hominem* argument is one directed against the person asserting a fact or making a claim rather than against the fact or claim itself. A rape victim who takes the stand is grilled about her personal life, not necessarily to disprove that the rape occurred but to suggest that she is immoral and therefore not credible. Attacks on the character of a person are not responsive to the merits of the case, so you should be particularly on guard when you encounter character assassination in your adversary's arguments—or are yourself tempted to make such an argument on behalf of your client.

4. Post hoc, ergo propter hoc

From the Latin, *post hoc, ergo propter hoc* means "after this, therefore because of this." The argument asserts that because X came before Y it must necessarily have caused Y. While true causes do come before their effects, not everything that comes before something else is necessarily a cause of it. Because the dog was first put on a leash in the front yard and then bit the plaintiff does not mean that putting the leash on the dog caused the dog to bite. Nor does a variant of the *post hoc, ergo propter hoc* fallacy make any more sense—namely, that because X brought about Y, Y can be eliminated by doing away with X. It would not be logical to insist that to prevent people from being bitten the court should adopt a rule forbidding owners from putting their dogs on leashes.

These and other types of logical fallacies should be avoided because they open your argument to attack and call into question your logical abilities. On the other hand, by identifying fallacies in your adversary's position, you are better able to attack his arguments. An argument convincingly attacked as illogical loses all persuasive credibility. In the end, the success of an appellate advocate stands or falls on her ability to persuade.

Do Exercises 19-A and 19-B on p. 327 Now

EXERCISES

Exercise 19-A

List the similarities between a legal office memorandum and an appellate brief.

Exercise 19-B

List the differences between a legal office memorandum and an appellate brief.

CHAPTER 20

The Appellate Brief: The Argument Section

When you master this chapter, you will understand:

1. the purpose of the Argument section;

2. how to find a basis for an appellate argument;

3. how to write a clear, persuasive argument on an issue;

4. how to write persuasive point headings for your argument; and

5. how to sequence arguments on different issues.

I n an appellate brief, the advocate attempts to persuade the court to grant the requested relief. To succeed, the advocate must identify sound bases for the relief. In a criminal appeal, for instance, a defense lawyer seeking a new trial might argue that the verdict was against the weight of the evidence, that prejudicial evidence was improperly admitted, or that the trial judge incorrectly charged the jury.

Each of these bases poses one or more legal issues that the appellate court must resolve. In an appeal, the advocate's task is to persuade the court to resolve the legal issue in his client's favor. To achieve this objective, he must provide the court with a logical, well-supported analysis of the issues in the form of a persuasive argument.

This chapter focuses on the Argument: the component of the appellate brief that presents the advocate's analysis. Although other sections precede the Argument, you will study them in later chapters because their content and organization are largely dictated by the analysis in the Argument.

A. Finding a Basis for an Appellate Argument

To find a basis for an appeal, the advocate must carefully review the trial record to locate grounds for the requested relief by identifying possible errors upon which the appellate court may grant the relief. Identifying errors at the trial level is often a matter of applying the requirements of the law to the particular facts of the case, a skill you are familiar with from earlier chapters. Chapter 15 discussed the appeal of a conviction for aggravated robbery in *State v. Dunn*. (Dunn was convicted of aggravated robbery because the jury found that she had exhibited a deadly weapon during a robbery.) To determine whether Dunn had grounds for an appeal, her lawyer no doubt reviewed the trial record, relevant motions and objections, the judge's instructions to the jury, and the jury's verdict. She considered grounds relating to the rules of evidence, such as whether the judge improperly excluded relevant evidence or erroneously admitted prejudicial testimony. In addition, she assessed the sufficiency of the evidence at trial, including whether the evidence proved beyond a reasonable doubt (the standard of proof in a criminal trial) that Dunn exhibited a deadly weapon during the robbery. Then she reviewed the statutes and case law to determine whether she had a legal basis for appeal. After careful review, she decided that the only ground for Dunn's appeal was that the evidence did not support the jury's finding that Dunn exhibited a deadly weapon. The appellate brief addressing this ground is in Appendix D, p. 425.

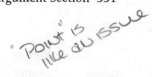
"Point" is like an issue

B. The Format of a Legal Point

The Argument section is composed of one or more points. A **point** is a legal proof that advocates a particular position. Like a legal proof in an office memorandum, a point in an appellate brief presents a logical, complete analysis of an issue. There is a crucial difference, of course. A legal proof is a *neutral* analysis, a *prediction* of how an issue might be resolved. A point is a *partisan* analysis, an *argument* that the court should resolve an issue in favor of the advocate's client. A point on fact-sensitive issues, which are usually briefed in first-year writing courses, often can be organized this way:

Point is an argument on how the should resolve an issue

the issue ✓ **Lead.** The lead identifies the issue considered in the point and persuasively asserts how it should be resolved.

— **Rule.** The rule explains the law that applies to the issue, including the relevant standard of review, and supports that explanation with a discussion of relevant authority.

— **Application.** By highlighting necessary facts, analogizing to favorable cases, and distinguishing unfavorable ones, the application demonstrates that the rule is satisfied.

spouds to otential attacks **Rebuttal.** The rebuttal section anticipates and responds to potential attacks on the analysis, showing them to be without merit.

w issue should be resolved **Conclusion.** The conclusion reasserts how the issue should be resolved.

Each of these sections is considered separately in this chapter.

The format of a point may be varied to accommodate sub-issues. For instance, the appellant's brief in *Dunn v. State* (Appendix D, p. 425) has two sub-issues. The point begins with one lead covering both sub-issues, continues with a separate rule, application, and rebuttal for each sub-issue, and ends with a single conclusion.

C. Writing a Compelling Lead

The lead is the appellate court's introduction to the point's analysis. After reading the lead, the appellate court should understand the issue, know the advocate's position, and conclude that the position is reasonable and fair. Also, the lead should capture the appellate court's attention, convincing the court that the advocate is advancing a meritorious appellate argument.

The lead often ties the theme of the case to the legal rule controlling the issue. For example, consider a point in a criminal appeal arguing that the evidence was legally insufficient to support a finding that the defendant aided or assisted in the sale of crack cocaine. The lead might summarize the relevant evidence introduced at trial and assert that it was insufficient to support the verdict. In doing so, it might portray the defendant as a passive observer who did not participate in the sale. It might begin this way:

> An undercover officer approached the appellant and an individual named Smith and asked for "nicks." Appellant asked the undercover officer "how many" and he replied "four." Appellant also asked her whether she was a cop, to which she unsurprisingly said, "no." Appellant did and said nothing more. Smith and the undercover officer then went into the building where they negotiated and consummated a sale of one "dime" of cocaine for $10, a different size from that initially requested by the undercover officer. This was the only evidence presented by the People and was legally insufficient to support an inference that the appellant provided any actual aid or assistance to Smith in her sale of cocaine to the undercover officer. [Based on the Brief of Defendant-Appellant at 3, *People v. Bello*, 92 N.Y.2d 523 (1998).]

Notice how the above lead fulfills its purpose. After reading this paragraph, the appellate court knows that the issue is whether the evidence was sufficient to prove that the appellant aided or assisted in a drug sale. The lead also advocates the appellant's position and gives the court reason to hold that the evidence in the case was legally insufficient to support a conviction.

In *National Treasury Employees Union v. Von Raab*, 489 U.S. 656 (1989), the question before the Supreme Court was whether the Customs Service could constitutionally require its employees to provide urine samples for drug testing as a condition to promotion. The lead in the Argument section in the employees' brief does not launch into a dry recitation of facts and case law but rather attempts to engage the Court with a forceful statement:

> As this case and others illustrate, the federal government has seized upon a relatively new technology, urinalysis, as an offensive weapon in its war on drugs. The Customs Service is using this weapon on its own employees, requiring them to produce urine samples for laboratory analysis to demonstrate that they are drug-free. It imposes this requirement without probable

cause to believe any individual tested is guilty of any work-related misconduct (in this case illegal drug use), without any reasonable suspicion that an individual is using drugs, and without even a reasonable generalized suspicion that drug abuse exists and constitutes a problem in the workforce. It freely admits that it has no such suspicions. [Brief of the Petitioner at 18-19, *National Treasury Employees Union v. Von Raab*, 489 U.S. 656 (1989).]

Here is another example of a lead from a brief for the appellants, the Clarks, in a hypothetical false imprisonment case. The appellants argue that the evidence was insufficient to support the verdict for the appellee, Taylor:

It is well settled that an employer may limit its employees' freedom of movement during working hours. *Randall's Food Market v. Johnson*, 891 S.W.2d 640, 645-646 (Tex. 1995). When supervising employees, the employer has the right to dictate the nature and location of the work. *See id.* In the instant matter, the Clarks were told that their employee, Taylor, stole a guest's wallet while she was working at a party in their home. Upon learning this troubling information, the Clarks took a reasonable step to separate Taylor from their guests for the remainder of her work shift: they told her to wait for them in the study until the party was over. Such an ordinary business decision of an employer does not, as a matter of law, give rise to a false imprisonment claim.

If your lead is effective, the appellate court will know the issue and your position, and believe you may be right. The court will then be ready for the detailed analysis to follow.

Do Exercise 20-A Now, p. 347

D. Stating and Supporting a Rule That Favors Your Client

1. Crafting a rule that is accurate and favorable to your client

In the rule section of a point, the advocate explains the law accurately and presents it from a perspective that favors his client's position. For instance, in *Dunn v. State*, Dunn's lawyer might present the rule on assertive conduct this way:

> The State must prove beyond a reasonable doubt that the defendant intended to inflict serious bodily injury or death. *See Lockett*, 874 S.W.2d at 814. Specifically, the evidence must establish that (1) the defendant wielded the object in an overtly aggressive manner by either actually injuring the victim or brandishing it at the victim, and (2) the victim believed the defendant would use the object to inflict serious bodily injury or death. *See id.; Lucero v. State*, 915 S.W.2d 612, 615 (Tex. Crim. App. 1996).

On the other hand, the State could present the same rule quite differently, stressing aspects of the law that favor its position:

> The appellate court must uphold a jury's finding of assertive conduct if, after considering the evidence, the jury might reasonably conclude that the defendant displayed the object in "a manner conveying an express or *implied* threat that serious bodily injury will result if the aggressor is not satisfied." *Hammons v. State*, 856 S.W.2d 797, 801 (Tex. Crim. App. 1993).

Notice the differences between these two rules and their support. Both rules are accurate, but each offers a different perspective on the law, one that favors the advocate's position on the issue. Dunn's lawyer mentions the State's heavy burden of proof, while the State emphasizes the standard of review restricting the appellate court's power to overturn the verdict. Dunn's brief presents the rule on assertive conduct as a two-part conjunctive test, thus making the finding of assertive conduct vulnerable on two independent bases. In contrast, the State's brief suggests that a conditional, implied threat is enough to establish assertive conduct. While each cites good law, Dunn's brief cites cases that overturned jury verdicts, and the State's brief cites a case that upheld one.

When drafting the rule, express it narrowly so its effect is limited to your client's case and factually similar ones. Generally, a court is more likely to accept a narrow rule than a broad one because the broad one could lead to unanticipated results when later applied to factually dissimilar cases. For instance, if you want a court to hold that your client had a "close relationship" with her niece, you should not argue that *all aunts and nieces* share that relationship. Rather, narrowly tailor the rule to cover the type of parental relationship shared by *this particular aunt and niece*. In other words, pitch the argument at the least vulnerable level by making the rule just broad enough to cover your case.

The rule, like all the parts of your brief, must persuade. Make sure that it not only accurately states the law, but also advocates your client's position. And always effectively support the rule by citing to and discussing the relevant cases.

Do Exercise 20-B Now, p. 347

2. Choosing supporting authority

Strive to support your analysis with relevant, binding authority. If possible, include the following:

- If the rule derives from a statute, administrative regulation, or constitution, be sure to cite to it and to quote its pertinent provisions.

- If the issue is about how the law applies to facts (in contrast to a question of what the law means), then you should support the rule with cases that are binding (*i.e.*, they were decided by higher courts in your jurisdiction), relevant (*i.e.*, they consider the same issue), factually similar, and favorable (*i.e.*, they have holdings that support your client's position). Whenever possible, the cases you choose should not only consider the same substantive issue but also should have the same procedural context. For instance, if you want to argue on appeal that a jury finding of negligence should be overturned because it was against the weight of the evidence, then look for support in appellate cases considering the same issue. A trial decision on a motion to dismiss a negligence complaint would not be as helpful, even if the substantive facts were similar. That decision would not take into account the standard of appellate review and would instead be limited by burdens and presumptions applicable only to a motion to dismiss.

If you find many binding, factually similar cases, choose ones most likely to influence the court. A decision's weight of authority, the persuasiveness of its language, and the degree of similarity of its facts to those of your case are among the things to consider when selecting cases to use. All other things being equal, it is better to cite a more recent case than an older one. Do not overburden the court with a citation to or a discussion of a case that adds little or nothing to the argument.

If you cannot find binding authority, support the rule with relevant persuasive authority (such as cases outside your jurisdiction). An appellate court is not likely to be influenced by persuasive authority, however, unless, it is well-reasoned or factually pertinent.

If a binding case does not favor your position, you may have an ethical responsibility to disclose it to the court. Specifically, rules of professional responsibility require an advocate to disclose to the court any controlling case that is directly adverse to his position if his adversary has not raised it. [ABA Model Code for Prof. Resp. DR 7-106(B).] In addition, bringing an adverse case to the court's attention has tactical advantages: you not only improve your credibility, but you also get the first opportunity to explain to the court why the case is not helpful to your adversary.

E. Applying the Rule

In the application part of the point, you must accomplish two things. First, having explained the law in the rule, you must persuade the court that the facts of your case justify the relief you are requesting. To do this, you must effectively "argue your facts" by presenting them in a light that applies the rule favorably, thereby convincing the court that the conclusion asserted in the lead is sound. Second, you must show that your case is consistent with existing cases by analogizing to favorable cases and, when necessary, distinguishing adverse ones.

1. Show that the rule applies favorably to your case

Apply the rule to your facts. Focus the court on the facts that are favorable to your position by relating them in detail. Here is an example of an application that effectively applies the rule to the facts. The case concerns false imprisonment, and the advocate for the appellant, having developed a rule on an element of false imprisonment, applies that rule by presenting facts to show that the appellee failed to satisfy it:

> Taylor failed to prove that the Clarks subjected her to oppressive circumstances. The uncontroverted evidence shows that Taylor was free to leave the study. Taylor testified that the door to the study was not locked, that she was left alone in the room

for three hours, and that no one was guarding her. Moreover, she even admitted that she knew how to leave the house and could have left.

Conversely, minimize the impact of unfavorable facts. You can do this by describing them more generally. Sometimes the impact can be minimized by placing an adverse fact in the middle of a paragraph or in a subordinate clause. Here is an example that might appear in the brief for the appellee in the false imprisonment case:

> Although Taylor was not physically prevented from leaving the house, the Clarks, who had the power to fire her and the ability to ruin her name in the community, had angrily and forcefully demanded that she remain there.

In this example, Taylor's freedom to leave is minimized by explaining it generally ("not physically prevented from leaving the house") and placing it in a subordinate clause (using "although") that is immediately followed in the same sentence by a more descriptive, favorable fact.

Do Exercises 20-C(1) and 20-C(2) Now, p. 348

2. Analogize to favorable cases and, if necessary, distinguish adverse ones

You must persuade the appellate court that your case is analogous to favorable cases and distinguishable from adverse ones. By doing so, you give the court a sound legal reason for ruling in your client's favor. When comparing your case to favorable cases:

- Analogize facts in favorable cases to the facts in your client's case.

- Show that the relief granted in the favorable cases is the same relief sought by your client.

- Explain why the reasoning in the favorable cases should be followed.

- Argue, when appropriate, that the weight of decisional authority supports your client's position.

- Argue that the public policy reasoning cited in the favorable cases supports your client's position.

An example from the appellant's brief in *Dunn v. State* (Appendix D) follows. In it, Dunn's attorney argues that Dunn's conduct closely resembled that of the defendants in two cases that overturned convictions for aggravated robbery:

> Like the defendant in *Lockett*, who intended to use a knife only to cut a purse strap, Dunn intended to use the crowbar as a tool, not a weapon. And like the defendant in *Lucero*, Dunn raised the crowbar defensively to ward off an attack, not to threaten injury. In fact, Dunn was far less aggressive than the defendants in *Lucero* and *Lockett*. The defendant in *Lockett* slashed the victim's fingers, and the defendant in *Lucero* swiped at the victim with the screwdriver. In contrast, Dunn's act of raising the crowbar, rather than striking the advancing Keyes with it, demonstrated, if anything, her reluctance to use the crowbar in any way that might harm Keyes.

In this part of the brief, Dunn's lawyer uses the logical device of comparison to argue that the facts of her case are at least, if not more, compelling than the facts of cases in which appellate courts held that assertive conduct was not sufficiently proved. She carefully draws factual parallels between her case and the analogous cases.

Sometimes you must analogize your case to a case with different facts. In this example, the advocate effectively draws an analogy between testing an employee's urine for drugs and testing a motorist's blood for alcohol:

> Although this Court has not yet had the opportunity to consider whether urine tests constitute "searches," the conclusion that they do finds strong support in this Court's decision two decades ago in *Schmerber v. California*. In *Schmerber*, the Court ruled that the extraction and chemical analysis of a motorist's blood to determine its alcohol content "plainly involves the broadly conceived reach of search and seizure under the Fourth Amendment." 384 U.S. at 767 . . . . Urine tests designed to detect drugs are materially indistinguishable from blood tests designed to determine alcohol content, since both involve an examination and analysis of body fluids to uncover illicit conduct. [Brief of the Petitioner at 23-24, *National Treasury Employees Union v. Von Raab*, 489 U.S. 656 (1989).]

In addition to highlighting favorable precedent, a persuasive, analytically sound brief also addresses adverse case law. You must argue whenever you can that your client's case is factually distinguishable from adverse cases. Here is an excerpt from the Dunn brief that shows how to distinguish adverse cases. Notice the level of detail used to show how the facts differ from those in adverse cases:

> This case is distinguishable from both *Hammons v. State*, 856 S.W.2d 797 (Tex. Crim. App. 1993) and *Compton v. State*, 759 S.W.2d 503 (Tex. Crim. App. 1988), in which the evidence was held sufficient to establish assertive conduct. In *Hammons*, the victim was robbed outside a gas station by three assailants, one of whom wielded a baseball bat. In marked contrast to Dunn, the defendant in *Hammons* was overtly aggressive, striking the victim repeatedly with the bat because he too slowly surrendered his wallet. And unlike Keyes, the victim in *Hammons* testified that he was "scared" and "thought [the defendant] was going to hurt . . . [him] bad" with the bat. 759 S.W.2d at 800. Similarly, in *Compton*, the defendant, while robbing a gas station, brandished a broken, jagged bottle and threatened, "Don't nobody move or I'm going to stab you with the bottle." 856 S.W.2d at 503. One of the victims, the cashier at the station, testified that he believed he would suffer serious bodily injury or death because of the broken bottle. *See id.* at 504. In contrast, Dunn carried the crowbar not to threaten injury, but to open the locked steel gate of the truck. Although Dunn threatened Keyes, she did so only to stop Keyes's advance. Dunn's reluctance to use the crowbar, even though Keyes was within striking distance, must have been obvious to Keyes, who neither retreated nor otherwise tried to protect himself.

F. Rebutting Your Adversary's Positions

In the rebuttal section of a point, you respond to arguments that your adversary might make that were not covered in the rule and application sections. For instance, if you anticipate that your adversary will rely on a case you did not use in your argument, you might distinguish or discredit it in the rebuttal section. If your adversary is likely to stress some unfavorable facts that you have not yet discussed, you might argue in the rebuttal section that these facts are irrelevant and explain why. If you think your adversary will advance a policy argument, you might contend that the argument is unsupported or speculative or that the policy's interests are outweighed by competing ones.

Anticipating your adversary's arguments and responding to them in advance accomplishes two things. First, by dealing with adverse authority, facts, and policy, you show you are trustworthy, thus enhancing the credibility of your entire argument. Second, by introducing the court to the argument, you give the court its initial impression of the issue by discrediting its persuasiveness, thus diminishing the effectiveness of your adversary's argument.

When drafting rebuttal arguments, be direct rather than defensive. For instance, if you anticipate that your adversary will argue that testing its employees' urine for drugs is needed to ensure a drug-free work force, do not begin by presenting your adversary's argument:

> *Defensive presentation (not recommended):*
> Respondent may argue that the drug test is needed to ensure the
> integrity of its employees. This argument is fallacious.

Instead, begin by stating *your position* directly:

> *Direct presentation (recommended):*
> The respondent's drug testing program fails to promote
> employee integrity.

more concise + succinct

create + reasoned statement

Similarly, if you anticipate that your adversary will rely on a case that is distinguishable, then do not begin this way:

> *Defensive presentation (not recommended):*
> Appellee may argue that appellant's claim is barred under
> *Tirano v. Salmon.*

Instead, begin this way:

> *Direct presentation (recommended):*
> This Court's recent ruling in *Tirano v. Salmon* does not bar the
> appellant's claim.

A rebuttal argument, like any argument, must be logical, accurate, and grounded in the law. Do not merely state that your adversary is incorrect. Rather, provide sound reasons and legal support that show why your adversary's position is incorrect.

G. Conclusion

The point's conclusion tells the court how it should resolve the issue. The conclusion should be short (one or two sentences). Its purpose is to formally close the argument, not to summarize it. Here is an example:

> The controlling case law and evidence presented at trial support the jury's finding that the jet ski was a dangerous instrument in the hands of young Tyler. This finding should be affirmed.

Note that the conclusion in a point is distinct from the formal Conclusion following the entire Argument. A conclusion in a point asserts how the court should resolve the issue covered in the point (*e.g.*, "Accordingly, the Court should hold that there was insufficient evidence to prove that the crowbar was objectively capable of causing serious injury or death."). The Conclusion following the Argument states the relief sought on appeal (*e.g.*, "For the foregoing reasons, the conviction of Appellant for aggravated robbery should be reduced to robbery, and the case remanded to the trial court for re-sentencing."). The Conclusion following the Argument is discussed in Chapter 22.

H. Point Headings

Every point in a brief is introduced by a **point heading**. A point heading is a sentence that persuasively summarizes the argument advanced in that point. Traditionally, point headings are designated by Roman numerals ("I," "II," "III," etc.) and written in full capital letters. For example:

Example 1

POINT I

SMITH'S SLURRED SPEECH AND AGGRESSIVE BEHAVIOR ARE SUFFICIENT EVIDENCE OF "VISIBLE INTOXICATION" UNDER THE STATE'S DRAM SHOP ACT.

The point for a lengthy or complex argument may be stated generally and then developed in more detail in two or more sub-headings. Traditionally, sub-headings are designated by capital letters ("A," "B," "C," etc.) and written in capitals and lower case. Here is an example of a general point heading that is developed in two sub-headings:

Example 2

POINT I

THE LOWER COURT CORRECTLY HELD THAT THE APPELLANT FAILED TO ESTABLISH A PRIMA FACIE CASE OF DISCRIMINATION UNDER THE AMERICANS WITH DISABILITIES ACT.

[Text summarizing the point's argument goes here, if appropriate.]

A.   The Appellant Failed to Prove That Her Moderate Loss of Hearing Substantially Limits a Major Life Activity and Therefore Constitutes a Disability.

[Text of argument related to sub-point A goes here.]

B.   Assuming That Appellant's Condition is a Disability, Appellee Did Not Discriminate against Her Because of Such Condition.

[Text of argument related to sub-point B goes here.]

In the preceding example, you could put a lead for the entire point (summarizing the argument developed in both sub-points "A" and "B") after the point heading and before sub-heading "A." Or you could have no text between the point heading and sub-heading "A," choosing instead to begin each sub-point with separate leads.

1.   Assert your conclusion and explain it with specific, necessary facts

A heading should assert the legal conclusion you want the court to reach and support it with necessary facts. Consider the effectiveness of the following headings:

Example 3

POINT I

THE APPELLANT CLEARLY WAIVED THE ATTORNEY-CLIENT PRIVILEGE.

Example 4

POINT I

THE APPELLANT WAIVED THE ATTORNEY-CLIENT PRIVILEGE BY DISCLOSING IT.

Example 5
POINT I
THE APPELLANT WAIVED THE ATTORNEY-CLIENT PRIVILEGE WHEN HE SENT THE ALLEGEDLY PRIVILEGED DOCUMENT TO TWO OF HIS BUSINESS ASSOCIATES.

Of these three versions, Example 5 is best. Example 3 merely asserts a conclusion. Example 4 is better than Example 3. It explains the conclusion with a general fact: the privilege was waived because the appellant "disclosed" it. But because this fact is expressed broadly, the appellate court may remain unpersuaded, unwilling to accept the implied assertion that the appellant's acts amounted to "disclosure." Example 5 is the best because it gives the court *specific* necessary facts—the appellant sent the document to two associates—to support the legal conclusion that the privilege was waived.

2. Keep it short.

To insure readability, point headings must be short, clear, and persuasive. Do not draft a point heading longer than a sentence, and strive to keep it under 35 words. If you find it difficult to stay within these limits, then state the point generally in a heading and give a more detailed presentation in two or more sub-headings. For instance, the following heading is too long and thus difficult to follow:

Example 6
POINT I
THE JURY'S VERDICT IN THIS CASE SHOULD BE REDUCED TO ROBBERY BECAUSE THERE WAS INSUFFICIENT EVIDENCE TO PROVE THAT APPELLANT USED A DEADLY WEAPON AS THAT TERM IS DEFINED IN TEXAS PENAL CODE § 29.03 IN THAT THE PROSECUTION FAILED TO PROVE THAT APPELLANT INTENDED TO CAUSE DEATH OR SERIOUS INJURY OR THAT IN FACT THE CROWBAR HELD BY HER WAS CAPABLE OF CAUSING SUCH AN INJURY.

The argument is more readable, and therefore more persuasive, if it is split into a general heading with two sub-headings:

Example 7

APPELLANT'S CONVICTION FOR AGGRAVATED ROBBERY MUST BE REDUCED TO ROBBERY BECAUSE THE EVIDENCE IS INSUFFICIENT TO PROVE THAT THE APPELLANT USED OR EXHIBITED A DEADLY WEAPON UNDER TEXAS PENAL CODE § 29.03.

A. The evidence is insufficient to prove that the Appellant intended to cause death or serious injury.

B. The State introduced no evidence proving that the crowbar used by the Appellant could cause death or serious injury.

3. Focus on the narrow issue

The heading should relate to the specific argument developed under it. If your heading is about a specific element or the meaning of a specific term, focus on that element or term, not on more general matters, such as whether the claim is established or whether plaintiff is entitled to the relief he requested. For example, consider the following two headings, dealing with the issue of whether the defendant waived the attorney-client privilege:

Example 8

POINT I

THE TRIAL COURT INCORRECTLY HELD THAT THE DOCUMENT WAS SUBJECT TO THE ATTORNEY-CLIENT PRIVILEGE AND THEREFORE NOT DISCOVERABLE.

Example 9

POINT I

THE TRIAL COURT INCORRECTLY HELD THAT THE APPELLANT WAIVED THE ATTORNEY-CLIENT PRIVILEGE WHEN HE SENT THE ALLEGEDLY PRIVILEGED DOCUMENT TO TWO OF HIS BUSINESS ASSOCIATES.

The heading in Example 8 has a misplaced focus: it informs the court only about the lower court's holding and the procedural context in which the issue arose. (The lower court was deciding whether the document was discoverable, that is, whether the plaintiff could require the defendant to give him a copy of it.) However, it neither asserts nor supports the point's main argument: that the privilege was waived. Example 9 is better because it asserts and supports the argument to be developed under it.

For some headings (particularly a heading with a point that is developed in subheadings), you may take a broader view, focusing on the lower court's decision (as in Example 2) or on the relief sought (Example 7).

4. Make sure your headings persuasively present your argument in the Table of Contents

When read together in the brief's Table of Contents, the point headings should present a coherent, comprehensive summary of the brief's entire argument. Review your headings in the Table of Contents to be sure they are consistent in form and style and that they present a complete, logical summary.

5. Do not put case citations in your headings

If you make an assertion about the law in your heading, do not include a citation to a supporting case. Support it in the point itself. You may however, refer to a case in short form in a heading if the case is well-known and its name is commonly associated with a particular rule or standard.

6. For statutory issues, cite the statute and, when appropriate, the relevant statutory language

If your issue is statutory, refer to the statute in the heading. (See Examples 1 and 2 of this section.) Moreover, if the issue involves the meaning of a word or phrase in a statute, include the word or phrase in the heading. (See Example 7, quoting the term "deadly weapon.")

Do Exercises 20-D(1) and 20-D(2) Now, p. 349

I. Arranging Points in a Multi-Issue Argument

If your Argument has more than one point, sequence the points to maximize your chances of winning the appeal. Advocates usually present their best arguments first. This order makes good sense: a judge who is unpersuaded by a brief's first point may be less willing to accept the later ones.

The two sub-issues in the *Dunn* brief (Appendix D, p. 425) are arranged in order of persuasiveness. The first point (there was insufficient evidence that

Dunn's conduct was assertive) precedes the second one (there was insufficient evidence that the crowbar was deadly) because the assertive conduct argument is much stronger. This order reverses the order in which most cases consider the issues. Most cases dealing with these sub-issues consider the deadliness sub-issue first, treating it as a threshold question. The brief's reverse order is nonetheless a good strategy. It is difficult to argue persuasively that the crowbar could not cause serious injury or death. Presenting that argument first could make a judge less receptive to the stronger argument on assertive conduct.

Although putting your strongest argument first is generally more sensible, in some instances you may decide to place a somewhat weaker point before a stronger one—for example, if the weaker point should logically precede the stronger one. Suppose you were arguing that your client did not intentionally interfere with his employer's contractual rights. This tort has two elements: (1) the employer had no enforceable contractual rights, and (2) even if he did have such rights, your client did not interfere with them. Even if the first point were slightly weaker than the second, you might decide to put it first if you concluded that the judge would be better able to understand the second argument after reading the first.

EXERCISES

Exercise 20-A

Nadine Jackson's husband Dwight was killed on a ride at an amusement park. Jackson sued the park for negligent infliction of emotional distress. A jury found in her favor, and the amusement park appealed.

You represent Nadine Jackson. Review the memorandum of law in Appendix B, p. 407). Prepare the lead for a point arguing that the evidence was sufficient to support the verdict.

Exercise 20-B

You represent Joseph Lake in his appeal of a conviction for criminal mischief in the fifth degree. Lake was arrested for breaking the window of a house, causing over $200 of damage. According to Lake's unchallenged testimony, he and his friends were attempting to throw rocks onto the roof of the house. The criminal mischief statute provides:

> A person is guilty of criminal mischief in the fifth degree when, having no right to do so, he recklessly damages the property of another in an amount exceeding $100. For the purpose of this section, a person acts "recklessly" if he is aware of and consciously disregards a substantial and unjustifiable risk of damage to another's property.

Lake has appealed on the ground that there was insufficient evidence of his recklessness. Review the following rule statements and decide which one best states the rule for this argument. Explain why the other rules are not as effective.

a. Criminal mischief in the fifth degree requires more than just mere damage to property. Rather, the defendant must have been consciously and substantially reckless.

b. A conviction for criminal mischief must be reversed unless the evidence proves beyond a reasonable doubt that (1) there was a substantial and unjustifiable risk of damaging property, and (2) the defendant knew the risk and consciously disregarded it.

c.   A conviction for criminal mischief in the fifth degree will not stand unless the jury had a reasonable basis for determining that the defendant acted recklessly, he damaged property, he had no right to do so, and the damage exceeded $100.

Exercise 20-C(1)

The following rule is from a brief appealing a conviction for reckless endangerment in the first degree. The evidence established that the appellant wove through traffic in a stolen car at 90 mph for over five minutes in an attempt to evade pursuing police.

> A person commits reckless endangerment in the first degree when he recklessly engages in conduct that creates a grave risk of death to another person under circumstances that evince a depraved indifference to human life.

Which of the following best applies the rule to the facts? Explain your choice.

a.   Clearly Appellant's high-speed flight from the police was an attempt to avoid capture, not to act recklessly. He had no intent or desire to hurt anyone. The conviction should be reversed because Appellant's motives are inconsistent with recklessness.

b.   Although Appellant's weaving through traffic to avoid the police may have been reckless, it does not evince a depraved indifference to human life.

c.   Appellant's driving created a risk of injury, but in fact he injured no one. He exhibited none of the inhumane, callous, or cruel behavior associated with a depraved indifference to human life.

Exercise 20-C(2)

You represent Roger Smith in his appeal of a trial court's dismissal of his negligence complaint against The Reformed Church of Arcadia. Read the Facts and Summary of the Law that follow. Identify the issue, and write persuasive rule and application statements. For the purpose of this exercise, do not include rule support or case comparisons.

Summary of the Law

The liability of a landowner to someone injured upon his property is governed by the standard of reasonable care under the circumstances, which employs foreseeability as a measure of liability. Such liability should rest upon a determination of the foreseeability of the plaintiff's presence in light of the frequency of the use of the area where the accident occurred, coupled with whether the defendant knew of the defective condition long enough before the plaintiff's injury . . . to have corrected it, or to give adequate warning of it. [Citations omitted.] *Demarrais v. Swift*, 724 N.Y.S.2d 766, 767 (2d Dept. 2001)

Facts

Roger Smith was injured on a Sunday morning when he entered the front porch of a house located on property owned by The Reformed Church of Arcadia. The house, which had been the pastor's residence, had been partially torn down by House Wreckers, a demolition company hired by the church. No work was being done on the house that weekend. The house was encircled with yellow tape. The entrance to the front porch was blocked with red tape with the word "Danger" written on it. Smith was trying to enter the house because he needed a demolition contractor and wanted to leave a note with his name and telephone number at the site. Smith sued the church to recover damages for his injuries, alleging the church was negligent. The church moved to dismiss. The trial court granted the motion.

Exercise 20-D(1)

Choose the more effective point heading for each of the following pairs. Explain your choice.

a.   THE LOWER COURT CORRECTLY DISMISSED THE APPELLEE'S COMPLAINT FOR NEGLIGENCE BECAUSE IT DID NOT STATE AN ADEQUATE GROUND UPON WHICH RELIEF COULD BE GRANTED.

b.   THE LOWER COURT CORRECTLY DISMISSED APPELLEE'S NEGLI-
GENCE CLAIM BECAUSE APPELLEE FAILED TO ALLEGE FACTS ESTAB-
LISHING THAT APPELLANT HAD A DUTY TO PROTECT APPELLEE FROM
THE INTENTIONAL ACTS OF THIRD PARTIES.

c.   APPELLANT'S WEAVING THOUGH HEAVY TRAFFIC AT 90 MILES
PER HOUR FOR OVER FIVE MINUTES TO AVOID CAPTURE CREATED A
GRAVE RISK OF INJURY TO INNOCENT DRIVERS AND PEDESTRIANS.

d.   THE APPELLANT'S CONVICTION FOR RECKLESS ENDANGER-
MENT IN THE FIRST DEGREE WAS CLEARLY WARRANTED BY THE EVI-
DENCE.

e.   THE COURT HAS JURISDICTION OVER THE APPELLANT BECAUSE
SHE HAD SUBSTANTIAL BUSINESS DEALINGS HERE.

f.   THE COURT HAS JURISDICTION OVER THE APPELLANT BECAUSE
HER ANNUAL SALES TO RESIDENTS OF ARCADIA CONSTITUTE SUBSTAN-
TIAL BUSINESS DEALINGS IN THE STATE.

Exercise 20-D(2)

Thomas O'Rourke, an employee of Gideon Construction, was injured when
a scaffold he was working on toppled and fell to the floor from a height of twenty
feet. O'Rourke knew the scaffold had a defective hoist, but he used it anyway
because no other scaffold was available. Arcadia Labor Law § 240 provides that
owners are strictly liable for injuries caused by unsafe scaffolding equipment.
O'Rourke moved for summary judgment against Gideon on the issue of liability,
and the trial court granted the motion. Gideon appealed.

*Review the following headings, which appear in the brief for Appellee O'Rourke.
Reorganize and number them as point headings and sub-point headings to make a
logical, coherent argument.*

a.   An employee's negligence does not preclude recovery for personal
injuries under § 240.

b.   The trial court correctly granted Appellant's motion for summary judgment.

c.   The undisputed fact that the scaffold toppled and caused Appellant to
fall twenty feet to a concrete floor establishes that the scaffold was defective.

d. Appellant did not act negligently by using the sole scaffold provided to him by Appellee.

e. Arcadia Labor Law § 240 imposes strict liability on contractors whose workers are injured by falls from defective scaffolding.

f. Appellee cannot avoid strict liability for its defective scaffold by alleging that appellant was negligent.

CHAPTER 21

The Appellate Brief: The Statement of the Case Section

When you master this chapter, you will understand:

1. the purpose of the Statement of the Case in an appellate brief;

2. how to write the Procedural History; and

3. how to write the Statement of Facts.

T he Statement of the Case is the section of the appellate brief that sets the stage for the Argument. It explains what happened between the parties, their legal claims, the lower court's disposition of those claims, the basis for the appeal, and the relief requested. The Statement of the Case prepares the appellate court to accept the reasoning in the Argument.

The heading for the Statement of the Case and its format depend on the jurisdiction. But all jurisdictions require the brief to recite the procedural history and facts in some form. Court rules also require the brief to support procedural and factual information by citing to the record. Law school assignments may dispense with this requirement. Before writing your appellate brief, check the applicable court rules or the instructions for your assignment to determine the required format for your brief. The format presented in this chapter divides the Statement of the Case into two parts: the Procedural History and the Statement of Facts.

A. The Procedural History

The Procedural History relates the significant procedural events that occurred in the case in the lower court. A chronological organization often works best in this part of the brief because it is a logical and efficient way to lead the reader through what may be complicated terrain. Introduce the parties and explain the basis for the action. Include key dates and the name of the court where the action was filed. Recount summarily the counterclaims, defenses, and motions that relate to the appeal. Do not, however, overburden the appellate court by littering your Procedural History with procedural minutiae that are not the subject of the appeal. Identify the judgments, orders, rulings, and decisions that are being appealed. Explain who is appealing, the basis for the appeal, and the relief requested.

The following is a sample Procedural History. Notice how key procedural events are chronologically presented.

Sample Procedural History

On August 18, 1999, Alison Alexander ("Alexander") filed a two-count complaint in Arcadia Superior Court against BKL Corp. ("BKL"), her former employer, alleging breach of contract and slander. BKL denied the allegations in their entirety and asserted a counterclaim for misappropriation of trade secret information.

On June 12, 2001, the jury returned a verdict for Alexander on both claims and awarded her $1,500,000 in compensatory damages. BKL moved for judgment notwithstanding the verdict and, in the alternative, for a new trial because of alleged jury misconduct. Judge Herbert denied these motions in an order dated July 29, 2001, and entered the verdict as a final judgment against BKL on July 31, 2001.

BKL timely appealed the order and final judgment. On appeal, BKL requests the court to reverse the order denying its motion for judgment notwithstanding the verdict. In the alternative, BKL requests that the verdict be set aside and a new trial granted on the ground of jury misconduct.

B. The Statement of Facts

1. Developing a theme

The Statement of Facts should persuasively relate your client's position. Think of yourself as a storyteller and develop a theme for the case—a way of looking at the facts—that supports the legal arguments advanced on appeal. The theme of the case often is conceived at the trial level and further refined on appeal. The theme should enable you to highlight favorable facts and minimize the impact of unfavorable ones. The theme must be anchored in the reality of the case. A lawyer cannot craft a theme from whole cloth and then simply write it up with a dramatic flare. The starting point for a powerful theme is careful study of the record and exhaustive research of the law. The following is one approach you can follow to develop a strong theme.

a. Identify the issues for appeal. Study the trial record and search for possible legal errors which may compel an appellate court to reverse, modify, or remand the lower court's decision. These legal errors enable you to identify appealable issues. Suppose, for example, a lawyer represents a client who wants to appeal her forgery conviction. The trial record shows that the judge permitted the prosecutor to cross-examine the client about her fifteen-year-old conviction for endangering the welfare of a minor. The lawyer believes that the judge may have incorrectly allowed this line of questioning and that the testimony may have prejudiced the jury against his client. Hence, the lawyer has identified a possible legal error which raises an issue to argue on appeal.

Issues are often identified for you in law school assignments. If so, do not conjure up issues but rather focus on those identified in the assignment.

b. Research the law to identify meritorious legal arguments. Once you have ferreted out a potential issue for the appeal, research to assess its merit. In the forgery example, the lawyer researches Arcadian law on the admissibility of a criminal defendant's prior convictions. He learns that the courts determine the admissibility of a prior conviction by balancing its probative value against the prejudicial effect it may have on the trier of fact. As a general rule, Arcadian courts do not allow testimony about a conviction that is more than ten years old. Research also reveals that the appellate court may set aside the defendant's conviction and order a new trial in a case in which such testimony is admitted.

Knowledgeable about the law, the lawyer now concludes that the trial judge likely committed a legal error by permitting the prosecutor to cross-examine his client about her fifteen-year-old conviction. The lawyer has found a meritorious legal argument for the appeal.

c. Search the record for necessary facts. After you have researched the law and selected the issues and legal arguments for the appeal, you will be ready to identify the necessary facts. You learned in previous chapters that necessary facts are those the court considers conclusive on the legal issues. Remember, nonoccurrences—things that did not happen—may be necessary facts too (*e.g.*, a seller's failure to notify his buyer of asbestos contamination before selling his home).

In the forgery appeal, the lawyer reviews the record and decides that the age of the prior conviction is a necessary fact because in Arcadia a conviction older than ten years is generally inadmissible. In addition, the nature of his client's prior conviction—endangering the welfare of a minor—is a necessary fact: the conviction is not probative of forgery, the crime with which his client was charged.

d. Devise a theme. Your next task is to create a theme that leads the court to view your case sympathetically and to conclude that your argument is legally correct and inherently fair. The theme encapsulates your view of the story (*e.g.*, that the appellant was denied his day in court; that the appellant is a disgruntled employee seeking to extort money from his employer). The theme, while usually implicit, shapes the selection and placement of the facts in the Statement of Facts.

In the forgery appeal, the lawyer develops the following theme: his client was denied a fair trial because the judge improperly allowed the jury to consider her fifteen-year-old conviction. The admission of testimony about the prior conviction poisoned the jury, prejudicing it against his client. The Statement of Facts should advance this theme.

2. Organizing the facts

The Statement of Facts must contain all the necessary facts, both favorable and unfavorable. It should also include supporting facts that will assist the appellate court in understanding the dispute and enable you to present a compelling story. Although the Statement of Facts should relate the facts in a way that supports the legal arguments, it should not include legal arguments.

Begin the Statement of Facts with a concise context statement that identifies the parties, summarizes the events or transactions central to the lawsuit, and introduces your theme. Here is an example of a context statement for Joe Weiss, an appellee in a negligence action:

> Joe Weiss ("Weiss"), an artist, permanently lost the use of his left arm when Nicholas King ("King") struck him with his car. Instead of watching the road, King was talking on his cellular telephone when he went through a red light and hit Weiss, who was walking across the street in the crosswalk with the light.

Follow the context statement with your client's story. Organize the facts in a way that promotes your theme, facilitates the appellate court's understanding of what happened, and prepares it to accept your client's legal arguments. The facts can be arranged in a chronological, topical, or mixed chronological and topical scheme.

A chronological scheme relates the facts in their order of occurrence, much as a story-teller tells a story. A topical scheme groups facts by claim or element to show how they fit together. It works well with multiple claims or elements. A mixed organizational scheme may be appropriate in complicated cases that involve a series of events or transactions.

The facts in a mixed organizational scheme are arranged by topic and then chronologically within each topic. For example, if a defendant is appealing his conviction on multiple counts of robbery, the prosecutor, in his Statement of Facts, might organize the facts first by topic—each robbery—and then within each topic, chronologically, describing the specifics of each robbery. A mixed organizational scheme may also be used to highlight favorable aspects of a case. The Statement of Facts for a doctor appealing a medical malpractice judgment might, for instance, begin with a context statement and then continue with one or more paragraphs describing a topic—e.g., the extensive training and excellent reputation of the doctor—before launching into a chronological presentation of the facts.

These organizational schemes are illustrative, not mandatory or exhaustive. The facts, law, and theme will determine how you arrange the Statement of Facts.

Regardless of its organization, always end the Statement of Facts on a strong note by concluding with information that supports your client's position.

3. Emphasis

The Statement of Facts should showcase favorable facts and diminish the impact of unfavorable ones. Display favorable facts prominently, relate them in detail, and use descriptive words to further your theme. Deemphasize unfavorable facts in your story, by skimping on supporting details and by using simple words to describe them.

Consider the following excerpts from Statements of Facts written on behalf of an employer who is appealing a decision finding him liable for age discrimination:

> *Version A*: The malcontent employee griped about what he considered to be workplace inequities—the lack of health club privileges for the administrative staff, limited vacation days for probationary employees, and required Friday afternoon meetings for his department. He never complained, however, about his employer's alleged age-biased comments.

> *Version B*: Although he did not express displeasure about allegedly offensive comments, the employee indicated that he disagreed with many things.

Version A makes a stronger statement than does Version B. Version A is concrete, providing the court with examples of the employee's complaints about ordinary business policies and practice. The characterization of the employee as "malcontent" in Version A is therefore well-founded. Unlike Version A, Version B provides no detail and does not portray the employee as a chronic complainer. When describing how the employee complained, Version A uses a strong verb—"griped"; in contrast, Version B uses a weak verb—"indicated." Finally, Version A clearly states that the employee never complained about his employer's alleged age-biased comments. Version B does not make this point, but rather, in a subordinate clause, tells the reader that the employee ". . . did not express displeasure about allegedly offensive comments." This example illustrates how attention to detail, word choice, and the arrangement of words and phrases can help you persuasively present your case.

4. Tone

The tone of the Statement of Facts should be persuasive and professional; appeal to emotion and common sense in a reasonable, measured voice. The nature of the case will dictate the appropriate level of drama and imagery. Indeed, a restrained tone is probably necessary if you are defending a corporate polluter, but a more emphatic tone is acceptable if you are representing a young child maimed in a school shooting. Regardless of the strength of your case, always characterize your client and key events in the most favorable light consistent with the facts. Always include concrete facts supporting your characterizations. It is unethical, not to mention strategically unwise, to mischaracterize the record or to omit important adverse information. Finally, do not personally attack the opposing party. If you do, your credibility will suffer.

5. Conforming the facts

Every fact you mention in the Argument must be in the Statement of Facts and come from the trial record. After you have written the first draft of your appellate brief, you must conform the document: read through the completed Argument carefully, noting each fact that has been mentioned. Return to the Statement of Facts as you come across each fact in the Argument to make sure it appears in the Statement of Facts as well.

C. An Example of How Lawyers Craft a Statement of Facts

Krista and Michael Hathaway's twelve-year-old son Tyler fatally injured George Kline in a jet ski accident. Kline's estate brought an action against Krista and Michael Hathaway. A jury found the Hathaways liable for negligently entrusting a dangerous instrument, their jet ski, to their son. The Hathaways appealed, asserting that the evidence did not, as a matter of law, support the verdict. The Summaries of the Trial Testimony, Summary of Arcadian Law, and the parties' Statements of Facts follow.

Summary of Tyler Hathaway's Trial Testimony

> We live on Lake Serenity, and just about every local kid does lots of water sports. Ever since I was little, I loved the water. My parents signed me up for swimming lessons at the recreation center when I was a year old. I was so good that by the time I was eight I made the town swim team. I compete in

county and state meets and have won many trophies. I swim in the lake all the time.

About three years ago, when I was nine, my friends on the swim team started jet skiing by themselves. I really wanted to try it, but my mom said I was too young. My friends called me a baby and wouldn't hang out with me at the lake. In June 2000, when I turned eleven, my parents finally agreed to let me use my father's jet ski by myself.

I already knew how to use the jet ski because my dad has been taking me out on it since I was five. Although my parents didn't make me take lessons, they did set down a lot of rules. I can't take the jet ski out unless I ask them first, can't ride faster than 20 mph, and can't race.

I broke my parents' rules a few times. Last summer my mom grounded me twice after she found out that I had been racing. This summer Roger Duke, who's on the Lake Police, stopped me because I was jet skiing too fast. He brought me back to the house and told my parents that I was going 40 mph. They were furious. They grounded me for two weeks and said I couldn't use the jet ski for the rest of the summer if anything like that happened again. I admit that after that I took it out without asking permission. Both my parents work and it was hard to resist taking it out, especially since all my friends jet ski, and the keys to our jet ski were hanging on the key peg in the kitchen. A couple of weeks before the accident, my parents found out from a neighbor that I was jet skiing without permission. I promised them I wouldn't do it again. But I did. Except for what happened to Mr. Kline, I've never had an accident or hurt anyone.

It is really hard for me to think about the accident. On August 23, 2001, my friend Josh asked me to go jet skiing with him. I said sure, and we walked a couple of blocks to the lake. When we got there, Josh bumped into Alyson, a popular girl from school, and started talking to her. He told me to go ahead and said he'd catch up with me later. Although no adults were around—my parents were at work—I got my jet ski and hit the water. I felt bad about not asking my parents, but I really felt like going out on the lake. I waved to Josh and Alyson—I guess I was showing off a bit. I didn't spot Mr. Kline in his kayak because I was looking towards the shore. By the time I did see him, it was too late. I was going really fast, about 40 mph, and was too close to him to slow down in time. Mr. Kline's kayak turned over as soon as I hit him. They told us his head crashed into a rock under the water, killing him instantly. The Lake Police brought Mr. Kline's body to the shore. The ambulance drivers put his body on a stretcher, draped a sheet over it, and took it away.

I still can't believe what I did. Mom and Dad tell me they love me and everything will be okay, but I know they are very sad and angry. I go to a psychologist because I have nightmares about the accident and can't eat or sleep.

Summary of Michael Hathaway's Trial Testimony

While some kids in our neighborhood started jet skiing when they turned nine, my wife Krista and I made Tyler wait until his eleventh birthday. I've had our jet ski, a red and black Sea Whiz, for years. It weighs 550 pounds and is 106 inches long, 46 inches wide, and 37 inches high. It can travel up to 45 mph.

Because Tyler is such a great athlete and already knew how to operate the jet ski, we didn't think he needed lessons. Although we believed that Tyler followed our rules on jet skiing, Krista did catch him racing our Sea Whiz with his friends twice last summer. We didn't make a big deal about it because he seemed so contrite, but we grounded Tyler for a week each time. This June, the Lake Police brought Tyler back to the house when they caught him speeding on the jet ski. We grounded him for two weeks and told him we wouldn't let him jet ski anymore if we caught him speeding again. We never caught him speeding again, but in late July my wife and I learned that he had been jet skiing without our permission. We made him promise not to do it again.

Tyler is a wonderful kid and is devastated by what happened. Our family is very sorry about Mr. Kline and can't begin to imagine what his wife and kids are going through now. For Tyler's sake, however, we feel that we have to put this whole thing behind us as soon as possible. What happened is horrible, but it was an accident.

Summary of Arcadian Law

A parent is liable for negligently entrusting a dangerous instrument to his child if
1. the child's use of the instrument is negligent and causes injury;
2. the instrument, because of its physical characteristics, is dangerous when used by the careless child;
3. a parent could foresee that his child would use the instrument carelessly and cause injury; and
4. a parent fails to restrict his child's use of the instrument despite having the ability to do so.

1. Statement of Facts from the Appellant's Brief

Statement of Facts

Krista and Michael Hathaway closely supervised their son Tyler's use of their jet ski. They established a series of rules for the twelve-year-old's operation of the water craft. The Hathaways had no reason to believe that Tyler would improperly operate the jet ski and fatally injure a boater, George Kline.

Tyler is an excellent athlete. He began swimming when he was only a year old. By the time he turned eight, Tyler, already an accomplished swimmer, was competing on the local swim team. The determined young man won many trophies in county and state meets. Tyler's talent in water sports is not limited to swimming. When he turned five, Tyler began riding with his father on the family's jet ski. The jet ski weighs 550 pounds and can travel up to 45 m.p.h. After riding for years with his father, Tyler knew how to operate the water craft. While most of Tyler's friends started jet skiing by themselves at age nine, the Hathaways, strict and cautious parents, made their son wait until he was eleven. By then, Tyler was a strong and experienced athlete ready to ride the water craft on his own.

The Hathaways established rules for Tyler's use of the jet ski: he could not race or ride faster than 20 m.p.h. and had to ask his parents for permission to use the water craft, the keys to which were hanging in the family's kitchen. Although Tyler used the jet ski frequently, almost daily during the summers, he departed from these rules on only a few isolated occasions. In the summer of 2000—a year before the Kline accident—the Hathaways grounded Tyler twice, one week each time, for racing. The following year Tyler once rode the jet ski more than 40 m.p.h. The Hathaways punished Tyler immediately. They grounded him for not one but two full weeks. The Hathaways had good reason to believe that this enhanced punishment was effective: while they learned that Tyler subsequently had taken the jet ski out without their permission, he did not, prior to the Kline accident, ever speed again.

Most significantly, Tyler never had an accident in the year he used the jet ski on his own. Nor did he ever hurt any boaters or swimmers while using the jet ski. The August 23, 2001, incident on Lake Serenity was a tragic accident. The Hathaways had no reason to believe that their son would look toward the shore and not be able to slow the jet ski, traveling at about 40 m.p.h., in time to avoid colliding with Kline's kayak. There was no evidence that Tyler, when riding the jet ski, had ever before failed to pay attention to the boaters and swimmers in the waters around him.

a. *Theme.* A strong theme is developed in the Hathaways' Statement of Facts. Tyler's collision with Kline's kayak is portrayed as an unforeseeable, unfortunate accident. Therefore, the Statement of Facts emphasizes that Tyler had never before injured anyone with the jet ski. It also points out that there was no evidence that he had previously endangered boaters and swimmers while using the water craft. This theme advances the Hathaways' legal argument that they had no reason to foresee that their child would use their jet ski carelessly and injure a boater. The Hathaways' argument challenges the jury's finding on the third element of negligent entrustment of a dangerous instrument (i.e., the parents could foresee that their child would use the instrument carelessly and cause injury). On the other hand, the evidence establishing the other elements is overwhelming: Tyler's negligent use of the jet ski—speeding and lack of attention to boaters and swimmers—caused Kline's death (the first element); the 550 pound motorized jet ski was dangerous in the hands of a careless child (the second element); and the Hathaways could have prevented Tyler from using the jet ski by securing it or hiding the keys, but failed to do so (the fourth element). The only viable argument, therefore, is to challenge the sufficiency of the evidence on the third element of the claim. This insufficiency is the basis for the theme of the case.

b. *Context statement.* The context statement identifies the parties, explains what happened, and introduces the theme. Krista and Michael Hathaway are presented in a favorable light.

c. Organization. The facts are arranged by topics relevant to the third element of negligent entrustment of a dangerous instrument. The second paragraph describes Tyler's expertise in water sports and his training on the jet ski. The third paragraph recounts the rules for Tyler's use of the jet ski, his violation of the rules, and his punishments for violating them. The final paragraph mentions the accident and explains why it was unforeseeable.

d. Characterizations. Tyler is characterized as an excellent athlete and an accomplished swimmer. He is also called a determined young man and a strong and experienced athlete. The Hathaways are characterized as strict and cautious parents because they made their son wait until he was eleven to ride the jet ski by himself even though most of his friends started jet skiing by themselves at age nine. Tyler's violations of the rules are described as isolated. The Hathaways' decision to ground Tyler for two weeks is characterized as an enhanced punishment because they previously had grounded him for only one week. Although it is clear that Tyler caused Kline's death, the word kill is never used.

e. Emphasis of favorable facts. Favorable facts are consistently featured and elaborately recounted. The second paragraph is devoted to a description of Tyler's expertise and training in water sports. The topic sentence of the third paragraph recites the Hathaways' rules for Tyler's use of the jet ski. Similarly, the topic sentence in the final paragraph proclaims that Tyler had never had an accident in the year he had used the jet ski on his own.

f. Deemphasis of unfavorable facts. Unfavorable facts—Tyler's violations of the rules—are sandwiched in between the strong topic and concluding sentences in the third paragraph. The frequency of Tyler's infractions is diminished by providing a contextual time frame: Tyler used the jet ski almost daily during the summers, but departed from the rules on only a few isolated occasions. The description of the big powerful jet ski, information that certainly is not helpful to the Hathaways, is mentioned briefly in the second paragraph. Tyler's access to the jet ski's keys ("the keys to which were hanging in the family's kitchen") is an aside at the end of the topic sentence in the third paragraph. The accident is described in a single sentence in the middle of the final paragraph and is surrounded by information favorable to the Hathaways.

g. Strong conclusion. The final sentence in the Statement of Facts conveys information favorable to the Hathaways and reiterates and emphasizes the theme: "There was no evidence that Tyler, when riding the jet ski, had ever before failed to pay attention to the boaters and swimmers in the waters around him."

2. Statement of Facts from the Appellee's Brief

Statement of Facts

Twelve-year-old Tyler Hathaway killed George Kline, the father of two, with his parents' jet ski. Krista and Michael Hathaway, Tyler's parents, gave Tyler unrestricted access to the water craft even though they knew he had a history of using it carelessly.

On August 23, 2001, young Tyler took the Hathaways' jet ski without asking his parents' permission and set off on his deadly ride on Lake Serenity. At trial Tyler admitted that he was speeding and "showing off" to his friends who were on the shore. He disregarded the safety of boaters on the lake by riding the 550 pound jet ski at 40 m.p.h. and not watching where he was going. Instead of looking out for boaters, the child deliberately fixed his gaze on the shore and waved to his friends. He did not see Mr. Kline until it was too late. Unable to slow the speeding water craft in time, Tyler crashed the jet ski into Mr. Kline's kayak. The kayak turned over on impact. Mr. Kline's head violently struck a rock under the water, killing him instantly.

Tyler's daredevil antics were well-known to his parents. Since he began riding the jet ski by himself at age eleven, Tyler repeatedly violated his parents' rules on his use of the water craft. The child, who had no formal training on the use of the jet ski, had a history of racing and speeding. He was caught racing with his friends on two separate occasions in the summer of 2000. The Hathaways' only reaction was to ground the boy for a week for each episode of potentially deadly behavior.

Only two months before Tyler killed Mr. Kline, the Lake Police caught him speeding. Officer Roger Duke brought Tyler home and told the Hathaways that their son was riding their jet ski at 40 m.p.h., twice the 20 m.p.h. speed limit the Hathaways had imposed on Tyler. The Hathaways, busy working parents who were not around to supervise their son, repeated the same ineffective punishment of the preceding summer: they grounded Tyler, this time for two weeks. Not surprisingly, even after the incident with the Lake Police, Tyler continued to violate his parents' rules. The Hathaways learned that he took their jet ski out in late July without their permission.

Although the Hathaways knew that Tyler had a propensity to use their jet ski in a dangerous manner, they did not lock, chain, or otherwise physically secure it. Moreover, they left the keys to the jet ski dangling on a peg in the family's kitchen, tempting the youngster to continue his perilous course of conduct. Tyler admitted at trial that the temptation to take the freely accessible jet ski without permission proved irresistible. The Hathaways failed to effectively restrict their reckless child's use of their jet ski, and, as a result, Mr. Kline is dead.

a. *Theme.* A forceful theme is developed in this Statement of Facts: the Hathaways' irresponsible entrustment of a dangerous instrument to their careless son caused Kline's tragic death. The theme derives from the elements of the claim: the Hathaways should have foreseen that Tyler would use the jet ski carelessly and cause injury (the third element); they could have restricted his access to the water craft, but failed to do so (the fourth element). Moreover, it responds strongly to the unforeseeable accident theme developed in the Appellant's Statement of the Facts.

b. *Context statement.* The context statement identifies the parties, explains what happened, and introduces the theme. It portrays Tyler and his parents as irresponsible and evokes sympathy for the victim, Mr. Kline.

c. *Organization.* The facts are arranged in a mixed chronological and topical scheme. The second paragraph is a detailed chronology of the accident. The third, fourth, and fifth paragraphs develop topics relevant to the elements of negligent entrustment of a dangerous instrument. The third and fourth paragraphs focus on Tyler's violations of the rules, his parents' knowledge of his careless behavior, and his parents' failure to discipline him effectively. These facts relate to the analysis of the third element of the claim (*i.e.*, the parents could have foreseen that the child would use the instrument carelessly and cause injury). The fifth paragraph chronicles the Hathaways' failure to restrict Tyler's access to the jet ski, information relevant to the fourth element of the claim (*i.e.*, the parents failed to restrict their child's use of the instrument despite having the ability to do so).

d. *Characterizations.* Tyler is characterized as reckless, irresponsible, and young. He is described as a child and a daredevil. The Hathaways are characterized as busy, working parents who were not around to supervise their son. Kline is presented as the deceased father of two. Tyler's violations of the rules are described as repeated. The Hathaways' punishments of Tyler are labeled ineffective. The verb kill is used three times to describe Tyler's conduct; it is in the first sentence of the context statement, the last sentence in the second paragraph, and the topic sentence of the fourth paragraph. The Statement of Facts ends with the powerful word dead.

e. *Emphasis of favorable facts.* Facts favorable to the Appellee's case are high-lighted by both their placement and the amount of space devoted to them. The tragic accident is recounted immediately after the context statement. Tyler's reck-lessness and the unfortunate drama of Kline's death are described in specific and vivid detail. The topic and concluding sentences in every paragraph relate infor-mation favorable to the Kline's estate.

f. *Deemphasis of unfavorable facts.* Kline's estate has a strong position on appeal: the jury has already found the Hathaways liable. A supporting fact that might enhance the Hathaways' argument, Tyler's expertise in water sports, is not included in this Statement of Facts.

g. *Strong conclusion.* The final sentence of the Statement of Facts conveys information favorable to Kline's estate in a forceful, direct statement: "The Hathaways failed to effectively restrict their reckless child's use of their jet ski, and as a result, Mr. Kline is dead."

Do the Exercises on p. 368 Now

Exercise 21-A

List the necessary and supporting facts in the Statements of Facts presented in Section C, pp. 362-363 and pp. 365-366.

Exercise 21-B

List similarities in and differences between the Statements of Facts presented in Section C, pp. 362-363 and pp. 365-366.

Exercise 21-C

Eighteen-year-old Joe Baker was convicted of criminal possession of stolen property in the second degree, for driving a 2000 BMW Z3 owned by Hilary Jefferson. He appealed, asserting that the evidence was, as a matter of law, insufficient to support his conviction. Read the Digest of the Trial Testimony and the Summary of the Law. List the facts that are favorable to Baker and those that are favorable to the prosecution.

Digest of Trial Testimony

1. Baker is a senior at West Mercedes High School.
2. Jefferson's car, valued at $25,000, was stolen three blocks from Baker's home.
3. The ignition and passenger-side door lock of Jefferson's car were damaged.
4. Baker was driving Jefferson's car at the time of his arrest.
5. The police arrested Baker about a half mile from his school on a Monday afternoon.
6. The police found a key in the ignition at the time of Baker's arrest.
7. Baker testified that he did not know the car was stolen. He said that Larry, his friend from the neighborhood, claimed to own the car and let him drive it after school.
8. Baker does not know Larry's last name or address.
9. The police recovered Baker's school books on the passenger seat of the car.

Summary of Arcadian Law

Arcadia Penal Law § 78.20: Criminal Possession of Stolen Property in the Second Degree

A person is guilty of criminal possession of stolen property in the second degree if

(1) he knows or has reason to know that he possesses stolen property;
(2) he intends to permanently deprive the owner of the property; and
(3) the value of the property exceeds $5,000.

Exercise 21-D

(1) Use the information in Exercise 21-C to write a Statement of Facts for Joe Baker. (2) Use the information in Exercise 21-C to write a Statement of Facts for the prosecution.

CHAPTER 22

The Appellate Brief: Ancillary Sections

When you master this chapter, you will understand:

1. how to prepare the opening sections of the appellate brief (the Title Page, Table of Contents, and Table of Authorities);

2. how to draft Questions Presented that frame the issues on appeal in a light favorable to your client's case;

3. how to write a concise and persuasive Summary of the Argument; and

4. how to prepare the closing sections of the appellate brief (the Conclusion, Signature, and Appendix).

I n preceding chapters, you learned how to draft the two principal sections of the appellate brief: the Argument and the Statement of the Case. This chapter covers the remaining sections.

A. The Opening Sections of the Appellate Brief: The Title Page, Table of Contents, and Table of Authorities

The appellate brief begins with a title (or cover) page, a table of contents, and a table of authorities. Like other parts of the appellate brief, their form and content are dictated by applicable appellate court rules. To familiarize yourself with the format of these sections, review the opening sections of the Dunn brief in Appendix D, p. 425.

1. The Title Page

The title page gives the name of the document (*e.g.*, "Brief for Appellant"), the name of the appellate court (*e.g.*, "New York Court of Appeals"), the name of the case (*e.g.*, "John Smith and Michele Smith, Appellants, v. Thomas Mercer, Appellee"), the court's docket number for the appeal, and the name and address of the attorney who prepared the brief. In addition, it sometimes refers to the judgment or order that is being appealed and the name of the lower court that entered it.

2. The Table of Contents

The Table of Contents lists each of the brief's sections and the page where they first appear in the document. (These sections are listed in Chapter 19 on p. 317.) The table also includes the text of the Argument's point and sub-point headings and the pages where they begin. When read together, these headings should give the court a clear, coherent outline of your Argument. The Table of Contents may be the appellate court's first exposure to your argument, so take the time to make it look professional.

3. Table of Authorities

The Table of Authorities lists, under separate headings, the cases, statutes, and other sources (primary and secondary) cited in your brief and gives the page numbers in the brief where these citations appear. Cite the sources in full citation form.

Begin with the cases. Under a heading for Cases, list the cases alphabetically, or if you have many cases, group them by court (*e.g.*, U.S. Supreme Court Cases) or court system (*e.g.*, Federal District Court Cases), starting with the highest court and moving down. Alphabetize case names within each group. Cases should be followed by a heading for Constitutional Provisions and Statutes (if there are any), grouping them by type (*e.g.*, "U.S. Constitution," "Federal Statutes," etc.). Other sources should be listed under a heading entitled "Miscellaneous Sources" or if appropriate, "Secondary Sources."

If a case is cited on more than three different pages in the brief, do not list the page numbers in the table; instead, put the term *passim* (a Latin word meaning *here and there*, used to indicate that it is referred to in many places) in the column where the page numbers would appear.

B. The Question Presented

The Question Presented focuses the court's attention on the issues. The goal is not just to identify the issues for the court but to present them persuasively so that the court will accept your positions.

Unlike the Questions Presented in legal memos, which are written for internal office purposes, Questions Presented in briefs must comply with applicable court rules. Most court rules dictate the form and placement of the questions.

Draft a Question Presented for each issue in your brief. Put the questions in the same order as they are discussed in the Argument. If you have a single Question Presented, do not number it. If you have multiple Questions Presented, then number them.

A Question Presented can be in the form of a question or a statement. In the following set of examples, the same issue is presented in both forms:

> **Question Presented as a question**
> Did the trial court correctly hold that Appellant had a sensory and contemporaneous observance of the accident when she heard the accident at close range and immediately witnessed its aftermath?
>
> **Question Presented as a statement**
> Whether the trial court correctly held that Appellant had a sensory and contemporaneous observance of the accident when she heard the accident at close range and immediately witnessed its aftermath.

Your legal writing professor may recommend a particular format. If not, choose a format and use it consistently.

Crafting an effective Question Presented requires you to strike a careful balance: you must make the question short, complete, and persuasive. A question is short and complete if it clearly and concisely imparts the issue, applicable law, and the pertinent necessary facts to the appellate court judges who are not familiar with them. A question is persuasive when it suggests a favorable response. Achieving these objectives requires a considerable amount of thought. Here are six drafting principles to help you succeed.

1.   Separate the law from the facts

In a legal memorandum, you crafted the Question Presented in three parts: the first giving the claim, crime, or defense and the relevant element of the law; the second giving the pertinent necessary facts; and the third posing the question itself. (See Chapter 9, p. 163.) This format required you to write several sentences. In an appellate brief, you must convey the law, facts, and issue in a single sentence. To make the Question Presented readable, think of it as having two parts, one describing the law and the other the facts. Present the law before the facts. In effect the question should ask, "Is this requirement of the law satisfied under these particular facts?" In the following examples, the law component is italicized and the fact component is bolded:

> Did *the trial court correctly find that Appellant had a sensory and contemporaneous observance of the accident* when **she heard the accident at close range and immediately witnessed its aftermath?**

> Whether *the jury properly found that Appellant exhibited a deadly weapon during the course of the robbery* by **brandishing a baseball bat at her victim and threatening to hit him with it if he interfered with the crime.**

> Was *the evidence legally sufficient to support Appellant's conviction for second-degree murder* when **three persons allegedly fired at the deceased and no ballistics or other evidence linked Appellants' firearm to the victim's fatal wound?**

This format is suited to appeals involving applications of law to fact. Questions of law would be styled differently, focusing exclusively on the proper interpretation of the law.

2. Present the facts in a favorable but measured tone

Do not overstate your client's position by slanting the facts in an overtly partisan way. Avoid judgmental adjectives and adverbs, and instead make your point with concrete facts that favor your position. Calling the appellant "cold-hearted" and the victim "helpless" is not as persuasive as reporting that the appellant inflicted multiple stab wounds on his eighty-year-old victim's face and chest.

3. Do not include legal conclusions in your facts

If the appeal is about whether the appellant slandered the appellee, do not describe the appellant's statements as "slanderous remarks." Similarly, in a breach-of-contract appeal, do not phrase the Question Presented this way:

> Did the lower court properly grant summary judgment for Appellant when the evidence showed that Appellee breached the contract by failing to timely deliver the goods?

The above question is poor because it makes legal conclusions. Rather than posing the question, it answers it for the court. Instead, ask:

> Did the lower court properly grant summary judgment on Appellant's claim for breach of contract when the contract required delivery no later than noon on January 15th and Appellee admittedly delivered the goods seven days later?

4. Do not refer to names, events, or other facts with which the court is unfamiliar

The court may read your Question Presented before it reads any other part of your brief. It may, therefore, be unfamiliar with the parties and the case. To avoid confusion, refer to persons by party name (appellant or appellee) or generically (testator, niece, co-worker). Do not allude to events or other facts that the court will not learn about until later in the brief. For instance, the question "Was Smith's search of Max Hart's trunk constitutional?" is bound to confuse a judge who does not know Smith and Hart or how and why the search happened. Instead, you should write:

> Whether the Constitution's prohibition against unreasonable searches is violated when a police officer stops a driver for

exceeding the speed limit and then makes him open his car's trunk for inspection.

5. Stress aspects of the law that favor your client

A Question Presented should emphasize the law that favors your client. For instance, in an appeal of a jury conviction for murder, the appellant and appellee might stress entirely different aspects of the law. The appellant might phrase the law component of the question to stress the State's high burden of proof: "Was the evidence sufficient to prove beyond a reasonable doubt that Appellant committed murder when . . . ." The appellee, on the other hand, might stress the strict standard of review: "Viewing the evidence in the light most favorable to the State, was there a reasonable basis for the jury to conclude that Appellant committed murder when . . . ."

In an appeal involving the dismissal of a complaint for intentional infliction of emotional distress, the parties might describe the law differently. The appellant might describe the conduct required to hold the defendant culpable as simply "extreme and outrageous," but the appellee, attempting to make the law's requirements seem more stringent, might describe the conduct as "outrageous conduct totally beyond all accepted social norms." Of course, you must state the law accurately. Make sure your description is grounded in a statute or a controlling case.

6. For Questions Presented involving statutes, identify or quote the relevant statutory language

If your question involves the construction of a statute, you should identify the statute. For example:

> Does a restaurant breach its warranty of merchantability under Uniform Commercial Code § 2-314 by serving cherry ice cream that contains a single cherry pit?

Moreover, if particular words in the statute are at issue, quote the pertinent statutory language:

> Did Appellant use Appellee's "portrait or picture" under Arcadia Civil Rights Law § 51 by manufacturing and selling a mannequin that was a recognizable likeness of her?

Do Exercise 22-A Now, p. 380

C. Summary of the Argument

In the Summary of the Argument, the advocate must accomplish three things. First, he must acquaint the court with the legal issues on appeal. Second, he must explain to the court, with minimal citation and other support, why the court should hold in his client's favor. Third, he should give a broad outline of the Argument, thereby providing a thesis for the Argument Section.

The Summary of the Argument should begin by stating the theory of the case and the relief requested. Unlike the Questions Presented, it may be overtly partisan. For instance, the Summary of the Argument in Dunn's appellate brief begins this way:

> Viewed in the light most favorable to the verdict, the evidence is insufficient to prove a principal element of aggravated robbery: namely, that Dunn used or exhibited a deadly weapon while committing a robbery. Because the State failed to present sufficient evidence establishing this element, Dunn's conviction must be reduced to robbery.

copied

Next, you should prepare the court for the Argument by summarizing your analysis. Again, be assertive: present the applicable legal rules in the light most favorable to your client and apply them favorably to your case. If your issue involves a statute, you should cite it, but you should avoid citing cases unless a case is controlling. The Summary of the Argument in Dunn's appellate brief continues as follows:

> To prove that Dunn used or exhibited a deadly weapon while committing a robbery, the State had to establish beyond a reasonable doubt that (1) Dunn displayed or used the crowbar in a manner which established her intent to cause serious bodily injury or death (the assertive conduct requirement), and (2) the crowbar was capable of causing serious bodily injury (the objective capacity requirement). First, even when viewed in the light most favorable to the verdict, the evidence fails to prove assertive conduct: Dunn used the crowbar only as a burglar's tool, not as a weapon. She did not advance on Keyes, and Keyes suffered no injury and showed no fear of physical harm. Second, the State presented no evidence on the objective capacity of the crowbar to cause death or serious bodily injury.

copied

The Summary of the Argument should be succinct and focused. Make sure it outlines the structure of the Argument. Presenting the analysis in the same order makes it easier for the court to follow the Argument's more detailed analysis.

Do Exercise 22-B Now, p. 380

D. The Closing Sections of the Appellate Brief: The Conclusion, Signature, and Appendix

The Argument is followed by a short conclusion and the signature of the attorney who prepared the brief. In addition, if you cite statutes or constitutional provisions in the brief, consult the applicable court rules to determine if you should include the relevant text of these laws in an appendix.

1. The Conclusion

The Conclusion following the Argument states the relief that the advocate is seeking on appeal:

> For the foregoing reasons, the Appellant's conviction for aggravated robbery should be reduced to robbery, and the case remanded to the trial court for re-sentencing.

Do not rehash your argument in the Conclusion. The Conclusion can often be stated in a single sentence.

2. The Signature

Consult the applicable court rules for signature requirements. Usually, the name of the attorney who prepared the brief should be typed and signed, together with the attorney's address, the date, and the city and state:

William Ward, Esq.
Attorney for the Appellant
[signature here]
201 Main Street
New City, Arcadia 01010
Dated: _____
New City, Arcadia

3. Appendix

Some courts require the particular text of the pertinent statutes or constitutional provisions to be reproduced in an Appendix. Others require that a separate section in the brief be included for the text. If your brief includes an analysis or discussion of a statutory section or constitutional provision, consult the court rules to determine where you should put the text.

A'ant should have privileged memo returned + be issued a prot. order b/c they took reasonable steps to prevent its disclosure.

Aant demanding return of the priv memo immediately after learing of its disclosure constitutes a prompt step to rectify the error

Exercise 22-A

Choose the most effective Question Presented for each of the following pairs. Explain your choice.

    a.   Whether the evidence convicting Appellant of reckless endangerment in the first degree was sufficient in light of the fact that Appellant's actions did not evince a depraved indifference to human life.

    b.   Whether the jury could find Appellant guilty of reckless endangerment in the first degree on the ground that he exhibited a depraved indifference to human life when the evidence established that he careened through heavy traffic at 90 miles an hour.

    c.   Was the evidence of Appellant's earlier arrest, ostensibly admitted to establish motive, unduly prejudicial when Appellant was facing a charge not requiring proof of intent, the earlier arrest occurred three months prior to the crime, and Appellant's motive was firmly established by other, admissible evidence?

    d.   Did the trial court incorrectly allow testimony about Appellant's arrest for driving without a license even though that arrest did not result in a conviction and the testimony was not probative on the issue of intent?

Exercise 22-B

    George Kline was killed in an accident involving a jet-ski operated by twelve-year-old Tyler Hathaway. Kline's estate sued Tyler's parents, Michael and Krista Hathaway, for negligently entrusting a dangerous instrument to their son. A jury found the Hathaways liable and they are appealing, asserting that the evidence did not support the verdict as a matter of law.

    You represent the Hathaways. Review the summaries of the trial testimony of Tyler and Michael Hathaway, as well as the summary of Arcadia law (Chapter 21, p. 359). Prepare the Summary of the Argument section for the Hathaways' appellate brief.

CHAPTER 23

The Reply Brief

When you master this chapter, you will understand:

1. the purpose of a reply brief;

2. the format of a reply brief; and

3. how to craft an effective reply brief.

L awyers in appellate practice write three types of briefs. The appellant writes the initial brief, arguing for reversing or modifying a lower court order. After reviewing the initial brief, the appellee writes an answering (or responding) brief, arguing that the lower court order should be affirmed. Usually, the answering brief has the same format as the initial brief, with its own Question Presented, Statement of the Case, Summary of the Argument, Argument, and Conclusion. Although called an "answering" brief, its purpose is not exclusively to rebut the arguments made in the initial brief. Like the initial brief, the answering brief presents a full argument of the issues raised on appeal and *in addition*, responds to points raised in the initial brief.

The reply brief is the third type of brief. In practice, it is written by the appellant. Unlike the other two types of briefs, the reply brief is purely responsive. It rebuts arguments made by the appellee in the answering brief.

In many legal writing and appellate advocacy courses, the actual practice is modified because of time constraints: often the appellant and appellee prepare and exchange initial briefs concurrently, and each responds to the other's brief in a reply. Thus, although in actual practice an appellee does not usually write a reply brief, an appellee in a mock appeal in law school often does. This chapter and the reply brief in Appendix E offer the law-school version of reply briefs.

A. The Purpose of the Reply Brief

The purpose of the reply brief is to respond to the arguments made by your adversary. The reply brief should not repeat or summarize the contents of your initial brief. Rather, it should identify deficiencies in your adversary's argument and, in doing so, convince the court that your client's arguments are meritorious.

While the reply brief should not repeat old arguments from the original brief, under many court rules it is not permitted to introduce entirely new arguments—that is, arguments not in the original brief—unless they respond to the adversary's arguments. For instance, if the appellant argued in his initial brief that the evidence showed that the appellee breached the contract, the appellant cannot argue for the first time in his reply brief that the contract is unconscionable, unless that argument responds to an argument in the appellee's brief.

B. The Format of the Reply Brief

Like all appellate briefs, the format of the reply brief is governed by court rules. Generally, it has the following format:

1. Title Page. The title page of a party's reply brief is identical to the title page of that party's initial brief, except for its title "Reply Brief for Appellant [Appellee]."

2. Table of Authorities. The Table of Authorities lists all statutes, cases, and other authorities cited in the reply brief, even if they were previously cited in the initial brief or your adversary's brief. Do not list your adversary's brief in the Table of Authorities, even though you probably will cite it in your reply.

3. Statement of Facts. Include a Statement of Facts *only* if the arguments in your adversary's brief require you to recite facts in the record that were not included in the initial brief, or if your adversary mischaracterized or omitted facts in his Statement of Facts.

4. Argument. The Argument is the core of the reply brief. Like the Argument section of an initial brief, it is divided into separate points, each with its own heading. Each point focuses on a different deficiency in your adversary's argument.

5. Conclusion. The Conclusion restates the initial brief's conclusion, briefly reiterating the relief requested.

An example of a reply brief in *Dunn v. State* appears in Appendix E, p. 441.

C. Crafting an Effective Reply Brief

There are four principal ways to rebut arguments in an adversary's brief. First, you can argue that your adversary's position is based on incorrect facts. Second, you can argue that his position is not supported by the law. Third, you can attack the substance of your adversary's argument, pointing out inconsistencies or logical flaws. Fourth, you can refute policy arguments that he relied on to support his position.

1. Refute your adversary's version of the facts

Your adversary may have neglected to include pertinent facts or included facts that are not supported by the trial record. If so, in your reply brief you should show that your adversary's arguments are based on a distorted or incorrect reading of the record.

If your adversary's Statement of Facts contains misstatements or omits facts, you may include a Statement of Facts in your reply brief to clarify and correct such imprecise characterizations of the record. Alternatively, you may decide not to include a Statement of Facts in your reply brief and rather refute your adversary's facts in the Argument section.

Even if you include a Statement of Facts in the reply brief, you should point out any factual inaccuracies in your adversary's brief in the Argument section. Your adversary may slant the facts, presenting them in a way that favors her position. If so, you should discredit your adversary's version by showing how it is at odds with the concrete facts in the record. Here is an example from the Argument section of the reply brief in *Dunn v. State* (Appendix E):

> In her brief, Appellant mischaracterizes the facts, casting her own conduct as defensive, and the victim's conduct as aggressive. According to Appellant, she did not intend to seriously injure or kill Keyes when she waved a crowbar at him and threatened to hurt him. Rather, she was trying to "stop" Keyes, who, Appellant insists, "boldly interrupted the robbery and approached" her. Appellant's Brief, p. 6.
>
> Appellant's spin on the facts—the crowbar-wielding robber protecting herself from her unarmed target—is contradicted by the evidence. Keyes's *uncontroverted* testimony established that Appellant waived the crowbar at Keyes and yelled, "Stop right there or you're gonna get hurt." *See* Appellant's Brief, p. 2. Further, uncontroverted evidence also established that Keyes, in response to Appellant's threat, stopped, permitting Appellant to complete her crime. In sum, the ample evidence here, viewed "in the light most favorable to the prosecution," *Lockett v. State,* 874 S.W.2d 810, 813 (Tex. Crim. App. 1994), proved exactly what the law requires: that Appellant displayed the crowbar "in a manner conveying an express *or implied* threat that serious bodily injury or death will result if the aggressor is not satisfied." *Hammons v. State,* 856 S.W.2d 797, 801 (Tex. Crim. App. 1993).

Arguments are often built on facts. If the factual foundation is shattered, the arguments built on them will crumble.

2.   Refute your adversary's legal support

An argument is not effective unless it is supported by law. You should review every authority cited in your adversary's brief to make sure that he has accurately quoted or summarized its provisions (if it is a statute) or its holding and reasoning (if it is a case). In addition, you should update all of his authorities (using Shepards or KeyCite) to determine whether they are still good law.

If your adversary relies on a case, determine whether he has mischaracterized it or whether the case is factually distinguishable. If so, then include this information in your reply brief. Here is an example from the Dunn reply brief:

> Attempting to make her case resemble *Lucero v. State*, 915 S.W.2d 612 (Tex. Crim. App. 1996), Appellant misconstrues that case. In her brief, Appellant states that the conduct of the defendant in *Lucero* was not assertive because he used the screwdriver "only to ward off the victim, who was chasing him." Appellant's Brief, p. 5. Appellant's reading of *Lucero* is wrong. The *Lucero* court reversed the defendant's conviction, not because the defendant was warding off the victim, but because the victim was not frightened by, or even *aware* of, the screwdriver held by the defendant during his robbery attempt. *Id.* at 614.

If your adversary has generalized a case's holding in an arguably incorrect manner, point this out and recast the holding in a narrower, more specific light:

> Appellant mistakenly relies on *Smith v. Jones*. Appellant cites *Smith* to support its contention that a witness cannot have a sensory and contemporaneous observance of an accident unless he sees it. *Smith*, however, involved a witness who neither saw *nor heard* the accident, but arrived at the scene ten minutes later. The *Smith* court did not consider the issue in this case, which is whether hearing the accident and immediately viewing its aftermath constitutes a contemporaneous sensory observance of it.

If your adversary quotes from a case, read the case to insure that the quotation does not present a false impression of the case. Review not just the quotation, but the case's facts, holding, and reasoning as well. If the case is not pertinent or is distinguishable, or if the quotation does not fairly represent the reasoning of the court being quoted, alert the court to the problem.

If your adversary has cited an irrelevant case, explain to the court why it is irrelevant. Suppose, for instance, your adversary cited a case that construes the term "sale" in a tax statute, but your appeal involves the meaning of that term under the Uniform Commercial Code. You could refute your adversary's position by arguing that the case he cited is not controlling because it does not relate to the UCC. You could further argue that the case is not persuasive because the meaning of "sale" for tax purposes is distinct from that term's meaning under the UCC.

3.   Refute the logic of your adversary's argument

Your reply brief should expose inconsistencies or logical flaws in your opponent's argument. For instance, in her initial brief, Dunn argues that her failure to use the crowbar proves she did not intend to use it. The logic of this argument is attacked by the State in its reply brief:

> In an attempt to convince the court that the jury's verdict was irrational, Appellant advances an illogical argument unsupported by the law. Appellant challenges the jury's finding that she *intended* to seriously injure or kill Keyes by asserting that she was "reluctan[t] to use the crowbar, even though Keyes was within striking distance" (Appellant's Brief, p. 7). However, the evidence points to a more likely reason why Appellant did not use the crowbar: by waving the crowbar at Keyes and threatening to hurt him, Appellant intimidated her victim and thereby prevented him from interfering with the robbery. Certainly the jury, which "may draw reasonable inferences from the evidence," *Lockett*, 874 S.W.2d at 813, could reasonably conclude that Appellant intended to use the crowbar *if* Keyes interfered.

4.   Refute your adversary's policy arguments

If your adversary has stated a policy argument, you should respond to it. Suppose your adversary is appealing a libel verdict against his client, a journalist, for including in a magazine article inaccurate and defamatory quotations attributed to your client. The adversary might advance a policy argument: imposing liability under these circumstances would have a chilling effect on free speech. You might counter that policy argument by asserting that a journalist's right to free speech is not impinged by requiring him to accurately quote his sources:

> [T]he writer need . . . not choose between silence and a lawsuit. Any professional reporter worthy of the name knows how to convey the gist of what he heard without resorting to fictional quotations—either by limiting quotation to verifiable

phrases or paraphrasing what was said. [Brief of Petitioner at 14, *Masson v. New Yorker Magazine, Inc.*, 501 U.S. 496 (1991).]

D. Tone

When writing your reply brief, be careful to maintain a professional tone. Do not attack your adversary by questioning his ethics or intelligence. Instead, attack the argument itself. For example, do not write: "Appellee's counsel cannot seriously expect the court to accept his ludicrous interpretation of the *Smith* case." Instead, write: "Appellee's brief incorrectly states *Smith's* holding." Moreover, do not harp on minor deficiencies in your adversary's brief. The court does not need you to point out inconsequential misstatements or grammatical or typographical errors. Concentrate on the important issues. Above all, keep your reply brief focused: discredit the opposing party's arguments and convince the court that your client's position is meritorious.

CHAPTER 24

Oral Arguments in an Appeal

When you master this chapter, you will understand:

1. the purpose of an oral argument in an appeal;

2. the procedure for an oral argument;

3. how to prepare for an oral argument; and

4. how to present an oral argument.

A. The Purpose of an Oral Argument

Oral argument is your last chance to persuade the appellate court to decide the case in your client's favor. Good advocates seize the opportunity to clarify and champion their position, answer the court's lingering questions, assuage its concerns, and discredit their adversary's arguments.

Many appellate cases are decided exclusively on the briefs. Oral argument is seldom granted as a matter of right; rather, it is within the discretion of the appellate court. To argue before the court, the lawyer probably must make a timely written request for it. Court rules prescribe the procedure for requesting an oral argument.

Appellate courts often grant oral argument when the merits of the case are uncertain or when the briefs raise questions or concerns. Oral argument is also usually heard in **cases of first impression**. Such cases require the court to decide an issue for the first time, and the decision may create a standard or rule for future cases within the jurisdiction. If there is an oral argument in a case, remember that an aspect of the case may be troubling or unclear to the appellate court.

B. The Procedure for an Oral Argument

Moot court competitions and court rules prescribe the procedure for the oral argument. The court gives each side a specific amount of time in which to present its argument. Usually, the appellant argues first and the appellee follows. Sometimes each side is permitted a short period to rebut his adversary's argument.

The oral argument is a formal, highly stylized process. Whenever possible, you should attend an oral argument in the court that will hear your appeal. Familiarize yourself with the court's conventions so that you will not be taken by surprise.

C. Preparing for an Oral Argument

The specter of an oral argument is intimidating. Even the most seasoned attorneys suffer from pre-argument jitters. Nervous energy, when channeled positively, will bring out your competitive edge and propel you to a peak performance. With preparation and practice, oral argument can be an exhilarating experience. The following advice will help you make the most of your potential.

1. Know the case

The key to a successful oral argument is knowing every aspect of your case. There are no shortcuts or substitutes for the intensive study that precedes an oral argument. A spellbinding orator will undoubtedly fail in her mission if she has not mastered the details and substance of her case. A weak public speaker can, however, present a competent oral argument if she knows every aspect of the appeal.

Study the record on appeal well in advance of your oral argument and compile a detailed outline of your presentation. Make sure you understand and can explain every nuance of the facts, procedural posture, and controlling law. Be prepared to intelligently discuss the issues; elements and sub-elements of claims, crimes, or defenses; the provisions in relevant statutes; and the necessary facts, holdings, and reasoning in key cases. Furthermore, be ready to explain how the law applies to the facts, to refute your adversary's arguments, and to argue that specific cases are analogous to or distinguishable from your case. (Do not, however, squander your time by memorizing case citations, because the court usually does not expect you to recite them.) Once you have a comprehensive understanding of every facet of your case, you will be well on your way to presenting an effective oral argument.

2. Organize the argument

Your presentation should contain in this order: a greeting, an introduction, the argument, and a conclusion. Each of these components is critical to an effective oral argument.

a. Greeting. Here is an example of a traditional greeting in a moot court competition by the advocate who argues first on each side:

> May it please the court. My name is John Doe. I represent WSD Corp., the appellant in this appeal. I will present the breach of contract issue, and my co-counsel, Jane Roe, will present the damages issue.

Co-counsel should, of course, omit the language "and my co-counsel . . . ."

b. Introduction. The introduction often consists of two parts: a recital of the important facts in the record and an outline of the main points of the argument. Although a persuasive presentation of the facts is necessary for an effective argument, resist the temptation to recite every detail. Explain the facts in enough detail to highlight your theme. In their introduction, appellees may identify omissions or inaccuracies in the appellants' recital of the facts.

After the advocate arguing first recites the facts, the court may excuse succeeding counsel from presenting the facts. Whether or not you present the facts, you must introduce your argument. State the issue and explain any essential elements of the claim, crime, or defense. Give the appellate court a clear outline of the points you will make in your argument.

  c. Argument. The argument is the core of your presentation. Keep your theme in mind, using it to unify your argument. Be sure to explain the legal rules by reciting the required elements of the claim, crime, or defense, and to support your application with references to cases or statutes. Analogize favorable precedent, distinguish adverse precedent, and use public policy to buttress arguments without favorable precedent. (See the discussion in Chapter 20, Section D, p. 334, on how to use authority.) The object is to give the appellate judges as many reasons as you can to rule in your client's favor. But remember that the judges have your brief or briefs—the purpose of the argument is not to repeat what you have written line for line but to insure that the judges understand your central points and to rebut your adversary's argument. Never read from your brief. You are engaged in a discussion with the judges.

  d. Conclusion. The conclusion is your last chance to focus the court's attention on your case. It should very briefly summarize the points emphasized in your argument and present a request for relief. The request for relief is traditionally stated as follows:

> For these reasons, the appellant [appellee] therefore requests
> that this Court affirm [reverse] the decision of the court below.
> Thank you.

3. Bring only key materials to court

Because the appellate oral argument is so formal and intimidating, you may find it helpful to bring a memory prompt to court. Use the detailed outline of your presentation to create a bare-bones outline of key points. This outline can be written on the inside of a manila file folder. Do not, however, bring individual pieces of paper to the podium. Judges find it distracting to watch an advocate shuffle through papers during an argument. The notes written on the folder might include:

a.   the procedural posture of your case;

b.   important facts (especially dates or easily forgotten details);

c.   a general outline of your presentation, including the greeting, introduction, argument, and conclusion;

d.   an outline of the argument, including the legal rules and support for your application;

e.   the names of cases which you plan to present in support of your argument or which you plan to distinguish;

f.   the desired outcome of your case (*e.g.*, affirmed or reversed).

Try to keep your notes to a minimum. Do not write a script. Never read from your notes. If you include too much information in your folder, you may not be able to locate necessary information in time to use it effectively.

In addition to a memory prompt, you may want to bring the briefs, copies of key cases, and important parts of the trial record with you to the argument for extra security. You can refer to these materials *before* your argument to refresh your memory on a particular point. However, do not use them *during* your argument. You are likely to lose your train of thought and the court's attention if you sift through a trial transcript or search for particular language in a case.

4. Practice

Fluency is essential to a successful argument. Practice with colleagues who are familiar with the case and can ask you about its intricacies. Practice with lawyers who are unfamiliar with the case, and with non-lawyers—their common sense questions will give you a fresh perspective on your argument. Rehearse your presentation in front of the mirror. Make sure you know your outline so well that you do not need it any more. The outline is just a memory prompt, not a substitute for practice. A lot of practice will not only alleviate anxiety, but also will help you to anticipate difficult questions and allow you to polish your performance.

Prepare for judges who ask few questions. Be ready to use all of your time meaningfully, even if you are not asked a single question. Also prepare for judges who will bombard you with rapid-fire questions. If the court relentlessly interrupts you, you must still cover the main points of your argument within the allotted time.

5. Dress appropriately

Wear conservative business attire to your oral argument. Dignified dress and good grooming show respect for the court and for your client. Moreover, you want the court to focus on your argument, not on your fashion statement.

D. The Presentation

With practice, you will develop your own style of oral advocacy. It will be informed by your personality and your strengths as an advocate. Regardless of your style, you will be expected to follow certain conventions.

1. *Speak slowly, audibly, and clearly.* Do not whisper or yell at the court. Use proper diction and inflections. Your argument will be effective only if the court can hear and understand it.

2. *Use simple, precise, and persuasive language.* Your tone and words should be formal—do not use slang or sarcasm. Select words and phrases that are powerful, but do not try to impress the court with legalisms, big words, or long sentences. Let your knowledge speak for itself.

3. *Speak with conviction.* Be sincere and enthusiastic about your argument. Emphasize important points, and show the court that you identify with and respect your client.

4. *Maintain eye contact.* You should be able to deliver your argument seamlessly. Do not read your memory prompt or stare blankly into space or at the floor when you are arguing. Rather, engage the judges by looking directly at them. Remember, you are having a conversation with them.

5. *Maintain a comfortable, but alert, body posture.* Do not fidget, rock the podium, or play with your glasses or pen. You may gesture to stress a point, but do not go overboard. Frantic movements will detract from your argument.

6. *Show deference to the court.* Be courteous and respectful. Address each judge as "Your Honor." Do not be surprised if the judges frequently interrupt you. When a judge interrupts you with a question, stop speaking immediately and answer the question. Do not ignore the judge, act annoyed, or respond evasively. Judges may be overbearing or even rude. Do not respond in kind. You can disagree with a judge, and should, when necessary, but always do so respectfully.

7. *Be responsive to the judges' questions.* Judges ask questions for two reasons: they either want information or they are sending you a message about how they view the issues. Listen to the questions carefully. Are the judges looking for information? Answer the question directly (yes or no), briefly explain your answer if necessary, and move back to your argument. Use the question to make a point in your favor and move to the next part of your argument. Are the judges expressing a concern through their questions? Address the concern and champion your position.

8. *Admit when you do not know an answer.* At times a judge's question may require you to concede a point or to admit that you have entered unfamiliar territory. Unanticipated questions should not divert you from your argument. Instead of becoming defensive or frustrated, address the point honestly. Admit that you do not know the answer or that the point does not support your case. Then, with as much enthusiasm as you can muster, seek to persuade the judges to consider a point or policy that is more helpful to your case.

9. *Cover all the main points of your argument.* Do not let the court's questions or hypothetical musings take you off track. Answer the questions as best you can, and return to your argument.

10. *Watch the time and pace your argument.* When your time is up, finish your sentence and ask for an opportunity to conclude. Do so with a formal statement, "Your Honors, I see that my time is up. May I briefly conclude?" Usually you will receive permission to conclude. If not, just say "Thank you" and sit down. Do not argue with the court.

11. *Maintain a professional, respectful demeanor when sitting at the counsel's table.* Do not fidget, whisper with co-counsel, roll your eyes, chuckle, or engage in any other inappropriate behavior when your colleagues are arguing. The judges will likely notice your behavior and disapprove of it.

Appellate oral advocacy challenges your intellect, strengthens your rhetorical skills, and increases your confidence. If you prepare and argue to the best of your ability, your experience before the appellate bench will be memorable and empowering, whether you win or lose the case.

Appendices

Memorandum of Law:

Criminal Charge

To: Michael Benitez

From: Blanca Alvarez

Date: September 12, 2000

Re: Jane Dunn: Likelihood of Conviction on Aggravated Robbery

         Charge

Question Presented

Under Texas Penal Code §29.03(a)(2), a person may be convicted
of aggravated robbery if she uses or exhibits a deadly weapon during
a robbery. Jane Dunn brandished a crowbar at the driver of a UPS
truck and threatened to hit him with it during the robbery of his
truck. Did Dunn use or exhibit a deadly weapon?

Short Answer

Probably. The prosecution is likely to prove that Dunn used or
exhibited a deadly weapon because the crowbar was objectively capable of causing serious injury, and her conduct demonstrated an
intent to seriously injure the driver with it.

Summary of the Facts

You asked whether Dunn is likely to be convicted of aggravated
robbery. On August 7, 2000, Dunn broke into a UPS truck by prying
open its steel gate with a crowbar. The truck's driver, Charlie
Keyes, caught Dunn taking packages from his truck. He walked toward
her yelling, "What the hell are you doin' in my truck?" Dunn turned
to him, shook the crowbar, and said, "Stop right there." Keyes, how-

ever, continued walking toward Dunn. She shook the crowbar again and yelled, "Stop right there or you're gonna get hurt." Keyes halted a few feet from Dunn. She then grabbed another package, shook the crowbar, and drove away. The police arrested Dunn minutes later. The stolen packages and the crowbar were in Dunn's car.

Discussion

In Texas, a person may be found guilty of the crime of aggravated robbery if the prosecution proves three elements beyond a reasonable doubt. *See Lockett v. State*, 874 S.W.2d 810, 813-814 (Tex. Crim. App. 1994). First, the person must commit theft by unlawfully taking property with the intent to deprive the owner of the property. Texas Penal Code Ann. §31.03(a) (West 1994). Second, while committing the theft, the person, with the intent to obtain or retain the property, must intentionally or knowingly threaten or place another person in fear of imminent bodily injury or death. Texas Penal Code Ann. §29.02(a)(2). Third, the person must use or exhibit a deadly weapon. Texas Penal Code Ann. §29.03(a)(2). The first two elements establish the crime of robbery; the addition of the third element elevates the crime to aggravated robbery. *Lockett*, 874 S.W.2d at 814.

The prosecution can probably prove the first two elements. Dunn committed theft because she unlawfully took property, the packages, with the intent to deprive the owner of the property. Texas Penal Code Ann. §31.03(a). Furthermore, to obtain the packages, she threatened Keyes with imminent bodily injury. Texas Penal Code Ann. §29.02(a)(2). In dispute is the third element: whether Dunn used or exhibited a deadly weapon, the crowbar. The prosecution is likely to prove this element because the crowbar had the objective capacity to cause serious injury and Dunn's conduct demonstrated her intent to use it to seriously injure Keyes. Therefore, Dunn is likely to be convicted of aggravated robbery.

The issue is whether Dunn used or exhibited the crowbar as a deadly weapon when she robbed Keyes. The Code defines a deadly weapon as "anything that in the manner of its use or intended use is capable of causing death or serious bodily injury." Texas Penal Code Ann. §1.07(a)(17)(B). An object is a deadly weapon under this provision if (1) its intrinsic characteristics make it objectively capable of causing death or serious injury when wielded within the effective range of the victim (the objective capacity requirement), and (2) the defendant demonstrates an intent to use it to cause serious injury or death (the assertive conduct requirement). *Lockett*, 874 S.W.2d at 814. The first requirement is met because the crowbar's intrinsic characteristics made it objectively capable of causing serious injury when Dunn wielded it within striking distance of Keyes. *See Hammons v. State*, 856 S.W.2d 797, 800-801 (Tex. Crim. App. 1993) (holding that the objective capacity requirement was satisfied when the defendant struck the victim with an aluminum baseball bat); *Compton v. State*, 759 S.W.2d 503, 504 (Tex. Crim. App. 1988) (holding that the objective capacity requirement was satisfied when the defendant waved a bottle with a broken, jagged edge at the victim). The second requirement — whether Dunn's conduct was assertive — is in dispute.

A defendant's conduct is assertive if her words and actions and the victim's perception of them establish an "intent to inflict serious bodily injury or death." *Lockett*, 874 S.W.2d at 815-816. When the defendant both physically and verbally menaces the victim, and the victim fears imminent harm, a finding of assertive conduct is warranted. *Compton*, 759 S.W.2d at 503-504. In *Compton*, for example, the defendant threatened to stab the victim with a broken bottle, and the victim feared serious injury or death. The court upheld the finding of assertive conduct. *Id.* at 504. Similarly, the *Hammons* court held that the defendant exhibited assertive conduct when he struck the victim in the groin and leg with an aluminum baseball bat and attempted to strike him a third time. Although the victim was not seriously injured, he feared serious injury. *Hammons*, 836 S.W.2d at 800-801.

In contrast to *Compton* and *Hammons*, in *Lockett* and *Lucero v. State*, 915 S.W.2d 612, 614-615 (Tex. Crim. App. 1996), the defendants did not demonstrate an intent to cause serious injury or death. In *Lockett*, the defendant used a pocket knife to cut a purse strap, incidentally cutting the victim. The victim testified that she did not fear the knife or even see it until after she was cut, but feared only being robbed. *Lockett*, 874 S.W.2d at 815. Similarly, in *Lucero*, the defendant was in possession of a screwdriver but did not brandish it or verbally threaten the victim. The victim in *Lucero* feared only that the defendant would hit her, not injure her with the screwdriver. *Lucero*, 915 S.W.2d at 614-615.

In this matter, Dunn threatened her victim both physically and verbally with the crowbar, and her victim may have feared imminent harm. Like the defendant in *Compton*, Dunn not only brandished the object at her victim but also verbally threatened him when she said, "Stop right there" and "Stop right there or you're gonna get hurt." Furthermore, like the victim in *Hammons*, Keyes may have feared serious injury: he halted his advance on Dunn.

Dunn's conduct is distinguishable from that of the defendants in *Lockett* and *Lucero*. While the defendants in both these cases did not display the weapons and made no verbal threats, Dunn not only openly displayed the crowbar so that Keyes could clearly see it, but she also made an explicit verbal threat. The prosecution is therefore likely to prove that Dunn used or exhibited the crowbar as a deadly weapon because it is capable of causing serious injury or death, and she demonstrated an intent to cause serious injury.

Conclusion

Dunn will probably be convicted of aggravated robbery because there is sufficient proof that she (1) committed theft, (2) placed Keyes in fear of imminent bodily injury to obtain the UPS packages, and (3) used or exhibited a deadly weapon.

Memorandum of Law:

Civil Claim

Memorandum

To: Senior Partner

From: Associate

Date: April 25, 2001

Re: Nadine Jackson's Potential Claim for Negligent Infliction of
        Emotional Distress

Question Presented

In Pennsylvania, a plaintiff claiming negligent infliction of emotional distress must establish that she suffered a direct emotional shock from a "sensory and contemporaneous observance" of an accident. Nadine Jackson saw her husband get on an amusement park ride, heard but did not see the ride crash, and moments later, saw him lying dead on the ground. Did Jackson suffer a direct emotional shock from a sensory and contemporaneous observance of the accident?

Short Answer

Probably. Jackson's visual awareness of the setting, simultaneous auditory perception of the accident, and her immediate observation of its aftermath most likely constitute a sensory and contemporaneous observance that caused her to suffer a direct emotional shock.

Summary of the Facts

You asked whether Nadine Jackson has a claim against Hi-Five Amusement Park ("Hi-Five") for negligent infliction of emotional distress. Jackson's husband Dwight was killed on a ride at the amusement park. Another associate has already determined that Hi-Five's negligence caused the accident.

On the day of the accident, Jackson watched her husband get on the Frenzied Ferret, a roller coaster. She then walked no more than ten feet away from the entrance to the ride and began talking to her friend, Alison Starr. Jackson had her back to the ride, but heard it gather speed. Suddenly, she heard a different sound, like metal parts screeching, and then a loud thud and frantic screaming. Jackson turned around, and Starr screamed, "Oh no, it's Dwight." Just then, Jackson saw that the ride had stopped and that Dwight was lying on the ground, close to a car that was turned upside down. She knelt down and held him in her arms. Jackson knew that he was dead when his head lolled unnaturally to one side.

Jackson now suffers from nightmares and has trouble eating and concentrating at work. She is seeing a therapist to cope with her extreme anxiety.

Discussion

Under Pennsylvania law, a plaintiff has a claim for negligent infliction of emotional distress against a defendant who injures or kills another person if the plaintiff can show that the defendant had reason to foresee her distress. To demonstrate foreseeability, the plaintiff must establish that (1) she was closely related to the victim, (2) she was near the scene of the accident, and (3) she had a sensory and contemporaneous observance of the accident that caused her to suffer a direct emotional shock. *Sinn v. Burd*, 404 A.2d 672, 685 (Pa. 1979). Here, Jackson was closely related to the victim

because he was her husband. *See Neff v. Lasso*, 555 A.2d 1304, 1308
(Pa. Super. 1989) (holding that the victim's wife was closely
related to him). Moreover, standing no more than ten feet from the
entrance to the ride, Jackson was near the scene of the accident.
See Bliss v. Allentown Public Library, 497 F. Supp. 487 (E.D. Pa.
1980) (holding that the plaintiff, who was about twenty-five feet
from the accident, was near the scene). The disputed issue is
whether Jackson had a sensory and contemporaneous observance of the
accident that caused her to suffer a direct emotional shock. A court
is likely to hold that she did because her emotional shock directly
resulted from her visual awareness of the setting, her auditory perception of the accident, and her immediate observation of its aftermath. Therefore, Jackson probably has a claim against Hi-Five for
negligent infliction of emotional distress.

The issue is whether Jackson had a sensory and contemporaneous
observance of her husband's accident that caused her to suffer a
direct emotional shock. A plaintiff has a sensory and contemporaneous observance if she (1) sees the victim immediately before the
accident, (2) sees or hears the accident, and (3) sees the victim
immediately after the accident. *See Bliss*, 497 F. Supp. at 489;
Neff, 555 A.2d at 1313-1314. Such a plaintiff qualifies as a "percipient witness" whose awareness of the accident causes her direct
emotional shock. *See Neff*, 555 A.2d at 1313. Conversely, a plaintiff
does not have a sensory and contemporaneous observance of the accident if she learns about it from a third party after its occurrence
and therefore has time to brace her emotions. *Mazzagatti v.*

Everingham, 516 A.2d 672,679 (Pa.1986). In this situation, the plaintiff's prior knowledge of the accident is considered a buffer that shields her from the full emotional impact of observing the accident's aftermath. *Id.*

The sensory and contemporaneous observance requirement was satisfied in *Neff* and *Bliss*. In *Neff*, the plaintiff, standing at her kitchen window, saw her husband's pickup being followed by a speeding car, heard a collision, and then ran out of the house to find her husband lying unconscious on their front lawn. *Neff*, 555 A.2d at 1313. In *Bliss*, the plaintiff, from a distance of about twenty-five feet, saw her daughter immediately before a statue fell, heard a crashing sound, and immediately looked up to see the statue lying on the injured child. 497 F. Supp. at 488-489. These plaintiffs were found to be percipient witnesses; their awareness of the accidents caused their emotional shock. *Neff*, 555 A.2d at 1313; *Bliss*, 497 F. Supp. at 488-489.

In contrast to the plaintiffs in *Neff* and *Bliss*, the plaintiff in *Mazzagatti* was not a percipient witness because she did not know that an accident had occurred until she received a telephone call informing her that her daughter had been injured in an automobile collision. *Mazzagatti*, 516 A.2d at 678-679. At the time of the accident, the plaintiff was at work, about one mile away from the accident scene. *Id.* at 673-674. The plaintiff then drove to the scene and arrived there a few minutes after the accident. The court held that the plaintiff did not have a sensory and contemporaneous observance of the accident, reasoning that she did not know about the accident until after it occurred and that the telephone call buffered the full emotional impact of observing her daughter's injury. *Id.* at 679.

In our case, Jackson saw her husband get on the ride, heard the ride crash, and, within moments after the accident, saw him lying dead on the ground. She was therefore a percipient witness because her awareness of the accident caused her emotional shock. Jackson's perceptions are analogous to those of the plaintiffs in *Neff* and *Bliss*. Like these plaintiffs, Jackson not only saw the victim immediately before the accident, but she also heard the accident, and immediately saw its aftermath.

Although Hi-Five may assert that Starr's scream was a buffer, Jackson's situation is distinguishable from that of the plaintiff in *Mazzagatti*. While Jackson heard her husband's ride crash, the plaintiff in *Mazzagatti* did not see or hear the automobile collision involving her daughter. And Jackson, unlike the plaintiff in *Mazzagatti*, did not learn of the accident from a third party. Jackson had already turned around when Starr screamed, "Oh no, it's Dwight." Finally, Starr's scream did not provide Jackson with sufficient time to brace her emotions; Jackson saw her husband's dead body within moments of hearing the ride crash. In contrast, the plaintiff in *Mazzagatti* learned of the accident from a third party and had a few minutes to brace her emotions when she drove a mile to the scene. Because Jackson was a percipient witness, a court will likely hold that she suffered a direct emotional shock from a sensory and contemporaneous observance of the accident.

Conclusion

Jackson probably has a claim against Hi-Five for negligent infliction of emotional distress. She was closely related to the victim, stood near the scene of the accident, and had a sensory and contemporaneous observance of the accident that caused her to suffer a direct emotional shock.

Memorandum of Law:
Possible Appeal of Conviction

Memorandum

To: Michael Benitez

From: Blanca Alvarez

Date: April 19, 2001

Re: Jane Dunn: Possible Appeal of Aggravated Robbery Conviction

Question Presented

Under Texas Penal Code §29.03(a)(2), a conviction for aggravated robbery may be reduced on appeal to robbery if the evidence is insufficient to prove that the defendant used or exhibited a deadly weapon. A jury convicted Jane Dunn of aggravated robbery. The evidence established that she brandished a crowbar at the driver of a UPS truck and threatened to hit him with it during the robbery of his truck. Was the evidence sufficient to prove that Dunn used or exhibited a deadly weapon?

Short Answer

Probably. The evidence established that the crowbar could cause serious injury and that Dunn intended to seriously injure the driver with it, thereby proving that she used or exhibited a deadly weapon.

Summary of the Facts

You asked whether Dunn can successfully appeal her aggravated robbery conviction and have it reduced to robbery, a crime that carries a lesser penalty, on the ground that the evidence was insufficient to prove that she used or exhibited a deadly weapon.

The trial record shows that on August 7, 2000, Dunn broke into a UPS truck by prying open its steel gate with a crowbar. The truck's driver, Charlie Keyes, caught Dunn taking packages from his truck. He walked toward her yelling, "What the hell are you doin' in my truck?" Dunn turned to him, shook the crowbar, and said, "Stop right there." Keyes, however, continued walking toward Dunn. She shook the crowbar again and yelled, "Stop right there or you're gonna get hurt." Keyes halted a few feet from Dunn. She then grabbed another package, shook the crowbar, and drove away. The police arrested Dunn minutes later. The stolen packages and the crowbar were in Dunn's car.

The State did not introduce the crowbar into evidence at trial. No testimony — lay or expert — was given as to its size, weight, or capacity. The only testimony about the crowbar came from Keyes, who said that he "recognized" the tool as a crowbar from his prior employment in construction, but that he had never used or even held one.

Discussion

In Texas, the crime of robbery becomes aggravated robbery when the robber uses or exhibits a deadly weapon. Texas Penal Code Ann. §29.03(a)(2)(West 1994). To succeed in her appeal — and thereby reduce her conviction to robbery — Dunn must show that there was insufficient evidence for any rational trier of fact to find beyond a reasonable doubt that she used or exhibited the crowbar as a deadly weapon. *Lockett v. State*, 874 S.W.2d 810, 813 (Tex. Crim. App. 1994). In reviewing the jury's verdict, the appellate court views the evidence considered by the jury in the light most favorable to the prosecution. *Id.*

An appellate court is likely to find that the evidence sufficiently established that Dunn used or exhibited a deadly weapon: the trial testimony demonstrated that the crowbar had the capacity to cause death or serious injury and that Dunn intended to use it to seriously injure Keyes. Therefore, an appeal will probably not succeed.

The issue is whether the jury had sufficient evidence to find that Dunn used or exhibited the crowbar as a deadly weapon when she robbed Keyes. Under the Texas Penal Code, a deadly weapon is "anything that in the manner of its use or intended use is capable of causing death or serious bodily injury." Texas Penal Code Ann. §1.07(a)(17). An object is a deadly weapon under this provision if (1) it can cause death or serious injury (the objective capacity requirement), and (2) the defendant demonstrates an intent to use it to cause death or serious injury (the assertive conduct requirement). *Lockett,* 874 S.W.2d at 814.

Objective Capacity. To prove the objective capacity requirement, the prosecution must show that the object's intrinsic characteristics (*i.e.,* its sharpness, size, shape, and weight) make it capable of causing serious injury or death. *See Hammons v. State,* 856 S.W.2d 797, 800-801 (Tex. Crim. App. 1993)(holding that an aluminum baseball bat was a deadly weapon); *Compton v. State,* 759 S.W.2d 503 (Tex. Crim. App. 1988)(holding that a broken bottle was a deadly weapon). In addition, the evidence must establish that the object

was wielded within the effective range of the victim. *See Compton,*
759 S.W.2d at 503, 504 (holding that a broken bottle was a deadly
weapon when "wielded by a person as a club"); *Lucero v. State,* 915
S.W.2d 612, 615 (Tex. Crim. App. 1996)(holding that a screwdriver
was not a deadly weapon when it was not held against a person's
body). Although objective capacity is sometimes established by
expert testimony, lay testimony may also be used. *See Compton,* 759
S.W.2d at 504 (holding that a police officer's expert testimony
established that a broken bottle could inflict serious injury or
death); *Hammons,* 856 S.W.2d at 801 (holding that a jury may rely
solely on the lay testimony of the victim to establish deadliness).

The crowbar's intrinsic characteristics and its proximity to
the victim could support the finding that the crowbar was objectively capable of seriously injuring Keyes. Intrinsically, a crowbar
is heavier and sharper than the aluminum baseball bat found to be a
deadly weapon in *Hammons.* Furthermore, Dunn was within striking distance of Keyes, putting the crowbar as close to her victim as the
bottle was to the victim in *Compton* and distinguishing her case from
that of the defendant in *Lucero.*

Dunn may, however, argue on appeal that the prosecution failed
to offer sufficient proof of the crowbar's objective capacity
because it did not introduce the tool into evidence and did not provide testimony, lay or expert, about its size, weight, or capacity.
An appellate court, however, is not likely to be persuaded by these
arguments because a crowbar's capacity to cause death or serious
injury is arguably self-evident.

Assertive Conduct. A defendant's conduct is assertive if the evidence establishes that her words and actions and the victim's perception of them established an "intent to inflict serious bodily injury or death." *Lockett,* 874 S.W.2d at 815-816. When the defendant both physically and verbally menaces the victim, and the victim testifies to a fear of imminent harm, an appellate court will uphold a finding of assertive conduct. *Compton,* 759 S.W.2d at 503-504. In *Compton,* for example, the defendant brandished a jagged broken bottle at the victim and threatened, "Don't nobody move or I'm going to stab you with the bottle." *Id.* at 503. In addition, the victim testified that he feared serious injury or death. The appellate court upheld the finding that the bottle was a deadly weapon. *Id.* at 504. Similarly, the *Hammons* court held that the defendant's conduct was assertive when he struck the victim in the groin and leg with an aluminum baseball bat and attempted to strike him a third time. Although the victim was not seriously injured, he feared serious injury. *Hammons,* 836 S.W.2d at 800-801.

In contrast to *Compton* and *Hammons,* in *Lockett* and *Lucero v. State,* 915 S.W.2d 612, 614-615 (Tex. Crim. App. 1996), the defendants did not demonstrate an intent to cause serious injury or death. In *Lockett,* the defendant used a pocket knife to cut a purse strap, incidentally cutting the victim. The victim testified that she did not see or fear the knife, but feared only being robbed. *Lockett,* 874 S.W.2d at 815. Similarly, in *Lucero,* the defendant was in possession of a screwdriver but did not brandish it or verbally threaten the victim. The victim in *Lucero* feared only that the defendant would hit her, not injure her with his screwdriver. *Lucero*, 915 S.W.2d at 614-615.

In our case, the evidence was probably sufficient to prove that Dunn threatened her victim both physically and verbally with the crowbar, and that her victim feared imminent harm. Like the defendant in *Compton*, Dunn not only brandished the object at her victim but also verbally threatened him when she said, "Stop right there" and "Stop right there or you're gonna get hurt." Furthermore, Keyes, like the victim in *Hammons*, may have feared serious injury: he halted his advance on Dunn.

In contrast, Dunn's conduct is distinguishable from that of the defendants in *Lockett* and *Lucero*. While the defendants in both these cases did not display the weapons and made no verbal threats, Dunn not only openly displayed the crowbar so that Keyes could clearly see it, but she also made an explicit verbal threat. Therefore, an appellate court is likely to conclude that there was sufficient evidence of assertive conduct.

Nonetheless, Dunn could argue on appeal that she intended to use the crowbar as a tool, not as a weapon. Like the defendant in *Lockett*, who used the knife to cut the victim's purse strap, Dunn used the crowbar to pry open the UPS truck. Furthermore, Dunn arguably was less aggressive than the defendants in *Lucero* and *Lockett*. The defendant in *Lockett* slashed three of the victim's fingers, and the defendant in *Lucero* swiped at the victim with the screwdriver. While Dunn raised the crowbar, she did not strike the advancing Keyes with it.

Notwithstanding these arguments, the jury could reasonably find that Dunn used or exhibited the crowbar as a deadly weapon because it was capable of causing serious injury, and she demonstrated an intent to cause serious injury.

Conclusion

Dunn will probably not succeed on appeal. An appellate court is not likely to reduce her aggravated robbery conviction to robbery because there was sufficient evidence that she used or exhibited the crowbar as a deadly weapon.

Appellant's Brief

In the

COURT OF APPEALS OF THE

STATE OF TEXAS

HOUSTON DISTRICT

Fall Term, 2001

No.44-01-91155-CR

JANE DUNN,

Appellant,

vs.

STATE OF TEXAS,

Appellee.

On appeal from the First District Court, Houston District

BRIEF FOR APPELLANT

South Galveston Legal Services
Attorneys for Appellant
101 Main Street
Galveston, Texas 42593

Blanca Alvarez, of Counsel

TABLE OF CONTENTS

TABLE OF AUTHORITIES

Cases

Statutes

QUESTION PRESENTED

Was the evidence legally sufficient to support Appellant's conviction for aggravated robbery under Texas Penal Code § 29.03(a)(2)
on the ground that she used or exhibited a deadly weapon, a crowbar,
even though she only used it to break into a truck and ward off the
driver?

STATEMENT OF THE CASE

Procedural History

On August 7, 2000, Appellant Jane Dunn ("Dunn") was arrested
and charged with aggravated robbery under Texas Penal Code
§ 29.03(a)(2). The complaining witness was Charlie Keyes ("Keyes"),
a U.P.S. truck driver. After a jury trial in the First District
Court, Houston District, Dunn was convicted on April 12, 2001, and
later sentenced to a forty-year prison term.

On May 1, 2001, Dunn appealed. Dunn seeks to reduce her aggravated robbery conviction to robbery on the ground that the State
failed to proved beyond a reasonable doubt an essential element of
aggravated robbery: that she used or exhibited a deadly weapon in
the commission of the crime.

Statement of Facts

The jury found that, on August 7, 2000, Dunn broke into Keyes's
locked UPS delivery truck with a crowbar and took five thousand dol-
lars worth of goods. Keyes interrupted the robbery and approached
Dunn. In response, Dunn raised the crowbar, warned him not to
advance, and fled. She neither struck nor attempted to strike Keyes

1

with it. Based solely on this evidence, Dunn was convicted of aggravated robbery.

The trial testimony established that Keyes, the UPS truck driver, walked toward the truck while Dunn was removing packages. He yelled, "What the hell you doin' in my truck?" Dunn, who was startled by Keyes's approach, turned to face him. Dunn was still holding the crowbar she had just used to open the truck's locked gate when she told Keyes, "Stop right there." Keyes was clearly not afraid since he continued to advance toward Dunn.

The undisputed evidence showed that Dunn did not move toward Keyes. Rather, she merely attempted to stop Keyes from approaching by raising the crowbar, shaking it, and yelling again, "Stop right there or you're gonna get hurt." Only then did Keyes halt, a few feet from Dunn. As Keyes conceded at trial, Dunn did not strike or even attempt to strike him. Instead, she nervously shook the crowbar in the air to prevent interference, grabbed the parcels, and ran to her car.

Most significantly, Keyes did not testify that he was in fear of imminent bodily injury or death when Dunn waved the crowbar. To the contrary, the uncontroverted evidence demonstrated that Keyes boldly confronted Dunn. In fact, Keyes conceded at trial that he never tried to retreat from Dunn, run away, or call for help, but rather purposely advanced at her. Keyes further admitted that Dunn did not, at any time, try to attack or restrain him.

2

The State did not introduce the crowbar into evidence at trial. No testimony, lay or expert, was given as to its size, weight, or capacity. The only testimony about the crowbar came from Keyes, who said that he "recognized" the tool as a crowbar from his previous employment in construction but that he had never used or even held one.

SUMMARY OF THE ARGUMENT

Viewed in the light most favorable to the verdict, the evidence is insufficient to prove a principal element of aggravated robbery: namely, that Dunn used or exhibited a deadly weapon while committing a robbery. Because the State failed to present sufficient evidence establishing this element, Dunn's conviction must be reduced to robbery.

To prove that Dunn used or exhibited a deadly weapon while committing a robbery, the State had to establish beyond a reasonable doubt that (1) Dunn displayed or used the crowbar in a manner which established her intent to cause serious bodily injury or death (the assertive conduct requirement), and (2) the crowbar was capable of causing serious bodily injury (the objective capacity requirement). First, even when viewed in the light most favorable to the verdict, the evidence failed to prove assertive conduct: Dunn used the crowbar only as a burglar's tool, not as a weapon. She did not advance on Keyes, and Keyes suffered no injury and showed no fear of physical harm. Second, the State presented no evidence on the objective capacity of the crowbar to cause death or serious bodily injury.

3

[handwritten marginalia: "put a colon here if there's more than 1" with arrow; "I"; "lead"]

ARGUMENT

APPELLANT'S CONVICTION FOR AGGRAVATED ROBBERY MUST BE REDUCED TO ROBBERY BECAUSE THE EVIDENCE IS INSUFFICIENT TO PROVE THAT APPELLANT USED OR EXHIBITED A DEADLY WEAPON UNDER TEXAS PENAL CODE § 29.03(a)(2).

Absent actual serious injury or death, a conviction for aggravated robbery is warranted only when there is sufficient evidence that the defendant used or exhibited a deadly weapon in a manner that establishes the defendant's intent to seriously injure or kill. *Lockett v. State*, 874 S.W.2d 810, 814 (Tex. Crim. App. 1994). This evidentiary requirement derives from Texas Penal Code §§ 29.03 and 1.07(a)(17)(B) and cases applying these sections. Under Texas Penal Code § 29.03(a)(2), a person commits aggravated robbery only if "he commits robbery ... and he . . . uses or exhibits a deadly weapon." Texas Penal Code § 1.07(a)(17)(B) defines a "deadly weapon" as "anything that in the manner of its use or intended use is capable of causing death or serious injury." The State must prove that an object was used or exhibited as a deadly weapon by establishing (1) assertive conduct (that the defendant displayed or used an object in a manner establishing the defendant's intent to use it to cause serious injury or death) and (2) objective capacity (that the object was capable of causing serious injury or death). *Lockett*, 874 S.W.2d at 814. Even when viewed in the light most favorable to the verdict, the State's evidence failed to prove either of these requirements.

4

A. The evidence is insufficient to prove that Appellant intended to cause death or serious injury.

The State must prove beyond a reasonable doubt that the defendant intended to inflict serious bodily injury or death. *Lockett*, 874 S.W.2d at 814. Specifically, the evidence failed to establish that (1) the defendant wielded the object in an overtly aggressive manner either by actually injuring the victim or by brandishing it at the victim, and (2) the victim believed the defendant would use the object to inflict serious bodily injury or death. *Id.; Lucero v. State*, 915 S.W.2d 612, 615 (Tex. Crim. App. 1996). Here, Dunn's conduct, together with Keyes's reaction to it, are insufficient to prove beyond a reasonable doubt that Dunn intended to—and that Keyes believed Dunn would—seriously injure or kill Keyes with the crowbar.

Dunn's conduct closely resembles that of the defendants in *Lucero* and *Lockett*, in which the evidence was held insufficient to establish assertive conduct. In *Lockett*, the defendant used a knife to cut the victim's purse strap, slashing three of the victim's fingers in the process. The appellate court reduced the defendant's aggravated robbery conviction to robbery on the ground that the defendant's conduct was not sufficiently assertive. The *Lockett* court reasoned that the conduct proved only intent to cut the strap, not intent to inflict serious injury or death. *Lockett*, 874 S.W.2d at 816. Similarly, in *Lucero*, although the defendant swiped at the victim with a screwdriver, the appellate court held that this conduct was not sufficiently assertive because he did so only to ward off the victim, who was chasing him. 915 S.W.2d at 614. Accordingly, it reduced the defendant's aggravated robbery conviction to robbery. *Id.*

Like the defendant in *Lockett,* who intended to use the knife only to cut the purse strap, Dunn intended to use the crowbar as a tool, not a weapon. And like the defendant in *Lucero*, Dunn raised the crowbar defensively to ward off an attack, not to threaten injury. In fact, Dunn was far less aggressive than the defendants in *Lucero* and *Lockett*. The defendant in *Lockett* slashed the victim's fingers, and the defendant in *Lucero* swiped at the victim with the screwdriver. In contrast, Dunn's act of raising the crowbar, rather than striking the advancing Keyes with it, demonstrated, if any-thing, her reluctance to use the crowbar in any way that might harm Keyes.

Moreover, Keyes's reaction to Dunn's defensive conduct resembles the reactions of the victims in *Lockett* and *Lucero.* In *Lockett*, the victim did not believe the defendant was going to harm her with the knife. She testified that she had "no idea what [the defendant's] intentions were, other than to rob me." 874 S.W.2d at 816. Similarly, in *Lucero*, the victim's fears during the crime did not stem from a belief that she would be injured by the screwdriver, but only from a general uncertainty about what the defendant "was going to do." 915 S.W.2d at 615. Likewise, Keyes never testified that he was afraid Dunn would seriously injure or kill him with the crowbar. In fact, he boldly interrupted the robbery and approached Dunn.

6

Keyes admitted that he did not try to retreat from Dunn or otherwise protect himself. His reaction to Dunn's conduct was to stop his advance on Dunn only after *he* approached *her*. The evidence points to one inescapable conclusion: Keyes obviously did not fear serious injury or death.

This case is distinguishable from both *Hammons v. State*, 856 S.W.2d 797 (Tex. Crim. App. 1993) and *Compton v. State*, 759 S.W.2d 503 (Tex. Crim. App. 1988), in which the evidence was held sufficient to establish assertive conduct. In *Hammons*, the victim was robbed outside a gas station by three assailants, one of whom wielded a baseball bat. In marked contrast to Dunn, the defendant in *Hammons* was overtly aggressive, striking the victim repeatedly with the bat because he too slowly surrendered his wallet. And unlike Keyes, the victim in *Hammons* testified that he was "scared" and "thought [the defendant] was going to hurt ... [him] bad" with the bat. 759 S.W.2d at 800.

Similarly, in *Compton*, the defendant, while robbing a gas station, brandished a broken, jagged bottle and threatened, "Don't nobody move or I'm going to stab you with the bottle." 856 S.W.2d at 503. One of the victims, the cashier at the station, testified that he believed he would suffer serious bodily injury or death because of the broken bottle. *Id.* at 504. In contrast, Dunn carried the crowbar not to threaten injury, but to open the locked steel gate of the truck. Although Dunn threatened Keyes, she did so only to stop Keyes's advance. Dunn's reluctance to use the crowbar, even though

7

Keyes was within striking distance, must have been obvious to Keyes, who neither retreated nor otherwise tried to protect himself.

The State's contention at trial that Dunn's words established her intent to use the crowbar as a deadly weapon is unsupported by the evidence. Taken in context, Dunn's words were nothing more than an attempt to keep Keyes from advancing. Dunn was more interested in obtaining the packages from the truck than in prolonging an unexpected encounter with Keyes. And as the evidence demonstrated, Keyes recognized that he had nothing to fear from Dunn.

B. The State introduced no evidence proving that the crowbar used by Appellant could cause death or serious injury.

The State failed to present sufficient evidence to satisfy the objective capacity requirement. This failure is in itself grounds for reducing Dunn's conviction to robbery, even assuming that the State could satisfy the assertive conduct requirement. *See Lockett*, 874 S.W.2d at 815.

A finding of objective capacity must be based on actual evidence of the object's characteristics. *See id.* In *Lockett*, although a police officer testified the defendant's knife cut the victim's fingers, the court held this testimony was insufficient, noting that the weapon was not introduced into evidence and that no one testified about the seriousness of the injury or the knife's ability to seriously injure or kill. 874 S.W.2d at 815. Here, as in *Lockett*, the evidence is insufficient to support a finding of objective capacity. As in *Lockett*, the crowbar was not introduced into evidence. Further, there was no testimony about its size or weight.

8

Both *Hammons* and *Compton* are distinguishable on the issue of objective capacity. In *Hammons*, there was ample evidence of capacity: the victim testified about the injuries inflicted with the baseball bat, the bat was introduced into evidence, and the defendant's use of the bat was demonstrated before the jury. *See* 856 S.W.2d at 801. Similarly, in *Compton,* the broken, jagged bottle used by the defendant in the robbery was described, and a police officer gave expert testimony about its deadly nature. Here, no such evidence was introduced. In contrast to *Hammons,* Keyes was not injured, the crowbar was not introduced into evidence, and the State failed to demonstrate the crowbar's alleged deadly nature to the jury. Furthermore, in contrast to *Compton*, the State introduced no testimony (expert or lay) about the crowbar's alleged deadly nature. Accordingly, Dunn's conviction for aggravated robbery cannot be permitted to stand.

9

CONCLUSION

For the foregoing reasons, Appellant's conviction for aggravated robbery should be reduced to robbery, and the case remanded to the trial court for resentencing.

Respectfully Submitted,
SOUTH GALVESTON LEGAL SERVICES
Attorneys for Appellant
101 Main Street
Galveston, Texas 42593

Blanca Alvarez

Of Counsel: Blanca Alvarez

Dated: June 17, 2001
          Galveston, Texas

APPENDIX

STATUTES INVOLVED

Texas Penal Code:

§ 29.03 **Aggravated Robbery**

   (a) A person commits an offense if he commits robbery as defined in Section 29.02, and he:

      .   .   .   .

      (2) uses or exhibits a deadly weapon;

      .   .   .   .

   (b) An offense under this section is a felony of the first degree.

§ 1.07. **Definitions**

   (a) In this code:

      .   .   .   .

      (17) "Deadly weapon" means:

      .   .   .   .

         (B) anything that in the manner of its use or intended use is capable of causing death or serious bodily injury.

Appellee's Reply Brief

In the

COURT OF APPEALS OF THE

STATE OF TEXAS

HOUSTON DISTRICT

Fall Term, 2001

No.44-01-91155-CR

JANE DUNN,

Appellant,

vs.

STATE OF TEXAS,

Appellee.

On appeal from the First District Court, Houston District

REPLY BRIEF FOR APPELLEE

OFFICE OF THE DISTRICT ATTORNEY
1200 Broadway
Galveston, Texas 42593

Alexander James, of Counsel

TABLE OF AUTHORITIES

Cases

ARGUMENT

POINT I

IN HER ATTEMPT TO DISCREDIT THE JURY'S FINDING THAT SHE
INTENDED TO SERIOUSLY INJURE OR KILL KEYES, APPELLANT
MISCHARACTERIZES THE FACTS, MAKES ILLOGICAL ARGUMENTS, AND
MISSTATES THE LAW.

A. Appellant mischaracterizes the facts by casting herself as the
victim of her own crime.

Appellant's first argument — that the State failed to introduce

sufficient evidence of Appellant's intent to seriously injure or

kill Keyes — is unsupported by the facts of this case and the appli-

cable law.

In her brief, Appellant mischaracterizes the facts, casting her

own conduct as defensive, and the victim's conduct as aggressive.

According to Appellant, she did not intend to seriously injure or

kill Keyes when she waved a crowbar at him and threatened to hurt

him. Rather, she was trying to "stop" Keyes, who, Appellant insists,

"boldly interrupted the robbery and approached" her. Appellant's

Brief, p. 6.

Appellant's spin on the facts — the crowbar-wielding robber pro-

tecting herself from her unarmed target — is contradicted by the

evidence. Keyes's *uncontroverted* testimony established that

Appellant waived the crowbar at Keyes and yelled, "Stop right there

or you're gonna get hurt." Appellant's Brief, p. 2. Further, uncon-

troverted evidence also established that Keyes, in response to

Appellant's threat, stopped, permitting Appellant to complete her

crime. In sum, the ample evidence here, viewed "in the light most

1

favorable to the prosecution," *Lockett v. State,* 874 S.W.2d 810, 813

(Tex. Crim. App. 1994), proved exactly what the law requires: that

Appellant displayed the crowbar "in a manner conveying an express *or*

implied threat that serious bodily injury or death will result if

the aggressor is not satisfied." *Hammons v. State,* 856 S.W.2d 797,

801 (Tex. Crim. App. 1993).

B. Appellant attacks the jury's verdict by advancing illogical arguments and misstating the law.

In an attempt to convince the court that the jury's verdict was

irrational, Appellant advances an illogical argument unsupported by

the law. Appellant challenges the jury's finding that she *intended*

to seriously injure or kill Keyes by asserting that she was "reluc-

tan[t] to use the crowbar, even though Keyes was within striking

distance" (Appellant's Brief, p. 7). However, the evidence points to

a more likely reason why Appellant did not use the crowbar: by wav-

ing the crowbar at Keyes and threatening to hurt him, Appellant

intimidated her victim and thereby prevented him from interfering

with the robbery. Certainly the jury, which "may draw reasonable

inferences from the evidence," *Lockett,* 874 S.W.2d at 813, could

reasonably conclude that Appellant intended to use the crowbar *if*

Keyes interfered.

Appellant's argument is not only illogical, but it is also con-

trary to existing case law. Courts allow juries to infer the rob-

ber's intent to inflict serious injury or death from the *threatened*

use of the object. *See, e.g., Compton v. State,* 759 S.W.2d 503 (Tex.

Crim. App. 1988). In fact, Appellant's conduct is very similar to the conduct of the Appellant in *Compton*, whose conviction for aggravated robbery was upheld. In that case, the defendant brandished, but did not use, a broken beer bottle in a robbery, yelling "Don't nobody move or I'll stab you with the bottle." 759 S.W.2d at 503. Here, Appellant brandished, but did not use, the crowbar, yelling "Stop right there or you're gonna get hurt." In *Compton*, the court upheld the defendant's conviction for aggravated robbery, holding that the weapon was displayed in a "manner which convey[ed] a threat, express or implied, that serious bodily death or injury will result." *Id.* at 504. This Court should reach the same conclusion.

Attempting to make her case resemble *Lucero v. State*, 915 S.W.2d 612 (Tex. Crim. App. 1996), Appellant misconstrues that case. In her brief, Appellant states that the conduct of the defendant in *Lucero* was not assertive because he used the screwdriver "only to ward off the victim, who was chasing him." Appellant's Brief, p. 5. Appellant's reading of *Lucero* is wrong. The *Lucero* court reversed the defendant's conviction, not because the defendant was warding off the victim, but because the victim was not frightened by, or even *aware* of, the screwdriver held by the defendant during his robbery attempt. *See* 915 S.W.2d at 614. The court noted that

> [The victim] testified that she saw the handle of the screwdriver in [the defendant's] hand but could not tell what kind of tool it was. . . She never testified that she feared bodily injury or death resulting from the use of the as yet unidentified tool, or that the tool frightened her in any way.

Id. at 614-615.

3

Lucero's holding is based on facts that are fundamentally different from the facts here. Unlike the victim in *Lucero*, Keyes testified, and Appellant does not contest, that Keyes saw the crowbar that Appellant waved in his face and that he knew it could seriously injure or kill him.

Accordingly, Appellant's first argument should be rejected.

<u>POINT II</u>

APPELLANT'S TECHNICAL ARGUMENT REGARDING PROOF OF THE CROWBAR'S CAPACITY TO SERIOUSLY INJURE OR KILL IS SPECIOUS.

Appellant's other argument — that the State failed to prove that the crowbar used by Appellant was capable of inflicting serious injury or death — is specious. The jury's finding of objective capacity must stand unless it is "irrational or supported by only a 'mere modicum' of evidence." *Lockett,* 874 S.W.2d at 813. There was ample evidence that the crowbar could seriously injure or kill Keyes. Keyes testified that he "recognized the tool as a crowbar from his previous employment in construction." Appellant's Brief, p. 3. Moreover, it is uncontested that Appellant used the crowbar to rip open the back of the truck. Certainly, the jury could reasonably infer that a crowbar that could rip through a metal lock could also seriously injure Keyes.

Finally, the crowbar's obvious capacity to seriously injure or kill a person makes any extended, technical evidence of its deadliness superfluous. The court's statement in *Hammons* about a baseball bat's deadliness applies with equal force to the crowbar in this case: "[W]e are inclined to believe that all mankind know that death

4

or serious bodily injury can be inflicted by a baseball bat in the hands of a grown man." 856 S.W.2d at 801.

Accordingly, Appellant's second argument should be rejected.

CONCLUSION

For the foregoing reasons, Appellant's conviction for aggravated robbery should be affirmed.

Respectfully Submitted,
Office of the District Attorney
Attorneys for Appellee
1200 Broadway
Galveston, Texas 42593

Alexander James

Of Counsel: Alexander James

Dated: August 1, 2001
          Galveston, Texas

5

Glossary

Affirm

To uphold a trial court's decision.

Analogous case

A case that applies the same law as and has facts similar to a particular case.

Annotated code

Statutes of a particular jurisdiction arranged by subject, with notes after each section on legislative history, related statutes, relevant books and articles, and cases construing the sections.

Appellant

The party appealing a lower court's decision, sometimes referred to as the petitioner.

Appellee

The party defending a lower court's decision in an appeal, sometimes referred to as the respondent.

Balancing of the interests test

A legal test in which the court weighs competing interests to resolve an issue.

Beyond a reasonable doubt

The government's burden of proof in criminal actions.

Binding authority

Law that a judge must follow.

Black-letter law

The text of a law; a statement of a well-settled legal principle.

Burden of proof

A rule that determines which party must prove particular facts.

Canon of statutory interpretation (or construction)

A rule that courts may use to determine the meaning of a statute that is unclear or ambiguous.

Case

(1) a court's written decision; (2) a lawsuit or other legal matter; (3) the arguments, law, and evidence that support a lawsuit.

Case brief

A concise written summary of a court's decision, usually used as a note-taking device.

Citation manual

A reference book that specifies the substance and format of citations.

Claim

A set of requirements, which, if proven, establishes a party's right to a judgment against another.

Clearly erroneous

The appellate standard of review for questions of fact.

Code

Statutes of a particular jurisdiction arranged by subject.

Common law

Law made by judges on a case-by-case basis.

Concurrent jurisdiction

Authority of both federal and state courts to hear the same claim.

Concurring opinion

An appellate judge's decision agreeing with the result reached by a majority of the judges hearing the case, but not fully agreeing with the majority's reasoning.

Controlling case

A prior written decision that dictates the resolution of a legal question in that jurisdiction.

Counterclaim

A claim asserted by a defendant against a plaintiff.

Court brief

A persuasive document submitted to a court that explains the law and facts supporting one party's position in a lawsuit.

Damages

A remedy in a civil case that gives a party money in compensation for harm suffered.

***De novo* standard**

A standard of review that allows the appellate court to freely substitute its judgment for that of the trial court.

Defendant

(1) the party who is sued in a civil case; (2) the party who is charged with a crime in a criminal case.

Defense

A set of requirements, which if proven, defeat the right to a judgment in a claim or counterclaim.

Dictum

A general pronouncement of law in a court's decision that is not part of its holding.

Digest

A secondary authority, organized by subject, which summarizes the holdings of cases.

Disputed issue

A question about what the law means that is the subject of a legal dispute.

Dissenting opinion

An appellate judge's decision disagreeing with the result reached by a majority of the judges hearing the case.

Distinguish

To assert that a prior decision is not applicable to a particular case because it has different facts, issues, or a different procedural posture.

Diversity jurisdiction

A federal court's authority to hear a case when the parties are from different states.

Diversity of citizenship

The parties to a lawsuit are from different states.

Element

A requirement for proving a claim, crime, or defense.

Factor

A criterion a court may consider to resolve an issue.

General jurisdiction

A court's authority to hear most substantive claims.

Headnote

A summary of the law about a specific legal issue, written by a book publisher.

Holding

A court's decision on how the law applies to the facts of a particular case.

Injunctive relief

A remedy in a civil case requiring a party to act or refrain from acting.

Interlocutory appeal

An appeal taken before a final judgment is reached in a case.

Judgment

> The formal determination of a lawsuit by a judge or jury.

Jurisdiction

> (1) the geographical location of a court or government entity; (2) the authority of a particular tribunal to hear cases; (3) the legal authority to hear a case involving the parties.

Key number

> The numbered subcategories of West Publishing Co.'s digest topics.

Legal issue

> A question about what the law means or how (or whether) it applies to the facts of a particular situation.

Legislative history

> The proposals, drafts, debates, committee reports, and other materials that document how a particular statute became law.

Majority opinion

> A decision by a majority of an appellate court's panel when all of the judges cannot reach a unanimous decision.

Mixed question of law and fact

> A question about whether the facts establish requirements set out in the law.

Necessary fact

> A fact that determines the outcome of the case.

Objection

> A formal request by a party during a trial or hearing, asking the court to rule on a substantive or procedural matter that affects the trial or hearing.

Opinion

> A court's written decision.

Ordinance

> A law passed by a local legislature.

Overrule

> To find that a court's holding in a different case was incorrect and is no longer good law.

Parallel citation

> A citation that includes citations to other reprints of the same authority.

Penal code

> A compilation of a jurisdiction's crimes in a statute.

Pendent claim
> A state claim in a federal action that derives from the same incident as the federal claim.

Persuasive authority
> Precedent that is not binding on a court but nonetheless is instructive because it involves a legal question that is identical or similar to the one before the court.

Petitioner
> The party appealing a lower court's decision, sometimes referred to as the appellant.

Pinpoint citation
> A citation that includes the specific page(s) on which a quotation is found or the specific page(s) in an authority that supports a proposition in the text.

Plagiarism
> Using another's ideas, facts, or language without correct use of quotation marks, citation, or other attribution.

Plaintiff
> The party who starts a lawsuit in a civil case.

Pleadings
> The written outline and explanation of each party's claims and defenses submitted to the court in civil actions (*i.e.*, The complaint, answer, reply).

Plenary standard
> A standard of review that is a *de novo* review—when the appellate court can freely substitute its judgment for that of the trial court.

Preponderance of the evidence
> A burden of proof in civil cases that requires a party to prove that a contention is more probable than not.

Primary authority
> Research materials that reproduce the actual text of the law.

Procedural fact
> A fact that describes how the parties got to court and the court's rulings.

Procedural legal question
> A legal question about the procedure to be followed in a lawsuit.

Procedural posture
> The stage of the proceedings at which a legal issue is raised.

Prosecution
> A criminal action against a person who is charged with committing a crime.

Question of law
> A question about what the law means.

Question of fact
> A question about what happened in a lawsuit.

Reasoning
> The court's rationale for its holding in a case.

Regulation
> A detailed guideline that explains a statute's general provisions, usually drafted and adopted by the agency charged with enforcing the statute.

Remedy
> A means by which a violation of a right is redressed.

Reporter
> A set of books that publishes court and/or administrative decisions.

Respondent
> The party defending a lower court's decision in an appeal, sometimes referred to as the appellee.

Reverse
> To find that the trial court's decision is incorrect and cannot stand.

Rule
> (1) a statement of law defining or explaining a claim, crime or defense; (2) a statement that accurately and consistently explains the holdings in similar cases.

Secondary authority
> Research materials that help you to understand and/or find the actual text of the law.

Session law
> Statutes passed during a particular legislative session.

Specific performance
> A remedy in a civil case requiring a party to do what was promised.

Standard of proof
> The amount or degree of proof a party must produce to prevail.

Standard of review
>The degree to which the appellate court will examine the jury's verdict or the trial court's decision.

Stare decisis
>Latin for *stand by things decided*. A judge in one court must follow decisions of judges in courts to which his decision could be appealed.

Statute
>A law enacted by a legislature.

Sub-issues
>Subsidiary issues stemming from the same element of a claim, crime, or defense.

Substantive legal question
>A legal question about what the law means.

Supporting fact
>A fact that helps explain what happened but does not determine the legal outcome of the case.

Term of art
>A word or phrase that has an exact meaning within the legal system.

Title
>A separate listing for each subject in a code.

Topic
>The broad areas of law into which West Publishing Co. divides its digests.

Trier of fact
>The entity responsible for finding facts in a trial: either the trial judge in a bench trial or the jury in a jury trial.

Undisputed issue
>A question about what the law means that has a definitive answer.

Acknowledgments

When we began work in 1997, Elaine P. Mills, then the Writing Specialist at New York Law School, actively participated in the scores of meetings stretching over more than a year during which we outlined the themes and structure of this book. She also contributed initial drafts of a few sections, and we are grateful for her help.

Our thanks to the NYLS Writing Program staff, Billie Coleman, José Noguerez, and Blanca (Nyasia) Batista, who aided us in ways large and small as we wrote, rewrote, and edited manuscript chapters over and over again. Thanks also to Writing Program student assistants Thomas Baglione, Lauren Ruff, Alex Mojica, '01, Alex Gomez '02, and Erin Parnell, '03, who provided research assistance along the way; and to Arundhati Satkalmi, at the St. John's University Law Library, who helped obtain copyright permissions.

During the 2000-2001 academic year, students in the NYLS first-year course Legal Reasoning, Writing, and Research used a draft of Parts I and II. We thank them collectively for their forbearance in providing us with the means of testing and refining these materials. During the year, we received innumerable comments and helpful guidance from all their teachers, and we acknowledge with thanks Adjunct Professors Vincent Chirico, David Cohen, Julie Cort, Julia Davis, Tracee Davis, Mark DeWan, Rosemary DiBenedetto, Karen Eisen, David Epstein, Natalie Feinstein, Michele Gartner, Eleanor Glanstein, CaraMia Hart, Tom Hughes, Sandee Janin, Natalie Kabasakalian, Judy Kaufman, Sabena Leake, Andrew Levi, Robert Marino, Maurice Mathis, Deirdere Newton, Jeannie Olivo, Jill Shapiro, Andrew Turro, and Nan Waite.

Special thanks to David Epstein, Jill Shapiro, and Elizabeth Rosen, who pitched in whenever asked, and to Camille Broussard, head of Reference Services at the New York Law School Library, who vetted our research chapters.

Special thanks to Jay Tribich and Tribich Design Associates, of New York City, who took the typescript of the manuscript and in a very short time transformed it into the page design and cover that you hold in your hands.

CG, JKL, RAR, LBS
October 23, 2001

About the Authors

Cathy Glaser

is the Associate Director of New York Law School's Writing Program. She has worked with the Writing Program since 1986, preparing the curriculum, supervising the adjunct faculty, and teaching both the first-year course and various upper-class writing courses. Before that, she taught legal writing at Syracuse University College of Law and Rutgers Law School-Newark as an adjunct professor. Prof. Glaser attended Cornell University's NYS School of Industrial and Labor Relations and Syracuse University College of Law, where she was a Staff Writing Editor of the Law Review and a member of the Order of the Coif, Justinian Society, and Phi Kappa Phi. After graduating from law school, Prof. Glaser practiced labor relations and employment law before moving to academia full time.

Jethro K. Lieberman

is Associate Dean for Academic Affairs, Professor of Law, and Director of the Writing Program at New York Law School, where he teaches Advanced Writing Skills, Constitutional Law, and Law and Society, and adjunct professor of political science at Columbia University, where he teaches the basic undergraduate constitutional law course. He is a graduate of Yale (B.A., 1964, *cum laude*), Harvard Law School (J.D., 1967, *cum laude*), and Columbia University (Ph.D., political science, 1995). Dean Lieberman practiced law for six years, including three years as a Navy lawyer from 1968-1971, and was founding editor of Business Week Magazine's Legal Affairs Department from 1973-1982. He is the author of 23 books, including *The Lawyer's Guide to Writing Well* (with Tom Goldstein, McGraw-Hill, 1989; University of California Press, 1991; 2nd edition forthcoming, 2002); *The Litigious Society* (Basic Books, 1981; Harper Colophon, 1983) and *The Enduring Constitution* (Harper & Row and West Publishing Co., 1987), both of which won the American Bar Association's Silver Gavel Award; and *A Practical Companion to the Constitution: How the Supreme Court Has Ruled on Issues from Abortion to Zoning* (University of California Press, revised paperback edition, 1999).

Robert A. Ruescher

is an Assistant Legal Writing Professor at St. John's University School of Law. From 1991-2001, he taught the first-year writing course, introductory research, and various upper-class writing courses at New York Law School, and helped develop and administer N.Y.L.S.'s Writing Program courses. In 1999-2000 he served as Assistant Director of the Program. From 1980 to the early 1990s he practiced banking, corporate, and securities law at several New York law firms. He is a graduate of Columbia College (B.A., 1976) and Columbia Law School (J.D., 1980, Harlan Fiske Stone Scholar).

Lynn Boepple Su

is an Assistant Director of the Writing Program, the Writing Specialist, and an Adjunct Professor at New York Law School. In addition to teaching courses and workshops, she works with students individually on legal analysis, writing, and editing. Prof. Su is a graduate of New York University (B.A., 1982, *magna cum laude* and Phi Beta Kappa) and Washington & Lee University (J.D., 1985, *cum laude*). In her third year of law school she was a Burks Scholar, serving as a teaching fellow for the first-year legal writing course. From 1986-1990, she was an Assistant District Attorney in Bronx County, New York, prosecuting cases in the Criminal Courts, Felony Evaluation Case Unit, and Investigations Bureaus. Prof. Su also was an associate attorney at several New Jersey law firms. In private practice, she concentrated in employment litigation, assisting in the representation of management in wrongful termination and discrimination cases and in matters of employer-employee relations.

General Index